Bittersweet Legacy is the dramatic story of the relationship between two generations of black and white southerners in Charlotte, North Carolina, from 1850 to 1910—a time usually characterized as racially antagonistic. Janette Greenwood describes the interactions between black and white business and professional people—the "better classes," as they called themselves.

The black members of this class were born in slavery and educated in freedmen's schools; they came of age in the 1880s with high expectations of being full-fledged members of New South society. They defined themselves against what they called the "masses" of the black community, and their alliance with their white counterparts helped shape their outlook.

Greenwood argues that concepts of race and class changed significantly in the late nineteenth century. Documenting the rise of interracial social reform movements in the 1880s, she suggests that the black and white "better classes" briefly created an alternative vision of race relations. But this alliance disintegrated under the pressures of New South politics and the rise of a new generation of leaders, leaving a bittersweet legacy for Charlotte that would weigh heavily on its citizens well into the twentieth century.

BITTERSWEET LEGACY

· · · · · · · · · ·

BITTERSWEET LEGACY

The Black
and White
"Better Classes"
in Charlotte,
1850—1910

JANETTE THOMAS GREENWOOD

The University of North Carolina Press

Chapel Hill and London

© 1994 The University of North Carolina Press
All rights reserved
Manufactured in the United States of America

Library of Congress Cataloging-in-Publication Data
Greenwood, Janette Thomas.
Bittersweet legacy : the black and white "better classes"
in Charlotte, 1850–1910 / Janette Thomas Greenwood.
p. cm.
Includes bibliographical references (p.   ) and index.
ISBN 0-8078-2133-0 (cloth : alk. paper)
1. Afro-Americans—North Carolina—Charlotte—Social
conditions. 2. Social classes—North Carolina—
Charlotte—History. 3. Charlotte (N.C.)—Social
conditions. 4. Charlotte (N.C.)—Race relations.
I. Title.
F264.C4G73   1994
975.6'76041'08622—dc20   93-32060
CIP

The paper in this book meets the guidelines for
permanence and durability of the Committee on
Production Guidelines for Book Longevity of the Council
on Library Resources.

98 97 96 95 94   5 4 3 2 1

For Elizabeth and Susannah

CONTENTS

· · · · · · · · · ·

ILLUSTRATIONS

· · · · · · · · ·

MAPS

. . . .

ACKNOWLEDGMENTS

. . . .

The roots of this project are deep, and I have accrued many debts researching and writing this book. I wish to thank the Charlotte-Mecklenburg Historic Landmarks Commission, which, under the direction of Dr. Dan Morrill, first assigned me the task of researching Charlotte's black history in 1983. That assignment turned out to be the beginning of a long-term relationship with Charlotte's history, and I am deeply indebted to Dr. Morrill and the commission for their interest and support. Thomas Hanchett, my onetime colleague at the Landmarks Commission in Charlotte, also provided unbounded enthusiasm and interest in this project from its earliest days. In addition, he has generously shared his own research and ideas about Charlotte's past with me. Professor William Bluford of Charlotte introduced me to many men and women who shared their memories with me. I am especially indebted to Rosa Smith, the daughter of W. C. Smith, a central character in this story. She generously shared her copies of the *Charlotte Messenger* with me, and without her help this book could never have been written. Jack Claiborne also proved to be an invaluable source of information, and I appreciated discussing ideas with him as this project unfolded.

A number of people at the University of Virginia critiqued this book in its dissertation form. My adviser, Edward L. Ayers, shepherded this study from its inception as a seminar paper through the dissertation phase and finally to its becoming a manuscript and patiently critiqued numerous revisions. I am deeply indebted to him for his insight and encouragement as well as for his humane and subtle approach to southern history. Cindy Aron, Stephen Innes, Armstead Robinson, and Daphne Spain all gave my dissertation a careful read and provided helpful suggestions for improvement. At the university, I greatly benefited from many conversations about southern history with the Dixie Diners, Larry Hartzell, Beth Schweiger, and John Willis, as well as with Patricia Minter.

I am especially grateful to the Carter G. Woodson Institute for Afro-American and African Studies at the University of Virginia, which supported me for two years as a predoctoral research fellow. The support of the institute greatly facilitated the completion of this work. I also benefited immensely from many informal conversations around the coffeepot in the Woodson Annex with colleagues Charles Dew, Terry Epperson, Julia McDonough, and Kay Mills.

At the University of North Carolina Press, Executive Editor Lewis Bateman, editor Pamela Upton, copyeditor Paula Wald, and outside readers Paul D. Escott and Raymond Gavins patiently read and reread my manuscript with great care. Their enthusiasm for this project buoyed my spirits through the long process of producing a book. They all offered me excellent advice for improving this work. Any shortcomings in this book reflect on me, not them.

At Clark University, Lisa Hauptmann and Michelle Reidel took time from their own hectic graduate studies to read the manuscript and offer suggestions.

I wish to thank the North Caroliniana Society for an Archie K. Davis Fellowship and the Clark University History Department for travel funds that expedited the completion of this book.

Numerous librarians and archivists deserve thanks for their aid over the years. I am especially indebted to the staffs of the Robinson-Spangler Carolina Room, Public Library of Charlotte and Mecklenburg County; Special Collections, J. Murrey Atkins Library, University of North Carolina at Charlotte; Southern Historical Collection and North Carolina Collection, University of North Carolina at Chapel Hill; North Carolina Division of Archives and History; and Goddard Library, Clark University.

I am grateful to my Charlotte friends who fed, housed, and entertained me during innumerable research trips to their city. I would especially like to thank John and Polly Andrews, who generously provided me with a home away from home; they made my research expeditions not only tolerable but lots of fun. Donna Stafford also provided me with a place to stay, numerous meals, and good conversation. Jennifer Johnston tracked down a number of key facts for me in Charlotte libraries.

Family and friends have provided everything from moral support to child care over the course of this project. I would like to thank my parents, Carl and Fern Thomas; my sisters, Jean Cober and Judy Swank; Merritt Greenwood; Mary Logan Greenwood and the late Walter Greenwood; Sallie Greenwood; Donna Alexander; Jim Alexander; Ken Bayse; Sally Deutsch; Debbie Merrill; and Marc Steinberg.

Finally, my daughters, Elizabeth and Susannah, insured that I would not lead the life of a lonely scholar. Neither of them remembers a time when this project did not exist; they have grown up with it, at times have competed with it, and too many times have had to put up with a preoccupied mom because of it. This book is for them.

BITTERSWEET LEGACY

· · · · · · · · · ·

INTRODUCTION

· · · · · · · · ·

If you take a walk down Charlotte's Tryon Street today, you will see the dreams of New South proponents come true, manifested in towering glass skyscrapers, the homes of regional banks and international corporations. A few streets away are two buildings practically rendered miniature by the massive First Union Tower that stands nearby. These small red-brick buildings, Grace African Methodist Episcopal (AME) Zion Church and the Mecklenburg Investment Company Building, are the last remnants of what was once the center of Charlotte's principal black business and residential district, known as "Brooklyn." Redevelopment forces leveled Brooklyn in the 1950s and 1960s, and its inhabitants scattered to a variety of neighborhoods in Charlotte.

Charlotte's urban landscape, including the seemingly incongruous fragments of Brooklyn, is a monument to the city's "better classes" of the nineteenth century, the focus of this study. The glass skyscrapers that house banks and corporations are the legacy of ambitious merchants, businesspeople, and cotton brokers who, with the aid of railroads, built their town into a regional trading center in the 1860s and 1870s and then parlayed their wealth into cotton mills, making Charlotte the center of the Piedmont textile industry by 1900. The remnant of Brooklyn reflects a different past, but a past inextricably linked to the white progenitors of New South Charlotte. Brooklyn was home to many members of Charlotte's black business and professional classes. Members of the black better class shared many of the same values as their white counterparts. They, too, sought economic advancement in the New South and prized hard work, discipline, and ambition. Indeed, Grace AME Zion Church and the Mecklenburg Investment Company Building attest to the mixture of spiritual and economic values that the black better class embraced. But their agenda included a key element that their white counterparts never had to worry about: they aspired to be full-fledged participants in New South society, politically, socially, and economically.

In their attempt to achieve this goal, the black better class frequently interacted with the white better class, at times forming alliances that challenged the seemingly intransigent mores of southern race relations. For a brief period in the 1880s, their association suggested an alternative vision of race relations. The Byzantine politics of the New South, as well as generational shifts in leadership in the 1890s, ultimately shattered the cross-racial coalition of the black and white better classes. Although short-lived, the alliance of the better classes had significant consequences in the way that these men and women responded to and shaped the racial politics, Jim Crow laws, and disfranchisement of the late 1890s. The rise and fall of the interracial cooperation of the better classes created a bittersweet legacy for Charlotte and the New South that would weigh heavily on its citizens well into the twentieth century.

·   ·   ·   ·   ·   ·   ·

The better classes played a central role in the unfolding story of the South between 1850 and 1910. During that time the world of black and white southerners changed at a vertiginous pace. They weathered secession and a civil war as well as the reconstruction of their war-torn society. They experienced severe shifts in the social and economic order induced by emancipation and industrialization. Moreover, they participated in fierce political battles over the control and direction of the postwar South.

By focusing on these two groups in the context of a booming New South city, this study reveals a surprisingly complex portrait of race and class relations in the New South, a portrait of fluidity, of strange and sometimes unsettling alliances. Concepts of race and class changed significantly over the second half of the nineteenth century, reflecting volatile economic and political transformations in the New South. Race and class relations were a kaleidoscope of shifting alliances and strategies as men and women attempted to make sense of their rapidly changing world. At times, barriers of race and class were porous, at other times, they were impermeable. At some moments, the fluidity of race and class lines depended on gender. Social relations in the New South were far from static as blacks and whites, men and women, rich, poor, and middling forged a range of associations in their daily lives. Like many other aspects of life in the New South, issues of race and class were hotly contested, never settled, and not simply defined or easily understood.

My study of Charlotte's better classes also suggests that class development followed a different pattern and proceeded at a different rate than in the North, despite some fascinating parallels. Whereas historians of the antebellum North have described how the middle class was "made" in a sequential process, class in New South Charlotte was constantly made and unmade with the changing economic and political landscape. Moreover, compared to the antebellum North, class development in the New South was both abbreviated and intensified, a reflection of the rapid economic changes in postbellum southern society, the timing of economic development, and the fact that by the 1890s definitions of class derived, in part, from northern examples. Issues of race also affected patterns of class formation in the New South. Class development followed different trajectories for whites and blacks in the New South, symbolized in the stark contrast between Charlotte's corporate glass towers and the small red-brick Grace AME Zion Church and Mecklenburg Investment Company Building. Racial issues, grounded in the context of social reform and partisan politics in Charlotte, also served as an impediment that ultimately separated the black and white better classes, complicating the meaning of class in the New South.[1]

In 1955 C. Vann Woodward in his now classic work, *The Strange Career of Jim Crow*, suggested that there was a window of time between the end of Reconstruction and the establishment of rigid segregation when race relations appeared to be more fluid. Although never a golden age for blacks in the South, the period from the 1880s through the mid-1890s nonetheless represented, according to Woodward, a season of "forgotten alternatives" in race relations. My study of Charlotte supports Woodward's thesis and explores the "forgotten alternatives" implemented by the black and white better classes in Charlotte and why those alternatives broke down, ushering in the harsher climate of the Jim Crow South.

My examination of Charlotte also supports Woodward's contention in his *Origins of the New South* (1951) that there was, indeed, much that was new about the New South. Woodward's thesis has been challenged and revised by subsequent generations of southern historians, creating rival "discontinuity" and "continuity" camps that represent the division between those who contend that the New South represented change in class and power relations and those who argue that the New South continued to be dominated by Old South elites. Charlotte's history between 1850 and 1910 lends credence to Woodward's claim that one of the most significant developments in the New South was the emergence of what he called a middle-class "new man" who "adjusted to his shoulders the mantle of leadership that had descended from the planter," shaping the region's economy and its culture.[2]

While narrowing my study to a single New South town, I have also attempted to build upon, broaden, and give detail to Woodward's portrait of influential "new men" and the New South that they built. First, I have explored how women of the better classes helped shape and build the New South. I have paid special attention to the way that women of both races helped define class in New South Charlotte and have examined how, at times, gender affected attitudes about race.

Second, my story of the New South includes the black better class, heretofore largely neglected despite being crucial players in the drama of the New South. Indeed, the emergence of the black better class represents much of what was new about the New South. Different from the "aristocrats of color" in older southern cities and Reconstruction-era black leaders, Charlotte's black better class emerged in the 1880s as a new generation of self-defined "race leaders." Not only did the men and women of the black better class, like their white counterparts, help build the New South, but they also engendered a strategy of "race progress" with long-term consequences, a moderate and flexible philosophy articulated long before either Booker T. Washington or W. E. B. Du Bois expounded competing racial strategies. Their ideology anticipated that of Martin Luther King, Jr., as they sought to "not be judged by the color of their skin but by the content of their character." The better class's attempts to convert the rest of the black community to their strategy engendered severe class-based conflict that manifested itself in fiercely fought battles for control of the black community.[3]

Finally, by tracing the activities and relationships of the black and white better classes in Charlotte, I have attempted to give names and faces to participants in this enigmatic period of southern history, to show the interplay of local, state, and national events in the lives of ordinary people and how ordinary southerners grappled with and shaped those events. The study of men and women in a single city over several generations also throws the significance of generational shifts into relief. Indeed, the seemingly puzzling trajectory of class and race relations in the New South cannot be understood outside of the examination of formative generational experiences, the lessons that blacks and whites of several generations drew from slavery and the Civil War, Reconstruction, Redemption, and fusion politics.

In reconstructing the story of Charlotte's better classes, I have tried to be especially sensitive to the ways men and women talked about class. Because the New South's economic and social transformation took place during the Gilded Age, the historical record teems with references to class. People in the New South, like other Gilded Age Americans, spoke openly and unapologetically about class. By paying attention to the class-related vocabulary and terminology of the men and women of the New South, we can begin to see how and when concepts of class formed—and were transformed—over the course of the late nineteenth century. Moreover, the fact that men and women in the New South talked so much, and so openly, about class suggests that concepts of class were contested and had no clear-cut definitions.

The "better class" is the term that both black and white business and professional people first used to describe themselves in the 1870s and 1880s. Not only does the term tell us a great deal about the sense of moral and social superiority these men and women presumed, but the common usage of this term by blacks and whites reflects a shared definition of class and an affinity that allowed the black and white better classes to build coalitions in the New South period.

Indigenous definitions of class also reveal the class-based bonds that existed between blacks and whites in the New South era, confirming the importance of studying both races concurrently. Not only were concepts of class dynamic in the New South, but they were also relational. Especially for the black better class, class identity depended in part upon their relationship with their white counterparts and the recognition the white better class afforded them.

Sensitivity to the vocabulary of class in the New South also helps avoid many problems surrounding the usage of the terms "middle class" and "elite." To be "middle class," as described in northern antebellum studies, is to be part of a class with significant economic and political power. But to describe the black professionals and business men and women of New South Charlotte as "middle class" ascribes a degree of power to this group that they did not have. Moreover, the term suggests a class in the middle, sandwiched between an elite and a working class. Yet Charlotte's black community in the late nineteenth century did not reflect a tripartite division; rather Charlotte's black society was two-tiered, divided between a small better class of businesspeople and professionals and their spouses and a large class of laboring men and women.

Likewise, the term "better class" fits the social and economic reality of white business and professional men and women in the 1870s and 1880s. A New South city that before the war was no more than a tiny trading town, Charlotte had no significant "upper class" in the decades following the war. Not until the 1890s did the town have a clearly recognizable manufacturing elite and a middle class that defined itself as separate from both the elite and the working class.

· · · · · · ·

Charlotte, the focus of this study, is in many ways a quintessential New South city whose development parallels that of many other cities of the era. Until the coming of the railroad in 1852, it was little more than a small crossroads town and county seat. Linking Charlotte to the coast, the railroad suddenly transformed the town into a regional trading center, and in the ten years before the Civil War, the town more than doubled in size, to 2,000 inhabitants. Charlotte continued to grow during the war as local entrepreneurs engaged in war-related industry. After the war the town's population surged, augmented significantly by war refugees and ex-slaves. By 1880 Charlotte had a population of over 7,000, six railroads, and a flourishing economy based on the cotton trade. In 1881

Charlotte entered a new phase of development when two local cotton merchants built the town's first cotton mill; by 1900 it boasted more than a dozen mills and could claim to be the center of the Piedmont's burgeoning textile industry. Ten years later, it was the largest city in the state, with 34,000 people, outstripping the older coastal city of Wilmington. Charlotte, then, seems representative of a type of New South city with relatively shallow antebellum roots that experienced rapid growth over the last half of the nineteenth century. Moreover, it epitomizes the dynamic development of inland cities in the New South that were built on railroads, commerce, and industry.

Charlotte stood in the mainstream of two of the New South's most significant economic developments: the growth of cotton culture and industrialization. Both developments transformed social relations in the town. The origins of the white better class lay in the burgeoning cotton economy of the 1870s, which conferred both definition and power to Charlotte's businesspeople and professionals. Less than twenty years later, by the 1890s, a second economic transformation—the establishment of the textile industry—threw class relations into flux again. Like other Piedmont cotton mill towns, Charlotte divided between "town people" and "mill people," the poor, landless men and women who migrated from the countryside to work in the mills. But Charlotte's "town people" also divided by class. The white better class bifurcated into a manufacturing elite and a middle class, often bitterly at odds with each other over issues relating to the "mill people."[4]

Class formation followed a different trajectory among the town's black residents. The origins of the black better class lay not in the cotton economy of the 1870s but in the churches and schools of the Reconstruction era that trained a generation of black teachers, preachers, and businesspeople. Born in the final decade of slavery, this generation of men and women came of age in the 1880s and asserted their leadership against an older generation of political leaders that had emerged during Reconstruction. The "better class" of blacks, as they referred to themselves, saw themselves as the new race leaders, promulgating a philosophy of race progress based on education, property ownership, and moral propriety. In the 1880s the black better class forged alliances with their white counterparts, alliances that helped define them as separate from the rest of the black community and Reconstruction-era leaders. In the 1890s whereas the white better class divided with the emergence of a manufacturing elite, the black better class found its economic opportunities circumscribed. Unlike their white counterparts, they remained economically weak, barred from the feast of New South industrial development.

While Charlotte stood in the mainstream of economic and social development in the South from 1850 to 1910, the town's residents participated in the explosive politics of the era, much of which was generated and molded by social and economic upheaval. The politics of secession and the Civil War, the painful transition of Reconstruction, the angry revolt of Grangers—and later Populists—against Charlotte's businesspeople, fierce battles over Republican party loyalty in the black community, the prohibition movement and experiments with nonpartisan reform, the rise of fusion politics, the white-supremacy campaigns, and progressivism were all played out in Charlotte. By examining the better classes' participation in these events and the political alliances they formed, we can begin to unravel the often tangled and hidden connections that informed political engagement and gave rise to the complex and explosive politics of the New South.

The story of Charlotte's better classes incorporates both the tragedy and the triumph of the New South. It is the story of unlimited promise reduced to bitter disappointment, of seemingly fresh beginnings stifled by eruptive racism. But it is also the story of men and women who had the courage to build bridges across the chasm of race, of black and white southerners who identified with each other across race lines and for a short time embodied an alternative vision of race relations. At the same time, it is the tale of the black men and women who, even after seeing their dreams of equality crushed at the turn of the century, managed to keep their vision alive until another generation of blacks and whites would once again join forces to restore their rights in the civil rights movement.

"A Magic Influence"

On the morning of 28 October 1852, the people of Charlotte and the surrounding countryside gathered to witness one of the most memorable events of their lives—the coming of the railroad. A crowd of about 20,000 people engulfed the tiny crossroads town, swelling the village to nearly twenty times its normal size. Men, women, and children jostled for position in the depot yard as a parade of Odd Fellows, the Sons of Temperance, and a brass band marched through the village. By mid-morning the steam engine from Columbia, South Carolina, roared into Charlotte, conveying passengers and freight and, most significantly, hopes for a prosperous future.

It was "the most brilliant and glorious day that the history of Charlotte has furnished in seventy odd years," reported the local newspaper, describing the inspired addresses of local dignitaries, the sumptuous barbecue, the fireworks at the depot, and the dance in the long room of Williams's dry goods store. The railroad celebration symbolized the beginning of a new era, and the enthusiasm generated that day gained momentum over the next few months as the people of Charlotte saw their town miraculously transformed. "The completion of the railroad to this place seems to have exerted a magic influence over the energies and enterprise of our people," wrote the editor of the local newspaper. "The streets of the town, which a few months ago presented the appearance almost of a deserted village, are now thronged with wagons and carts laden with the rich productions of our prosperous country, and strangers of every tongue are now in our midst seeking the profits of trade and active enterprise." The railroad linked Charlotte—an isolated backwater village only a few months before—to the urban centers of the East Coast, altering the significance of both time and space. Within only a few months, the railroad helped realize "the wildest and most extravagant dreams of those who prophesied five years ago upon this subject."[1]

Those who prophesied and diligently worked to bring about the coming of the railroad to Charlotte were motivated by both hope and fear. The fortunes of Charlotte and Mecklenburg County had been in decline since the late 1830s. Founded in 1768 at the crossroads of two ancient Indian trading paths—one of which became part of the Great Philadelphia Wagon Road—Charlotte served as the county seat of Mecklenburg. In its early days, the town housed a number of taverns for weary travelers and boasted a few stores and tradespeople. As late as 1791, according to the diary of one traveler, the village had about 300 residents and consisted "only of a wretched Court House, and a few dwellings falling to decay." Spending the night in the village as part of his southern tour in 1791, George Washington referred to Charlotte as "a trifling place."[2]

The discovery of gold in adjacent Cabarrus County in 1799, and later in Mecklenburg, breathed life into the region, and Charlotte suddenly found itself strategically located in the center of the Piedmont's mining activity. Several gold mines were established in and near Charlotte, and the village attracted fortune seekers from both the North and abroad in what was at that time the United States' most significant gold strike. Mecklenburg's population jumped by nearly 4,000 people between 1820 and 1830, the largest ten-year increase it had ever experienced. The trifling crossroads village took on the trappings of town life as Charlotte got its first newspaper, the *Catawba Journal*, in 1824 and two banks opened in the 1830s. Property values increased, and new buildings were erected. Blacksmith shops and sawmills, taverns and stores proliferated, providing goods and services for the mines and the miners. Gold mining proved to be so successful in the region that in 1835 the U.S. Congress established a branch of the U.S. Mint at Charlotte. The halcyon days of gold mining ended with the panic of 1837, however, which closed down many mining operations and rendered others marginal.[3]

The decline in gold mining left a huge void in the region's economy. Although Mecklenburg was one of the leading cotton-producing counties in North Carolina by mid-century, farmers found it difficult and expensive to get their crop to market. With nearly unnavigable rivers nearby, produce had to be transported over rough and sometimes treacherous roads to Fayetteville, over a hundred miles from Charlotte, and then shipped down the Cape Fear River to Wilmington. Flat-bottomed scows also carried produce down the Catawba River to Cheraw, South Carolina, nearly seventy miles away, where cotton merchants shipped the crop to Georgetown via the Pee Dee River. Some farmers hauled their crop on wagons directly to the Charleston market, over 250 miles distant. The difficulties faced by farmers in marketing their crop led many to abandon the Carolina Piedmont for greener pastures to the west. Mecklenburg County's population dropped by 7,000 people between 1830 and 1850, making it one of many North Carolina counties that experienced a declining population.[4]

By the late 1840s several leading citizens of Charlotte and Mecklenburg began to search for new ways to rejuvenate the area's stagnant economy. They seized upon the railroad as the panacea for the region's economic ills. Railroad promoters were mostly businesspeople and professionals who lived in Charlotte and had seen their fortunes deteriorate in recent years. They were joined by some of the county's wealthiest farmers who would benefit greatly by a direct rail link to a coastal market. Moreover, many of the most avid railroad promoters, such as physician Charles J. Fox and lawyers James W. Osborne and William Johnston, were ambitious young men in their twenties and thirties who saw their futures, and that of their town, inextricably linked to the railroad. Although many of the railroad men, such as Johnston and Osborne, were active Whigs, one of the most ardent boosters was Democrat Charles Fox. Thus railroad promoters joined forces above the din of partisan politics, fearful of the consequences of the region's economic decline and confident about the ameliorative influence of the railroad.[5]

In 1847 promoters of the Charlotte and South Carolina Railroad, led by Fox and Osborne, organized a series of public railroad conventions in Charlotte and nearby towns to promote a rail line that would link the town to the Charleston market by way of Columbia, South Carolina. In a highly publicized report, the railroad boosters argued that a rail line was "the only scheme by which a convenient Market can be afforded for our Agricultural products—the development of our Manufacturing and Mineral resources be promoted, and a participation be secured to our people in the improvements and advantages of the age in which we live." Although the people of the Charlotte area found themselves surrounded "with natural advantages," such as a fertile countryside, "the interests of our country are rapidly declining." Real estate prices had fallen by 50 percent in the last few years, and "many farms are lying waste and desolate, all improvement is arrested." Moreover, "enterprising citizens have left us in the thousands," especially young people. "Scarcely a young man is commencing life in any branch of business, but is directing his attention to some other State," noted the promoters.[6]

The railroad, and the new markets it would bring, could provide the remedy for rehabilitating Charlotte and Mecklenburg. Prosperity, wrote the railroad promoters, depended on a town's proximity to the sea. Although Charlotte could not be transplanted to the coast, the railroad "annihilates distance and equalizes the advantages of all countries." Not only would Charlotte gain better access to markets, but the railroad would also allow diversification in the local economy as it would encourage the growth of industry. Railroads "are designed as hand-maidens to capital and labor" and "augment every source of prosperity." The boosters claimed that only the railroad could save the area "from poverty and from ruin . . . and provide a home in which we and our children may participate in the enlightened spirit and social advancement in the age in which we live."[7]

The Charlotte promoters preached the gospel of the rail in the surrounding countryside, addressing gatherings in Lincolnton, Salisbury, and Concord, Rutherfordton, Monroe, and Jefferson, their altar call an opening of subscription books. In Mecklenburg County the farmers of the Providence section held a barbecue to champion the railroad, subscribing $14,000 for the road. By August 1847 well over $300,000 had been pledged for the railroad, with all but $28,000 from Mecklenburg. In September, with sufficient funds in hand, the Charlotte and South Carolina Railroad held an organizational meeting, elected directors, and began letting contracts for the road.[8]

When the railroad reached Charlotte five years later, linking the town to the up-country of South Carolina and Charleston, plans were underway for more rail lines. The largely state-financed North Carolina Railroad would link Charlotte to Goldsboro by way of Raleigh, Greensboro, and Salisbury. In September 1854 the road's first passenger service trains steamed through Charlotte, and two years later the railroad was completed. Not satisfied with two railroads, boosters began organizing conventions to bring more railroads to the town. In May 1854 Charles Fox chaired a meeting to organize support for the ambitiously named Atlantic, Tennessee, and Ohio Railroad. Promoters envisioned the road connecting, by way of Charlotte, "Wilmington by the most direct route with the Mississippi Valley," and promoters once again opened subscription books to raise funds for the effort. A year later, the Wilmington, Charlotte, and Rutherford Railroad was incorporated and subscriptions were enrolled (see map 1).[9]

The flurry of railroad-building activity that agitated Charlotte in the 1850s was part of a larger crusade in North Carolina and the South. Between 1835 and 1850, Whigs controlled state government in North Carolina and adopted an agenda of improvements, with railroad building the centerpiece of their program. The state's first railroads were built in the east, but by the late 1840s legislators in the west demanded their own roads. The state then partially funded the North Carolina Railroad to connect east and west. In the 1850s North Carolina built over 641 miles of track, a 258 percent increase in railroad mileage in one decade. Southern states built railroads at such a furious pace that the South actually outstripped the North in the relative increase in railroad mileage

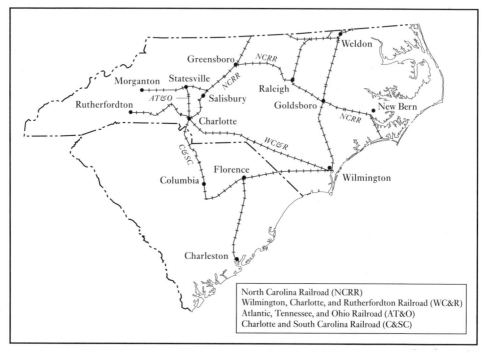

North Carolina Railroad (NCRR)
Wilmington, Charlotte, and Rutherfordton Railroad (WC&R)
Atlantic, Tennessee, and Ohio Railroad (AT&O)
Charlotte and South Carolina Railroad (C&SC)

Map 1. Charlotte's Rail Connections, ca. 1865
Sources: Stover, *Railroads of the South*, 25;
Powell, *North Carolina through Four Centuries*, 54.

between 1850 and 1860. Across the South, towns like Charlotte vied for railroads as the key to prosperity.[10]

It is little wonder that the people of Charlotte and Mecklenburg embraced railroad schemes so enthusiastically. They had seen their town and county transformed almost immediately by the railroad. The "magic influence" of the railroad seemed to leave nothing untouched. "Our people seem to be inspired with new life and new energies amounting almost to intoxication," remarked the *North Carolina Whig* in December 1852. The railroad reversed the precipitous population drop of previous years. Mecklenburg grew by nearly 4,000 people in the decade of railroad building, and the town of Charlotte more than doubled in size, from a population of 1,065 in 1850 to 2,265 in 1860, making it North Carolina's sixth largest town. Wilmington and New Bern still ranked as North Carolina's most populous municipalities in 1860, reflecting the dominance of coastal cities in both the state and the rest of the country. But Charlotte's growth demonstrated the power of railroads to stimulate the development of interior towns. Inland towns with new rail connections surged in population, outstripping coastal towns in growth. Fayetteville, which declined railroads in favor of plank roads, grew only negligibly during the 1850s (see table A.1).[11]

Not only did Charlotte and Mecklenburg grow dramatically in the 1850s, but railroads transformed Charlotte into a regional commercial center. Just as one railroad promoter had predicted, new stores began to spring up as the railroad diverted "the trade from this portion of the State from its old time worn channels." Instead of hauling their produce over hazardous dirt roads to distant markets, farmers flocked to the village of Charlotte to sell their harvest to the town's merchants, who then shipped the crop to the sea by rail. The farmers, in turn, stocked up on food, dry goods, hardware, and clothing. Townspeople found the streets "constantly crowded with wagons laden with cotton, flour, wheat, corn, meal, tobacco, potatoes, apples, poultry, and all manner of produce raised in the country," which was "nearly all bought up by our Grocers and Produce Buyers, and shipped to Atlantic markets." Between 1850 and 1860 the number of merchants in Charlotte more than doubled, from twenty-four to fifty-three, and the number of professionals living in Charlotte more than doubled as well (see table A.2).[12]

Charlotte merchants zealously contended for the trade of the upper Piedmont. Appealing to "our Mountain friends" and "our friends in the Country," they claimed that they could compete with merchants in older trading centers. The stores in Charlotte "are literally groaning under the weight and pressure of new goods," the *Whig* claimed in 1853. By luring the region's farmers to the village to trade, the railroad allowed merchants to improve their stock, selling items previously unavailable in the town. Moreover, merchants began to specialize in various goods and services. General merchandisers such as Elias and Cohen offered "Foreign and Domestic Dry Goods, Gentlemen's Ready Made Clothing, Ladies Dress Goods of All Kinds, and Negro Ware," while William W. Elms concentrated on groceries and E. Nye Hutchison sold pharmaceuticals. J. W. Sanders offered "furniture at Charleston prices," and T. H. Brem and Company sold "British, French, and American dry goods." The contest for trade sometimes grew bitter. Vying for the patronage of farmers to the North, Charlotte merchants accused the Salisbury newspaper of deliberately misrepresenting Charlotte's market prices in an attempt to divert trade back to Salisbury.[13]

Because of the brisk, expansive nature of Charlotte's commerce, local merchants organized a second bank in 1853 to finance even more economic development. Seven townspeople—five merchants and two lawyers—served on the Board of Directors of the Bank of Charlotte. "Having the money of two Banks at their service," announced the *Whig*, "our merchants and traders will be enabled to give the largest prices for country produce." Yet merchants and bankers found trade so vigorous in the fall of 1854 "that our Banks find it difficult, without cramping their other operations to furnish the merchants money to buy produce."[14]

In addition to a bank, a number of other new enterprises, including manufactures, followed in the wake of the railroad, just as the railroad boosters had predicted. Charlotte entrepreneurs enthusiastically embraced small industry. In 1854 Taylor and Allison began manufacturing brick, and in January 1855 merchant Leroy Springs opened a steam flour mill near the railroad tracks in Charlotte "on a scale commensurate with the capacity of the country to supply it with grain for manufacturing into flour." The Ozments established a furniture manufactory in January 1857, and that same year Rudisill and Whisnant opened a sash, door, and blind factory. In 1858 Captain John Wilkes, a native of New York, established the Mecklenburg Iron Works. The 1860 census also listed a tobacco factory.[15]

Not only did the town gain some small-scale manufactures in the 1850s, but new buildings improved the town's appearance. "With our citizens, the tide and the spirit of improvements are still as high as ever," bragged the *Whig* in 1853, commenting on the "great improvement in architectural taste, as displayed in our buildings." Merchants invested their profits in expanding operations and improving their facilities. A group of shopkeepers, including jeweler Thomas Trotter and merchants Elias and Cohen, constructed Granite Row, five large shops on South Tryon Street that compared favorably with any stores "this side of Charleston."[16]

At the same time that the town's merchants and professionals expanded their business activities, they promoted town improvements through local government. Many of the same men who served as railroad and bank directors, invested in manufactures, and built large and prosperous businesses also served as town commissioners, using their influence to improve Charlotte. In 1854 the town macadamized the main streets, enhancing Charlotte's appearance as well as making it easier for farmers to market their goods. That same year the telegraph linked Charlotte with the outside world, causing the *Whig* to marvel that "we will . . . be able to hold sweet converse on wires with our neighbors in New York, and the rest of man-kind." Four years later, gas lights illuminated the streets, giving Charlotte the countenance of a well-established city.[17]

Like boosters in small towns across the mid-nineteenth-century United States, Charlotte's leaders sought to establish cultural institutions that would elevate their town. In 1853 town leaders formed a joint-stock company for a female academy, and Charlotte Female Institute opened in the fall of 1857, another testimony to the town's prosperity and bright future. Two years later a male academy, the North Carolina Military Institute, opened in Charlotte, headed by Major Daniel Harvey Hill and supported by a subscription of $10,000 in public funds.[18]

Large and elegant homes constructed by merchants and professionals added to the town's improving appearance and served as a symbol of the increasing wealth and status of businesspeople. Merchant R. F. Davidson and John A. Young, owner of the Rock Island Woolen Mills, built new homes "according to the latest and most approved models of modern architecture." Merchant W. W. Elms's stylish new home attracted the attention of northern visitors who "pronounced the execution of the job as good as could be found in the Northern cities." So many residences were being built in Charlotte in the mid-1850s that brickmakers Taylor and Allison could not meet the demand, although they manufactured 40,000 bricks a day.[19]

As merchants and professionals distinguished themselves from other townspeople by building fashionable new residences, some began to dress in the sumptuous fashions of the day, now available by rail from coastal cities. The *Whig* noted that "it is the policy of the merchant to dress himself well, and to make an advertisement of his wife, and thus display in the most fascinating form the richness, elegance, variety, and splendor of his stock at hand."[20]

The stylish homes and dress of Charlotte's businesspeople, professionals, and their spouses suggest that they were beginning to set themselves apart from fellow townspeople. The growth of clubs and associations also reflected and reinforced this growing self-consciousness. In 1854 the town's leading citizens formed a Thespian Club to perform plays in Charlotte. A few years later, pharmacist E. Nye Hutchison and Dr. M. B. Taylor, with the aid of local ministers, formed the town's first YMCA.[21]

The activities of women in the 1850s also imply a growing self-consciousness among Charlotte's business and professional people. In the overwhelmingly rural, evangelical antebellum South, female organizations were rare; kinship and community ties as well as demanding work routines undercut the formation of all-female voluntary associations. But in the South's few towns and cities, where the wives and daughters of business and professional men enjoyed more leisure than their rural sisters, female organizations emerged before the Civil War. Charlotte, although still a small town in the 1850s, saw the rise of female associations similar to those formed in larger cities of the South, such as Petersburg, Virginia. Moreover, in creating female organizations, Charlotte's women played a key role in helping define their rapidly changing town.[22]

Charlotte women, like their southern sisters, created their first organizations within the confines of the church. Women made up the majority of churchgoers in the antebellum South, and churches depended on women for financial support. Through most of the 1850s, the activities of town women centered on fund-raising fairs for their churches. Episcopal, Presbyterian, and Methodist women all participated in these functions.[23]

The formation of the Charlotte Presbyterian Ladies' Tract Society in 1858 marked a significant expansion in the activities of women. The society aimed to ameliorate "the spiritual destitution of a large class of the white population of the town & its suburbs, which cannot be breached by the ordinary ministrations of the Gospel." The members hoped to alleviate this "destitution by the circulation of a cheap religious literature" for "the glory of God and the salvation of men and women." They pledged to canvass, at least once a month, "every destitute family" in Charlotte, to speak with them about spiritual matters, and to leave a book or tract at every house. A year later, society members augmented their efforts by furnishing religious literature to travelers on railroad cars, reaching out to strangers passing through their midst.[24]

The Ladies' Tract Society represented an amalgam of both tradition and innovation. Framing reform within the confines of evangelical religion, the society reinforced nineteenth-century ideals of womanhood, emphasizing the spiritual and nurturing qualities thought to be unique to women. At the same time, the society represented a new self-consciousness among wealthier women and an exalted sense of their place in the rapidly growing town. The wives of some of Charlotte's most prominent men organized and headed the society, including Mrs. J. H. Wilson, the wife of a leading lawyer; Mrs. Robert Burwell, whose husband headed the Charlotte Female Institute; and Mrs. Thomas W. Dewey, a banker's wife. Their organization represented the formal emergence of a select female group in Charlotte dedicated to reaching out to needy strangers. As a developing market town, Charlotte attracted many new people in the 1850s, men and women without kinship ties to older residents or roots in the area. Troubled by the growth of an unfamiliar "large class of the white population," the ladies took on the responsibility of incorporating these strangers into the religious life of the community.[25]

By focusing their attention on poor strangers, the women of the Ladies' Tract Society also articulated a growing awareness of social difference in the growing market town. The women helped define the burgeoning town of Charlotte during the decade of the railroad; they divided the white population into two categories—the churched and the unchurched, the affluent and the destitute. The society's emphasis on "cheap literature" and "destitute families" suggests that these women equated being materially needy with being spiritually destitute. Unlike women in larger towns, like Petersburg, Charlotte's wealthier women did not form poor relief organizations in the antebellum period. But by ministering to the spiritual lives of the needy residents of their town, the women of the Ladies' Tract Society set themselves apart as members of the more affluent, rooted, churchgoing group.

Despite a growing self-consciousness among Charlotte's professionals and businesspeople and their spouses, other developments undercut class awareness. The town's businesspeople and professionals did not define their interests as distinct from those of the county's planters. After all, many of Mecklenburg's largest planters had entrepreneurial interests and had promoted railroads, commerce, and industry. In addition, many of Charlotte's businesspeople and professionals owned farms in the county. A serious town-versus-country split did not yet exist in Charlotte and Mecklenburg in the 1850s.[26]

Charlotte's business and professional people were also a numerically small group. In 1860 there were still only 246 businesspeople and professionals living in the town and 340 skilled artisans. Moreover, by the mid-1850s, when their wealth and power began to increase, Charlotte's business and professional people found themselves divided by party politics. In the late 1840s and early 1850s, most of the town's professionals and merchants appear to have been members of the Whig party. Whiggery depicted itself as active, energetic, and progressive, compared to the "Chloroform stupefaction" offered by the Democratic party. The Whig party appealed to the spirited boosters of Charlotte, "Young America," those committed to "improvement" through active control. As Thomas J. Holton, publisher of the Whig newspaper in Charlotte, argued, "Whiggery addresses the rational intelligence of the American people," while "the very term Democracy appeals to the wildest and most tumultuous passions of an illiterate populace."[27]

Charlotte itself was a bastion of Whiggery, like many county seats and small towns in North Carolina and the South. But Mecklenburg County, unlike some other Piedmont counties, was "a stronghold of Democracy, the tenth legion." Whigs in Mecklenburg found themselves continually frustrated in their attempts to break the Democracy's stronghold in the state legislature and Congress; Whigs were simply outnumbered. Commenting on the 1853 election, the *Whig* remarked, "Our defeat has not been owing to the want of ability, industry, or energy . . . but to the strong and over-ruling power of numbers." Banker Thomas Dewey, writing to his wife after the 1854 election, described his chronic disappointment as a Charlotte Whig, bemoaning the fact that "the whole democratic ticket for this county is elected, and it seems to be my fate to be always in a democratic county."[28]

Despite perpetual losses, Whiggery remained an active political force in

Charlotte and Mecklenburg in the early 1850s. When the Kansas-Nebraska Act of 1854 effectively broke the back of the Whig party by dividing it into short-lived northern and southern factions, Charlotte's businesspeople and professionals lost a viable and coherent political voice. Elsewhere in the antebellum United States, the Whig party helped give shape to the interests and concerns of an emerging middle class. At a crucial moment in the development of the business and professional class in Charlotte, the Whig party shattered, leaving merchants and professionals divided among themselves and without a political party or a unified political voice.[29]

Out of the remnants of their party, Charlotte's Whigs tried to refashion a new party to address their interests. Many former Whigs in Charlotte, such as lawyer and railroad promoter William Johnston, manufacturer John A. Young, and banker Thomas W. Dewey, allied with the American party, or the Know-Nothings, the successor of the collapsed Whig party. The American party seemed at first the ideal solution for southern Whigs who hoped to paper over sectional animosities. By castigating Catholics and foreigners, southern Whigs hoped to re-create a Unionist coalition. "Foreigners, Catholics, Abolitionists, Secessionists, all Democrats that oppose the American Party," wrote "Civis" to the *Whig*, "are arrayed against true Americans." But few voters in Charlotte seemed roused by such appeals. The nativist rhetoric of the Know-Nothings rang hollow in Charlotte, where Catholics and the foreign-born made up only a tiny percentage of the population. Although the Whigs in Charlotte tried to resuscitate their party in 1856 and in 1859, they had little success at the polls. Thus many members of the nascent business and professional class drifted through the final years before the Civil War without a viable party to advance their concerns.[30]

Charlotte's merchants and professionals divided over the issue of temperance as well. The temperance movement swept across many towns and cities in the antebellum United States as men and women sought to control what they viewed as the root of all social evil—alcohol. By the 1850s the temperance movement in Charlotte and Mecklenburg was well over twenty years old. As early as 1833, townspeople and county dwellers, men and women, began forming temperance organizations at the behest of the American Temperance Society. Prominent townspeople, such as merchant John Irwin and Whig newspaper editor Thomas Holton, played an instrumental role in these efforts. The movement appears to have gained momentum during the gold-mining boom, when grog shops catered to miners and fortune seekers in the village, but waned during the economic decline of the 1840s.[31]

By the 1850s, when Charlotte again verged on prosperity, the temperance movement grew stronger. Soon the liquor issue polarized municipal politics in Charlotte as it did in many other antebellum American towns. Liquor flowed bountifully in Charlotte's taverns and grocery stores, where farmers from the country spent part of their hard-earned profits from the sale of their crops. Yet visiting farmers and traders alone did not account for the town's alcohol problem. Even some prominent church members succumbed to the lure of the bottle. Bessie Dewey, who moved to Charlotte from Raleigh in the 1850s with her banker husband, Thomas Dewey, wrote to her mother that Charlotte was not a "pleasant place" because "there are a great many more erring members of the church here than in Raleigh," with several church members "who get on the rarest sort of drinking sprees & half a dozen who are drinkers by habit—not frolickers but soakers." Temperance advocates aspired "to free our beloved flourishing village from the withering blighting curse" of alcohol.[32]

In December 1852 "the friends of order, morality, and Temperance" nominated a "No License" ticket of candidates for town intendant and the council, pledged to "oppose the granting of licenses" to liquor dealers. Headed by Dr. L. G. Davidson, the ticket included dentist E. H. Andrews, merchant R. C. Carson, mint coiner Emor Graham, jeweler Thomas Trotter, and lawyer J. W. Osborne.[33]

The opposition slate, the Independent ticket, also included leading merchants and professionals. Lawyer W. F. Davidson headed the Independents, joined by fellow lawyers W. R. Myers and William Johnston as well as a brickmason, a saddler, and the mint's assistant coiner. Friends of the wet ticket argued that No License candidates would "deprive us of our liberties," while others argued that North Carolina law protected investment in the liquor trade as much as it did ventures in dry goods or railroads. After an acrimonious campaign, the No License ticket lost the election by twenty-one votes.[34]

Despite the failure of the No License ticket, the liquor issue gave women a platform for public debate they did not have before. Antebellum southern women typically kept a low public profile; but the temperance issue touched directly on family life, allowing women to voice opinions in the public arena in the decade before the Civil War. Although local women apparently did not form their own temperance societies or hold offices in Charlotte's temperance organization—as they would in the 1880s—they made themselves heard in the local press. Women typically addressed their pleas specifically to men, calling for the obliteration of "the tyrant Alcohol" in order to secure family life. One female letter writer discussed the pain of being married to a drunkard, whose family "he drags down with sorrow and degradation with him to the grave."[35]

With some of Charlotte's women publicly supporting the cause, temperance advocates ran No License candidates again in the municipal election of 1856, and, as it would thirty years later, temperance became hopelessly entangled in partisan politics. In an attempt to discredit the Know-Nothing party, which Democrats claimed was the driving force behind the No License candidates, a group of local Democrats formed the Anti-Know-Nothing ticket. The ticket, according to temperance advocate Thomas Holton, was a ploy by Democrats, "a ruse of the license men to bring politics to bear upon the license or no license question." The Know-Nothing party in North Carolina had refused to take sides on the temperance issue. Still, the *Western Democrat*, the voice of the Democracy, claimed that since the Know-Nothing party had no strength of its own, it "seeks on all occasions to unite itself to the cause of temperance, religion, and everything else which promises to give it vitality."[36]

Despite attempts by temperance advocates to disentangle the issue from partisan politics, businesspeople and professionals divided over the issue. A number of church leaders, to the disgust of temperance advocates, sided with the Democratic Anti-Know-Nothing ticket. The temperance ticket lost again, and the Democrats declared the result "a Democratic triumph."[37]

Instead of binding Charlotte's businesspeople and professionals in collective action and self-definition, temperance splintered them. Elsewhere in the antebellum United States—such as Rochester and Utica, New York, Jacksonville, Illinois, and Providence, Rhode Island—the temperance movement served as a rallying point for an emerging middle class. But many of Charlotte's businesspeople and professionals, a small, amorphous group, were just beginning to experience long-sought prosperity. They seemed unwilling to commit themselves to the temperance movement, perhaps fearful that the loss of liquor sales would threaten the town's burgeoning good fortune. Moreover, the divisive nature of temperance discouraged many of the town's boosters, who diligently labored to make Charlotte a prosperous and harmonious place. Finally, the identification of temperance with the muddled, unpopular Know-Nothing party probably dampened active participation in the movement as well.[38]

After the explosive municipal elections of 1853 and 1856, temperance advocates moderated their approach. To avoid "partisan squabbles" that "embarrass our cause," they resolved simply to lobby for a state law to control liquor sales more tightly.[39]

Although partisan politics and temperance divided Charlotte's white population, the presence of slaves, free blacks, and perceived threats to slavery united all white townspeople regardless of their political stripe or stance on temperance. The size and composition of Charlotte's African American population mirrored many other towns in North Carolina (see table A.1). In 1850 Charlotte had approximately 456 slaves, constituting 44 percent of the town's population. When Charlotte more than doubled in size in the 1850s, its slave population did not quite keep pace, accounting for 36 percent of the population in 1860, a decrease experienced by many towns in North Carolina and the South. Charlotte's free black population was smaller than most other towns in the state, especially those in the eastern part of North Carolina, where the free black population clustered. But the town's free black population grew significantly from 1850 to 1860. In 1850 Charlotte had only 36 free black inhabitants; ten years later the census listed 139.[40]

Many of the town's leading merchants and professionals owned slaves, apparently having purchased them as both an investment and a symbol of status in the decade before the Civil War. Some of these slaves may have worked on farms owned by their masters in the country, while many others were "hired out" as house servants or laborers. In addition, some town slaves probably worked in their masters' manufacturing enterprises. John Wilkes, proprietor of the Mecklenburg Iron Works, had ten slaves, and lawyer and railroad promoter William Johnston, who also owned a sawmill, had eleven. Employed as industrial workers and hired out as servants, slaves in Charlotte, as in other southern towns, experienced an independence unknown to slaves on the plantation. The relative autonomy of town slaves along with the threatening presence of free blacks contributed to an uneasy relationship between the races.[41]

White residents attempted to control the activities of slaves through town ordinances. Slaves were barred from the streets after 9:30 P.M. unless they had written permission from their owners. They also were not allowed to buy or sell alcohol and were forbidden to assemble without the permission of the mayor or town commissioners. The town guard patrolled the streets from 9:00 P.M. until daylight and had permission to "visit all suspected negro houses." A severe lashing awaited blacks found guilty of breaking any of these ordinances.[42]

Even though free blacks in Charlotte made up only a tiny percentage of the town's population in both 1850 and 1860, their presence created tension in the town. Anomalous citizens in a society built on race-based slavery, free blacks served as a constant reminder to enslaved blacks of the possibility of freedom. Moreover, white citizens feared them as perpetrators of revolt, and white laborers resented competing with them for employment. They lived a precarious and circumscribed existence, neither slave nor fully free.

In 1860 free blacks made up less than 10 percent of North Carolina's population. In Charlotte the free black population by 1860 had never exceeded 6 percent of the town's population. Yet both state and local authorities over the previous decades had carefully restricted the activities of free blacks, reducing them to a state of quasi freedom. In 1830, fearful of the growing abolitionist movement, the General Assembly passed the Free Negro Code, which attempted to restrict free blacks' contact with antislavery advocates and slaves. The code prohibited the movement of free blacks in and out of the state, forbade their teaching slaves to read and write, and circumscribed their contact with black seamen. In 1835 the General Assembly disfranchised the state's free black citizenry. Although the courts remained open to free blacks, the competency of their testimony could easily be called into question.[43]

Like their counterparts in other southern towns, Charlotte's commissioners passed laws supplementing state statutes that regulated the lives of free blacks. Town ordinances often lumped free blacks and slaves together, affirming the inferior status of the free black citizenry. Neither slaves nor free blacks could smoke a pipe or a cigar or carry a weapon or a club. Moreover, ordinances restricted the economic sphere of free blacks, who were prohibited from being employed as clerks or retailers or selling alcohol.[44]

Despite economic restrictions, Charlotte's free black community boasted a handful of men who were skilled artisans, including three barbers, a brickmason, a housepainter, a wheelwright, and several apprentices, some of whom managed to amass considerable property. Barber Jerry Pethel ranked as the wealthiest member of Charlotte's free black community. In 1860 Pethel claimed $2,300 in real property and $1,250 in personal property, making him the richest free black in town as well as one of only fifty-three free blacks in the entire state who owned more than $2,500 worth of property. By contrast, most of the town's free blacks, like free blacks across North Carolina, owned no property. Women predominated among the town's free blacks, and nearly all of them worked in menial positions as servants or laborers. Yet some were able to amass significant amounts of property. Laborer Nancy Jones, for example, claimed $550 worth of property in 1860. The ownership of property held special significance for free blacks. Owning property was one of the few ways free blacks could exercise their rights as citizens. Moreover, many free blacks in the South saw the accumulation of property and economic advancement as ways to guarantee their freedom.[45]

Unlike older and larger antebellum towns and cities, Charlotte had no deeply entrenched free black community before the Civil War. Cities such as Charleston, New Orleans, Mobile, and Savannah contained highly stratified free black communities crowned by an elite who were defined largely by ancestry, color, education, and wealth. Charlotte's free black community, by contrast, was small and largely undifferentiated, lacking a black "aristocracy." Most of its members were propertyless, recent arrivals to the town.[46]

Small in number, Charlotte's free blacks lived among the white residents and were dependent on them economically. Whereas free blacks in larger southern cities established separate black neighborhoods as well as churches, benevolent societies, and schools, Charlotte's free black population was too small to sustain separate institutions. Free blacks lived interspersed among the white population—in separate residences in white neighborhoods, in boardinghouses and hotels with white residents, and in the households of white employers. Most free blacks in Charlotte managed to establish their own households. More affluent free blacks, such as the Pethels, maintained their own homes, as did some laborers and household servants, such as Nancy Jenkins and her two children. Whereas single free black women tended to establish their own places of residence, single free black men usually lived in the households of their employers. For example, apprentice Joe Johnston resided in the household of his employer, John Harty.[47]

Despite the fact that Charlotte's free blacks lived among white citizens and must have been well known to them, free blacks in Charlotte, like their counterparts across the South, suffered daily indignities and humiliations and lived with the constant fear of enslavement. Sectional tensions in the 1850s exacerbated uneasy relations between blacks and whites across North Carolina and in Charlotte. During the decade, the General Assembly received a barrage of petitions from white citizens demanding the removal of free blacks from the state. In 1852, after a number of Charlotte slaves attempted to escape to the North with the aid of forged papers, white citizens angrily blamed the town's handful of free blacks. Noting "a growing spirit of insubordination among our slaves," some town leaders called for the deportation of Charlotte's entire free black population to Liberia. If free blacks, "this unhappy class of our population," were "removed from our community," claimed the *Whig*, "the cords of slavery would certainly be slackened to some extent."[48]

Through the course of the 1850s, the people of Charlotte reluctantly found themselves pulled into the orbit of national affairs. In 1854 the Kansas-Nebraska Bill initially elicited only passing interest in the local press and from politicians. Indeed, the formation of the Atlantic, Tennessee, and Ohio Railroad that year received far more attention in the press than the pending bill. After New England abolitionists protested the bill, however, the *Whig* lashed out angrily against "Northern fanaticism." By November 1854 the *Whig* pronounced that the late elections "plainly indicate that a large and dangerous majority of the people" in the North "are opposed to Southern institutions."[49]

Fear of northern interference resulted in several confrontations with suspected abolitionists. In 1854 a "Yankee" who had been "giving vent to his abolitionist sentiments" was "called upon by a committee" and "politely in-

formed that if his 'pretty face' was visible in the town of Charlotte at the end of
the hour, he would be made a bird of"—that is, tarred and feathered. According
to the local press, "he took the hint and vamoosed," after "tampering with one
slave at least." A few years later "a man by the name of Thompson" came to
Charlotte, and "from his intercourse with some negroes," local citizens concluded that he was an abolitionist. Also threatened with being tarred and feathered, Thompson was escorted to the railroad depot "with drum and fife."
Abolitionists, warned the local press, "had better be on their guard when they
come to this place."[50]

John Brown's raid at Harpers Ferry in October 1859 intensified the fears of
Yankee interference and slave revolt in Charlotte and the South. The *Whig*
labeled Brown's raid an abolitionist plot "to aid in murdering the people of the
South by causing an insurrection of the Negroes." Slaves "are becoming un-
manageable now, and with the prospect of being set free they would become
worse." In response to perceived threats from abolitionists and slaves, the men of
Charlotte and Mecklenburg formed new militia units, including the Charlotte
Light Infantry and the Mecklenburg Dragoons.[51]

In a decade of rapid social and economic change and political turmoil, tension
between blacks and whites as well as the presence of slavery served to bind
together the town's white population. Despite differences in status, professionals, merchants, farmers, artisans, and the small group of mechanics and
laborers were all bound by their whiteness. Moreover, their hatred of outside
agitators coupled with a chronic fear of black revolt united white men and
women of various social groups.

The coming of the Civil War also blunted emerging social distinctions among
Charlotte's white population, even though North Carolina, a state with especially
strong Unionist sentiments, was racked with class-based conflict during the war.
Committed to secession by February 1861, Charlotte and Mecklenburg remained staunchly dedicated to the war even in the darkest days of the Confederacy, avoiding the internal civil war that tore apart much of the rest of the
state and even neighboring counties.[52]

On the eve of the war, Charlotteans seemed divided over the issue of disunion.
In July 1859 Alabama fire-eater William Yancey delivered "the first Disunion
Speech ever heard publicly in Charlotte." Although the Unionist *Whig* hoped
that "the atmosphere of Charlotte is too pure for spreading such pestiferous
doctrines as he advocates," Yancey's speech, to the dismay of some townspeople,
"was welcomed . . . with great cordiality . . . and his Disunion sentiments
applauded."[53]

With both the Whig and Know-Nothing parties moribund, moderate Unionists cast about to find a party and candidate to represent their sentiments as the crucial presidential election of 1860 approached. Most of the town's ex-Whigs and Know-Nothings supported John Bell and the Constitutional Union party, while the majority of Democrats endorsed John Breckinridge, even as they called for calm and moderation. A handful of Charlotte Democrats formed a club supporting Stephen Douglas, the candidate of northern Democracy.[54]

As the election drew near, tensions increased as party men held torchlight parades and erected banners in the town square. The *Whig* appealed to all "Union Men" to go to the polls "to cast the most important vote of your life." But holding with Mecklenburg tradition, Democrat Breckinridge overwhelmingly carried the county, with Bell and Douglas a distant second and third. Mecklenburg's vote for Breckinridge, however, did little to block Abraham Lincoln's election even though his name did not appear on the ballot in North Carolina and other southern states. "The election of Lincoln," noted the *Whig*, "has unsettled the foundations of everything, . . . [and] has accomplished an universal alienation of love for the Union among the Southern people."[55]

Nevertheless, in the wake of the election of 1860, the people of Charlotte and Mecklenburg, like many other North Carolinians, remained divided over what course North Carolina should take. Unlike their neighbors to the South, North Carolinians took a far more moderate stance on the issue of secession. Lacking a large, wealthy planter class and containing significant numbers of small farmers and nonslaveholders, North Carolina generally approached the question of disunion with restraint.[56]

At a public meeting a few weeks after Lincoln's election, the people of Charlotte passed a series of resolutions of a "dignified, mild, and conservative character" calling for "the preservation of our Union and our Federal Government in its original integrity." But at the same time, "in the event the States of the South should withdraw from the Union," the citizens resolved that "the best interest of North Carolina demands a similar course of action." In the county, public meetings were held representing each end of the political spectrum.[57]

By early 1861 Mecklenburgers grew increasingly impatient with the federal government and more shrill in their anti-Union sentiments. The secession of neighboring South Carolina in December 1860—with which the area had powerful economic bonds—thrust many of Charlotte's businesspeople and professionals to the forefront of the secession movement. Indeed, because of rail connections to Columbia and Charleston, Charlotte and Mecklenburg's economic interests in 1861 were far more oriented to South Carolina than to North Carolina.

Moreover, by 1861, many local citizens identified the current conflict with the

American Revolution, a particularly powerful association for Mecklenburgers. The revolution provided a potent metaphor for many secessionists by 1861; they portrayed themselves as the new American revolutionaries who, like their ancestors, wished to declare their independence and throw off the shackles of tyranny. The allusion to the American Revolution especially resonated among the people of Mecklenburg. As they struggled to make sense of the friction between the federal government and the southern states, local citizens constantly drew on the heritage of their forebears, who allegedly wrote a Declaration of Independence from Britain in 1775—a full year before Thomas Jefferson's declaration—and who valiantly repulsed British troops who marched through Charlotte and Mecklenburg. The present generation, they believed, needed to defend the honor of their ancestors who had fought to maintain liberty. Just as Mecklenburg had been a "hornet's nest," in Lord Cornwallis's words, of revolutionary activity during the American War of Independence, so too would it be a stronghold of insurrection against the perceived tyranny of the federal government.[58]

In late January 1861, soon after Mississippi, Florida, Alabama, and Georgia joined South Carolina in leaving the Union, North Carolina's General Assembly called for the state's voters to decide on 28 February whether to hold a convention to address the issue of secession and to choose delegates to the proposed convention. In Charlotte and Mecklenburg, secessionist sentiment crystallized as the county voted overwhelmingly in favor of a convention and elected two delegates—who had run unopposed—both of whom pledged to vote for immediate withdrawal from the Union: J. W. Osborne and William Johnston.

Both delegates represented Charlotte's economic interests, with strong ties to South Carolina through their involvement with the Charlotte and South Carolina Railroad. Johnston served as president of the railroad, and Osborne had been an early promoter and investor in the road. In ratifying their delegates, local citizens appealed to what they called the "Spirit of 1775," calling upon Mecklenburgers to show in the present crisis the "same determination to maintain and defend our rights." The *Western Democrat* confidently asserted "that the stout hearts and strong arms of the sons of old Mecklenburg will be ready, as ever, to maintain the right." But Mecklenburgers proved to be in disagreement with their fellow Tarheels in advocating a secession convention. Although the county voted by a landslide—1,448 to 252—to hold a convention, strong Unionist sentiment in the state blocked the proposed assembly.[59]

As the people of Charlotte and Mecklenburg discussed secession in the spring of 1861, news arrived of the Confederate bombardment of Fort Sumter in April. Delighted citizens fired cannons and celebrated "with demonstrations of joy." Although North Carolina would not officially secede until May 1861—and although a majority of North Carolinians would not support secession until after Lincoln's call for troops from the state several days after the Fort Sumter bombardment—the *Whig* proclaimed that "the war has begun and it becomes the duty of every true friend of the South to be up and doing." In a show of solidarity, Democrat W. R. Myers and former Whig J. A. Young made speeches in the public square, and the local militia fired a salute "in honor of the victory at Charleston."[60]

Building on the militia units formed in the wake of John Brown's raid in 1859, local men quickly mobilized for action, displaying "the chivalry which distinguished the heroes of Old Mecklenburg in days gone by." By late April several military units, including the Charlotte Grays and the Hornet's Nest Rifles, headed for Virginia after receiving emotional send-offs.[61]

Charlotte's women, like women across the South, played a key role in sending fathers, sons, and brothers off to war. Flag-presentation ceremonies provided a symbolic ritual whereby women gave their blessings to departing warriors. Continuing a tradition begun with antebellum militia units, young women made public speeches at the flag-presentation ceremonies. The speeches were laden with language that stressed the active masculinity and gallantry of the soldiers and the passive, feminine, spiritual ideals of southern women. Miss Sadler sent off the Hornet's Nest Rifles with "the prayers, the hopes, the heart, of our ladies," noting that she and other Mecklenburg women were "proud that the chivalry which distinguished the heroes of old Mecklenburg in days gone by, still animates her gallant sons." Likewise, Hattie Howell, who dispatched the Charlotte Grays, lauded the bravery of the "sons of Mecklenburg," whose "sires have written the brightest pages of history with their blood . . . which you are now called upon to defend."[62]

The war expanded the activities of Charlotte's women far beyond public ceremony. As the men of Charlotte left to do battle, women organized societies to assist them. Soon after the battle of Bull Run in July 1861, the women of Charlotte formed the Ladies' Hospital Association to collect clothing, bandages, and food for the Confederate wounded. Several months later, leading townswomen established the Soldiers' Aid Society of Charlotte to sew clothing for Confederate troops.[63]

Charlotte women also served as nurses to sick and wounded soldiers. In the summer of 1861 two members of the Ladies' Hospital Association, "ladies of skill and experience," traveled to Yorktown, Virginia, accompanied by five servants whose expenses were paid by the association, to work in a Confederate hospital. By July 1862 Charlotte had its own hospital "for the care of transient, sick and wounded soldiers." Confederate officials established a second hospital at the fairgrounds in July 1863. Besides nursing the infirm, the townswomen sewed and washed bedding and bandages, solicited contributions of fresh food, and gathered herbs and barks for medicinal purposes.[64]

Work in hospitals and soldiers' aid societies expanded the role of women while confirming traditional gender roles. Wartime activities brought the women of Charlotte together for the first time in secular, females-only organizations outside the home and church. Yet the services women provided in aid societies and hospitals stressed the auxiliary role of women and underscored traditional feminine virtues, such as healing and caretaking. As the *Whig* remarked, "The ladies cannot shoulder the musket and march to the field, but in their sphere may do much to furnish the sinews of war, and hold the hands of those who stand in the deadly breach or the perilous edge of battle."[65]

Women's relief organizations, although founded and headed by affluent women, bound women of various social groups. Several officers of the Charlotte Presbyterian Ladies' Tract Society of 1858 also directed the Ladies' Hospital Association, including Mrs. J. H. Wilson and Mrs. T. L. Dewey. These women applied the organizational skills they had mastered in their antebellum mission group to the exigencies of wartime. They were joined by other prominent Charlotte women, including Mrs. C. J. Fox, Mrs. J. W. Osborne, and Mrs. John Wilkes. But unlike the denominationally based Ladies' Tract Society, the Ladies' Hospital Association appealed to all women of the county for aid and received an overwhelming response. The local press noted that women "of all classes and conditions" threw themselves into the war effort, ministering "to the comforts and necessities of those who have gone to defend our rights on the tented field." Young and old, rich and poor, Charlotte and Mecklenburg's women carded, spun, stitched, and knitted for Confederate troops. "No one should feel satisfied," wrote a woman to a local newspaper, "who does not devote one half her time towards assisting in the manufacture of the necessary amount of clothing for our soldiers."[66]

Besides uniting women of various social groups in a common effort, aid associations, and the support for the war that they engendered, also cut across race lines. In 1861 the Soldiers' Aid Society received a donation of $25 from "the coloured ladies of Charlotte," probably the spouses of the town's handful of free black artisans. The society thanked the black women "for their testimonial of fidelity and attachment to the South." The association received a second donation from free black townspeople later that year, a gift of $30. Secretary Bessie Dewey praised the contributors and used the occasion to make a public political statement: "Our country's cause is a common one with master and servant alike," she contended, "and it behooves us all to . . . show the fanatics of the North that we of the South, regardless of colour, stand as a unit to sustain and strengthen the arm of the soldier of our glorious Confederacy."[67]

The public support of Charlotte's free blacks for the Confederate cause reflected their precarious position in southern society, which only worsened with the war. Public displays of Confederate patriotism, replicated by free blacks across the South, helped distance them from the slaves. More importantly, patriotic acts demonstrated to their white neighbors that their loyalties lay with the Confederacy and that they indeed posed no threat to the slave order.[68]

While the wives of Charlotte's businesspeople and professionals directed relief efforts, many of their husbands also volunteered their services to the war effort. A contingent of the town's physicians went to Richmond to tend to sick and wounded North Carolina soldiers. By the fall of 1861 the local press remarked that "the sudden departure of so many leading citizens leaves a vacuum in the business and social circles of their respective places of business and residence which is silently but painfully felt."[69]

Businesspeople who remained in the town struggled to keep their enterprises alive as the blockade curtailed commerce, the lifeblood of Charlotte. As commerce shriveled, some businesspeople began investing in war-related industries. The war did not dampen the entrepreneurial spirit of Charlotte's businesspeople and professionals so evident in the 1850s but instead fueled it. Like their counterparts who had promoted economic diversification since the 1850s in other southern towns and cities, Charlotte's businesspeople took advantage of wartime opportunities to create new industries and convert existing industries to war production.[70]

Prominent antebellum entrepreneurs invested in two new wartime industries: a powder-manufacturing company and a gun factory. Patriotic and profit-driven Charlotte entrepreneurs happily embraced the opportunity to take advantage of well-paying government contracts and the Confederacy's lucrative offer to subsidize powder and arms manufacturing. Local businesspeople, headed by lawyer S. W. Davis, established the North Carolina Powder Manufacturing Company on Tuckaseegee Road. That same year, William Phifer and J. M. Springs called a public meeting to form a joint-stock company to manufacture ordinance and shells. The company, noted the *Western Democrat*, was made up of "a goodly number of our wealthy and most influential citizens," who subscribed $15,000 for the factory. Dr. J. H. Gibbon served as president of the Mecklenburg Gun Factory, and the board included lawyer J. H. Wilson and planter A. B. Davidson.[71]

Charlotte's war-related industrialization received a major boost when the town became the site of a Confederate navy yard. When Union troops threatened the Norfolk yard in the spring of 1862, Confederate secretary of the navy Stephen Mallory chose Charlotte as the location of a new inland yard. With an established ironworks and rail connections to the coast, Charlotte seemed a logical location. The Confederacy took over John Wilkes's Mecklenburg Iron Works at Trade and College streets, constructed a number of large frame structures as well as coke ovens and a foundry, and began manufacturing marine engines, gun carriages, anchors, iron projectiles, and propeller shaftings.[72]

War industries attracted skilled labor to Charlotte, an element largely missing before the war. Approximately 300 workers moved from Norfolk to Charlotte to work in the navy yard, and Chief Engineer Ramsay employed local men as well. Charlotte finally got the "mechanic class" that town leaders had yearned for since the late 1850s. So many navy yard workers lived in the town's First Ward that it became known as "Mechanicsville."[73]

As entrepreneurs created new industry in wartime Charlotte, several manufacturing concerns in and near the town converted to war-related production. J. A. Young's Mountain Island Woolen Mill, located on Tuckaseegee Road, manufactured "soldiers' round jackets." The army's demand for the jackets was so great that the mill ran an advertisement in the newspaper in 1863 calling for 200 women workers to produce the jackets. The New Manufacturing Company, located on East Trade Street opposite the Confederate navy yard, produced wooden canteens for the army.[74]

The Confederate government's insatiable need for guns, powder, and supplies provided unprecedented opportunities for creating new industries and converting old ones, diversifying the local economic base. Indeed, because of the war, Charlotte shifted from being a commercial center to being both a commercial and industrial hub. Meanwhile, war-related industry broadened Charlotte's social base as skilled workers flocked to the town for employment during the war. As in other southern towns and cities, war industry promoted urbanization in Charlotte, as the town flourished with the influx of newcomers. War-related industrialization and urbanization not only diversified the local economy and social fabric, but also would provide an important precedent for New South Charlotte.[75]

Besides bringing new workers to Charlotte, the war also brought a large influx of refugees. Beginning in the spring of 1862—after the fall of Norfolk and Portsmouth—Charlotte experienced the start of a deluge of homeless and uprooted people who flocked to the town during the war years. In May 1862 the *Western Democrat* commented, "The town is about all filled up, and it is almost impossible to accommodate more."[76]

Yet Charlotte did manage to accommodate a large, fluid wartime population.

Soldiers on their way to and from battle regularly passed through the town, sometimes causing problems for local residents. Dandridge Burwell wrote to his brother about a drunken regiment of Georgians who "stole everything they could lay their hands on. It is said that they would jerk your hat off and walk off with it and you had to stand or whip twenty or thirty of them."[77]

The crowding of the city with strangers, the deaths of local soldiers, and uncertainty sapped the spirits of many residents of the town. The *Western Democrat* devoted a regular column, "Loss of North Carolina Troops," to listing killed, wounded, and missing Tarheels by regiment. Like countless other citizens of the North and South, the men and women of Charlotte mourned the deaths of their sons, husbands, and fathers. Mrs. Robert Burwell, an organizer of the Soldiers' Aid Society, fretted about what the future held for her sons and wrote in 1863 to her son, Edmund, "If this horrid war does not cease all the men who are young & from whom our country expects great things will be killed & you young ones that are coming on must be qualified to take their places."[78]

Food shortages and inflation exacerbated war weariness. As early as December 1861, the *Whig* noted that "hard times is the cry at every corner" and that "our country is infected with land sharks who buy up everything that comes within their reach from a pint of chestnuts up to a sack of flour." The *Western Democrat* contended that "no town in the State beats Charlotte in high prices although we are in the midst of a fine producing section."[79]

Speculation, inflation, and food shortages helped stimulate class-based resentment across much of the South during the Civil War. But in Charlotte resentments over shortages and high prices cut across social groups, defusing class consciousness. All "town people"—regardless of occupation or position—suffered. Indeed, deprived Charlotteans directed their wrath not at their richer neighbors, who also suffered, but at the producers—the farmers in the countryside.[80]

Growing antiwar sentiment in the state also did not stimulate class-based conflict in wartime Charlotte. For the duration of the war, Charlotte and Mecklenburg remained firmly in the secessionist camp, committed to the Confederate cause despite deprivation, war weariness, and a robust antiwar movement in North Carolina. In many other parts of the Tarheel State—particularly in the mountains, parts of the coastal region, and the Piedmont area in and around Randolph County—Confederate policies helped trigger massive disaffection from the government and the war effort. The Conscription Act of 1862, which called for the draft of white males between the ages of eighteen and thirty-five, contained massive loopholes that allowed for substitutes and exemptions by the rich and well connected. The draft law seemed to underscore the growing belief among poorer citizens that the war was indeed a rich man's war and a poor man's fight. Moreover, many North Carolinians viewed the draft law as unconstitutional, an infringement on their civil liberties. The Confederacy's suspension of the writ of habeas corpus in 1862 only accentuated fears that the government had little concern for protecting constitutional rights.[81]

The 1862 governor's race helped focus growing bitterness against the Confederacy in North Carolina. In March 1862 Mecklenburg citizens held a meeting nominating Charlotte's William Johnston as a candidate for governor. An ardent secessionist and enthusiastic advocate of the war, Johnston received the spirited backing of several secessionist newspapers in the state. William Holden, editor of Raleigh's *North Carolina Weekly Standard* and a vocal opponent of secession and the Davis administration, immediately seized upon the chance to transform the election into a referendum on the actions of Tarheel secessionists in 1861. Holden condemned Johnston as a "Destructive" who had helped lead North Carolina to war, a fanatic, and a "rabid precipitator" who had favored "war and bloodshed in February 1861, when two-thirds of the people were for peace and an honorable adjustment of our difficulties." Moreover, Holden contended that Johnston, as president of the Charlotte and South Carolina Railroad, was "nearly as strongly attached to South Carolina as he is to his own state." Not only did he conduct most of his business in Columbia, but he also built a railroad from Charlotte to Statesville on "the South Carolina gauge," forcing local farmers to ship their produce to Columbia and Charleston rather than east to Wilmington, a North Carolina market.[82]

To oppose Johnston, Holden drafted Confederate colonel Zebulon Vance to run for governor on the Conservative ticket. Vance, dubbed by Holden as one of North Carolina's "old Union men," had opposed secession until Lincoln's call for troops from the state. To many Tarheels, Vance represented former Unionists who now found themselves fighting a war that secessionists such as Johnston—who stayed at home in Charlotte—had precipitated. Moreover, compared to Johnston, Vance was, in Holden's words, "a North Carolinian, in all his instincts, sympathies, and habits." Holden pronounced the governor's race a contest to overthrow the secessionist domination of the state.[83]

The campaign for governor sparked heated political discourse in Charlotte and across the Tarheel State, revealing deep fissures over support of the war. Both the *Whig* and the *Western Democrat* backed Johnston, claiming that Vance's candidacy represented nothing more that an attempt "to build up a Holden party in North Carolina in opposition to the true friends of the South." But some residents took the opportunity offered by the campaign to criticize men like Johnston who led the South to war and then did not volunteer to fight. "Confederate," a Charlotte resident, wrote a bitter letter to Holden's newspaper just before the 1862 election attacking "that class of political leaders and speech-makers who promised the people peaceable secession, and if there was any fighting they would do it." Yet, noted the writer, "they are at home, and now that they have urged their neighbor's children to fight, they refuse to go and stand by them." Reflecting growing rancor toward the secessionists, the writer contended that "every town in the State is cursed with these political warriors who would whip the Yankees before you could spell secession."[84]

Despite "Confederate's" caustic criticism, Johnston, the native son, over-whelmingly carried Mecklenburg County in the election. His wide margin of victory, in which he received 1,335 votes to Vance's 425, suggests that in August 1862 the county remained firm in its support of secession and the war. Yet Mecklenburg found itself in a distinct minority in North Carolina. Vance carried the state by a landslide, burying Johnston 58,070 to 14,491; among soldiers, Vance defeated Johnston 2 to 1. Counties that harbored large numbers of army deserters and where alienation from the Confederacy prevailed—such as Chat-ham, Guilford, Randolph, Forsyth, Yadkin, and Wilkes counties, as well as adjacent Iredell County—gave Vance twenty times the number of votes cast for Johnston. As a result, Vance's Conservative party wrested control of the General Assembly from the secessionists.[85]

Union victories at Vicksburg and Gettysburg in July 1863 coupled with Confederate domestic policies fueled further alienation from the war in North Carolina. A tax-in-kind, instituted in 1863, required farmers to tithe a tenth of their produce to the government in Richmond. The Impressment Act, also passed in 1863, proved especially odious to southern producers. The act allowed the Confederacy to take produce, slaves, and livestock from farmers for use by the army; in many cases, farmers had to accept below-market prices for their property. Although farmers across the South protested the Impressment Act and its arbitrary and inequitable enforcement, North Carolinians were inordinately affected by the law. With an unusually high proportion of white men serving in the military and a relatively small slave population, the Impressment Act only increased the suffering of the already strapped population.[86]

By mid-1863 William Holden channeled growing anti-Confederate senti-ment into a peace movement in North Carolina that called for a negotiated settlement to the war. Holden's crusade for peace spawned acrimonious debate across the state, dividing the citizenry to an unprecedented degree. Thousands of North Carolinians, including some rural residents of Mecklenburg, gave their support to the peace movement. A public meeting held at Long Creek in Mecklenburg in August 1863 not only endorsed Holden's plan but also condemned the tax-in-kind, the suspension of habeas corpus, and Confederate draft laws.[87]

Voters in Charlotte and Mecklenburg had a chance to vote on the peace movement in the fall of 1863. Across the state Holden promoted several peace candidates for the Confederate Congress who pledged to demand that the Congress pursue a negotiated settlement with the Union. In North Carolina's Eighth District, which included Mecklenburg, Dr. James G. Ramsay ran as a Conservative peace candidate against incumbent William Lander.[88]

Charlotte's business and professional men virulently opposed Ramsay and the peace movement. Maintaining their secessionist stance, they threw their support behind Lander, the Davis administration, and the Confederate cause. The *Charlotte Bulletin* called Ramsay's supporters, "with few exceptions, the scum of society—men who have done very little if anything towards supporting the Confederate government since the war began, and are ready to accept any sort of a compromise with the Yankee government."[89]

As peace meetings proliferated across the Tarheel State in the summer and fall of 1863, Charlotte's business and professional men countered by organizing public assemblies pledging support for the Confederacy. In August they headed an assembly at the county courthouse that resolved "that the citizens of Mecklenburg county have unabated confidence in the justice of the cause" and that there was "no cause for despondency"; the southern people would win their independence if they presented "a united and undivided front in support of the war."[90]

In the November election, peace candidate Ramsay defeated Lander in the Eighth District—but not with the aid of Charlotte and Mecklenburg. Whereas voters in the surrounding counties of Rowan, Cabarrus, Lincoln, and Gaston demonstrated their disapproval of the war by supporting Ramsay, Charlotte and Mecklenburg remained secessionist strongholds. In Charlotte Ramsay polled only 54 votes to Lander's 389; countywide, Lander defeated Ramsay 933 to 371. In only two county voting districts—Long Creek, the site of Mecklenburg's only recorded peace meeting in August 1863, and Deweese—did the peace candidate receive a majority.[91]

As southern hopes for victory dwindled in 1864 and fatigue and conflict engulfed North Carolina and the South, Charlotte and Mecklenburg remained committed to the war and the Confederacy. In 1864 Confederate critic William Holden challenged Zebulon Vance for the governorship of the splintered Tarheel State. Once a staunch ally of Holden, Vance had finally split with the peace advocate in August 1863 over what he viewed as Holden's excessively vicious and treasonous attacks on the Confederate government. Like the congressional elections of the previous year, the governor's race severely divided the state's voters into bitter factions.[92]

In the election, Vance overwhelmingly defeated Holden, whose increasingly extreme attacks on the Davis administration had alienated many moderate Tarheels. Notably, Holden received the least support in Mecklenburg County. Soon after the election, Holden bitterly acknowledged that "Old Mecklenburg has given Governor Vance the largest vote he has received in any county in the State, and has also given him a larger majority than any other county in the state." Holden charged that "there was no free ballot in the town of Charlotte, either for citizens or soldiers." He angrily labeled Mecklenburg "the foremost *secession* County in the State."[93]

As white residents of Charlotte and Mecklenburg tenaciously clung to the Confederate cause, concerns over the loyalty of blacks in their midst increased their anxieties. In an attempt to control the free black population—a long-standing source of concern—the town required free blacks twelve years of age and older to appear before the mayor and have their names registered. "Upon satisfactory evidence of a peaceable character and industrious work habits," Charlotte's free blacks would obtain a certificate that they were to carry with them at all times. At the same time, town authorities also cracked down on the slave population. An 1861 ordinance made it illegal for slaves to "go at large as a free person exercising his or her discretion in the employment of their time." Moreover, slaves were forbidden to "keep house . . . as a free person."[94]

Despite the attempts of town authorities to control the black population, many slaves took advantage of the chaos and confusion of wartime to escape. In June 1863 the *Western Democrat* reported that "portions of this county have been infected for sometime with runaway Negroes." Although the *Democrat* tried to assure readers that slaves "were true to their masters and 'loyal' to the cause," the press simultaneously commented on the number of runaways. Slave patrols hunted missing slaves and tried to keep them from "committing depredations" and causing "terror to the neighborhood."[95]

By early 1865 in the declining days of the Confederacy, Charlotte braced for an invasion. In February 1865 General William T. Sherman and his troops burned Columbia, terrifying Charlotte residents, who feared that their town might be Sherman's next target. Refugees from Sherman's March flooded the strapped town, and, confirming the accounts in the local press, Mrs. Robert Burwell reported that "there is the greatest crowd of refugees from South Carolina passing into Charlotte" and "we are importuned every day to take Boarders—I hate to hear the bell ring."[96]

But Sherman never came, opting instead for a path to the east through

Cheraw, South Carolina. Although a temporary refuge in April 1865 for the fleeing Confederate cabinet and Jefferson Davis and his family, Charlotte was spared destruction. The town entered the postwar years physically intact and with a population augmented by the ravages of war.

$$\bullet \quad \bullet \quad \bullet \quad \bullet \quad \bullet \quad \bullet \quad \bullet$$

In the spring of 1865, when the Confederacy came to an end, the Charlotte and South Carolina Railroad lay in ruins as a contingent of Stoneman's Raiders had burned a key bridge over the Catawba River outside of Charlotte. The railroad, the progenitor of prosperity, the embodiment of Charlotte's hopes and aspirations, lay temporarily lifeless, its steam engines halted by the devastation of war. The ruined railroad stood as a fitting symbol of the shattered fortunes and dreams of Charlotte's leaders in the spring of 1865. The war they had enthusiastically supported terminated their prosperity and delayed their dream of making Charlotte the leading inland trading center. But soon after Appomattox, workers began to repair the railroad, and Charlotte's businesspeople resumed building up their town—this time in a much more complicated world.

2

"The New State of Things"

In the spring of 1866, a year after the Confederacy's defeat, journalist and former Confederate general D. H. Hill of Charlotte contemplated the South, past and present, in the first issue of his newly established journal, *The Land We Love*. Although the past should be venerated, Hill asserted, southerners needed to adjust to the profound alterations brought about by the defeat of the Confederacy. "But we of the South," wrote Hill, "however much we may revere our ancestors and their time-honored usages . . . must yet of necessity change our minds upon many subjects, else our very name and nation will be taken away." Hill continued, "Our system of labor has been abolished, our currency destroyed and our whole social organization has been overturned . . . and we must make our minds correspond to the new state of things."[1]

In the aftermath of the Confederacy's subjugation, the townspeople of Charlotte, black and white, grappled with the new state of things as described by Hill. Many of the town's white residents seemed anxious to put the war behind them and resume the business of town building and creating a diversified local economy. "We are seriously desirous of letting by-gones be bygones," wrote newspaper editor W. J. Yates. "We are tired of turmoil and disputes, and want to do all in our power to promote peace." Picking up where they had left off in 1861, the people of Charlotte lured more railroads to their town and built banks, iron-front buildings, and fashionable Italianate homes. In the years from 1865 to 1880, town leaders saw their dream come true as Charlotte emerged as one of the leading trading centers of the Piedmont.[2]

However, the town they sought to shape after the war was far more complex than the one they had known in 1861. Refugees flooded Charlotte from the surrounding countryside, seeking employment, food, and shelter. More importantly, emancipation threw race relations into flux. Former slaves left nearby plantations to live in Charlotte, where they struggled to establish their own communities and assert their rights as full-fledged citizens. The black and white townspeople of Charlotte clashed repeatedly as blacks tested the limits of their freedom and whites tried to enforce customary rules of race relations. Moreover, as freedpeople enthusiastically entered the political arena, many whites furiously fought against what they deemed "Negro domination," maintaining that even in the new order, white supremacy must be preserved. The fact that so many white townspeople demanded a continuation of their control at the same time that blacks insisted on political equality guaranteed that politics would be waged on a bloody battlefield through most of Reconstruction.

While Charlotte's black and white citizenry struggled with the implications of emancipation, class lines in the white community became more distinct. Not only did the town's white merchants, professionals, and businesspeople grow in power as the town flourished, but they also became aware of themselves as a distinct class—with their own special interests—in a series of bitter disputes in the mid-1870s that pitted the "town people" of Charlotte against the "country people" of the county. Moreover, the wives of town leaders helped delineate class lines through their benevolent activities, particularly poor relief. Postbellum Charlotte, then, represented a "new state of things" as men and women, blacks and whites shaped postwar society and were, in turn, fashioned by it.

• • • • • • •

In the immediate aftermath of the Confederacy's demise, the prospects for Charlotte looked grim indeed. Captain Morris Runyon, commander of the Ninth New Jersey Volunteers, found the town "filled with rebel soldiers." Mobs looted stores and "drunkenness and disorder" abounded. Sick and wounded soldiers, housed in makeshift hospitals, taxed the town's slender resources, and war refugees struggled to find food and shelter. As newly freed black men and women gathered in the town, white residents eyed them warily, fearing "that trouble will result." Most townspeople actually welcomed the arrival of federal troops from New Jersey and Ohio who soon restored order in Charlotte.[3]

In June 1865 William Holden, recently appointed by President Andrew Johnson as provisional governor of North Carolina, reestablished civil authority in Charlotte by naming a provisional mayor and town council. Holden, the Unionist propagator of North Carolina's peace movement, generally rewarded like-minded people with appointments across the state in the summer of 1865. Holden named physician H. M. Pritchard, a longtime resident of the town, as mayor and appointed eight aldermen, including merchant H. M. Phelps and cotton buyer J. E. Stenhouse, who had both served on the town council during the war; farmer William Windle; carpenter David Barnhardt; and dry goods dealer J. C. Burroughs. The new town officials helped keep the peace by prohibiting the sale of alcohol and by enforcing vagrancy laws. The commissioners also organized a town patrol, enrolling all white male citizens between the ages of eighteen and forty-five to guard the town against lawbreakers.[4]

Whereas many towns in the South languished in the wake of the war, Charlotte seemed to be on the road to economic recovery only a few months after the fighting ended. Charlotte escaped the severe damage suffered by many towns and cities of the South, such as Atlanta, Columbia, and Richmond. Although the rail line to Statesville had been dismantled during the war to furnish sorely needed rails to the Confederate cause, other lines remained intact. Thus Charlotte continued to be linked to the hinterlands and the coast and emerged from the war relatively unscathed, a clear advantage in the war-torn South. In August 1865—only four months after the end of the war—the *Western Democrat* boasted that business had increased to such an extent that it "reminds one of old times to pass through our streets and see the bustle caused by the receipt of New Goods and the Stores crowded with buyers." Houses for both stores and dwellings, reported the *Democrat*, were in great demand. "There's life in the old land yet," crowed the newspaper.[5]

Several encouraging developments in the next few months supported the *Democrat*'s claims. In September 1865 the First National Bank inaugurated operations. Replacing the defunct antebellum banks, the First National Bank provided desperately needed capital for Charlotte's recovery. Another promising sign was the number of prominent North Carolinians who settled in Charlotte after the war. Zebulon Vance, the state's beloved wartime governor, moved to Charlotte early in 1866, upon his release from federal prison, to practice law. Likewise, Confederate general Rufus Barringer, a native of nearby Cabarrus County, moved to the town and established a law practice. Other lesser-known figures flocked to Charlotte and aided the town's recovery. R. Y. McAden, who would become a leading cotton mill owner later in the century, left Alamance County in 1867 to head Charlotte's First National Bank. Similarly, R. M. Miller, who would play a major role in the economic development of Charlotte, moved to the town from the stagnant Lancaster district of South Carolina.[6]

The fact that so many enterprising and established men from both North and South Carolina left older, once-prosperous rural districts for the bustling town reflected, in a palpable way, the shift from the Old to the New South. The South's brightest economic prospects no longer existed in the countryside, in the old plantation districts built on slavery, but in dynamic towns and cities like Charlotte, built on railroads, commerce, and fledgling industry.

These newcomers, along with a core of men who had antebellum roots in the town, became New South Charlotte's business leaders. Like New South Nashville and Atlanta, most of Charlotte's postbellum business leaders had been born in the 1820s. Some had fought in the Civil War and were experienced businesspeople. Well over half of Charlotte's New South business leaders were active in the town before the war. William Johnston, W. R. Myers, John Wilkes, and J. A. Young all continued to play an active role in the town's economic development, as they had since the 1850s. Yet a significant number of "new men"—over 30 percent of the town's business leaders in the 1870s—migrated to Charlotte after the war, mostly from the hinterlands of the Carolina Piedmont. Some, like Clement Dowd of Moore County and R. Y. McAden of Alamance, had well-established careers as lawyers and businesspeople before the war. Seeing greater opportunity in the booming town of Charlotte, they relocated there after the war. Dowd and McAden headed two of the town's banks in the 1870s and by the 1880s were involved in Charlotte's industrial development. Others were like John W. Wadsworth, who moved to Charlotte from Davidson County in 1865 as "a poor man," according to a biographical sketch, and made his fortune in livery stables, becoming one of Charlotte's wealthiest citizens. Thus Charlotte's New South economic leaders, like those in Atlanta and Nashville, were far from being all "new men," but many new men soon climbed to the top of Charlotte's economic ladder and, with the town's previously established business leaders, helped shape Charlotte into a vital New South city.[7]

The cotton trade served as the key to Charlotte's rapid economic recovery and growth. Since Charlotte continued to be able to boast superior transportation facilities, the town's merchants were able to pick up where they had left off at the outbreak of the war, aggressively pursuing the trade of the upper Piedmont. Merchant T. H. Brem promised "Old Times at His Old Stand," while commercial merchant J. Y. Bryce guaranteed "the highest market cash price for cotton." In November 1866 the *Western Democrat* reported as "evidence that the Charlotte market is the best in the State" that cotton and other produce "is brought here from within seven miles of Cheraw, twenty miles of Camden, and five miles of Winnsboro, South Carolina"—all major antebellum markets. Editor Yates proclaimed that the streets of Charlotte reminded him of Fayetteville in the days of his youth, "filled with wagons from all directions—some from Fairfield, Kershaw and Chesterfield Districts, South Carolina," as well as the North Carolina mountain counties of Watauga, Caldwell, and Burke. The Reverend Robert Burwell wrote to his son in November 1866 that "the town is improving very fast and business is very active. The quantity of goods brought here is amazing and yet they are all sold."[8]

Charlotte's wholesale trade also boomed and attracted country merchants from upper Piedmont North and South Carolina. Expanding the specialized trade of the 1850s, merchants declared that the Charlotte market offered everything available in larger cities. New red-brick, two-story double stores served as tangible symbols of Charlotte's affluence.[9]

By 1869 Charlotte had made such serious inroads into antebellum cotton and wholesaling markets that Charleston merchants fought back. They declared they were "determined to make an effort to regain what they lost to a considerable extent by the changes of the war: the trade of this section of North Carolina." Charleston businesspeople published thirty advertisements in Charlotte newspapers extolling the advantages of trade in their market. But because of rail connections and wartime destruction on the coast, the tide of trade had shifted significantly to interior markets all over the South. The advertisements of the Charleston merchants could not stem the new flow of trade.[10]

Whereas Charlotte and its businesspeople adjusted smoothly to the new state of things in strictly economic dealings, the broader social and political order did not accommodate such a peaceful transition. Black and white townspeople struggled in the aftermath of abolition to redefine their relationship. Like their compatriots across the South, ex-slaves in the Carolina Piedmont asserted their newly won freedom by abandoning plantations and heading for town, leaving the past behind. To many whites, the migration of ex-slaves from the countryside to towns and cities seemed frenzied and aimless. In June 1865 a Charlotte Freedmen's Bureau agent remarked that "the whole population of Blacks" seemed "completely wild," proof, in his view, that "the sudden transition from Slavery to Freedom had caused them to become a restless and wandering People Straggling over the country in Search of Freedom." But many freedpeople migrated to towns like Charlotte with clear intentions. Like white southerners in the new order, many African Americans viewed towns and cities as the best place to make a new start after the war. Employment and educational opportunities certainly seemed greater in Charlotte than in the countryside. In addition, Charlotte provided some security and protection—not found in the countryside—through the Freedmen's Bureau. The bureau in Charlotte occasionally distributed clothing and rations to the most impoverished ex-slaves and, soon after the end of the war, established a camp and hospital for destitute freedpeople. Moreover, in town newly freed men and women had the chance to live among and socialize with people like themselves. Ex-slaves helped make Charlotte the fastest-growing town in North Carolina between 1860 and 1870, as the population swelled to over 4,400 residents, more than doubling in a decade (see table A.3).[11]

White Charlotteans, who had lived in a precarious relationship with blacks even before emancipation, feared the black men, women, and children who swarmed to their town. They complained incessantly about blacks who crowded the streets, loitered around the courthouse, and lived in makeshift shacks in low-lying areas of Charlotte. Like white town dwellers in other parts of the South, they insisted that their town was no place for freedpeople. The *Western Democrat* griped about ex-slaves who left the countryside to "come here to town and lie about . . . in idleness," preferring "to do a day's work in town for their dinner." Especially irritating to many whites was the fact that the migration of African Americans to their town resulted in a severe labor shortage in the countryside, forcing many whites "to discontinue farming for the want of labor, while hundreds and thousands of able-bodied negro men are lounging about the towns and cities." They argued that "compulsion is necessary" to make blacks work and called for civil authorities to force black labor. Others could not imagine a stable society populated with large numbers of free blacks and called for black emigration to Liberia. Many blacks left the area on their own, lured by planters in Mississippi and Georgia, further exacerbating the labor shortage in Mecklenburg County.[12]

Freed blacks often found their high expectations for a new life dashed in the early years of Reconstruction. In the fall of 1865 a rumor circulated among the freedpeople in Charlotte and across the South that the government would supply them with forty acres and a mule by Christmas. Freedmen's Bureau agents in Charlotte tried desperately to quash the rumor, bluntly cautioning freedpeople, "The Government has given you your freedom and you must not expect anything further from it."[13]

Many freedpeople found that loyalty and honesty did not get them very far in the new free labor economy. Despite being backed by the Freedmen's Bureau, ex-slaves struggled to obtain fair labor contracts from white employers. In 1866 a bureau official reported that "disputes are daily arising between blacks and whites" in settling accounts for the year's labor and that "there are but few cases where the terms of the contract are respected" since "there seems to be a determination on the part of the whites to deprive if possible the Freedman out of his just claims." As a result, "many blacks find in settling that instead of having something to keep them through the coming winter, they are in debt to their employers." Many "are out of work, and are without food or shelter, and much suffering is anticipated."[14]

Even when ex-slaves procured their just wages, many still found themselves mired in poverty since wages were "scarcely sufficient to keep soul and body together where there is the usual family." In 1867 a bureau agent reported that many ex-slaves would "soon be at the point of starvation, unless food is furnished by the Government." Even though the bureau issued rations throughout 1866 and 1867, the Charlotte bureau agent in 1868 callously recommended that "it would be worse than folly to attempt to better their condition by issuing provisions, for the reason that these people have always been on the brink of starvation."[15]

Despite economic intimidation and warnings to behave compliantly, many former slaves demanded that they be treated with respect by whites. Some white citizens responded with contempt and physical abuse. A Charlotte freedman filed a complaint with the Freedmen's Bureau against N. Q. Johnson for clubbing him with an axe "in front of the mayor . . . with a crowd of spectators who did not interfere" because he "did not reply quite so respectfully as Johnson thought he should." Alexander Wagstaff attacked freedman Alec Hall with a hoe after Hall bravely asserted that his wife was Wagstaff's equal. Equality entailed sexual rights for one freedwoman. When newspaper editor J. C. Britton attempted to rape his thirteen-year-old servant Georgiana Boyd, Boyd had Britton arrested by bureau authorities and held on $1,000 bond.[16]

Despite the nearly insurmountable problems they faced, freedpeople immediately began to lay the foundations for their own community in Charlotte. Moreover, they did so without the guidance or legacy of a free black elite. Charlotte's antebellum free black population had been too small and too new to sustain an "old upper class" and separate, elite free black institutions, such as churches or clubs. Also, few free blacks remained in Charlotte after the war. Of the 139 free blacks listed in the town's 1860 census, only 18 appeared in the 1870 census. The fact that women, who cannot be traced due to marriages, predominated in the free black population of 1860 may account for the small number recorded in the 1870 census. Nevertheless, Charlotte's postwar black community contained only a handful of free blacks from the antebellum era. Several free black artisans remained in the town, most notably the Pethel family, headed by barber Jerry Pethel, the wealthiest member of Charlotte's free black population before the war. Wheelwright William Foster and his family also stayed in the town. By 1870, Foster had advanced to the position of coachmaker. The remaining members of the antebellum free black community who stayed in Charlotte consisted of laborers, servants, and washerwomen.[17]

The absence of an old free black community and a dominant free black elite allowed newly freed men and women to create a new postwar black community in Charlotte unencumbered by prewar social patterns or divisions. In older and larger southern towns, such as Charleston and New Orleans, a free black elite continued to dominate the black community, controlling political power, leadership, and wealth and doing all they could to set themselves apart from the recently freed slaves. But in Charlotte no elite maintained control after the war to shape and define the black community.[18]

Freedpeople laid the cornerstone of the postwar black community by organizing churches. Churches not only accommodated religious services but also housed schools, political meetings, and social functions. In May 1865, only a month after the defeat of the Confederacy, African Methodist Episcopal Zion (AMEZ) missionary E. H. Hill reached Charlotte and organized Clinton AME Zion Chapel, the town's first postwar black institution. Clinton Chapel, established independently of white influence, nurtured many of the town's future black leaders. The same year that black missionaries organized Clinton Chapel, black Presbyterians revolted against their treatment in the town's Presbyterian church, where they were relegated to the balcony as they had been in slave times. Kathleen Hayes, a freedwoman, summoned the black members of the church to "come out of the gallery and worship God on the main floor." A year later the Reverend S. C. Alexander, a white Presbyterian missionary from Pittsburgh, aided Hayes and her followers in founding the Seventh Street Presbyterian Church.[19]

The establishment of black churches led to the creation of black schools. Northern missionaries and teachers trooped to Charlotte to bring both the gospel and education to ex-slaves. In 1867 the Reverends S. C. Alexander and Willis L. Miller of Pittsburgh, missionaries of the Northern Presbyterian church, founded a school for freedpeople. Early students wore greatcoats and trousers from the U.S. cavalry and infantry, donated by the Freedmen's Bureau. Alexander and Miller moved the school slightly west of Charlotte in 1868 onto land donated by W. R. Myers. Myers, who had been a Whig in the early 1850s and briefly a Democrat before the war, joined the upstart Republican party after the Civil War and became a benefactor of the freedpeople. The school was named Biddle Memorial Institute after Mrs. Henry Biddle of Philadelphia made a donation to the school in honor of her husband, who had been killed in the Civil War. The institute aimed to prepare "Teachers, Catechists and Ministers for the education of the colored race," and drew hundreds of freedmen from the surrounding area. It served as the training ground for Charlotte's "race leaders" who emerged in the 1880s.[20]

Joining the Presbyterians from Pittsburgh were Quakers from Philadelphia. The Friends Freedmen Association of Philadelphia established a day school in the Third Ward that supported four teachers who taught fifty-five pupils. By September 1867 eleven schools had been established in the Charlotte area, five of which were "conducted by Charitable institutions at the North." Most of them, however, had been built "by individual efforts of the Freedmen." The

William R. Myers, Republican benefactor of Biddle Memorial Institute.
(Courtesy of the Robinson-Spangler Carolina Room,
Public Library of Charlotte and Mecklenburg County)

efforts of local freedpeople to build schools "proves beyond a doubt," wrote bureau agent A. W. Shaffer, "that the negro is susceptible of great improvement mentally, morally, and physically." By mid-1868 thirty freedmen's schools operated in the Charlotte area, serving approximately 700 students.[21]

Clusters of black settlement formed around the churches and schools. The town of Biddleville developed in the vicinity of Biddle Memorial Institute, and concentrations of African Americans occurred in the town's Second and Third wards. But blacks were not confined to these wards and settled throughout Charlotte; residential intermingling—not segregation—continued to be the rule in Charlotte and many other southern cities through the late nineteenth century.[22]

Ex-slaves sacrificed their meager earnings to educate themselves and their children, often boarding teachers and paying "50 cents per scholar" to be schooled. Despite having eager pupils, teachers and parents fought an uphill battle to maintain and operate freedmen's schools. Teachers often felt isolated and frustrated by the lack of support they received from the Freedmen's Bureau, state and local governments, and the white public. One teacher, writing to the bureau for more support, stated that "the pupils are already doing all they can, the Parents of the pupils are too poor to do anything more," while "the state Government is in such a transient state that nothing can be expected from it." In response to a questionnaire asking how the bureau could aid local schools more, the Reverend Willis Miller testily replied, "I should like to know what they have done. Will the Bureau inform me?" A local teacher noted that although the public demonstrated "little active open opposition, few men of influence cooperate, and many secretly oppose" the freedmen's schools.[23]

Opposition to black schools stemmed from several concerns. Many whites worried that education would prevent blacks from accepting a subservient role in southern society and would fill their heads with thoughts of equality. To many whites, going to school represented an act of black rebellion against white authority. Still others feared that Yankee schoolteachers, with the aid of the Freedmen's Bureau, sought to use the schools to organize ex-slaves for political purposes. Although the federal government ordered bureau agents to be nonpartisan, agents were encouraged to inform blacks of their political rights; many of them undoubtedly crossed the line into partisan politics and guided freedmen into the Republican party. The freedmen, wrote Confederate veteran and local journalist D. H. Hill, "might become useful citizens, if let alone by the fire-and-fee loving bureaux and incendiary agents, who are seeking to perpetuate their power by using these unfortunates as their tools."[24]

Whether influenced by bureau agents and teachers or not, Charlotte's blacks entered the political arena with a passion. In September 1865 the state's fledgling black political leaders met in Raleigh, demanding the right to vote as well as the right to testify in court and to serve on juries. From that gathering emerged the North Carolina State Equal Rights League. Aiming to promote political rights as well as education and aid to the poor, the league served as an organizing vehicle for political action and a training ground for Charlotte's first black political activists, such as John T. Schenck. In September 1866 the State Equal Rights League, with Schenck as Mecklenburg's representative, met again in Raleigh. Claiming to be "the only recognized organization we, as a colored people, have," the convention stressed "that we must learn to rely upon ourselves." While emphasizing the importance of education, the convention did not hesitate to take a political stance, endorsing the Civil Rights and Freedmen's Bureau bills as well as the Fourteenth Amendment. The convention also called for the formation of Equal Rights Leagues across the state. Schenck served on the executive board of the State Equal Rights League and probably organized a league chapter in Charlotte.[25]

As a free mulatto before the war, an artisan, and a veteran, Schenck fit the profile of many other black political leaders in the Reconstruction South. Born a slave in Cleveland County in 1824, he learned to read and write and managed to save enough money as a carpenter to buy his freedom and that of his wife before the Civil War. He traveled around the world, supporting himself with his trade. Returning to the South as the Civil War began, Schenck worked at the Wilmington breastworks before joining Stoneman's Cavalry—as a member of the Union army—in Tennessee. Returning to the North Carolina Piedmont with Stoneman's Raiders, Schenck was credited with influencing Stoneman not to destroy his ex-master's property. At the end of the war, he settled in Charlotte, where he immediately began to build a political career.[26]

Although Schenck was not a native of the town, his travels and experience as a Union soldier undoubtedly enhanced his reputation among the ex-slaves who would constitute his political constituency. Moreover, his rapid ascension to the political leadership of Charlotte's black community attests to the absence of an entrenched free black population in the town to dominate the African American community after emancipation. Black newcomers to Charlotte—whether previously free, like Schenck, or newly freed ex-slaves—found opportunity unimpeded by an older black elite.[27]

Late in 1866 Schenck and his fellow black Tarheel political activists received support from an unlikely source—William Holden. As provisional governor in 1865, Holden had originally argued that blacks needed to earn their political rights gradually; indeed, black rights ranked low on Holden's agenda as governor in 1865. But after losing the governor's seat to Jonathan Worth in December 1865, Holden changed his opinion about the rights of ex-slaves. The enfranchisement of black men by the Radical Congress seemed a foregone conclusion in 1866, and Holden seized the opportunity to curry black support for the revival of a Unionist party in North Carolina. In December 1866 Holden announced his support for black political rights and soon began making contacts with Tarheel blacks.[28]

In March 1867, after Congress passed the Reconstruction Act granting black North Carolinians the right to register to vote for the first time since 1835, Holden organized North Carolina's Republican party. In the state's first racially mixed political assembly, the party praised the Radical Congress, championed unionism, and condemned the defiant Confederate spirit that they believed still plagued the Tarheel State. Finally, the party specifically endorsed black political rights.[29]

Built on a coalition of black voters, old Unionist Whigs, and northern carpetbaggers, North Carolina's Republican party developed into the most broadly based and successful Republican party in the South. Although constantly racked by intraparty disputes—most of which centered on the role of blacks in the party—the Republican party remained vital in the state until the late 1890s.[30]

Two months after the formation of the state Republican party, Mecklenburg's Republican party was born. In May 1867 John Schenck, black tinner John C. Davidson, and farmhand Armstead Brown, along with a diverse group of white citizens, organized Mecklenburg County's Republican party. Charlotte Republicans chose 20 May—Mecklenburg Declaration of Independence Day—to declare their liberation from traditional politics. In a dramatic show of African American voting strength, the town's Colored Union League formed a procession one-half a mile long and led party followers to a speaker's stand on Tryon Street. Formed at the same time as the state party, the Colored Union Leagues were secret societies that organized black voters. As a participant in state black organizations, John Schenck likely had a hand in the creation of Mecklenburg's Colored Union Leagues. Dr. H. M. Pritchard, who had been appointed by Holden as provisional mayor in May 1865, addressed the meeting, declaring "a new era in the history of man in this vicinity." Advocating political equality for freedpeople, Pritchard proclaimed that "we are here upon equality under the law, as American citizens." The Mecklenburg party also underscored its support for the state Republican platform, formulated a few months earlier.[31]

In Charlotte the makeup of the Republican party mirrored that of the party statewide. Dominated by freedmen, it also included a handful of northern-born townsmen as well as several of Charlotte's most prominent native-born white citizens—some of whom were affiliated with the Whig party before the war. Painter Charles A. Frazier and tailor Edward Fullings, both of whom were born in the North, joined Northern Presbyterian missionaries Alexander and Miller as founders of the party. Lawyer and entrepreneur W. R. Myers helped found the party in Charlotte. Myers had been a Whig before 1854 and then served in the state senate as a Democrat. But his loyalty to the Democracy seems to have been thin, as he became an outspoken Republican during Reconstruction. Joining his fellow renowned townsmen was Civil War general Rufus Barringer. Barringer prided himself on his independent thinking. Before the Civil War, he had been an outspoken Whig and Unionist in Cabarrus County, serving as an elector for John Bell in 1860. As the debate over secession raged in North Carolina in late 1860 and early 1861, Barringer vociferously attacked the Democracy and secessionism. Despite his disapproval of the war, Barringer raised a cavalry company when North Carolina joined the Confederacy and fought valiantly for the southern cause. After the war, however, he again opposed his traditional foes, the Democrats, and worked wholeheartedly for the Republican cause. Barringer's association with the Republican party served as a constant source of irritation to the local opposition, which worked hard to portray the Republican party as a coalition of carpetbaggers, ignorant blacks, and scalawags.[32]

"Union, Liberty, and Equality" became the rallying cry for the town's Republicans. "Safety, peace and prosperity," claimed Rufus Barringer, were "to be found no where outside of the Republican Party." The Republicans took the initiative in the political debate, voicing a moderate position that endorsed universal education, a uniform currency, and payment of the debt while opposing property confiscation from former Confederates. The party offered "the right hand of fellowship to all good and true men who, abnegating past hostility, come forward . . . [to] help us push on the good work of early reconstruction."[33]

But few whites were in such a conciliatory mood. To many white Tarheels, Republicanism represented black rule and Yankee domination. North Carolinians who opposed the Republicans attempted to unite under the banner of the Democratic-Conservative party. As the first election opened to freedmen approached in the fall of 1867—to choose delegates to a state constitutional convention—Conservatives found themselves bitterly divided over whether they should even participate in the contest. As a result, the state's Conservatives failed to organize a party before the election.[34]

Despite the lack of a statewide organization, Charlotte and Mecklenburg's Conservatives managed to establish a county party just prior to the convention election. As the editor of the *Western Democrat* commented, "The white people of the South . . . do not intend to voluntarily consent to be governed by the colored

Rufus Barringer, Confederate general and postwar Republican.
(Courtesy of the Robinson-Spangler Carolina Room,
Public Library of Charlotte and Mecklenburg County)

people." Faced with the threat of black Republican rule, the local Conservative party managed to unite disparate political elements, including old secessionists, some ex-Whigs, and even a leader of Mecklenburg's anti-Confederate peace movement. Despite the fact that many Tarheel secessionists had been discredited during the Civil War, William Johnston, a leader of the state's secessionist faction during the war, reasserted his political leadership in 1867. At the organizing convention, Johnston gave a rousing speech in support of the party. Planter A. B. Davidson, an ex-Whig, served on the nominating committee. Perhaps in a symbolic act of reconciliation, the convention nominated Captain Thomas Gluyas as one of two party nominees to attend the state constitutional convention. Gluyas had served as chair of Mecklenburg's only recorded peace meeting in August 1863.[35]

Most of the town's whites tried to discourage black voting. The *Western Democrat*, echoing the sentiments of many of the town's white citizens, suggested "that the negro will be more benefitted by large crops of corn, etc. than by all the political harangues from this until doomsday." Black men should "attend to their work and strive to make money. . . . Money in the pocket or corn in the crib, and plenty of meat in the smoke house, will be found to be better friends to the colored man than all the political speakers in constitutional conventions in the land."[36]

Despite discouraging words from local Conservatives, freedmen flocked to the polls in late November 1867, and Conservatives got their first bitter taste of the power of the freedmen's vote. Mecklenburg's Republican nominees to the state constitutional convention, Edward Fullings and Silas Stillwell, routed their Conservative opponents. They then joined a large majority of Republican delegates at the convention that ratified the state's new constitution in 1868, paving the way for North Carolina's readmittance to the Union.[37]

The outcome of the 1867 election stunned the Conservative party. Intraparty squabbles and disorganization diluted the potential power of the Conservative vote; moreover, many white voters approached the election tepidly, fearing that bloody partisan battles would only delay the South's recovery. White voters, noted editor Yates, seemed confused about how to cast their votes, while freedmen displayed no such hesitation, appearing "to have voted en masse for the Republican candidates."[38]

In the spring of 1868 Republicans and Conservatives geared up for an even more serious confrontation. In the upcoming election, voters were asked to approve or reject the new state constitution as well as to elect state and county officials and representatives to Congress. The Colored Union Leagues, the core of both the state and the local Republican party, met frequently in Charlotte and

Mecklenburg and elected delegates to the Republican State Convention, including black party men Armstead Brown and Richard Smith. In February 1868 the
two men helped nominate William Holden to head the Republican ticket as
candidate for governor.[39]

The state's Conservatives finally organized officially in February 1868, intent
on recapturing control of North Carolina from Holden and the Republicans.
Defining themselves as the "white man's party," the Conservatives hoped to split
the electorate on the basis of race and sunder Holden's carefully fashioned
Republican coalition. Racked by division between old Unionists and secessionists, the Conservatives finally chose Thomas S. Ashe to head the Conservative
slate to oppose Holden for the governorship.[40]

As Holden campaigned across the state in March 1868 to drum up support for
the Republican ticket, he faced his most savage resistance in Charlotte. Hatred
of Holden, generated in secessionist Charlotte during the Civil War years, found
new expression in the Reconstruction era as local Conservatives burned Holden
in effigy on the night he arrived in their town. Although the mayor and town
commissioners condemned the incident and apologized to Holden, the old
Unionist exploited the episode to attack his longtime enemies in Charlotte.
Addressing a crowd of around 2,000 people, Holden proudly pointed out that in
1860 "he was hung in effigy, in this same city, because of his Union sentiments."
Eight years later, he again found himself "assailed by a set of desperate politicians, who are resolved to rule or ruin." Waving the bloody shirt, the ex-governor
accused Conservative leaders of "enacting the scenes of 1860–61," which "must
lead to another war."[41]

Tension escalated across the state as the election approached. The Ku Klux
Klan appeared for the first time in several North Carolina counties, although
apparently not in Mecklenburg. Thomas D. McAlpine, the Freedmen's Bureau
agent in Charlotte, wrote his superior in Raleigh that "the excitement growing
out of state elections in this and adjoining counties is very great." McAlpine was
so worried about violence that he requested half a company of infantrymen "as a
preventative measure . . . to remain well after the pending election," a request his
superior granted. The presence of federal troops, however, did little to intimidate Conservatives determined to vanquish the Republican party and keep
blacks from the polls. Republican officials, aware of possible threats to freedmen,
instructed black voters to "avoid all quarrels and fights" and not to "strike any
man unless he strikes you." Offering words of encouragement, party leaders
exhorted freedmen to "GO TO THE ELECTION! Go, if you have to walk fifty miles.
Go, if you starve for it. It is better to suffer now than to endure hereafter the
intolerable burdens which the Rebel leaders would put upon you." Conserva-

tives, on the other hand, tried to keep freedmen from the polls with threats and intimidation. But the new voters went anyway. Their ballots played a key role in bringing about a statewide Republican victory in which the party carried fifty-eight of eighty-nine counties and saw Holden elected governor and the new constitution ratified. North Carolina Conservatives managed to elect only one judge, one solicitor, and one representative to Congress. Yet Conservatives demonstrated remarkable strength in Mecklenburg, a reflection of the area's old secessionist sentiment. The hated Holden lost to Conservative Ashe in the county, and Mecklenburgers voted against the ratification of the state constitution.[42]

Many freedmen in Charlotte and Mecklenburg paid a heavy price for the Republican victory. Indeed, as bureau agent McAlpine pointed out, they brought upon themselves "the wrath of the people among whom they have got to live the remainder of their lives." Conservatives did not hesitate to use economic coercion as well as violence to punish blacks for voting Republican. Drayman Allen Cruse fired five black employees for voting the Republican ticket and then openly bragged about it. Likewise, carpenter Jonas Rudisill dismissed his black employee, Elam Henderson, for the same offense. A black voter in the county had his mule killed the night of the election. Even white Republicans suffered abuse at the hands of their fellow townsmen. McAlpine reported that William Shelton, "a quiet, industrious citizen," not only lost his job but "at almost every step he took in the street . . . boys and half-grown men would assail him with cries of Scalawag, etc." McAlpine called the pressure placed upon blacks to vote the Conservative ticket "almost resistless." Charlotte's freedmen, he wrote, "are entitled to the highest credit for the manner in which they withstood it," even though "hundreds of colored people would have voted the Republican ticket at the late election, had they not been afraid of the consequences." Freedmen who voted the Conservative ticket, on the other hand, had their names published in the local press, and white men were "called upon to patronize them."[43]

Despite the injuries incurred by many party men during the election, Republicans gloried in their hard-won achievement and enjoyed the spoils of victory. Governor-elect William Holden especially savored ridiculing his Charlotte nemeses. He hooted in his *North Carolina Weekly Standard* that "the rebels in Charlotte, unfortunately for themselves, showed their teeth a little too soon" in predicting a Conservative victory. He exclaimed, "With their usual conceit they mistook Charlotte for Mecklenburg and Mecklenburg for North Carolina."[44]

Governor Holden must have particularly relished replacing Charlotte's mayor and town commissioners in the summer of 1868 with his own appointees. Determined to supplant secessionists who had regained power by 1868, Holden used the new state constitution, as well as the political disbarment clause of the

Fourteenth Amendment, to remove town and county officials across the state
and replace them with Republicans until new elections could be held. In Charlotte Holden once again rewarded local Republicans and Unionists. He named
Dr. H. M. Pritchard mayor, as he had in 1865, and appointed Rufus Barringer,
Dr. William Sloan, and missionary Willis Miller to the town commission. Repay-
ing the loyalty and courage of the town's black Republicans, the governor
appointed Charlotte's first black town officials, naming laborer J. N. Hunter and
tinner J. C. Davidson to the town commission. Budding Republican politician
John T. Schenck became the town's first black policeman. New justices of the
peace for Mecklenburg included two blacks, Richard Smith and Washington
Grier. In the spring of 1868, in the glow of Republican victory, black Charlotte
experienced a degree of representation in town and county offices that it would
not know again until the late twentieth century.[45]

Holden's appointment of black officials outraged many local whites. Journalist
and ex-Confederate general D. H. Hill wondered whether the ratification of the
state constitution in May 1868 and the subsequent readmittance of North
Carolina to the Union in June was a blessing or a curse. Even rule by federal
officers, argued Hill, was better than being governed by "the vilest of mankind,
whom no gentleman would allow to enter the kitchen." But white Republicans
like Rufus Barringer instead saw in Holden's appointments a new beginning for
the New South. The "new men" who now governed Charlotte and many other
southern towns "have given us the 'results of the war,' all at once; and with the
plowshare of reform they struck deep into the musty institutions, habits and
customs to which we clung." But such a blow to tradition seemed unbearable to
many white townspeople.[46]

By the fall of 1868, as the presidential campaign approached, some white
Charlotteans channeled their anger at the new state of things by resorting to
extreme tactics. The campaign pitted Republican Ulysses S. Grant against
Democrat Horatio Seymour and proved to be one of the most contentious in the
state's history because the stakes in the contest seemed inordinately high to both
sides. Conservatives shuddered at the thought of another Republican president
who would back the Radical Congress and guarantee what they perceived as
Yankee and black rule at the expense of white civil rights. On the other hand,
Republicans feared that a Democratic victory would mean the end of congressional Reconstruction, the loss of political rights advanced to blacks in the
past several years, and ultimately the end of their party. In October bureau agent
McAlpine reported to his superior that sixteen rifles had "lately come into the
possession of a prominent extreme Democrat in this city" as part of a statewide
scheme, reported by the *North Carolina Weekly Standard*, to import arms into the

state to be distributed to Democratic organizations. Local Conservatives denied the charges. The *Western Democrat* claimed that if boxes of guns had been spotted, "they no doubt belonged to merchants who bought them for sale and who publicly advertise that they have such articles." Or, the *Democrat* weakly suggested, "a number of axes with handles have been brought here in gun boxes" and may have been mistaken for illegally smuggled weapons.[47]

Such tactics, supplemented by Klan activity in other parts of North Carolina, helped reduce the Republican majority across the state in the 1868 election. Despite the inflammatory rhetoric and tactics of both parties, Republicans still managed to carry the day. North Carolina helped elect Grant to the presidency, and the Republicans took every congressional seat except one.[48]

Political battles in Charlotte would continue to be hard-fought. Editor W. J. Yates's sentiments after the presidential election undoubtedly reflected those of other white townspeople for years to come. "We are in favor of treating colored people kindly, fairly and justly," he wrote, "but at the same time we warn them, as a friend, against thrusting themselves forward as the rulers of the white race."[49]

In the face of such attitudes, Charlotte Republicans tried to maintain their grip on municipal politics. But, like Republicans in larger southern cities, such as Richmond and Nashville, Charlotte's Republicans found their control of local politics tenuous and wholly dependent upon provisional appointments; they never managed to elect a single Republican mayor. In 1869, in the first town election since Holden's appointments the year before, Charlotte voters repudiated imposed Republican rule, and Conservatives once again took charge of the town government. Perhaps in a personal swipe at Holden, Conservatives elected John A. Young as one of the new town commissioners. Young, with William Johnston, had been elected as a secessionist delegate to the state convention in 1861. Young later served as mayor in 1871, as did Johnston from 1873 to 1877.[50]

Despite Conservative domination, the Republican party remained robust in Charlotte and Mecklenburg through the Reconstruction era. Interestingly, Conservatives never attempted to gerrymander the town to guarantee their domination, as their compatriots did in Raleigh—perhaps a reflection of Republican strength in Charlotte. Instead, changes to the city's charter in January 1869, establishing an aldermanic system, guaranteed that Republicans would control at least a few seats on the town council and practically insured black representation. Each of the city's four wards selected three aldermen, and in the heavily African American Second and Third wards, Republicans usually achieved representation. Through the 1870s, Republicans typically held two and sometimes three seats on the twelve-man Board of Aldermen, with John Schenck representing the Second Ward for four terms.[51]

By the 1870s Charlotte, like much of the New South, comprised both the old
and the new. While accommodating new economic growth, new business leaders, a vigorous Republican party, and black political participation, the town
continued to be dominated by the secessionists of the Civil War era. In 1870 an
exasperated Charlotte Republican noted the explosive mix of old and new in his
town. "This flourishing town," he noted, boasted "new buildings, and considerable enterprise mark it." Charlotte seemed "destined to be the great central trading place of all this region." But "whilst so much may be said in its
praise," Charlotte and Mecklenburg bore "some bad fruit in the way of strong
and bitter conservatism." Like so many southerners during Reconstruction, the
people of Charlotte, black and white, Republican and Conservative, grappled
with the changes brought by the war, simultaneously elated and terrified at the
prospects.[52]

•   •   •   •   •   •   •

The contentiousness of politics did not, however, divert the attention of Charlotte's white businesspeople and professionals from fostering economic growth.
By 1870 Charlotte not only had made inroads into coastal markets such as
Charleston but also had developed a lucrative trade with the Midwest, via rail
connections to Cincinnati and St. Louis.[53]

Trade with midwestern states reflected the changing economy of Charlotte
and of the South generally. With cotton prices at a high level immediately after
the Civil War, and hard cash in great demand to pay taxes and debts, many
farmers began to grow more cotton at the expense of grains. Compared to the
cultivation of other crops, cotton cultivation after the Civil War represented far
more value per acre. Cotton had been a leading crop in Mecklenburg and
surrounding counties since the invention of the cotton gin, but after the war the
crop grew in importance. In 1869, when cotton prices hovered around 28 cents
per pound, the editor of the *Western Democrat* remarked that he hoped "our
farmers will not allow the high price of cotton to cause them to neglect the
production of enough corn, wheat, oats, etc., for their own use, and a little to sell
at least." However, farmers did just that. Between 1860 and 1880, cotton
production increased threefold in Mecklenburg and nearly as much in adjacent
counties and districts; wheat, on the other hand, declined precipitously, and corn
barely maintained antebellum levels. Although Charlotte's antebellum markets
had brimmed with a variety of produce, cotton dominated after the war. As early
as 1870, the *Democrat* feared that farmers grew too much cotton. "Buying corn
and bacon is a terrible strain on the pocket," noted editor Yates, "and certainly
ruinous when cotton rules low in price." But cotton prices remained high for

another three years, and many farmers of the region enthusiastically embraced the cash crop.[54]

The expansion of rail lines also quickened the growth of cotton culture. The need for more railroads was one issue that both Conservatives and Republicans in Charlotte wholeheartedly agreed on during Reconstruction. In the spring of 1870 leaders of both parties began to drum up support among county residents for a subscription of $200,000 to build the Air Line Road to link Charlotte with Atlanta via Spartanburg and Greenville, South Carolina. An advocate of the Atlanta road bluntly contended, "Railroads give us all better chances to make money, and that is all independent folks ask for." After a zealous campaign, Mecklenburg voters—black and white, Conservative and Republican, town and country—overwhelmingly approved the Atlanta road and ratified the payment of an additional $100,000 to repair the Atlantic, Tennessee, and Ohio Railroad from Charlotte to Statesville, which had been dismantled during the Civil War. By the spring of 1871, an observer noted, no one could "pass out from the centre of this little City, in any direction, without crossing a Railroad track."[55]

Along with the expansion of railroads, the availability of guano, a cheap commercial fertilizer, made the cultivation of cotton possible for many Charlotte area farmers for the first time. In addition to fortifying the soil and enhancing cotton yields, guano extended the growing season of the cotton crop. During the 1870s cotton production spread to the north half of Mecklenburg County as well as to the nearby counties of Rowan, Iredell, Lincoln, Catawba, Cleveland, and Rutherford. Charlotte merchants sold guano in such great quantities that the air of the city became saturated with its pungent smell and citizens complained to the Board of Aldermen of "the nuisance in storing Guano & Fertilizer in town."[56]

As laborers completed segments of track through the South Carolina Piedmont and farmers enthusiastically purchased guano, merchants in Charlotte immediately felt the impact. The railroad passed through sections "heretofore almost inaccessible to markets, but capable of selling a large amount of produce." By March 1873 Charlotte merchants received hundreds of bales of cotton, "all of which formerly went to the Columbia or some other South Carolina market." Charlotte attracted even more trade in 1874 when the Carolina Central Railroad linked the town with Wilmington, drawing trade from the east. As a result of the growth of the cotton trade, the Board of Aldermen built a cotton-weighing platform adjacent to the train depot in 1870. In 1874 the town built yet another cotton platform to accommodate the large volume of trade.[57]

Charlotte's merchants and businesspeople not only grew richer as the railroads funneled trade to the town, but they found their power greatly augmented by the growth of cotton culture. Farmers became dependent on merchants and cotton buyers not only to purchase their crop but also to extend them credit. Moreover, many of the town's businesspeople and professionals also served as directors and officers of several railroads that set the rates farmers had to pay to get their crop to market. William Johnston, J. A. Young, and A. B. Davidson had all served on the board of the Charlotte, Columbia, and Augusta Railroad since the 1850s and were joined in 1870 by Rufus Barringer. Johnston and Young were also board members of the Atlantic, Tennessee, and Ohio, and R. Y. McAden was a member of the board of both the Atlantic, Tennessee, and Ohio and the Air Line. In 1873 Barringer and W. R. Myers, who served on the Atlantic, Tennessee, and Ohio board in 1871, became members of the board of directors of the North Carolina Railroad.[58]

The relationship between town dwellers and country people grew increasingly uneasy as the cotton economy added new stresses and strains to their association. Cotton prices, which peaked in Charlotte in 1869 at 28 cents per pound, began to decline precipitously in the spring of 1870, dropping to 22 cents. By the fall, when farmers from the surrounding countryside brought their cotton to the Charlotte market, they received a paltry 14 cents per pound, a sum that placed many farmers on the brink of economic disaster.[59]

Stung by low cotton prices and feeling the grip of the merchant and banker tighten as they fell into the depths of debt, local farmers fought back. To counter the Board of Trade formed by businesspeople to promote their own interests in 1870, local farmers created their own organization, the Farmer's Mutual Aid Society of Mecklenburg County. The organization called upon farmers to culti-vate at least one-half acre on behalf of the society, donating profits from the designated land to the farmers' group. Donations would go toward organizing a farmers' bank that would grant loans to farmers, allowing them to hold their crops until market conditions were more favorable. "Organization," wrote a passionate founder of the society, was the farmer's "city of refuge and to that he must flee if he would save himself from the insatiable avarice and withering touch of bloated, bigoted and mammoth combinations that are to-day sweeping over the land with the poisonous breath of the deadly."[60]

Over the next several years, cotton prices climbed by a few cents but by the spring of 1873 reached a plateau of 17 cents per pound. In March 1873, as debt-ridden farmers faced the humiliating task of asking for more loans from bankers and merchants to plant their crop, the cotton buyers of the town announced a seemingly innocuous change in purchasing procedures. Concerned with the problem of falsely packed cotton, the buyers stated that "in no instance will we bid on cotton cut by any other than a Charlotte buyer or his agent." After farmers

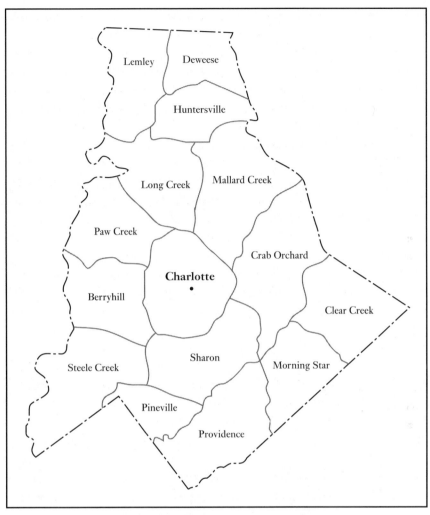

Map 2. Mecklenburg Townships, ca. 1870
Source: Vertical files, Robinson-Spangler Carolina Room,
Public Library of Charlotte and Mecklenburg County.

had their cotton sampled, they were expected to carry a slip of paper, indicating the grade, to the cotton buyers, who would then bid on the cotton.[61]

Area farmers reacted angrily to the new procedures, setting off a bitter dispute that reflected the deep-seated discord between merchants and farmers. In the Mallard Creek, Steele Creek, Lemley, and Deweese townships, as well as adjacent Iredell County, farmers called meetings to denounce "the nefarious, sordid, and malicious action in the sale of our cotton." Especially upsetting to farmers was the requirement that they had to carry a slip of paper to the cotton buyers. Referring to this as "the pass system," farmers likened it to slavery, calling it "humiliating to the farmer." Moreover, the farmers threatened to abandon the Charlotte market. Since they had assisted in paying for the construction of the railroads to Charlotte, they protested being "driven away from the market of our choice," but they nevertheless threatened to desert Charlotte if the rules were not changed.

The cotton-selling controversy provided the opening wedge for further demands from the farmers. They insisted that since farmers helped pay the salary of the cotton weigher, they "should have a voice in his election." Moreover, they expressed anger toward the railroads, especially the bloated salaries of railroad officials. The Steele Creek farmers also complained of being detained from two to five hours, even in cold and inclement weather, before being allowed to deliver their cotton to the weigher.[62]

Soon after organizing neighborhood meetings, farmers channeled their anger by joining the Grange. Founded in 1867 by Oliver Hudson Kelley, the National Grange of the Patrons of Husbandry, popularly known as the Grange, espoused cooperative efforts among farmers and attempted to alleviate their economic plight by circumventing the powerful "middle man" as well as regulating railroads to maximize the profits of farmers. Originating in the Midwest, the Grange found fertile soil in the South beginning in the early 1870s as farmers became entangled in the cotton economy. In the spring of 1873, the order began making huge strides in North Carolina. Under the direction of South Carolinian D. Wyatt Aiken, approximately twenty Granges were founded in the state by May 1873; less than a year later, 243 Granges were in operation, among them a cluster organized in Mecklenburg. In June 1873 Aiken, finding "great enthusiasm" in Mecklenburg, established five Granges in the county and one in Charlotte. At the organizational meeting of the Grange in the county, Aiken addressed "a large and appreciative audience of the most substantial farmers of this county," telling them "that their seclusion as a class had made them selfish and wanting in public spirit," that "as a class they were ignorant." Farmers "needed to organize to resist the rings formed by capitalists," implored Aiken.[63]

Aiken's exhortations resonated among Mecklenburg farm men and women who felt abused by Charlotte's merchants. Not only did the Grange provide a vehicle to fight the growing power of town-based merchants, but the order offered educational and social opportunities as well. A sorely needed antidote to the monotony and loneliness of rural life, the Grange sponsored picnics and agricultural fairs. Regular meetings, often held on a weekly basis, featured secret ritual, lectures on agriculture, literary and musical programs, refreshments, games, and informal conversation. Women played a particularly active role in the order. Grange women toiled shoulder to shoulder with men in the farmers' organization. Reflecting the economic realities of farm life, the Grange admitted women as equals, with separate but corresponding degrees or ranks, while reserving a number of offices in the order exclusively for women. Moreover, women were guaranteed a place—and vote—in state and national meetings.[64]

In Mecklenburg, according to local journalist D. H. Hill, "our most wide-awake and progressive farmers have gone into the Order." The children of wealthy antebellum Mecklenburg farmers, who found their family fortunes and status diminished by the war, played a particularly active role in the Grange. The order promised not only to alleviate the financial suffering of farmers but also to shore up their eroding rank in postbellum southern society. Richard and John A. Torrance, heirs to the elegant plantation Cedar Grove, which boasted 3,200 acres and 109 slaves before the war, served as officers in the Lemley Grange, as did their wives. Another Grange activist, M. L. Davis, was the only son of James H. Davis, one of Mecklenburg's wealthiest antebellum planters. The war wrecked the Davis family fortune, and M. L. Davis and his wife helped found the Providence Grange, where they both served as officers. By January 1874 nineteen Granges had been established in Mecklenburg, and they spearheaded the attack on Charlotte's merchants.[65]

As the Grange gained momentum in the county, cotton merchants and farmers settled their dispute over cotton-selling procedures. Merchants withdrew the previous procedural changes and recommended the employment of an assistant cotton weigher as well as "improvements around the platform" to facilitate the selling of cotton. The editor of the *Charlotte Democrat* remarked that "we hope the little 'misunderstanding' between the seller and the buyer is now forever settled" since "all classes having an interest in thrift and prosperity should dwell together in harmony and work all-together."[66]

The "little 'misunderstanding' " proved to be far more profound, rooted in the ascendancy of town-based businesspeople at the expense of county farmers. The dispute over selling procedures served as the opening volley in a protracted battle between merchants and farmers that raged in the 1870s and helped give shape to Charlotte's previously amorphous commercial and professional class. Attacked as hated "middlemen," "shoddy sharpers," and "the cotton ring," Charlotte's businesspeople were forced to defend themselves and the interests of "town people," as they began to refer to themselves by the fall of 1873, against the interests of "country people." The Grange, argued Yates in the *Charlotte Democrat*, did nothing but "array the country people against the town or city people" and was a movement of "Western Yankees and cunning officeseekers." By contrast, D. H. Hill, editor and publisher of Charlotte's *Southern Home*, joined the Grange and used his paper to defend the farmers and their organization. Hill pointed out, "Editors have had Press Associations; Doctors have held Medical Conventions; Merchants have established Boards of Trade. . . . Not a word of dissent has ever been uttered by the ring of robbers about these things; but when the class that feeds all other classes has an eye to its own interest, *this* is denounced as an atrocious crime." The local press raged with the debate between "town" and "country" people; animosity was so widespread that businessman S. G. Howie played on the division to promote his local eatery, touting it as a "Refreshment Place for Country and Town People."[67]

Hostility between "town people" and "country people" spread as the Grange attempted to undercut the power of Charlotte's merchants through cooperative strategies. In June 1874 the order appointed "a purchasing and business agent" to represent Grangers in negotiations with local merchants concerning discounts on goods. That fall the Grange also began participating in the Direct Trade Union, whereby area farmers could bypass local cotton merchants and sell their crop directly to the Liverpool and Savannah markets, a plan originally implemented by the Georgia state Grange. The Direct Trade Union, according to the Grange, allowed farmers to avoid "the combinations made against them by Northern shylocks and moneyed rings." The probusiness *Charlotte Democrat* contended, however, that the union was nothing but "humbugging talk" and "will not amount to much" after "two or three of our farmers are cheated out of their cotton by home and foreign agents." Against the criticism of the *Democrat* and the town's merchants, Hill and the *Southern Home* outspokenly supported the union. In response, angry Charlotte merchants denounced Hill "as an enemy of the interests of Charlotte" and withdrew their advertising from his newspaper. Fifty area Granges endorsed Hill's fearless stance in the face of the powerful town merchants.[68]

As merchants and farmers battled over the cotton trade, the election of 1875 reflected the deep rift between town and country people. At the Mecklenburg Conservative convention that summer, country dwellers protested that the ticket overwhelmingly represented town interests at their expense. Party officials then decided to appoint one candidate "from town and the other from the county to the end that the agricultural and commercial classes should each be represented." If county voters could select town candidates, the *Charlotte Observer* feared, they "might select a town man with county prejudices and pursuits—a granger middleman." Editor Charles R. Jones urged that in the coming election, Mecklenburg Conservatives "smother class feuds," promising "as a journalist to spare neither middlemen or granger when either is acting . . . against the interest of the whole community."[69]

Sensing a rare opportunity to divide the opposition, Republicans immediately jumped at the chance to bring disaffected farmers into the Republican fold. Noting that "there has long been a spirit of unfriendliness existing between the city and rural elements" in nominating Conservative candidates, the Republicans extended "a cordial greeting to our country friends" to join the Republican convention and help select candidates.[70]

On election day, county Conservatives crossed party lines. Despite racial appeals from Conservative leaders to the "white men of Mecklenburg" to vote the Conservative ticket, farmers rejected the party in droves. They overwhelmingly voted for the despised Republican party, which consequently swept every single precinct in Mecklenburg for the first and only time in its history. Their renunciation of the Conservative party foreshadowed the willingness of farmers in the 1890s to abandon an unresponsive Democratic party for the People's party. Reeling from the devastating defeat, editor Jones remarked that "one fact is certain, and that is that it will never do for the Conservative party to go into any campaign divided among themselves."[71]

By 1876 Conservatives healed the rift in their party, and country and town party men joined together to "redeem" the state by electing Democrat Zebulon Vance as governor of North Carolina. But the cotton economy had built an impenetrable wall between town and country people. Throughout the rest of the decade, townspeople defended their economic interests in the local press and kept up a relentless assault on the "secret class combination" of farmers against townspeople even as the Grange began to fade in the late 1870s.[72]

Economic and political battles between merchants and farmers represented only one facet of the division between town and country people. In the 1870s New South towns like Charlotte eclipsed the countryside, casting a long shadow over the plantations that had once been at the pinnacle of southern society, a shift that exacerbated hard feelings between town and country people. As farmers watched their fortunes wane in the 1870s, Charlotte seemed to abound with energy and opportunity. Many ambitious young people flocked to Charlotte in the 1870s from the surrounding countryside as well as from less vigorous towns, such as Lincolnton and Fayetteville. Rather than stay on the farm, enterprising young men came to Charlotte to work their way up the economic ladder. "Industrious and steady Clerks," observed the *Charlotte Democrat*, "are frequently 'taken in' as members of the firm—a reward to good boys."[73]

Others sought the cultural opportunities available in Charlotte, which increasingly distinguished the town from the countryside. The Charlotte Female Institute regularly offered recitals, readings, and lectures to the public. In 1874 the town got its first Opera House, which hosted a variety of dramatic productions, comedy troupes, and musical events open to all who could afford a modest admission. A roller-skating rink also provided "a pleasant place to spend an hour or two," and circuses and traveling animal shows frequented the town.[74]

Country people criticized the apparently soft and easy life of town dwellers, and townspeople defended themselves against such attacks. "If *country* people think Town people live easy without work let them come here and try it for a few years," wrote W. J. Yates in the *Charlotte Democrat* in 1875. "We assert without fear that the hardest working people in the land are those who live in towns and who meet their obligations as required between man and man in an honest manner."[75]

As white townspeople grew in self-consciousness in the 1870s, they also began to separate by class. Through the 1870s representatives of the townspeople, such as newspaper editor W. J. Yates, defined "town people" in broad terms. "Suppose there were no 'middle-men' in Charlotte," he asked, "such as merchants, mechanics, doctors, lawyers, preachers, etc., where would our neighboring farmers find purchasers for their farm products?" But as Yates and others spoke of the common interest of townspeople, the cotton economy helped draw the line between the nonmanual business class of merchants and professionals and the town's artisans and mechanics.[76]

The New South business class—not the town's artisans—held the reins of economic power in postbellum southern society. As bankers, brokers, and board members of railroads, they largely controlled the local economy. Reflecting a growing sense of class difference, businesspeople and artisans created separate organizations to promote their class-based interests. After the town's businesspeople formed a Board of Trade in 1870, artisans created their own Mechanics' Association a year later for their "mutual benefit and protection." Moreover, like their counterparts in the rapidly developing towns and cities of the antebellum era, Charlotte's businesspeople in the 1870s outstripped artisans and laborers in wealth. Nonmanual and manual laborers diverged markedly in wealth by 1870, and businesspeople invested their money in ways that physically separated them from manual workers, further delineating them as a distinct class (see table A.4). They built stylish new stores modeled on those in New York City. Four-story iron-front buildings appeared in the early 1870s and were the pride of the city. Businesspeople and professionals also built architecturally fashionable homes, "substantial and splendid residences" that set them apart from manual workers. In 1872 a visitor from Augusta commented on the "numerous elegant and stately mansions, with scores of bright, handsome and tasty cottages" that "afforded a panorama . . . reflective of the wealth, taste and enterprise of the different classes resident in this sprightly city." The visitor noted "the more attractive and elaborate private grounds and residences" of railroad president and lawyer William Johnston, merchant Thomas Brem, cotton merchant Allan Macauley, and lawyer and entrepreneur W. R. Myers.[77]

Growing wealth also distinguished the leisure activities of Charlotte's businesspeople, professionals, and their families, who vacationed at fashionable resorts. Cleaveland Springs in the mountains and the Atlantic Hotel in Beaufort on the coast were especially popular vacation spots where they played croquet and tenpins and "promenaded" at night. Charlotte "rather thinned out" in the summer months, noted Bessie Dewey; the crowding of mountain and beach resorts "is a sign that there is plenty of money among the people," suggested the *Charlotte Democrat*. At vacation resorts, Charlotte's white business and professional class also participated in an extralocal New South social network through which they mingled with people like themselves from other parts of the South.[78]

Leisure activities at home in Charlotte also reflected growing class divisions and distinctive social worlds among the town's citizens. Merchant W. H. H. Gregory, proprietor of the town's roller rink, made no bones about the fact that his establishment catered exclusively to Charlotte's more prosperous citizens. He reserved "the right to refuse admission or use of skates to any objectionable or untidily dressed person," welcoming only the "genteelly dressed." He set aside Monday, Wednesday, and Friday mornings "exclusively for Ladies to learn and practice" and occasionally hosted "Fancy Dress Entertainments" at the rink. Although the Opera House offered affordable "lowbrow" diversions, many performances were geared to the wealthier, better-educated townspeople. Only "the elite of the city" could afford to see famous comedian John E. Owens in 1875, and a lecture on "Science and Christianity" probably appealed only to the educated class.[79]

Separate class-based organizations also reflected the division between the commercial class and manual laborers. Like their counterparts in the antebellum North, business and professional men and women began to form voluntary organizations that separated them even more from manual workers and created a new and exclusive social network. A variety of clubs—drama troupes, singing societies, historical societies, and book clubs—appeared in the 1870s, all bound by the ethos of self-improvement. Founders of the Rip Van Winkle Book Club, for example, gave their organization that unusual moniker because "it was high time we waked from our lethargy as to our mental culture and mutual improvement." Members read and discussed Coleridge, Longfellow, Thackeray, and selections from *Eclectic Magazine*.[80]

Despite the fact that Charlotte was still a spatially small town in the 1870s—only a mile across—residents began to separate physically by class. Many of the town's elegant homes were situated on Charlotte's main streets, Trade and Tryon, and dwellings tended to get smaller toward the outskirts of the town. Although residential lines were not yet clearly drawn in the 1870s, wealthier residents appear to have had little contact with the town's poor. *Observer* editor Charles Jones noted the social and physical separation of classes in 1876, remarking "that one-half of the world does not know what the other half is doing." The "people of the better class, who confine themselves to the principal streets," contended Jones, "know nothing at all of the people with whom they live." Jones described "the countenances" of the poor, their "sallow, care-worn faces, their clothes . . . tattered and dirty," their unfurnished homes, "their children in rags [who] crawl over the floor." "These are the opposites of those who dress in their purple and fine linen," asserted Jones, "and who dash through the streets in their elegant equipages ignorant and careless of the fact that beggary lives next door to them."[81]

Yet women of the "better class"—as Charlotte's business and professional men and women began to call themselves in the early 1870s—had already called attention to the problem of poverty in Charlotte and had been the first to attempt to address it. As early as 1871 "certain ladies of the city" pointed out to the Board of Aldermen "cases of extreme poverty, . . . asking for relief for the same." The board appointed a committee to investigate "the suffering poor of Charlotte," and the mayor asked for "the assistance of one lady from each Ward in ascertaining the names of deserving objects of charity." Such efforts, however, proved to be ephemeral and inadequate.[82]

By the mid-1870s a group of Episcopal women, prominent members of the better class, took steps to create a permanent institution to help alleviate the suffering of the poor. Appalled at the lack of medical care available to impoverished citizens, particularly "aged, helpless women," the women formed the Church Aid Society in January 1876 to provide a "hospital and home" for destitute women. Jane Renwick Smedberg Wilkes, the wife of Mecklenburg Iron Works owner John Wilkes, led the crusade, with the aid of the wife of lawyer Hamilton C. Jones. By the end of the month, they had solicited enough money to rent a four-room house on Seventh Street, hire a cook and nurse, and begin to care for patients. They named their facility the Charlotte Home and Hospital. A year after the hospital opened, the women raised funds in Charlotte for a new hospital building, completed in 1878.[83]

Jane Wilkes, social reformer. (Courtesy of Special Collections,
J. Murrey Atkins Library, University of North Carolina at Charlotte)

The work of the Episcopal women in the 1870s, in some respects, represented a continuation of the nursing and relief activities of Charlotte women during the Civil War. Jane Wilkes had nursed sick and wounded Confederate soldiers in local military hospitals and now applied her expertise to aiding sick and destitute women. The Charlotte Home and Hospital also embodied a significant increase in female benevolent activity. During the war women like Wilkes had volunteered their services in government-operated hospitals and worked under the authority of male physicians. The Charlotte Home and Hospital, by contrast, was an all-female institution: it was planned by women, funded through public solicitation by women, and staffed and managed by women.

The efforts of Wilkes and her compatriots of the better class on behalf of their poorer sisters also marked, in a dramatic way, their entrance into the civic sphere of their town. Like affluent women in the burgeoning towns of the antebellum United States—such as Petersburg, Rochester, and Chicago—the women of Charlotte chose the female asylum as their first significant venture into public benevolence. The similarity is not a coincidence; in the 1870s Charlotte, like antebellum Petersburg or Rochester, found itself in the midst of rapid economic development with an exploding population and a discernible group of impoverished residents. When traditional "neighborly" enterprises could no longer meet the needs of a growing poor population, women in these towns helped establish institutions for the poor. By the mid-1870s Charlotte had grown large enough to warrant similar action.[84]

Notably, women's involvement in asylum work emerged just as the social and economic roles of more affluent women grew more confined. By the 1870s women of the better class in Charlotte—like their sisters in industrializing antebellum towns—no longer played a central role in the economy of their households; homes no longer functioned as units of production, and affluent women had easy access to servants. Although the cult of domesticity may have provided women with a sense of place and purpose, many women of the better class must have felt suffocated in the confines of their homes. Benevolent activities, such as female asylum work, allowed women to gain a public presence as well as a larger sense of purpose. Notably, the activities of Wilkes and her compatriots in Charlotte, like those of their antebellum sisters, did not challenge traditional female roles but instead extended the sphere of the home to include care for the destitute. The female asylum allowed women of the better class to participate in civic activism while reinforcing traditional gender roles.[85]

The activities of the Episcopal women sparked the formation of a poor relief committee in January 1879 that transcended denominational lines and included men for the first time as well. Although the committee was headed by manufacturer J. A. Young and the Reverend J. F. Butt, women of the better class, many of whom were active in the Church Aid Society, provided most of the labor for the committee. The poor relief committee remained active through the 1880s.[86]

The Church Aid Society and poor relief committee helped raise concerns among the better class about the town's less fortunate residents. But more importantly, poor relief served as an important rallying point for Charlotte's emerging white better class. The efforts of well-to-do women, and later men, in aiding the poor both reflected and reinforced class lines. The attack on poverty united businesspeople, professionals, and their spouses and helped define them as distinct from less fortunate members of Charlotte society. Poor relief efforts helped clarify who belonged to Charlotte's better class in the 1870s.[87]

· · · · · · ·

Hospitals and poor relief were, notably, for "whites only." Although blacks and whites lived in proximity to each other in the late 1860s and 1870s, they occupied distinct social spheres, continuing a policy of racial separation established before the Civil War. When Mike Lipman's Great Combination Show circus visited Charlotte in early 1867, it advertised "separate seats for Colored Persons." Although blacks could attend events at the Charlotte Opera House, they were relegated to the balcony, apart from white patrons. Saloons also served separate black and white clienteles. In 1871 saloonkeeper Lawrence Aletelier had "two separate bars in his establishment in different rooms—one for whites and one for Colored Persons." More elegant bars and restaurants, such as the Central Hotel, served white customers only. Segregated graded schools were established in Charlotte in 1874. Separation of the races extended even into death. By 1868 the town had established a separate cemetery for black citizens. Despite separation of the races, a degree of flexibility existed in race relations that would all but disappear by the late 1890s. When Alderman W. H. H. Gregory suggested in 1873, for example, that the black and white cemeteries be divided by a fence, Alderman J. F. Butt disagreed, stating that such a division "would prove objectionable to the Colored People," a position verified by black alderman Jefferson Hagler. As a result, Gregory withdrew his proposal.[88]

Like most urban blacks during the late 1860s and early 1870s, Charlotte's African American citizens seem to have accepted de facto segregation with little resistance. But the passage of the Civil Rights Act of 1875, requiring equal access to public accommodations, institutions, and educational facilities, inspired some of them to challenge the system, as did many blacks throughout the South. In April 1875 the *Observer* reported that a "colored civil righter" attempted to sit in one of the front seats at the Opera House during a minstrel show, but "as there was some resistance on the part of one of the ushers and a number of gentlemen" in the audience, the "civil righter" left "and the matter ended there." A month later, six black townsmen took seats in the "whites only" section of the theater. "No attention was paid them by the audience," noted the local press, but word of the incident "was not long in extending to the streets." A "crowd of young gentlemen" immediately trooped to the theater. The "gentlemen" collared the black men and kicked them down the steps of the theater, ending their protest.[89]

Charlotte's blacks failed to end segregation in 1875, but they continued to strive for economic advancement and to build up their own community organizations. Although white Charlotte began to separate into distinct classes in the 1870s, the African American community remained largely a one-class society. Like most blacks across the South, Charlotte's blacks toiled in low-paying, low-status jobs, doing "Negro work." Over 86 percent of the black labor force worked in unskilled positions, making up nearly half of the town's unskilled working force. Another 11 percent were employed as skilled workers, but they made up only 5 percent of Charlotte's craftsmen. In 1870 only a handful of blacks owned their own businesses. The census listed a single black grocer, a saloonkeeper, a boardinghouse proprietor, and a restaurateur; it is also likely that the town's two black barbers owned their own shops. Whereas white male youths had the opportunity to work their way into business partnerships by starting as clerks, Charlotte businesses employed only three black clerks. Moreover, Charlotte had a dearth of black professionals. In 1870 the black community boasted only three teachers and two ministers. Black women especially found themselves mired in low-status, low-paying, unskilled jobs. Of 406 employed black women listed in the 1870 census, only 5 held skilled positions, all as seamstresses. The census also listed a lone black female boardinghouse owner, an eatinghouse proprietor, and a schoolteacher. The rest of Charlotte's black females labored in unskilled positions, as domestics, farm laborers, washerwomen, and cooks.[90]

Yet in the first five years after emancipation, a handful of Charlotte's black citizens were able to accumulate both real estate and personal property. Although their wealth paled in comparison with Charlotte's most affluent white citizens, their resources reflected a major achievement in the immediate wake of emancipation (see table A.5). Skilled artisans, such as carpenter John T. Schenck and butcher Burwell Johnston, were the town's richest black residents. As a leading black Republican, Schenck reaped the spoils of political patronage, and in the early 1870s Republican leaders rewarded him with the job of mail agent. A few laborers, like drayman Frank Alexander and day laborer Malinda Sloan, managed to buy real estate and amass some personal property. The Freedmen's

Bureau gave an economic start to some of the town's black citizens by granting contracts to them soon after the war ended. Carpenter Anderson McKnight, for example, landed a $250 contract for building a smallpox hospital in 1867 and built coffins for the bureau as well. Similarly, the bureau contracted with blacksmith Washington Ross to build a wall at Biddle Memorial Institute in 1868. Notably, only one member of Charlotte's antebellum free black society, Nancy Jones, ranked among the ten wealthiest black residents in 1870, a reflection of the absence of an entrenched or dominant free black elite.[91]

Black social life, like that of the white community, centered on church activities and social organizations but in the 1870s reflected no class divisions. Churches, fraternities, sororities, and benevolent societies consolidated the black community while serving valuable welfare functions as well. The Odd Fellows and Masonic lodges were especially popular. In 1876 Charlotte blacks founded a chapter of the Independent Order of Good Samaritans and Daughters of Samaria, a national black benevolent order. Black fraternal, sororal, and benevolent organizations often paraded through the streets, dressed in top hats, broadcloth coats, sashes, and badges. Black men and women also participated in railroad excursions to other lodges in nearby towns and frequently hosted visitors from other southern cities. Special celebrations occurred on 1 January, Emancipation Day. The Fourth of July, seldom celebrated with much enthusiasm by southern whites after the Civil War, had special meaning for African Americans. On the nation's centennial, 8,000 area blacks gathered on the grounds of Biddle Memorial Institute for a "jolly time" and to hear political speeches by black politicians against the Democratic candidate for governor, Zebulon Vance.[92]

Politics was never far from the surface in any gathering of the town's blacks; partisan concerns continually fed tensions between the races. White Democrats, threatened by the power of black voters in Charlotte, continued to insist throughout the 1870s—as they had in the early years of Reconstruction—that political participation distracted blacks from earning a living. "Instead of organizing political leagues and societies," wrote the *Charlotte Democrat* in 1871, "we hope the colored people will organize societies for the encouragement and promotion of industry, temperance, and honesty." Whites blamed "a few boss negroes" who "want to live by holding office, or preaching, or teaching school, and who hope to succeed by keeping up excitement and agitation among the negroes." W. J. Yates of the *Charlotte Democrat* contended that blacks "must make up their minds to occupy subordinate positions in the world. The man who leads them to believe anything else is a deceiver and an enemy to the negro race." Yet participation in the political system concretely symbolized equal rights; politics was the only

sphere in which blacks and whites met each other on an equal footing. "Boss
negroes," such as John Schenck, continued to demand their place in the political
system, organized the black vote, and fearlessly stood up for the interests of the
African American community. When a white policeman interfered with a black
prayer meeting in the Second Ward, for example, Schenck demanded an inves-
tigation. The board ordered Mayor John A. Young "to tell the Policeman that they
disapproved of any interference with any Religious meeting" and to reprimand
him for the intrusion. But by the crucial election of 1876, politics divided blacks
among themselves, splintering the unity that they had largely maintained since
emancipation.[93]

Through the mid-1870s the Republican party had commanded the town's
black vote almost unanimously. But in 1876 the black voting bloc began to
crumble, reflecting both disillusionment with the Republican party and the
economic pressures placed upon blacks by powerful whites. The gubernatorial
campaign of 1876, one of the most contentious in the state's history, pitted
Charlotte lawyer Zebulon Vance, the popular Civil War governor of North Carolina, against Republican candidate Thomas Settle. North Carolina Democrat-
Conservatives hoped that Vance could defeat the Republican candidate and
"redeem" the state from the hated Republicans, who had maintained their grip
on the governorship since Holden's election in 1868. To insure victory, Democrats needed to neutralize the black vote.

In the spring of 1876 some black voters in Charlotte began to voice their
disenchantment with the Republican party and its corruption. The unscrupulous
machinations of the Grant administration soiled the reputation of the Republican party for many voters, including freedmen who had originally embraced the
party of emancipation. In North Carolina, railroad and bond scandals plagued
Republican administrations during Reconstruction, buttressing the case for the
successful impeachment of governor and party leader William Holden in 1871.
The behavior of John Schenck also may have fueled concerns among town and
county blacks about corruption in the party. In June 1872 federal authorities
arrested Schenck, who worked as mail agent on the Atlantic, Tennessee, and
Ohio Railroad, on the charge of stealing tobacco, which was found in his
possession. According to the local press, "leading Republicans" were so convinced of Schenck's guilt that they refused to bail him out.[94]

In March 1876 J. W. Poe took the lead in publicly criticizing the Republican
party. In a letter to the *Observer*, Poe petitioned his "colored fellow citizens and
friends" to "cut loose from a party that proves so false to its supporters and
constituents (I mean the Republican Party) for she is becoming the constant
advocate of corrupt principles." The party, insisted Poe, was "only striving to

enrich or make rich a few men. . . . I find it time to support a new order, the old one proving a slander and disgrace to herself."[95]

As Poe denounced the party of emancipation, some Charlotte blacks enlisted in a national movement to reject the Republican party. S. A. Hudson organized local black support for a crusade headed by the Reverend Garland H. White, a black minister from Washington, D.C. White hoped to organize black voters against the Republican party, calling upon Hudson to "bring your friends and the colored people together and organize to combat corruption in the coming election" since "Colored men all over the country are now prepared to do battle against corruption in high places."[96]

Such sentiments must have seemed blasphemous to black Republican politicians such as John Schenck, yet even he seemed frustrated by his own party. The glittering promise of equal political participation, evident in the early years of Reconstruction, seemed badly tarnished to many blacks by the mid-1870s. Schenck joined a growing number of southern black Republican leaders who openly began to censure the party, largely on the grounds that party leaders rarely ran black candidates for office and that blacks seldom enjoyed the spoils of political patronage—even though they made up practically the entire party.[97]

Although in no position to rail against corruption, Schenck angrily denounced the shabby, second-class treatment of blacks in Mecklenburg's Republican party. In April 1876 black Republicans, led by Schenck, openly revolted against white Republican leadership when they caucused at Burt Schenck's Third Ward store. According to the local press, a leading white Republican had angered blacks by boasting "that he *knew* the darkies would go for whom he wanted them to." Instead, blacks held their own caucus to determine their course of action. "The proceedings would seem to indicate that the white leaders are rather losing hold of the colored followers," the *Observer* hopefully speculated. Two months later, in June 1876, when county Republicans held their convention, white Republicans attempted to renew the loyalty of black voters by reminding them that "it was the Republican party which had given them their liberty." John Schenck, chairman of the Republican party executive committee for Mecklenburg, refused to be stirred by the reminder and instead castigated white party leaders for keeping African Americans in a subservient position. He proclaimed that "he was tired of being dictated to as to his course in all matters political." In a forceful declaration infused with bitterness and rage, Schenck attacked white party chief W. R. Myers and proclaimed his refusal to be treated as a slave in the party. "If the Republican party belonged to Mr. Myers," he decreed, "then I had better go back to Henry Schenck, and all the balance of you niggers to the men you used to belong to." Schenck railed against the patronage system that rewarded whites for their support of the party almost exclusively. "I want to know," asked Schenck, "if Jenkins [the white candidate for postmaster] gets the postoffice, if he will put a colored boy on there as clerk." Blacks "have been Republicans for nine years, and what have you got to show for it? I am getting tired of this thing," proclaimed an exasperated Schenck, "and want to throw off the yoke."[98]

Democrats played on the frustrations of black voters. Since 1870, moderates within the state party had called for a "new departure" by which the party would finally acquiesce to black political rights, reject racial extremism, and attempt to lure valuable black voters. Stressing Republican corruption and contending that they would guarantee black voting rights, Democrats through the "new departure" caused a political upset in 1870 when the party regained the state legislature and elected nearly all of its congressional candidates.[99]

By 1876 the Democratic party in Charlotte openly vied for black voters. The *Southern Home* commented on the "hatred of White Republicans to the Colored Race," noting that although there were approximately 2,500 black Republicans in Mecklenburg compared to 190 whites, whites had been given every slot on the Republican ticket. "Mr. John Schenck, who is considered to be the smartest man in the county," remarked the *Southern Home*, "was not even thought of." The *Observer* asked black voters, "Will you bend your backs longer as pack-horses to carry those unscrupulous whites to power?"[100]

To some blacks, the answer was a resounding "no." In August servant John Henderson became the first black member of the Democratic Tilden and Vance Club. Henderson promised to bring scores of other disenchanted African American voters with him, all of whom promised to vote a straight Democratic ticket in support of Samuel Tilden's presidency and Zebulon Vance's governorship. Henderson's defection elicited an angry response from many blacks. When he entered church one Sunday morning in August, he was accosted "by a number of negroes who told him they had sworn to kill any d—d negro who wore a Vance badge." Henderson pushed his way into church, but when he attempted to leave, he was "surrounded by about a hundred negroes who threatened his life." A few days later, the *Observer* reported that another black Democrat, Lee Moore, also a member of the Tilden and Vance Club, was badly beaten near Charlotte "by 12 or 15 negroes."[101]

Despite such intimidation, some black voters founded their own clubs. Barber Grey Toole headed the Vance Colored Democratic Club. Toole catered to an exclusively white clientele, and his support of Vance reflected the economic pressures that the white community placed on black businesspeople such as himself, which Toole publicly acknowledged. He remarked "that if whites would refuse to give employment to the Radicals, both white and black, they would flock over to Vance in crowds, and give no trouble at any future election." Club members wore badges to "indicate their determination not to vote against the interest of men who give them employment and support." A few weeks before the election, the town's leading businesspeople, "the most influential citizens and some of the largest property holders in the city," attempted to tighten the economic screws in an appeal published in the *Observer* imploring black voters to cross party lines. "We declare to you that we have never desired your reenslave-ment, nor to deprive you of the full protection of the laws," they argued. "We have a common destiny and common interest. . . . Let race antagonism cease to exist, so that our judgement of public affairs may not be worked by passion or prejudice." William Johnston and J. A. Young, two of the wealthiest and most powerful men in Charlotte, also spoke to the Colored Tilden and Vance Club just before the election.[102]

Yet for many blacks neither economic pressure nor the corruption and unre-sponsiveness of Republican leaders could break their nearly spiritual bond with the party of emancipation. Even African American women, who had no vote, demonstrated their passionate engagement in the political process and their allegiance to the Republican party. Some did not hesitate to use the only weapon that they possessed—their labor—to try to influence the outcome of the elec-tion. A black cook, for example, informed her employer that if he voted for Vance, "he would be under the necessity of looking out for some body else to do his cooking." Fifteen minutes after her confrontation with her employer, re-ported the *Observer*, "the ebony mistress of the culinary art was walking out of the yard carrying her bed," having willingly sacrificed her job for her political principles.[103]

On election day, most of the town's blacks remained loyal Republicans, with Charlotte's largely black Second and Third wards voting for Settle over Vance. But enough black voters crossed over to the Democratic party to insure a Vance victory. The former governor carried Mecklenburg and the state, a victory that marked the symbolic end of Reconstruction in North Carolina. Savoring the sweet Democratic triumph, the *Observer* remarked that victory would not have been possible "without the aid of a large number of colored voters . . . who have at last been convinced that the interest of the employer and the employed is identical." Blacks who voted Democrat "have thus earned the friendship of every white democrat in the land." Party leaders rewarded J. W. Poe, who initiated the black migration to the Democratic party in Charlotte, with a job as messenger in the state House of Representatives at three dollars a day.[104]

The political fissures in Charlotte's black community did not easily heal. Al-though the Republican party would continue to be unresponsive to its black constituents, politicians like John Schenck, despite their own frustrations, worked to keep black voters in the Republican camp. But the charges of corruption in politics, first sounded by black voters in the campaign of 1876, would be amplified by a new generation of black leaders a few years hence, temporarily reconfiguring local politics in innovative—and threatening—ways.

•   •   •   •   •   •   •

By 1880 Charlotte's white businesspeople and professionals had built their town into one of the most important trading centers of the Carolina Piedmont. Simultaneously, the economic transformation of the postbellum South, particularly the growth of the cotton economy, had created a self-conscious and powerful class of white businesspeople, professionals, and their spouses, defined initially by their feuds with angry "country people" and reinforced through social networks and voluntary associations. The end of the Civil War brought about a "new state of things" not only in politics and race relations but in class development as well. As Charlotte's whites separated by class, the black community remained fundamentally a one-class society. Yet the churches and schools of the Reconstruction era spawned a new, self-conscious generation of black teachers, preachers, and businesspeople who would come of age in the 1880s. Calling themselves "the better class of Negroes," they would form an alliance with the town's "better class of whites," asserting their leadership in the black community and challenging John Schenck and the leadership that had emerged in the Reconstruction era.

3

BLACK AND WHITE TOGETHER

In June 1882 twenty-six-year-old William C. Smith published the premier edition of the *Charlotte Messenger*, the city's first black newspaper. The newspaper represented "an honest effort on our part to promote the moral, intellectual, and material standing of our people." Smith and his newspaper exemplified a new generation of black leadership—"the better class" of blacks, as they referred to themselves—that came of age in Charlotte during the 1880s, and the paper served as the mouthpiece for this newly emergent group. "The negro," wrote Smith in a typical column, "must become owners of more land" and "stop smoking cigars, drinking whiskey, pleasure riding, wearing jewelry, fine dress." The creation of "an educated, wealthy and moral colored population" would, he believed, keep the race "safe at all times and places."[1]

Born in the last decade of slavery and able to take advantage of educational opportunities offered during Reconstruction, the black better class united around values of morality, self-discipline, and social decorum, seeking respect from the white community and influence in their own. Like their white counterparts, the better class of blacks developed social networks and associations that helped define them as separate from the rest of the black community. Furthermore, they embraced many of the same values as the white better class.

The prohibition movement of the 1880s, the preeminent reform movement of the late nineteenth-century South, provided members of the black better class with their first opportunity to assert their authority in Charlotte's African American community. Moreover, the black better class and their white counterparts, men and women who identified each other across race lines, bridged the chasm of race in an attempt to institute social reform. In the prohibition movement, the better classes briefly shaped a new kind of politics outside of traditional party channels.

Although the prohibition movement galvanized and bonded the white and black better classes, it severely divided the black community. Prohibition was an especially explosive issue among Charlotte's blacks, for it entailed issues of freedom as well as leadership of the African American community. Prohibition sparked a fierce battle for control of Charlotte's black community, a battle that left the community severely divided by class.

An examination of the prohibition movement and subsequent social reforms reveals the internal dynamics of race, class, and gender in the New South in the 1880s. In the brief period between the end of Reconstruction and the emergence of Jim Crow, race and class relations proved to be remarkably fluid in Charlotte; the values and social vision of the better classes—black and white—provided them with enough common ground to wage a war for social improvement. For most of the prohibition movement, class interests overshadowed the importance of race as whites and blacks of the better class cooperated in their battle against alcohol.

•   •   •   •   •   •   •

"Like Banquo's ghost," wrote editor Smith in 1887, "prohibition will not 'down' at any man's bidding." Prohibition proved to be one of the New South's most persistent and divisive social reform issues. Prohibition petitions clogged state legislatures; local-option elections separated towns and counties, churches and clubs, into virulent "wet" and "dry" factions; agitation over alcohol reduced many local elections to hotly contested battles over the alcohol problem. Whereas drys argued that alcohol was the root of all social evil and that prohibition would advance the South's social and economic progress, wets asserted that buying and consuming alcohol constituted a fundamental right.[2]

In North Carolina, prohibition led to the presentation of more petitions to the legislature than any other issue in the state's history. In the 1870s prohibition agitation came from both rural areas and the state's rapidly growing towns. Of these, Charlotte soon became one of the focal points of prohibition activity.[3]

It was no accident that the burgeoning towns of North Carolina fostered prohibition agitation in the 1880s. Town dwellers came into daily contact with alcohol-related problems such as poverty, crime, and public drunkenness in town squares and railroad stations. Moreover, by the 1880s, North Carolina's town-dwelling better class rallied around prohibition as the fundamental reform to improve their towns morally and economically.[4]

In 1881 prohibition sentiment in Charlotte crystallized after a series of incidents explicitly demonstrated the calamitous consequences of alcohol abuse— particularly on "respectable" young men of the white better class. In July 1880, after spending an evening in one of the town's saloons, two young clerks got into a knife fight that left one of them critically injured. A few months later "an intoxicated young man" fell from the second story window of the Springs Building, one of Charlotte's main business houses, severely injuring himself. Then on Christmas Day 1880 some of the town's young men "presented a carnival of intemperance," in the words of prominent local attorney and Civil War veteran General R. D. Johnston, as the streets "filled with reeling, drunken youth."[5]

Public drunkenness was not limited to holiday celebrations. Thomas Henry Lomax, a black bishop of the AMEZ church, claimed in 1881 that "Charlotte was haunted with more drunken men, in proportion to the population, than he had ever seen and he had traveled in every State of the Union except three." A flourishing commercial center of over 7,000 people in 1880, Charlotte had seventeen saloons and a beer garden; drug stores also dispensed liquor. Although the Board of Aldermen made efforts to curb the growth of saloons in 1880 by raising the tax on alcohol sellers from $125 to $500 per year, a number of citizens mobilized to take even stronger measures. Disgusted with the social problems created by alcohol, especially the impact on the younger generation, they pledged themselves to destroy what they viewed as the root of the problem—the saloon itself.[6]

In January 1881, as the state legislature considered a law ending the liquor traffic, T. L. Vail, a farmer and bank cashier, initiated a movement to start a prohibition club in the city. On 28 January, Vail and a number of other prominent white Charlotte citizens—including merchants M. L. Barringer and J. H. Weddington, wholesale grocer Calvin Scott, and lawyer T. M. Pittman—organized the Prohibition Association and served as its officers.[7]

While men served as officers in the club, women served as footsoldiers, collecting signatures for prohibition petitions. Moreover, women served as the inspiration behind the movement. Prohibition was "born of women's prayers and mankind's high resolve." The movement could not fail, argued leader R. D. Johnston, because "the women were in the cause." Indeed, the involvement of women in prohibition, like their participation in the earlier temperance movement, was a natural extension of their roles as homemakers and moral protectors of the family. Destroying the curse of alcohol, prohibitionists believed, would help protect the home.[8]

Charlotte's fledgling prohibition movement soon had a powerful ally in Charles R. Jones and his *Charlotte Observer*. Jones heartily endorsed the battle against "the great evil of intemperance." Other prominent community leaders soon jumped on the prohibition bandwagon as well, including R. D. Johnston; R. Y.

McAden, president of the town's First National Bank; lawyer Rufus Barringer; and farmer and merchant A. B. Davidson.[9]

Within weeks of its founding, the prohibition movement had attracted the better class of white businesspeople, professionals, and their spouses, the men and women who had grown in power, prestige, and self-consciousness in the 1870s. As a class-based movement, prohibition cut across denominational lines, uniting Presbyterians, Methodists, Baptists, and Episcopalians alike. Although sentiment against alcohol had long been a tenet of the Baptist, Methodist, and Presbyterian faiths, Episcopalians, who traditionally did not advocate abstinence from alcohol, played a key role in the prohibition movement of the 1880s. Prominent Episcopalians, such as John and Jane Wilkes and Mr. and Mrs. Hamilton C. Jones, joined Presbyterians, such as A. B. Davidson and Rufus Barringer, as well as Charlotte Baptists, led by the Reverend Theodore Whitfield.[10]

Notably, the Prohibition Association represented the first large-scale reform movement in Charlotte that originated outside of the church and was Charlotte's first reform association open to both men and women. The establishment of the Charlotte Home and Hospital, the most notable social reform of the 1870s, and subsequent poor relief efforts had been initiated by Episcopal women. Indeed, prohibition was a natural outgrowth of the poor relief efforts of the 1870s since many members of the better class associated poverty with alcohol abuse. Two of the women who directed the hospital and poor relief efforts of the 1870s, Jane Wilkes and Mrs. Hamilton Jones, became leading prohibitionist activists in the 1880s. Yet the Prohibition Association differed from the hospital movement in that it was a secular organization that enlisted both men and women of the better class from a variety of denominations.

The Prohibition Association resolved to pressure the state legislature "to enact an absolute prohibition liquor law . . . effective in suppressing the drink traffic." Circulating petitions throughout the town and county, men and women of the association gathered over a thousand signatures demanding a statewide prohibition law. Charlotte's women prohibitionists also drafted a special appeal to the legislature.[11]

Engulfed by an avalanche of petitions from prohibition organizations all over the state, the North Carolina legislature passed a prohibition law in March 1881 outlawing the manufacture of spirituous liquors, wines, and ciders. The legislature, however, decided that the law could not go into effect unless approved by the voters in a statewide referendum to be held on 4 August. The Charlotte prohibitionists, poised for battle, were not willing to wait for the August election. In February they decided to run "no-license" candidates for mayor and aldermen in the May municipal election. Charlotte thus became the first city in the state to transform a local election into a referendum on the saloon.[12]

The decision to form a dry slate invigorated the Prohibition Association and prompted cooperation between the white better class and the fledgling black better class. White prohibitionists realized that Charlotte's black voters would be the deciding factor in a prohibition election; without their support, no-license candidates could never be elected. By the spring of 1881 some black residents had already formed their own prohibition association. Recognizing the common concerns of black and white prohibitionists as well as the strength of the black vote in Charlotte, R. D. Johnston instructed the executive committee of the white association "to confer with the association among the colored people with a view to presenting . . . a ticket for mayor and board of aldermen." In exchange for their support, blacks would "be given a division of candidates on the ticket."[13]

In addition to the obvious political reasons to enlist blacks in their cause, the white prohibitionists may have been motivated by benevolent, paternalistic feelings as well. Charlotte's white prohibitionists appear to have been part of a wave of liberalism that appeared in the South in the 1880s. Liberals challenged the reactionary mentality of the Reconstruction era that insisted on the natural inferiority of all blacks. Instead, liberals, as Joel Williamson has pointed out, called "for a return to the paternalism of late slavery when the best masters had cared for and raised up the best blacks." By enlisting the best of the black community in the prohibition movement, the white better class could do their part to uplift the black race while simultaneously instituting a crucial social reform.[14]

Like their white counterparts, the black men and women who joined the prohibition crusade were mostly businesspeople, professionals, artisans, and their spouses. They included newspaper editor William C. Smith, teachers J. E. Rattley and Mary Hayes, merchant A. W. Calvin, and minister D. R. Stokes. Although still a small group within Charlotte's black population, and small in number compared to their white counterparts, they nonetheless represented an emerging black better class. Vocal, young, and determined, they aspired to be the new leaders of Charlotte's black community.[15]

The men and women of Charlotte's emergent black better class were bound largely by their generational experience, education, and values. Most of them were born in the final decade of slavery and in the 1880s were in their late twenties and early thirties. They had known slavery only briefly as children, had experienced emancipation at a young age, and had embraced unprecedented educational opportunities offered during Reconstruction; most received their

William C. Smith, editor of the *Charlotte Messenger*.
(Courtesy of the Charlotte-Mecklenburg Historic Landmarks Commission)

education in freedmen's schools and colleges. W. C. Smith, who was born in 1856 near Fayetteville, attended freedmen's schools there in the late 1860s, earning a teaching certificate while learning the printing trade. Similarly, J. E. Rattley enrolled in the Charlotte Parochial School, a freedmen's school operated by Northern Presbyterian missionaries, at the age of fourteen and graduated with honors from Biddle Memorial Institute in 1877. A. W. Calvin, born in North Carolina in 1853, attended Hampton Institute in the 1870s. D. R. Stokes, born in North Carolina in 1854, was an 1878 graduate of Biddle Memorial Institute.[16]

Schooled largely by northern, middle-class white missionaries, these black men and women imbibed the values of their teachers, who stressed the importance of self-discipline, morality, and property ownership. W. C. Smith exhorted every black citizen to "live an upright Christian life, learn all he can in good books, educate his children, acquire all the property he can." As a result, Smith contended, the black citizen "will discover in a few years that he himself is much more like the class he would like to pattern after."[17]

The black better class absorbed another important belief from their northern teachers: that the destiny of the black race lay in their own hands. Blacks could earn the respect of white citizens and full participation in southern society only if they proved themselves worthy. Thus education and morality played key roles in race progress. "Unless we educate our children in letters and morals," charged Smith, "our race will continue in dissipation and disgrace." Smith summed up the faith of the black better class in self-help: "Just give us time and we will show the world that the Negro is the equal of anyone."[18]

The black better class also contended that they were the new race leaders, that "the destiny of the Negro race is in the hands of our preachers and teachers" as well as those involved in "trades and professions"—not politicians. Explicitly rejecting the leadership of Reconstruction-era politicians, the black better class maintained that they were the first generation of African Americans fully prepared to participate as full-fledged citizens in southern society. "We must all admit," wrote Smith, "that the colored men were not so well fit for important places five or six years ago as they are to-day." The last several years saw "two or three hundred young men graduated from the different institutions of our State and country, who are better versed in the duties and responsibilities of citizens."[19]

Repudiating the leadership and strategy of the Reconstruction generation, the black better class argued that the salvation of the race was not in politics but in personal improvement. Although far from rejecting political involvement outright—as Booker T. Washington would a decade later—the black better class of the 1880s placed far less emphasis on politics as a means of gaining full-fledged citizenship. Indeed, spokespersons for the black better class, such as Smith, often exhibited deeply ambivalent feelings about politics. As a child of Reconstruction, Smith constantly stressed his loyalty to the Republican party, "the good old principles as set forth by Garrison, Greeley, Sumner, and Lincoln." At

"Miss Poe," a member of the black "better class," ca. 1890. (Courtesy of the Robinson-Spangler Room, Public Library of Charlotte and Mecklenburg County)

the same time, he often criticized the unresponsiveness of the party to blacks as well as the corruption of the system and political leaders. Smith and other members of the black better class generally viewed the machinations of politics as unseemly and beneath their station. While attempting to remain aloof of party politics, the black better class found itself drawn into the political maelstrom in their pursuit of "race progress."[20]

Although they placed less emphasis on politics than on self-improvement, members of the black better class vocally protested unequal treatment of African Americans in their society. Far from being silent accommodationists, members of the better class served as vigilant and outspoken defenders of black rights. Smith and the *Messenger*, for example, vociferously protested the lack of black jurors in Mecklenburg County, the presence of black women on the county chain gang, and the unfair taxation of black shoeshine boys in Charlotte.[21]

Emphasizing race pride, self-help, and economic advancement, the moderate and flexible strategy of race progress advocated by Charlotte's black better class was growing in popularity among blacks across the United States in the 1880s. After the disappointments of Reconstruction, African American leaders generally had less confidence in effecting change through politics and instead emphasized self-help and racial solidarity. Newspaper editor Smith summed up this strategy for progress in his typically didactic manner: "Get knowledge. Get money. Get land. Use these things properly taking Christ as our guide, and all will be well."[22]

Acting as the self-appointed leaders and advocates of Charlotte and Mecklenburg's blacks, members of the black better class nonetheless did what they could to distinguish themselves from the rest of the black community, which they typically referred to as the "poorer sort" or the "masses." The better class criticized the activities of poor blacks, especially those that reinforced white stereotypes of blacks or undercut advancement. They expressly targeted camp meetings, public baptisms, and excursions—"three of the strongest agents in the demoralization and breaking down of our people." Editor Smith reserved special vitriol for blacks who idled away their time at the courthouse square. Smith urged "the better class, those who have the good of our race at heart, to turn their attention to this matter," arguing that "the morals of our people *must* be improved," since "that class of people so much exposed to the world would do the better class a great hurt."[23]

As Smith's appeal suggests, the better class attempted to distance themselves from the rest of the African American community, articulating disgust and occasionally revulsion for "the masses" even as they stressed race pride, solidarity, and uplift. As the fortunate few, many felt a deep obligation to uplift the "poorer sort," yet to gain the respect of whites, and advance race progress, the better class had to prove to the white world that they were not like the rest of the black community. As Smith wrote, "Our conduct should teach white people that we are not to be judged as a people, by the vulgar, rough set that loafs around the streets in filth and idleness." At the same time, the better class "ought to labor and pray to raise the fallen and save others from falling." Theirs was a weighty responsibility, fraught with tension. Nothing less than the future of the race in the South, they believed, rested on the conduct of the black better class and the propagation of their values. Yet by defining themselves as a class apart, the better class created a gulf between themselves and the rest of the black community that limited both their leadership and the acceptance of their social vision.[24]

Unlike the "aristocrats of color" in older and larger southern cities, Charlotte's black better class consisted of few natives of the town. Instead, nearly all of them were young, educated men and women who had flocked to the town in the 1870s and 1880s in search of opportunity; very few could trace their ancestry to local antebellum free black families. William Pethel, an active prohibitionist, was one of the few blacks with local roots. His relatives were skilled free black artisans in Charlotte before the Civil War, and Pethel appears to have been the lone representative of the free black community involved in the prohibition cause. Moreover, light skin color—a prerequisite of admission to the African American elite in many American cities, particularly Washington, D.C., Charleston, and New Orleans—seems to have played little, if any, role in determining membership in Charlotte's black better class. Newspaper editor W. C. Smith, the voice of the black better class, was dark-skinned, and his nemesis, politician John T. Schenck, who rallied the rest of the black community against the better class, was a mulatto. African American prohibitionist leaders included both blacks and mulattos, as did antiprohibitionists.[25]

Like their white counterparts in the 1870s, blacks of the better class in the 1880s created an exclusive social network of clubs and organizations that helped differentiate them from the rest of the black community. Black clubs, like the clubs of the white better class, stressed self-improvement while providing opportunities for entertainment and socializing. The Winona and the Oriole book clubs, organized in the early 1880s, helped "to advance the social and intellectual standing of our people," according to the *Messenger*. Held in the homes of members of the black better class, such as brickmason William H. Houser and Bishop Thomas Lomax, book clubs were open to both men and women of the better class. Other clubs were single-sex organizations that sponsored entertainment and social events. In 1887 editor Smith listed eight social clubs, "the rage of the day," including the Winona and the Oriole book clubs, the Young Men's

Pleasure Club, the Young Ladies' Independent Club, and the Married Ladies' Social.[26]

Besides participation in self-improvement and social clubs, church membership also helped define the status of the black better class. By the early 1880s many members of the black better class belonged to the Clinton AME Zion Chapel—the city's oldest black congregation—or the Seventh Street Presbyterian Church—founded in conjunction with Biddle Memorial Institute by Northern Presbyterian missionaries. Moreover, a social web linked church-related institutions of higher education and their graduates, such as Biddle Memorial Institute in Charlotte and Scotia Seminary in Concord, both Presbyterian institutions, and Zion Wesley Seminary (later renamed Livingstone College) of the AMEZ church in Salisbury. Charlotte's better class of blacks, along with their counterparts from neighboring towns, attended commencements, debates, and addresses by prominent black leaders as well as other social gatherings at these institutions.[27]

While the black and white better classes shared many similar values, institutions, and social networks, aspects of their domestic life were similar as well. The black better class seem to have embraced gender roles that corresponded to those of the white better class. Women of the black better class, unlike the overwhelming majority of black women, had the luxury of staying at home to tend to their households and children. Concepts of separate spheres for men and women as well as the cult of domesticity appear to have been every bit as strong among the black as among the white better class. W. C. Smith contended that "woman is the noblest piece of God's work" and that young girls should be taught "to occupy their proper sphere—next to angels." Similarly, Annie Blackwell, wife of an AMEZ minister, articulated such sentiments in an article directed at women of the better class. A graduate of Scotia Seminary, Blackwell asserted that woman's place was "in the home dispensing those virtues and graces that are her God-given right and privilege." Smith went as far as telling black women to "follow the example of our best white women and let them not do things or go places white ladies of standing don't visit."[28]

Regardless of their conception of their place and role in their own community, the better class of blacks suffered daily reminders that white southerners seldom recognized class difference in the African American community. Like the "poorer sort," members of the better class, despite their gentility, often found themselves subject to racial segregation and restricted to second-class accommodations in Charlotte and the New South. They, like their white counterparts, enjoyed partaking in the cultural events offered at Charlotte's Opera House, but they found themselves relegated to the balcony because of their color. Many simply chose not to attend events at the Opera House in order to avoid the indignity of being seated with poor blacks. Even though they were "free American citizens, and many of them are free born, educated, and as refined as they may be," noted Smith, "they are compelled to take back seats or none at all" among "rude, noisy boys" and "all manner of male and female roughs." In ameliorative tones, Smith appealed to the management to recognize the good breeding of the black better class and not relegate them to the cheap seats. But Smith's request fell on deaf ears. As he lamented in 1882, "Cursed is the man whose skin is black, for he can scarcely be a gentleman in America."[29]

Despite the frustrations engendered by segregation and racial attitudes, members of Charlotte's black better class, like their counterparts in other towns and cities across the United States, insisted that they could earn respect and acceptance. Ultimately they believed they would earn full-fledged citizenship by demonstrating their capacity to function and prosper as moral, cultivated, hardworking citizens.

The prohibition movement provided the black better class with the chance to prove their respectability, giving the crusade against alcohol a special urgency. When prominent whites in the spring of 1881 approached them to form a political alliance on behalf of prohibition, members of the black better class leaped at the opportunity. Besides helping them gain respect from whites, prohibition could also serve as a vehicle for young, educated blacks to assert their values in their community. The movement granted them the chance to shape the African American community in their own image, to enforce their values of self-help, discipline, and social propriety—all of which they believed would better the condition of southern blacks. Finally, the prohibition movement might allow them to take their places as the "rightful" leaders of Charlotte's black community, supplanting the black political leaders of the Reconstruction era, whom they viewed as corrupt and uncouth.

The prohibition movement surmounted the segregation and second-class citizenship that the black better class usually suffered. In early April black and white prohibitionists convened a joint Prohibition Association. They elected both black and white officers and committee members, who on 16 April presented a biracial slate of dry candidates, made up of eight whites and two blacks, that reflected the class composition of the prohibition movement. Bank cashier Frank De Wolfe headed the ticket as the mayoral candidate. White candidates for aldermen included prominent merchants R. M. Miller and D. W. Oates, attorney E. K. P. Osborne, iron manufacturer John Wilkes, and insurance agent D. P. Hutchinson. Brickmason and contractor William Houser and merchant A. W. Calvin served as the two black candidates.[30]

Revealing the liberal and innovative spirit of the prohibition movement, the Prohibition Association also repudiated traditional racial etiquette by presenting both black and white speakers, who took turns addressing the crowds at rallies. They shared the same speaker's rostrum and platform at integrated public rallies in an attempt to whip up enthusiasm for the prohibitionist slate.[31]

The prohibitionists ran their candidates on a carefully articulated platform, arguing their case against the saloon at public rallies and in the local press. Prohibition, they stressed, was the key to maintaining social order and a morally upright society. "Dens of vile indulgences," saloons destroyed "life, morals, happiness, peace and property." Closing saloons, they argued, would protect innocent women and children who were "denied even the *necessities* of life that the rum seller and his family should have comfort and luxury." Prohibition leader George E. Wilson, a local attorney, claimed that compared to war, pestilence, and famine, "liquor had spread wider havoc, made more distress, caused more tears to flow, ruined more men, and made more heart-broken wives and mothers, and more ruined children orphans and beggars."[32]

Not only would prohibition protect the family, but it would also assist in improving the "laboring classes"—an obvious concern of the better classes. Laboring men, banker McAden claimed, are "among our greatest sufferers" and spent far too much of their income on alcohol. The Reverend Stephen Mattoon, the white president of Biddle Memorial Institute, underscored McAden's argument. A veteran of "work among the colored people," Mattoon believed that prohibition would serve the black man "as a powerful agent in the elevation of the standard of morals and citizenship."[33]

Black prohibitionists amplified Mattoon's message with their own pointed arguments aimed at the African American community. Rejection of alcohol, they contended, was essential in achieving progress and respect from the white community. C. C. Pettey, a Lancaster, South Carolina, minister and graduate of Biddle who played an active role in the Charlotte movement, described alcohol as "the accursed brutalizer and destroyer of humanity." Pettey claimed that blacks had "only three great battles to fight, and three victories to win . . . ignorance, prejudice and whiskey," the fight to give up alcohol being the key battle. Similarly, D. R. Stokes, a student at Biddle, argued that if blacks were to "prosper and command the respect and confidence of their white fellow-citizens," they must "prove that they are capable of thinking and acting for themselves." Teacher J. E. Rattley made an impassioned plea to his "fellowmen of color" in which he associated racism with the saloon and racial respect with the town's leading institutions—all represented in the prohibition movement. "During strong political struggles," asked Rattley, "from what walls and fronts do you most frequently or altogether hear the infamous blasphemous epithet 'd—d nigger'? Does it come from the Mecklenburg Foundry, Observer office, First National Bank, Second Presbyterian Church, or does it come from those temples of propriety and virtue, the Retail Saloons?" In emotional tones, Rattley challenged the black community: "Will you use your influence for Reform and Race Pride, or willfully blinded, will you irreparably use it for positive evil?"[34]

While prohibitionists, black and white, contended that banning the saloon would bring social and moral progress, they also believed that prohibition would guarantee economic prosperity. The prohibitionist cause undergirded the booster rhetoric of the town's business leaders. "This city," wrote a longtime Charlotte resident in the spring of 1881, "has been cursed and handicapped with the dead weight of grog-shops." Because too many promising young men of Charlotte "fill drunkard's graves" and "many of the very best families of the State have been prevented from making their home in our midst" because of alcohol-related problems, "Charlotte looks more like a little shriveled dwarf than a giant."[35]

Prohibitionists provided an array of justifications for their crusade, but a number of common threads held their ideas together. Prohibitionists of both races were bound by the belief that alcohol was the root cause of social and moral problems. As Prohibition Association officer R. D. Johnston stated simply, "When this reform is accomplished, all others will follow." Moreover, Charlotte prohibitionists believed that theirs was a righteous battle between good and evil, God and Satan. It was "a contest against evil, wickedness, and crime began in High Heaven by the Great Omnipotence."[36]

Prohibitionists also stressed that their movement was not tied to a political party. Their crusade, they asserted, was too weighty to be left to the vagaries of party politics. Reflecting a disaffection with political parties that had emerged during Reconstruction, black and white prohibitionists, Republicans and Demo-crats, fashioned a new style of politics in the 1880s. Stressing the importance of reform over party labels, their new politics anticipated the progressive movement of a few decades later.[37]

Prohibitionists were also bound by their class awareness. Both black and white prohibitionists continually stressed that their movement represented "the wealth and intelligence of Charlotte." Despite their racial differences, black and white prohibitionists identified themselves as the "better class" and closed ranks under the prohibition banner. Their stress on the uplift of the "poorer sort" and the "laboring" classes and their self-definition as the "better sort," "the substantial men," and "the best element" reflected the class dimension of their movement.[38]

As prohibitionists mobilized for the May election, antiprohibitionists united to oppose the movement. Although never as organized as the drys, the wets nonetheless held rallies, publicized their views in the local press, and formed their own slate of municipal candidates. Like prohibitionists, antiprohibitionists joined forces across race lines and represented a class-based movement. The wet ticket, although headed by mayoral candidate William Johnston, one of the city's wealthiest residents, was made up mostly of the "poorer sort," like drayman Allen Cruse, saloonkeepers John Schenck and C. L. Adams, and laborer Alexander Allison. Describing themselves as the "poor men" fighting the rich and influential, the antiprohibitionists contained a much larger component of unskilled workers than the prohibitionists. Although unskilled laborers accounted for only 4 percent of all prohibitionists, they made up nearly a third of the antiprohibitionist ranks, which were swelled by saloonkeepers and grocers whose livelihood depended on the sale of alcohol.[39]

The rhetoric of the antiprohibitionists also reflected the fact that the battle over alcohol was integrally related to class. Antiprohibitionists described prohibition as "the rich man's license and the poor man's prohibition." In April black gardener Manuel Lord, in a speech before a wet rally, placed the battle over alcohol squarely within the context of class, warning his listeners of "the intention of the wealthy class to abolish the rule of whiskey as a first step toward encroaching upon their liberties." Mayoral candidate Johnston argued that the prohibition law "might protect rich young men who had been allowed to roam around on the streets with money to spend" but would "bring hardships upon another class." Turning the prohibitionists' economic arguments on their head, Johnston argued that prohibition would injure Charlotte's businesses, pointing out that liquor taxes supported nearly half of Charlotte's educational budget.[40]

Along with class issues, party politics soon came to the fore in the prohibition debate. Soon after the legislature passed the conditional prohibition law in March 1881, the Republican leadership in North Carolina decided to take advantage of a rare opportunity to divide the Democratic party. Sensing a growing backlash against prohibition, the Republicans championed the wet position. Although the vote on the prohibition bill had not been along party lines, Republicans reasoned that Democrats would bear the blame for the prohibition law since they controlled both houses of the legislature that had passed the bill. Fearful that prohibition could threaten their political dominance, and thrown off balance by the Republicans' wet stance, the Democrats insisted that prohibition was not a political issue.[41]

In Charlotte, prohibitionists continued to insist that their cause was apolitical. Arguing that prohibition had nothing to do with party loyalty, they showcased Democrats as well as Republicans, blacks as well as whites, at their rallies. Black minister C. C. Pettey told his "colored brethren" that "this is not a conflict between the two great national parties but a war between the heroes of virtue and the advocates of vice." Similarly, *Observer* editor Charles Jones, a leading spokesman for the drys, stressed that prohibition was "a matter not so much of politics as it is of economics and morals."[42]

The political implications of prohibition bitterly divided the town's African American community. As members of the black better class entered the political sphere by forming an alliance with white prohibitionists, they ran up against John Schenck, Charlotte's leading black politician and saloonkeeper, who campaigned vigorously against prohibition. Schenck, in his late fifties, was significantly older than the black prohibitionists and, unlike them, had no formal education—and probably lacked the hallmark cultivation of the black better class. His political career, although blemished by scandal, was at its apex in the early 1880s. Schenck had reason to resent the self-righteous black prohibitionists who intruded on his political turf. They challenged his authority by running dry aldermanic candidate William Houser against him in the Second Ward. Moreover, Schenck must have viewed the black prohibitionists as traitors to the Republican party, which opposed prohibition.

To counter the black prohibitionists, Schenck helped organize antiprohibitionist rallies, attended by both black and white wets. Schenck warned black voters that prohibition was "a Democratic dodge to get possession of their votes." According to Schenck, "The last resort was to divide the preachers from the common negroes, and then get them to lead them in a body to the fold."[43]

Besides engendering political and class struggle, the prohibition debate was especially explosive in the black community because the right to drink held special significance for black men and women who had experienced slavery. During the slave era, alcohol had largely been forbidden to slaves and in most cases was available only during holiday celebrations. Charlotte's town ordinances, like those of most other southern towns and cities, explicitly forbade slaves from purchasing or selling alcohol (see chapter 1). Many black men and women prized the right to buy and consume alcohol, viewing it as a fundamental right granted along with freedom. While the black better class imbued prohibition with symbolic meaning, the "poorer sort" also perceived prohibition in symbolic terms—it meant the loss of their cherished independence. Indeed, many blacks of the "poorer sort" remained adamantly vigilant in defense of their citizenship rights, believing that if they lost their right to drink, the loss of other liberties would inevitably follow. A rumor circulated during the campaign that after prohibition "the next step will be to pass a law to prohibit the poor colored man from voting for his president." A white prohibitionist scoffed at the rumor, in words that twenty years later would seem hopelessly naive—or cynical: "Do not colored men and white men, not versed in politics, even know enough to know that the United States gives the right [to vote], and the little State of North Carolina, if she desired, could not take it away?"[44]

As the 1881 municipal election approached, the prohibition issue consumed Charlotte's citizens—particularly African Americans. The *Observer* reported that "the campaign gets hotter as the election draws near." The city's black population "seemed particularly exercised and those who are announced for prohibition appear to be equally balanced by those in favor of cheap whiskey." Both wets and drys passed out leaflets on the streets, and each side registered voters to support their cause. In addition, ministers of various denominations devoted their Sunday sermons to the upcoming election. Also, to prove that they were not spoilsports, prohibitionists opened a "prohibition billiard hall."[45]

On 2 May voters flocked to the polls to cast their ballots on the burning issue of the day. Dry mayoral candidate De Wolfe barely defeated wet candidate Johnston by a vote of 667 to 642. In the election for aldermen, Charlotte voters elected six wets and six drys. Notably, the six dry candidates were elected in predominately white wards whereas largely black wards elected wet candidates (see map 3). The First and Fourth wards, where white voters dominated, elected prohibition candidates grocer Calvin Scott, painter Charles A. Frazier, merchant R. M. Miller, manufacturer John Wilkes, attorney E. K. P. Osborne, and insurance agent D. P. Hutchinson. In the Second and Third wards, where black voters prevailed, Schenck routed the prohibitionists and retained his seat. In addition, voters elected saloonkeeper and liquor dealer James C. Long, John Smith, horse trader C. T. Walker, saloonkeeper C. L. Adams, and black farm laborer Alexander Allison.[46]

Despite a less than overwhelming show of support for prohibition, the drys proclaimed victory, ransacking Charlotte's hardware stores for cowbells and throwing "their hats into the air," whooping and shouting "until they were hoarse." Editor Jones described the triumph as "the result of the spontaneous uprising of the best element in our community." He especially praised black prohibitionists for their contribution. Even though "most of the colored men voted against prohibition, enough of them voted with the prohibitionists to lift the whole question out of the arena of politics and place it upon its merits." Another grateful white prohibitionist wrote a letter to the *Observer* proposing "that the names of such of our *colored fellow citizens* who were arrayed on the side of the victors, be collected and put upon a card for the further consideration of those among us who think that some grateful recognition of their services should be expressed." The writer contended that "it must be remembered that if they

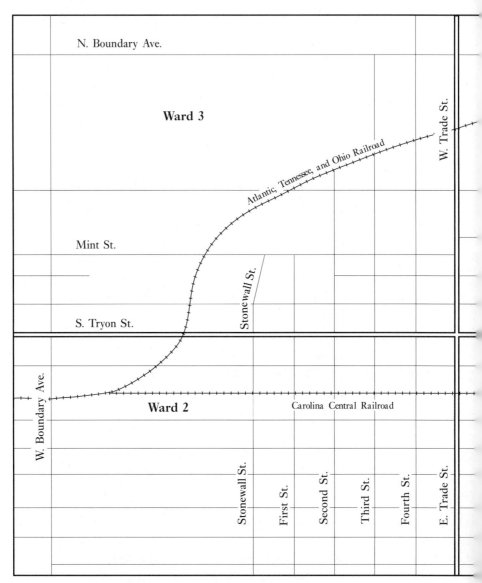

Map 3. Charlotte's Four Wards and Main Streets, ca. 1880
Source: *Gray's New Map of Charlotte, Mecklenburg County, N.C., 1882.*

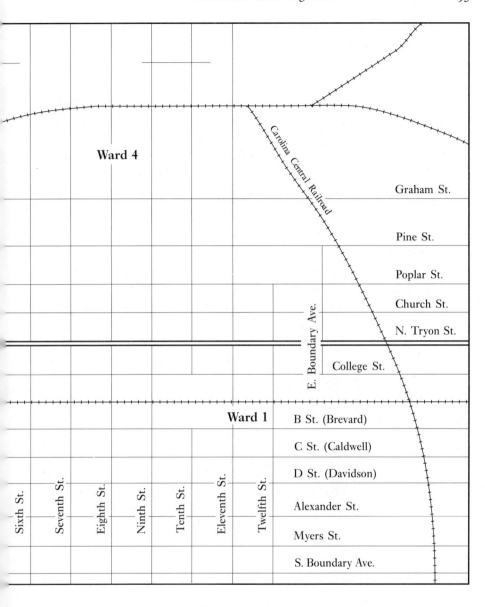

Ward 4

Carolina Central Railroad

Graham St.

Pine St.

Poplar St.

Church St.

N. Tryon St.

E. Boundary Ave.

College St.

Ward 1

B St. (Brevard)

C St. (Caldwell)

D St. (Davidson)

Alexander St.

Myers St.

S. Boundary Ave.

Sixth St.

Seventh St.

Eighth St.

Ninth St.

Tenth St.

Eleventh St.

Twelfth St.

had not cast their votes for Prohibition, the 'wet' ticket men would have ruled the city of Charlotte for the next two years and our side have been shorn of the prestige of success in the coming campaign next August."[47]

Such praise must have been heady for the black better class, who seemingly had played a key role in the prohibitionist "victory." Their alliance with the white better class in the spring of 1881 seemed to grant them what they so urgently desired: recognition by the white better class that they were valuable and responsible counterparts worthy of respect as well as validation that they were indeed the true leaders of the black community.

Although Jones and other prominent whites commended black prohibitionists for their contribution, a closer look at the election results reveals that the black better class had little political clout in their own community—despite their alliance with powerful whites and their contention that they were the new race leaders. The black better class had not been able to elect a single aldermanic candidate. John Schenck retained his seat—and his political influence—in both the Second and Third wards, where most of Charlotte's black citizenry resided, as black voters elected Schenck and fellow wets John Smith and Alexander Allison.

The 1881 municipal election results demonstrated a fundamental difference between the black and white better classes, despite obvious similarities. The better class of whites, as owners of banks, wholesale and retail stores, cotton brokerage houses, and small industry, translated economic power and status into political power. By contrast, their black counterparts had no such influence. The power of black prohibitionists may have been blunted not only by their political inexperience and age but also by their lack of economic power. Black business in the 1880s was small business, limited to grocery stores, meat markets, and the small shops of artisans. Black businesspeople, as well as ministers and teachers, found themselves largely dependent upon the black community for support, but the black community was not dependent on the black merchants and professionals of the better class. By contrast, politician Schenck had political patronage at his disposal. Moreover, as a saloonkeeper with cash on hand, he probably also functioned as a banker in the black community. In short, Schenck offered more to most of Charlotte's blacks than the better class could hope to offer. Moreover, unlike the black better class—which consciously distanced itself from the rest of the black community and built alliances with powerful whites—Schenck remained a man of the people, as both saloonkeeper and politician.

As prohibitionists claimed victory in Charlotte in May 1881, the wets proved far from gracious in defeat and immediately announced that they would prevent the newly elected Board of Aldermen from ever meeting. Wet aldermen threatened to refuse to enter the council chamber and thus to deny a quorum. Consequently, on 4 May, two days after the election, the mayor convened the old board and the aldermen passed a prohibition ordinance closing Charlotte's saloons and outlawing the sale of alcohol in the town—all before the new aldermen could be sworn in. The *Observer* pronounced that the ordinance meant that Charlotte had taken a decisive and unalterable step. "Not surer of execution were the laws of the Medes and Persians," editor Jones ardently proclaimed, "than is the resolution of the people of Charlotte to abate the nuisance of an always open bar-room. Charlotte is a dry town henceforth and no mistake."[48]

As authorities closed down the town's saloons, wets sought an injunction against the ordinance on the grounds that the old Board of Aldermen had instituted it illegally. Although a local judge refused their request, the wets vowed to fight on by preparing for the state referendum in August. At the same time, prohibitionists, not satisfied to rest on the laurels of their municipal victory, also prepared for the August showdown.

Women of the better classes played a key role in mobilizing prohibition sentiment for the state referendum. Their participation in the municipal election energized and empowered them. Although they had no electoral voice, they did all that they could to influence the outcome of the election. In late May Charlotte's white women of the better class "buckled on their armor," forming the Ladies Prohibitory Society. The organization, headed by the wife of grocer S. M. Howell, soon claimed 435 members. In July their black counterparts formed the Colored Ladies Prohibition Association. Led by teacher Mary Hayes, the members boldly proclaimed that they were "unqualifiedly opposed to drunkenness, believing the habit to be sinful in the sight of God and degrading," and called for the "speedy suppression" of alcohol.[49]

The statewide referendum significantly broadened the activities of reforming women. Both black and white women prohibitionists felt obligated to justify their unprecedented venture into politics by presenting it as an extension of their domestic role. One white woman prohibitionist explained in a letter to the local press that she and her compatriots recognized "that our true sphere is not in the political arena or public places, but the home, the fireside, and the privacy of the domestic circle." Yet prohibition seemed so critical, so "freighted with vital interest to ourselves and those most dear to us," that women had to be involved.[50]

Black women of the better class employed similar language in describing their place and role in this vital reform movement. When they formed the Colored Ladies Prohibition Association, they contended that it was women's place, as guardians of morality, to fight against drunkenness, a habit "sinful in the sight of God and degrading in the eyes of man." Thus, black and white women of the better class not only shared the same values but also shared common conceptions of their role as women and political activists.[51]

Despite class-based conceptions of womanhood that spanned race, black and white women prohibitionists worked separately, in their own institutions, for a common cause. Women prohibitionists wrote letters to the press, collected signatures for petitions, and drummed up membership for prohibition clubs. They also disseminated free literature, doing all they could to influence public sentiment.[52]

As the August referendum neared, wets and drys held public rallies and appealed to voters through handbills and public announcements. The *Observer* noted that the prohibition campaign, at a fever pitch in towns and counties across the state, was especially intense in Charlotte because of the May municipal election. "Never before," wrote the newspaper, "was there such a universal discussion of a campaign issue." A few days before the election, the *Observer* published "an earnest invocation" from the Ladies Prohibitory Society to the men of Mecklenburg. In language imbued with images of domesticity and woman's elevated moral status, the women stressed "the impulse of holy love, which God has implanted in the maternal bosom of animals as well as women." They appealed "to the true manhood of Mecklenburg" to heed "the cry of woman, suffering woman, that bids to you to contest with the evil which has brought this suffering upon us."[53]

Despite this emotional plea, the men of Charlotte, Mecklenburg, and North Carolina voted against state prohibition on 4 August 1881. An all-out effort by the wets, backed by the nearly limitless resources of the state's liquor dealers, defeated the underfinanced drys. The wets took all four of Charlotte's wards and won handily, 1,446 to 458. "The colored voters," noted the *Observer*, exercised their suffrage "with their usual eagerness" and "were more solid for license than was anticipated," once again defying the better class and giving the wets an easy victory. Across the state, only three mountain counties—Haywood, Transylvania, and Yancey—voted for prohibition.[54]

The election, mourned the *Observer*, represented "a New Prohibition Waterloo" and did, in fact, help end prohibition in Charlotte. Although prohibitionists hoped that the aldermen would continue to enforce the May ordinance banning saloons, the board reopened the city's bars on 19 September in response to the August referendum. Despite this defeat for the prohibitionists, the aldermen instituted a number of new controls over saloons, requiring liquor dealers to apply personally to the board for a license and to pay a sum of $500 if the board approved their request. Moreover, the aldermen confined saloons to Trade and Tryon streets, which formed Charlotte's central axis, and forbade any obstructions on windows or doors in an attempt to curb excessive drinking by making alcohol consumption as public as possible.[55]

Although prohibitionists continued to maintain that their cause transcended party lines, party politics focused on prohibition in the aftermath of the 1881 state referendum. A faction of state Republican leaders, led by Dr. J. J. Mott, interpreted the rejection of prohibition by Tarheel voters as vindication of their party's proliquor stance. Mott hoped to give shape to antiprohibition forces, molding wet sentiment into an effective weapon to defeat the Democrats in the statewide elections of 1882. Moreover, the Republican leader wished to form an alliance with both Liberal Democrats and the state's economically pressed farmers. By 1882, the Democratic party in North Carolina had divided into two factions—Liberals and Bourbons. Liberal Democrats had become increasingly vocal in their dissatisfaction with the Bourbon faction that dominated the party and that insisted on retaining the undemocratic county government system instituted in 1877. Hoping to impede "black rule" in black-majority counties in the east, the Democratic legislature had abolished the popular election of county commissioners, placing their selection, instead, in the hands of justices of the peace chosen by the legislature. Many Tarheels decried the change as elitist and demanded a return to direct election. In addition, North Carolina's farmers, who continued to suffer economic setbacks, displayed a willingness to buck Democratic authority in the short-lived Greenback movement of 1880. Mott hoped to capitalize on their discontent through a new coalition party.[56]

In June 1882 the State Anti-Prohibition Association met in Raleigh to hold a convention to construct a new political party, formulate a platform, and present a slate of candidates to North Carolina's voters. William Johnston, Charlotte's wet candidate for mayor in May 1881, served as chairman of the convention, attended by approximately 150 delegates: 80 white Republicans, 40 Democrats, and 30 blacks. The new party, dubbed with the unwieldy name of the Liberal Anti-prohibition party, promised to protect individual rights and liberties that, the party claimed, had been threatened in the August prohibition referendum. Moreover, the party promised a return to the direct election of county commissioners and nominated Republican Oliver H. Dockery for Congress and Liberal Democrat George N. Folk for the North Carolina Supreme Court.[57]

When the Republican party held its convention nearly a week later, Mott, against the protests of "pure" Republicans, engineered the party's endorsement of the platform and candidates of the Liberal Anti-prohibition party. The Republicans also promised to direct their candidates to vote against all prohibitionist legislation. That summer, the Liberal Anti-prohibition party held county conventions across the state, convening in Mecklenburg in August 1882, and

nominated a slate of candidates for the state legislature. According to the local
Democratic press, the convention was "fully as largely attended as was the
late Democratic convention." Nervous local Democrats soon resorted to race-
baiting, accusing whites and blacks at the convention of drinking from the same
pitcher. Chairman William Johnston called the charge "a deliberate falsehood
with all its base insinuations."[58]

The alliance of Republicans and Liberal Anti-prohibitionists reflected deep
disaffection among many North Carolinians with the two-party system. Prohibition, the county government system, and the worsening economic plight of the
state's farmers exacerbated the alienation felt by many citizens since Reconstruction. Neither the Democratic nor the Republican party seemed willing, or
able, to respond to their concerns.

Notably, North Carolina's new coalition party was one of a number of political
amalgamations taking place across the South in the early 1880s as black and
white voters desperately sought to create a more responsive political system.
Observer editor Charles Jones noted "a restiveness among the masses in political
matters," pointing out that "in the South the Republicans are playing the
game of coalition . . . joining hands with debt repudiators in Virginia, antiprohibitionists in North Carolina, Greenbackers in South Carolina, Independents in Georgia."[59]

The creation of a new coalition party presented a dilemma for many North
Carolinians, severely testing their party loyalty. Both white Democratic drys and
black Republican prohibitionists wrestled with the issue of the coalition party.
Democrat Charles Jones, a hearty and influential supporter of prohibition in
1881 as well as an avid critic of the county government system, admitted that the
Liberal Anti-prohibitionists displayed more "sympathy with the principles of the
Democratic party" than the Democracy itself, which had been "diverted from
those principles." Although Jones sympathized with the reform sentiments of the
coalition party, he refused to support it, fearing Republican rule. Instead, he
challenged the Democratic party to "loom up into the grand party of the people
which it should be."[60]

While Jones called for party loyalty and a more responsive Democracy, black
prohibitionist W. C. Smith also struggled with the question of whether to support
the new coalition party. As a member of the black better class, Smith attempted
to stay aloof of local politics, particularly as practiced by politicians such as
Schenck. At the same time, he often maintained his fundamental loyalty to the
traditional tenets of the Republican party as defined in the era of Abraham
Lincoln and the Civil War. Although Smith struggled to maintain pure, transcendent Republican principles above the unseemly political fray, his concerns

with prohibition and race progress continually drew him—and other members of the black better class—into the combat of New South politics.[61]

As an avid prohibitionist, Smith initially supported the Liberal Anti-prohibitionist party with deep reservations. Despite its support of the liquor interests, the party represented, in Smith's opinion, a chance to rid the state of Democratic Bourbon rule, and he adapted his beliefs accordingly. Moreover, he believed that blacks could parlay their support of the coalition party into patronage positions— especially for "worthy" members of the black better class. The new party, Smith surmised, would allow the better class to play a key role in party politics and to push aside the old, corrupt generation of African American leadership. Smith noted that blacks "have stuck to the [Republican] party like tar to a black cat's tail; and what have we profited by it?" Times had changed and the political loyalties of blacks should change accordingly, he contended. "There are too many intelligent colored men among us now to lead us as sheep to the slaughter as we were ten to twelve years ago," he wrote; "many of us think for ourselves now, and would like to vote our own interests." Speaking for the county's black voters, Smith proclaimed, "We are tired of being led by two or three men, to vote for the men of their choice . . . and whenever any one is rewarded, it is a white man." He continued, "To be plain, we want more colored men appointed to lucrative positions." Condemning "a chronic set unfit" to hold office, Smith asked for positions for "our better class," who are "more modest" and "will do credit to our race."[62]

As the summer wore on, Smith's enthusiasm for the movement waned. After the Mecklenburg coalition party hesitated to nominate black candidates for office, Smith complained that the party needed to demonstrate to blacks why it warranted support since there appeared to be "nothing in the move for the Negro." Smith feared that the party contained "the same vindictive element that has fought us in the Democratic party, fighting under new colors," and he bluntly exclaimed, "Till we become independent we will be boot-licks of all parties."[63]

Bourbon race-baiting soon forced Smith back into the coalition camp. After Senator Matt Ransom gave "a white-line, color-line, sectional speech" in Charlotte in September 1882 in an attempt to rally Democratic loyalty, Smith announced, "We are now ready to vote for anybody to best a Bourbon." Although the Mecklenburg coalition ticket remained entirely white, Smith and the *Messenger* endorsed the party slate. "Which is the better, a half a loaf or no loaf at all?," asked Smith. "Remember we have the same old enemies to fight."[64]

As the election neared, Smith amplified his support of the coalition party. He advised black voters, "Even if you take Bourbon money, don't vote for a single Bourbon nominee." Other members of the black better class supported Smith's

position. A. P. Hunter wrote a letter to the *Messenger* criticizing blacks for
questioning which party to vote for. Concurrently, Smith escalated his attack on
black politician John Schenck, intimating that a coalition victory would end
Schenck's unscrupulous reign as the leading black politician in the county.[65]

As Smith attempted to rally black voters to support the coalition ticket,
Charles Jones raised the specter of Radical Republican rule as a way to mobilize
white Democrats. A coalition victory, wrote Jones, "puts us back where we were
six years ago." As the election approached, race tensions flared in Mecklenburg.
According to the *Messenger*, mounted Red Shirts attempted to intimidate black
voters—much as they had during Reconstruction—to keep them from supporting the coalition ticket.[66]

After an emotional, race-baiting campaign, the Bourbon Democrats emerged
victorious. In Mecklenburg the Democratic ticket swept every office except
county treasurer. Statewide, the Liberal Anti-prohibitionists managed to elect
several U.S. congressmen and a representative to the state legislature. Despite
its poor showing, support for the party nonetheless reflected a deep-seated
alienation among a significant number of voters, both black and white. The
Liberal Anti-prohibitionist alliance with the Republican party foreshadowed the
fusion politics of the 1890s. Many disillusioned white Tarheel voters willingly
joined the coalition movement to protest the unsatisfactory rule of the state's
Democrats, a lesson not lost on Republican leaders.[67]

The Republican–Liberal Anti-prohibition alliance continued through the
election of 1884 in North Carolina but seems to have had little appeal in
Mecklenburg. Embittered by the defeat of the coalition and its inability to unseat
the race-baiting Bourbons, Smith retreated to his previous advocacy of pure
Republicanism, urging his readers to "stand upon Republican principles" and to
reject "liberalism or any other 'ism.'" Like many members of the black better
class, Smith, through the rest of the decade, advocated reforms that transcended
party politics, which, in his view, remained hopelessly corrupt. At the same time,
he called for an overhaul of the Republican party, demanding proper recognition
of blacks. "If it is not given them," he argued, "they should take it. We have
served as pliant tools of men too long already. If we are to remain serfs we should
throw off the name freemen." Again Smith appealed for new race leaders to
replace old, corrupt politicians. "The masses mistake by following bad white
men in preference to intelligent, good men of their own race," wrote Smith in
December 1882. "We must have our own leaders. They should be men of
reputable conduct, intelligent, good men."[68]

As the coalition disintegrated, Charlotte's prohibitionists began laying the foundations for the city's first local-option election, launched in the spring of 1886. In April 1886 the drys organized another biracial Prohibition Club, whose members gathered the required number of signatures to call an election, and an election was set for June. Along with Charlotte, fifty townships, including the towns of Greensboro, Durham, Asheville, Winston, and Salem, held local-option elections that spring.[69]

The Prohibition Club, chaired by lawyer John E. Brown, consisted of many veterans of the 1881 campaigns. As in 1881, the club emphasized its formation "irrespective of party lines and without reference to race or color." In a series of resolutions, the club reiterated many of the arguments made against alcohol five years earlier, including that the saloon impaired "the peace and order of society" and endangered "life, liberty, and property."[70]

In addition to participating in the interracial Prohibition Club, black prohibitionists also maintained their own club, led by brickmason and builder W. W. Smith and undertaker Henry S. Boulware. The Colored Prohibition Club held meetings that were "open for their white friends as well as colored" and featured both black and white orators.[71]

In 1886 women prohibitionists found themselves well prepared to play a vital role in the campaign, having been especially active in the five years since the last prohibition election. The Woman's Christian Temperance Union (WCTU) had established white and black branches several years earlier that supplanted the women's prohibition clubs organized for the 1881 referendum. Although maintaining separate clubs, the black and white WCTU organizations occasionally met together to coordinate their activities. By 1886 they had considerably expanded their labors. Concentrating on educating the public, the women organized two children's temperance societies, the Bands of Hope and the Juvenile Temperance Union. The WCTU also held temperance picnics, distributed thousands of pages of literature, and sponsored prohibitionist speech contests. By the time of the 1886 local-option campaign, women prohibitionists were well organized, had enhanced public prohibition sentiment, and stood at the forefront of the movement.[72]

The local-option election campaign again raised emotions to a fever pitch and bitterly divided the community. Militant in tone, the campaign, according to the *Observer*, opened "in a manner to be regretted by all." Wets and drys held impassioned rallies, often in the same vicinity. Tension in the black community again grew particularly strong as the better class tried to sway black voters to reject the saloon. Black wets, led by car greaser Mack Ross, defended their right to drink, bringing class animosities once more to the surface. The *Observer* noted that although the campaign stirred up the community at large, "the excitement is principally among the colored people" since the outcome depended "in great measure on the colored vote."[73]

The black vote and party politics played an even greater role in the 1886 election than in 1881 and divided the community—and prohibitionists themselves—even more severely. Although the Prohibition Club continued to argue that its cause transcended party lines, the formation of the Prohibition party of North Carolina politicized prohibition and split the dry ranks. Headed by farmer T. L. Vail of Charlotte, the Prohibition party, organized in December 1885, proclaimed the "imperative necessity for a new party, with prohibition of the [liquor] traffic its prime object." For the two major parties, argued the Prohibitionists, the liquor issue would remain secondary; affiliation with either party meant "endorsing saloon influences, encouraging the power of the saloon in politics, and aiding to perpetuate that power."[74]

The Prohibition party had little support in Charlotte, and the prohibitionist cause lost some of its most ardent supporters, including Charles Jones and the *Observer*, over the formation of the single-issue third party. An enthusiastic supporter of prohibition in 1881, Jones criticized prohibitionists in 1886 for politicizing the liquor issue. "We fought for prohibition five years ago when it was a moral issue," wrote Jones, but "it is a party issue now, made so by the temperance people themselves." Since the Democratic National Convention of 1884 had declared that prohibition was not a partisan concern, Jones argued, the creation of the Prohibition party meant that one could not be "a prohibition man and a Democratic party man at the same time." But Jones did not reject the prohibition issue on the grounds of loyalty to the party line alone. The Prohibition party, he argued, threatened to divide the Democratic party and usher in black Republican rule, just as the Liberal Anti-prohibition party had done a few years earlier. Resurrecting the ghost of Reconstruction, as he had in 1882, Jones proclaimed that "the Democratic organization . . . is all that has stood between the people of the State and chaos, which the rule of the Republican party meant in 1870 and still means in 1886."[75]

After a long and vitriolic campaign, the voters of Charlotte decided the prohibition issue on 6 June. As women held prayer vigils and dispensed ice water to voters, and as children paraded through the streets bearing prohibition banners aloft, voters rejected prohibition by a margin of 1,018 to 589. According to the *Observer*, black voters turned out in full force and voted almost solidly against prohibition, rejecting the pleas of their ministers, teachers, and merchants—to the disgust of white prohibitionists and in defiance of the black better class. "Their badge," noted the newspaper, "was a red, white, and blue ribbon, upon which was printed, 'Freedom and Liberty.'" In public displays that must have deeply embarrassed the black better class, many of the city's black voters "hailed with great delight" the outcome of the election and "paraded through the streets with bottles, jugs, and kegs aloft, and waving flags," led by the "colored cornet band." The Second and Third wards, which had the largest number of black voters, voted overwhelmingly for the saloon. Only the Fourth Ward, the city's most prosperous white neighborhood, supported the dry cause, and then by only thirteen votes.[76]

In the aftermath of the election, the *Observer* exhorted the local citizenry to bury the hatchet and to suppress hard feelings. But subsequent events, particularly in the black community, reflected the deep divisions created by the prohibition movement. Prohibition served as a wedge that divided the African American community's fundamental institution: the church. Although several of Charlotte's black churches were associated with the better class in the early 1880s—particularly Clinton AME Zion Chapel and the Seventh Street Presbyterian Church—by the mid-1880s, the prohibition movement helped define more precisely certain congregations as those of either the better class or the "poorer sort."[77]

In May 1886, during the local-option campaign, a conflict between the Reverend Powell and his congregation at the First Baptist Colored Church over prohibition defined the congregation as a wet church when members clearly rejected the prohibitionist guidance of their minister and the better class. The controversy was ignited after the women of the congregation were invited to attend a meeting at the church, which, unbeknownst to them, was called to garner support for the prohibitionist cause. When they realized the nature of the meeting, they "became indignant" and angrily contended that their church should not sponsor such meetings. The protest of the women culminated in an angry confrontation with their minister, whom they blamed for calling the meeting. "The entire congregation became excited over the matter," and church members threatened their pastor with dire consequences "should he take an active part in favor of prohibition." One irate parishioner warned that if Powell made any prohibition speeches, "they would do him like another was done, cease paying him."[78]

While black Baptists furiously rejected the direction of prohibitionists, muzzling their minister and maintaining their right to drink, the issue of alcohol actually split the city's oldest black institution, Clinton Chapel, and helped divide the AMEZ church by class in Charlotte. In January 1887 editor and prohibitionist W. C. Smith, a member of Clinton Chapel, reported that during the local-option campaign the previous May "the devil crept into our church . . . through whiskey." Smith recommended that those who opposed alcohol break from Clinton and form their own church. Once again asserting the leadership and social vision of the black better class, Smith maintained, "The building of a new church is essential with us now, to rid our youth of fogey ideas, sentiments, etc., and to bring them up to *proper moral sentiments* and religious beliefs."[79]

The following Sunday, approximately forty people met to form a new AMEZ congregation, which they named Grace Church. Grace's members, according to Smith, had been "dissatisfied with many things in the management of the old church, believing especially that the preacher . . . was not exerting enough influence with regard to temperance and Christian piety generally." Because of their vocal support of prohibition, he and others "were persecuted" and "insulted in class meetings" to such an extent that they "went out, forty-odd in number, determined to worship God in peace and the way they understood His direction." Although he maintained that the new church was not a prohibition church, "*every person* that did leave the old church is a prohibitionist, as we think all Christian and church people ought to be."[80]

Grace's founders represented a significant portion of Charlotte's black better class; in Smith's words, they were "progressive, being made up mainly of intelligent young people." The founders included Smith, two teachers, a livery stable owner, and fourteen skilled artisans, including three carpenters and three brickmasons and their spouses, a plasterer, a butcher, and a barber. Only two founders were unskilled laborers, a porter and a cook.[81]

The founding of Grace Church intensified hard feelings within the black community. Reflecting the suspicion that Grace was an elitist church, some critics referred to it as "the 'paler' church" or the "Winona Circle," the name of a select literary and social society. Some of the founding members were indeed mulattoes, including Jennie Sumner, wife of barber Jethro Sumner, and brickmason Horace Lynch and his wife Moriah. But other charter members, including Smith himself and brickmason W. W. Smith, were black. Although editor Smith ignored the charge that Grace was a church of the light-skinned, he replied that "only two of the male members of this church and about a dozen females belong to the Winona." Prohibitionist sentiment and belief in the values it entailed—not skin color or club membership—served as the necessary prerequisites for affiliation at Grace.[82]

Grace Church and prohibition served as a symbolic rallying point for the new generation of educated black leaders such as Smith who sought to assert their authority in the black community. The church was a concrete symbol of class division in Charlotte's black community by the mid-1880s, reflecting the fact that involvement in the prohibition cause functioned as a litmus test for progressive black leadership in the late nineteenth century. Opposition to alcohol and the pursuit of moral and race progress, according to the black better class, were inextricably entwined.

The congregation retained its image as the church of the better class through the 1890s. Referring to the church's "intelligent and high-toned congregation," a black visitor to Charlotte in 1893 wrote, "To say that you belong to 'Grace,' signifies almost as much as it did at one time to say, 'I am a Roman citizen.'" On the cornerstone of the congregation's second church, laid in 1900, are the words "Deo Religion Et Temperantiae"—meaning "God, Religion, and Temperance."[83]

Smith and his compatriots at Grace Church continued to be active in the prohibition movement and took a leading role in the next local-option election held in 1888. But controversy and fraud marred the 1888 campaign, the decade's final showdown between wets and drys. Following previous patterns, local citizens formed prohibition clubs, circulated petitions to invoke a June election, and held rallies, but allegations about the legality of election petitions cast a shadow on the campaign. Antiprohibitionists accused the drys of forging signatures on the petitions. An investigative committee found "doubtful signers," "repeaters," and the names of several convicts on the petitions. Although the number of valid names remaining after the questionable names were removed was less than the number required to call an election, the board decided to allow the election anyway.[84]

Compared to previous prohibition campaigns, the 1888 election proved to be surprisingly calm. According to the *Charlotte Chronicle*, an antiprohibition newspaper that replaced the *Observer* as the city's leading daily in 1887, most interest centered in the black community. "The darkey," asserted the *Chronicle*, "who in prohibition elections in Charlotte seems to hold the balance of power, felt his importance and was sought after by both pros and antis." Again Charlotte voters rejected prohibition, 780 to 705, with only the Fourth Ward voting in favor.[85]

Soon after the election, a bribery scandal rocked the prohibitionist ranks. At an interdenominational prayer meeting, the Reverend A. G. McManaway, pastor of the Second Presbyterian Church, accused the liquor interests of buying votes during the recent campaign. Rufus Barringer then proclaimed that election bribery was "not confined to immoral people, but was indulged in by some of the most respected people in town." During the 1886 local-option campaign, he charged, a caucus of prohibitionists had "almost unanimously" agreed to buy votes.[86]

The controversy over election fraud typified other serious fissures caused by the prohibition movement. The *Chronicle* recounted the story of two local churchwomen who, in the aftermath of a heated debate among church members about the use of wine in the communion service, both walked out of the church the next time communion was offered since "each feared that the liquid she stood in horror of would be placed before her." A few suggested that buttermilk or grape juice replace communion wine "since the communion is a commemorative service, and it makes no difference what is drunk."[87]

The bribery scandal and the communion wine controversy damaged the already splintered prohibitionist cause. By 1889, after nearly a decade of crusading against the saloon, the prohibition movement represented to many extremism and division. Furthermore, the politicization of the issue alienated many avid supporters who feared the demise of the Democratic party and the "unthinkable" consequences of its collapse. Thus prohibitionists themselves split over the viability of local-option campaigns. In March 1889 some prohibitionists circulated a petition for another local-option election in June, but local prohibitionists "of calmer judgement" opposed holding another election. Even T. L. Vail, the former state president of the Prohibition party, refused to sign the petition, and the drive failed.[88]

Chronicle editor W. S. Hemby summed up the sentiments of many citizens in his plea to the county commissioners to not allow the election. Local-option elections, he wrote, succeeded only in "stirring up the people. It is very unwise and inexpedient to carry to an excess a matter of this kind." Moreover, Hemby charged that blacks, who made up most of the petition's signers, only endorsed it "for the sake of an election to create a market for votes." His remarks reflected a growing backlash against black voters as well as against local-option elections.[89]

The end of the decade marked a turning point in the attempt to settle the prohibition question through local elections. Throughout North Carolina, prohibitionists began to question the local-option strategy. Even the WCTU, at the forefront of the cause, concluded that prohibitionists needed to try a different approach. "Local option is not satisfactory," argued the state WCTU president in 1889, since "all kinds of fraud and deceit are practiced to dupe the ignorant and irresolute." The state legislature agreed. To put an end to annual local-option elections, it passed a law in 1889 allowing elections to be held every two years only.[90]

Some citizens sought a middle ground between prohibition and a whiskey free-for-all. Advocating a return to moral suasion rather than coercion, Hemby and the *Chronicle* argued that "public opinion is stronger than any law. . . . Educate public sentiment, and more will have been accomplished than could be done under martial law in every hamlet in the land." The *Chronicle* urged the enforcement of city codes banning screens, signs, and obstructions in front of saloons in order to "place barrooms under the public eye." In addition, the newspaper called for the city's saloons to close at 10:00 P.M. rather than midnight. The Board of Aldermen responded to some of these requests. In 1889 they refused to extend the limit of liquor sales beyond Trade and Tryon streets and doubled the annual tax on the sale of malt liquor from $250 to $500.[91]

In the 1890s the antialcohol cause moved from the arena of local elections to local and state legislation and became inextricably entwined with disfranchisement and other progressive "reforms" (see chapter 7). The link between white and black prohibitionists proved to be fragile and short-lived. A wave of fears and frustrations soon washed away the bridge built by the black and white better classes in their crusade against the saloon. When prohibition threatened the dominance of the Democratic party, a number of influential white advocates withdrew support. In their opinion, the evils of the saloon could never outweigh the threat of black Republican rule.

Moreover, white prohibitionists blamed blacks for the failure of local-option elections in the 1880s. As the weight that could tip elections either way, black voters—and the black better class especially—found themselves in an extremely vulnerable position. Indeed, the black better class, by claiming to their white allies that they had influence over the black community, set themselves up for an angry backlash when they could not deliver black votes. Unable to traverse class difference in their own community, the better class failed to convince the majority of blacks to embrace their ideals. Although white prohibitionists publicly praised blacks for their role in the victorious municipal election in 1881, they also placed the subsequent failure of local-option elections squarely on the shoulders of black voters. In addition, charges of voter fraud and claims that blacks profited financially from the frequency of elections embittered the relationship between blacks and whites. As a result of fear, frustration, and community divisiveness, white prohibitionists shifted the arena of their activities from the public election to local ordinances and state legislation, where the black vote had no relevance or influence.

Thus the experience of the black better class in the prohibition movement of the 1880s proved to be bittersweet. The movement provided them with opportunities for unprecedented political alliances with powerful whites, which helped confer status on the black better class. In the spring of 1881 they had even received public praise and recognition for their role in the municipal prohibition victory. But when the black better class proved unable to rally the majority of black voters to the prohibitionist cause and their larger social vision—in the state referendum of 1881 and the local-option elections of 1886 and 1888—the white better class angrily jettisoned the black better class from the prohibition movement. Although the interracial cooperation of the prohibition movement proved to be short-lived, it served as a formative generational experience for the black better class.

In spite of the failures of the prohibition coalition, Charlotte's black better class gleaned several critical lessons from their experience, lessons that would shape their behavior in the battles over race, class, and politics that defined the crucial decade of the 1890s. They concluded that there were many good, paternalistic whites, benefactors willing to befriend their black counterparts in an effort to enhance race progress, better race relations in the South, and work for social reform. The prohibition movement of the 1880s—despite its ultimate failure and subsequent racial backlash—gave the black better class a taste of equality and recognition by powerful whites of their accomplishments. The movement seemed to prove that their strategy of promoting race progress was, indeed, the key to gaining full citizenship, recognition, and participation in New South society. They remained optimistic that the better class of whites would continue to recognize the black better class as the true leaders of the black community and that blacks in the New South could ultimately earn the full respect of whites as long as they followed the lead of the better class and embraced their values.

•   •   •   •   •   •   •

Despite the demise of the interracial prohibition movement in the 1880s, women of the better class continued to work for other social reforms in the 1880s. Notably, black and white women, not bound by partisan political considerations like their husbands, were able to sustain their reform efforts across race lines. At the same time that they transcended barriers of race, they helped delineate class lines through their reform efforts. While their activities spanned the race gap, their organizations set them apart from less fortunate members of Charlotte society and reinforced their self-definition as the better class.

In 1886, as the prohibition movement began to disintegrate, white and black women, nearly all of whom were active prohibitionists, channeled their reform energies into building hospitals for the black community. The hospital movement grew directly from the prohibition movement, in which women of the better classes were introduced to each other.

Charlotte blacks had long needed a medical facility. Barred from St. Peter's Hospital, founded as the Charlotte Home and Hospital in the 1870s, black residents had no place to go for medical care or treatment. W. C. Smith pointed out in the *Messenger* that "there are many cases of accident; a person is shot, injured in railroad accidents, a stranger is taken sick in our city, and we have no place for them to go for treatment, except the county poor house in the country."[92]

Black and white women of the better classes took up the cause of opening a black hospital late in 1886. Mirroring the paternalism of white prohibitionists, "a few benevolent ladies of Charlotte" initiated the establishment of a "hospital for the colored people." Following the model of cooperation established during the prohibition campaign of 1886, black and white women maintained separate organizations and committees while working for the same cause. Indeed, membership in the prohibition associations and the subsequent hospital committees was nearly synonymous. In 1887 the black hospital committee included Mrs. W. W. Smith, Mrs. Robert Johnston, Mrs. Dick Pethel, and Mary Lynch, all of whom were active in the Colored Ladies Prohibition Association. The white committee was headed by prohibitionists Mrs. R. D. Johnston and Mrs. E. K. P. Osborne. Moreover, many white male contributors to the hospital were active prohibitionists, including Rufus Barringer, E. K. P. Osborne, and George E. Wilson.[93]

Together—yet separately—black and white women canvassed funds, organized fund-raising events, and arranged free medical treatment for blacks by both black and white physicians. White women, led by Mrs. R. D. Johnston, sponsored an art exhibit to raise funds for the hospital and solicited subscriptions from "a number of prominent white citizens." Black women, headed by Mrs. W. W. Smith, solicited funds from black churches, clubs, and individuals in their community. The black women even sponsored a baseball game to benefit the hospital. The Colored WCTU performed a crucial role in supporting the hospital, reflecting the link between the prohibition and hospital movements. In March 1887 the Union Hospital opened its doors on Myers Street, a testament to the joint efforts of the black and white women of the better classes.[94]

The better classes of black and white women also cooperated in establishing the city's second black hospital, Good Samaritan Hospital. In 1882 veteran reformer Jane Wilkes, a former Confederate hospital nurse, founder of the Charlotte Home and Hospital, and member of St. Peter's Episcopal Church, began collecting funds from northern Episcopal congregations for a black hospital. In 1888 she had raised enough money to purchase a lot on Hill Street in the Third Ward, and in December 1888 she had the cornerstone laid for the hospital. Three years later the hospital opened. Although the funds for establishing Good Samaritan seem to have come almost exclusively from whites, black Charlotteans played a key role in administering the hospital. St. Michael's and All Angels, Charlotte's black Episcopal parish, managed the hospital along with a white board of managers that included Wilkes, Julia Fox, and Lizzie Clarkson. Moreover, Charlotte's black community bore most of the financial burden for running the institution, with funds coming "from the colored churches and the societies, besides subscriptions from white persons interested in the work."[95]

The black hospital movement was the capstone of interracial class-based cooperation in Charlotte. A religious revival in 1887 turned the reforming impulse of the better class of white women away from work in the black community to reform in their own community. In February 1887 Mississippi evangelist R. G. Pearson held a three-week revival in Charlotte that set the community ablaze with evangelical fervor. Dubbing the revival "A Great Awakening," the *Chronicle* remarked that "there has never been such a religious revival in the memory of the oldest inhabitants," as townspeople experienced "deep heart searchings" and "many tearful confessions."[96]

The Great Awakening of 1887 seems to have sensitized white women of the better class to problems among their own race. Soul-searching and Christian rededication inspired white women to attempt to ameliorate problems closer to home rather than aid in the "uplift" of the black community. During the revival, three prostitutes experienced conversion. In response, the newly formed Ladies Reformatory Society, energized by the revival, leased and outfitted a "House of Refuge" on Myers Street for "the especial benefit of reclaimed fallen women." Although one of the residents "returned to her old haunts," the house was "in a flourishing condition."[97]

The evangelical revival of 1887 not only shifted the trajectory of reform but also reinvigorated women's denominational reform organizations. With interest in religion rekindled, the better class of white women once again began to use church organizations as their vehicle for social reform—much as they had in earlier decades—rather than secular organizations, such as the Ladies Prohibitory Society. Episcopal women played a key role in establishing the Thompson Orphanage and Training School in May 1887 as a "home for orphan and destitute children." Presbyterian women of the city, led by Mrs. A. G. Brenizer, followed suit by establishing the Presbyterian Home and Hospital in May 1888 on Ninth Street in the First Ward, proclaiming it a "refuge to the poor and needy." Methodist women organized a day nursery for working mothers. With the anticipated opening of three cotton mills in 1888 (see chapter 4), "the Day Nursery will become more than ever a necessity," enabling "many a deserving woman to work, as she could leave her child at the nursery for safe-keeping during the day, and feel it was in good hands." Led by Mrs. Walter Brem, the women leased a cottage near the First Presbyterian Church in February 1888 and opened the nursery "with four little inmates." The women solicited high chairs, toys, books, and pictures from the community to furnish the nursery.[98]

The establishment of black hospitals and a plethora of benevolent institutions founded by white women of the better class embodied the nature of social reform in Charlotte in the aftermath of the prohibition movement. Moreover, these hospitals and benevolent institutions reflected the relationship between the black and white better classes at the end of the 1880s. Earlier in the decade, the prohibition movement invigorated and inspired cooperation by the black and white better classes in Charlotte. New South politics, however, splintered interracial cooperation. Although black and white women of the better class sustained their cooperative reform efforts longer than their spouses, their activities also demonstrated the limits of interracial cooperation in the New South. Black and white women, like their male counterparts, went their separate ways by the end of the decade. Yet both the prohibition and hospital movements had acquainted the black and white better classes; they had recognized common class interests that transcended race lines. Their collaboration in the 1880s, however temporary, continued to inspire the black better class to pursue their course of self-help and to seek alliances with powerful whites in the 1890s. Turbulent economic and political developments, however, would further separate the black and white better classes in the next decade.

INDUSTRIALIZATION

In 1881 cotton merchants Robert M. Oates and his nephews, D. W. and John E. Oates, opened the Charlotte Cotton Mill in the city's Fourth Ward. The opening of the mill, which employed eighty operatives, would prove to be as consequential to Charlotte's development as the coming of the railroad in 1852. The Charlotte Cotton Mill represented the beginning of a new era in the city's history, an era that not only would transform the nature of the local economy but also would recast class relations in the rapidly growing town. Many members of the white better class enthusiastically joined the crusade to establish cotton mills, investing the wealth they had accumulated from the growth of the cotton economy in the 1870s. Installment plans, in which subscribers contributed as little as 50 cents a week for a share, made cotton mill investment a possibility even for people of modest means. Cotton mill fever raged in Charlotte in the 1880s and 1890s, and by 1900 the town boasted a dozen mills and was the center of the Piedmont's burgeoning textile industry. At the turn of the century, industrialist D. A. Tompkins, who led the crusade to build cotton mills beginning in the mid-1880s, estimated that "one-half of the looms and spindles of the South are within a one-hundred mile radius of this city."[1]

Just as the growth of the cotton economy transformed concepts of class among Charlotte's white residents in the 1870s, industrialization threw class relations into flux again in the 1890s. Cotton mills generated a class of impoverished mill workers who resided in a ring of mill villages that surrounded Charlotte. Like other Piedmont cotton mill towns, Charlotte found itself divided between "town people" and "mill people." But Charlotte's townspeople were also divided by class. Industrialization led to the bifurcation of the white better class as it split between a manufacturing elite and a middle class.

Whereas industrialization provided new economic opportunities for the white better class, members of Charlotte's black better class found their economic prospects limited. Not only did black businesses have to compete with well-established white businesses, but African Americans also found their investment opportunities severely restricted when compared to whites. Although many of Charlotte's black businesspeople and professionals expressed an interest in industrial investment, only real estate and a few other economic ventures were open to them. Ultimately, industrialization separated further the paths of the better class of blacks and whites. Besides helping to differentiate white society into new, distinct classes, cotton mills also created a powerful manufacturing elite that had no counterpart in the black community. At the turn of the century, the influence and economic power of black businesspeople and professionals in their own community remained circumscribed, having improved little since the prohibition battles of the 1880s.

• • • • • • •

The cotton mill fever that swept Charlotte in the 1880s and 1890s had deep roots in the area's past. Local businesspeople had long recognized that large profits could be made by establishing mills in their cotton-rich area. In 1847 promoters of the Charlotte and South Carolina Railroad promised that new manufacturing enterprises, "factories of cotton," would be among the first fruits of railroad building in Charlotte. Soon after local citizens subscribed funds for the railroad, local entrepreneurs established the county's first textile mills. In 1848 William M. Neal of Charlotte founded the Catawba Manufacturing Company, which produced cotton yarn and cloth near Charlotte on the Catawba River. That same year, Charlotte businesspeople R. C. Carson, John A. Young, and Z. A. Grier established the Rock Island Manufacturing Company, which produced high-quality cotton and wool yarn sold throughout the South. The Catawba and Rock Island mills were among fifty textile mills operating in North Carolina when the Civil War began.[2]

In Mecklenburg only the Rock Island mill survived the conflict, and in the years following the war, it provided a model for a new industrial South. Soon after the end of the war, the owners moved the steam-powered mill from the Catawba River to a four-story brick building in Charlotte, where it employed about ninety hands. In the aftermath of the war, the Rock Island mill served as a shining example of "home industry," what many boosters viewed as the key to the prosperity of both the town and the region. The local press urged "our capitalists" to replicate the Rock Island mill, to "invest their surplus means in manufacturing," to "learn a lesson from the Yankees." Imbuing industrialization with a spiritual quality that it would retain for the rest of the century, the *Western*

Democrat claimed "that our only salvation is in our sustaining each other and keeping our capital at home."[3]

In 1870, only a few years after the press sang the praises of the Rock Island mill, the firm went bankrupt. However, mill boosters seemed undeterred. Farmers, benefiting from the high prices commanded by cotton in the years immediately following the Civil War, seemed to be potential investors. Rock Island founder John A. Young appealed to farmers to invest in mills as a means of "building a market for their own products, keeping their money at home and building up their own country." The *Western Democrat* even beckoned "Northern capitalists" to invest in local manufacturing, promising that "if men from abroad will locate among us and identify themselves with the material interests of our State and section, we know they will receive a hearty welcome, no matter whether they are Republicans or Democrats."[4]

Some northern capital did indeed come to the Charlotte area beginning in the late 1860s and early 1870s, but not in the form of cotton mill investment. Instead, northerners helped rejuvenate the area's gold mines, most of which had lain dormant since the 1840s. Gold mining aided in reviving the area's economy in the late 1860s and 1870s, and a plethora of small manufactures appeared in Charlotte, including a spoke and handle factory, a shoe and boot factory, and a cigar manufactory. But neither gold mines nor small industry seemed to offer the economic rewards associated with cotton mills. The cotton mill served as a preeminent symbol of the New South; in the minds of many New South advocates, only cotton mills signified true progress and insured economic prosperity.[5]

Yet the "monied men"—farmers and businesspeople alike—seemed hesitant to invest in mills. As cotton prices dropped precipitously beginning in 1870, most farmers found themselves in desperate financial straits, while local businesspeople seemed to prefer less risky ventures, such as real estate. The *Charlotte Observer* noted that "our people have capital, but they are slow to take hold of any new enterprise." In 1872 a local citizen criticized "the fogy notions which our men of capital have" that "are not exactly those which will realize the splendid destiny that nature and location design for this City." Although new buildings sprang up in the town, they represented little economic expansion. "Where are your workshops, your mills, your factories? . . . Where are enterprises that create wealth?"[6]

Other town leaders soon joined in the cry for the creation of cotton mills to guarantee Charlotte's continued growth and prosperity as well as the economic independence of the South. Both the *Charlotte Democrat* and the *Observer* agitated for the building of cotton mills throughout the 1870s. In the spring of 1873 W. J. Yates exhorted Charlotte businesspeople "to put the ball in motion," assuring potential investors that "no investment . . . will add more speedily and effectually to the common inheritance of our city than one or more well conducted cotton factories."[7]

In September 1873, a few months after Yates made his plea, a group of Charlotte businesspeople met at Miller's Hall to consider establishing a mill in Charlotte. Headed by cotton buyer J. E. Stenhouse, the businesspeople appointed a committee made up of banker R. Y. McAden, textile manufacturer John A. Young, farmer and businessman A. B. Davidson, and merchants S. M. Howell, Thomas H. Brem, and R. M. Miller to investigate the matter. But just as Charlotte's business leaders began to organize a cotton mill, the "unsettled state of financial affairs" resulting from the panic of 1873 delayed their plans.[8]

Nearly a year later, the same group of businesspeople organized the Charlotte Cotton Factory, headed by A. B. Davidson. Directors for the mill included bankers McAden and Thomas Dewey and lawyers John E. Brown and W. R. Myers. A month afterward, the bondholders of the Rock Island Mill, which had declared bankruptcy in 1870, organized a company to put a cotton mill in operation in the old Rock Island building. But the plans of cotton mill boosters foundered amid the tenacious national economic depression of the 1870s that resulted in money shortages and bankruptcies. The prominent cotton-buying house of Stenhouse and Macaulay went bankrupt in 1877, and a handful of Charlotte merchants closed their doors as the depression sapped the economy and made the funding of industrial enterprise nearly impossible.[9]

Although economic doldrums sidetracked the mill-building plans of local businesspeople, the depression inspired local Grange chapters to explore the possibility of pooling their resources and building cotton mills. Aggressively supported by D. H. Hill and the *Southern Home*, cotton mills seemed to be the panacea for the agricultural crisis squeezing the area's farmers. Area Grange chapters began to call for factories in the summer of 1875. Granger Jasper Stowe of Gaston County, who owned a small cotton mill, argued in a series of letters to the *Southern Home* that through cotton mills "a needy class would find employment . . . and the rural people would be taught the value of manly thought and enterprise." In another letter to the *Southern Home*, a local farmer made a heartfelt plea for the opening of cotton mills as the solution to local poverty. "Is there no hope for the poor women and children of Charlotte?" he asked. "Can we not devise some plan by which one or two cotton factories can be put into successful operation in this place?"[10]

The issue of cotton mills was soon swept into the bitter conflict raging between town and country people in the 1870s. Even though townspeople had made little progress in establishing cotton mills in Charlotte, some of them viewed the pleas of Stowe and Hill for farmer-built mills in the countryside as "exciting the country against the town." In the summer of 1875 the *Observer*, defending the interests of townspeople, charged Grange mill advocates of "agrarianism" and "communism," while the *Southern Home* defended Grange plans against the severe criticism of the *Observer*.[11]

Bickering between town and country people did little to advance the mill-building crusade in Mecklenburg. But as soon as the clouds of economic depression began to lift, cotton mill boosters resumed their work. The decline of cotton prices through the 1870s probably made industrial investment more attractive to local businesspeople. Charlotte merchants and professionals, like their counterparts in other areas of the South, sought new investment opportunities that would supersede the obvious limitations of the cotton-based economy. At the end of the decade, cotton merchants R. M. Oates and his nephews finally took the steps that mill enthusiasts had long called for. In December 1879 the Charlotte Board of Aldermen granted the Oateses a ten-year tax exemption for their proposed cotton mill. A few weeks later, they traveled north to buy machinery and then began building a mill in the city's Fourth Ward near the Air Line depot. Their Charlotte Cotton Mill began operating in 1881, with 6,240 spindles to make warps and yarns.[12]

The opening of the Charlotte Cotton Mill represented the beginning of a new industrial era in Charlotte's history. By the end of the 1880s, as cotton mill building in the South accelerated and even outstripped mill building in the North, three more mills had been built in Charlotte. The Victor, Ada, and Alpha mills were all founded in 1888, the Ada and Alpha mills financed through an installment plan whereby an investor could spend as little as 50 cents per week per share to be a part-owner of a cotton mill. By 1900 seven additional mills— the Highland Park Manufacturing Company, also known as the Gingham Mills (1891); the Atherton Mills (1892); the Louise Mills (1896); the Gold Crown Hosiery Mills (1897); the Magnolia Mill (1899); the Chadwick Manufacturing Company (1900); and the Elizabeth Mills (1900)—all operated in and around Charlotte.[13]

Besides initiating cotton mill building in New South Charlotte, the Oates family exemplified the course followed by most of the town's mill builders as they climbed the ladder from merchant or professional to mill owner. In the late 1860s Robert Oates had established a small store in Charlotte and by the mid-1870s had built it into a major cotton-buying house. His nephews had also established a cotton-buying house that flourished with the growth of the cotton economy. In addition to founding the Charlotte Cotton Mill, R. M. Oates invested in the Victor Mill, and D. W. Oates helped found the Gold Crown

Hosiery Mills. Similarly, R. Y. and J. H. McAden had come to Charlotte after the war, forging successful careers as bankers, and in 1881 built the McAden Mills in adjacent Gaston County, the same year the Oateses opened their Charlotte mill. The McAdens also invested in the Victor Mill in 1888. Lawyer E. K. P. Osborne, organizer of the Alpha Mill, had moved to Charlotte from Alabama in the mid-1870s and established a lucrative law practice before entering the textile business in 1888.[14]

Charlotte's mills, then, like those of Piedmont South Carolina, were built almost entirely by local merchants and professionals, apparently with local capital (see table A.6). Northern capital did not play a major part in Charlotte's mill-building efforts until 1892, with the construction of the Atherton Mills. Like their counterparts in neighboring Piedmont South Carolina, over half of Charlotte's cotton mill investors were merchants or were involved in other commercial enterprises. Another 44 percent were professionals, predominately lawyers. Only one farmer is listed as a mill stockholder in the late nineteenth century, A. B. Davidson, and he had been involved in entrepreneurial enterprises since before the Civil War (see chapter 1).[15]

In addition, Charlotte's New South cotton mill builders, unlike those in other parts of North Carolina, had no connection with the antebellum textile industry. Whereas the Holt family dominated textiles before and after the Civil War in Alamance County and the Worths and Odells continued to command the industry in Randolph County, no such continuity in mill ownership existed in Mecklenburg. None of the men involved in the county's antebellum textile industry played a role in Charlotte's New South cotton mill building. Charlotte's mill builders were, for the most part, merchants and professionals who had arrived after the Civil War, established flourishing businesses in the 1870s, and invested their wealth in cotton mills in the 1880s and 1890s. They represented a new, postbellum generation of industrialists, a generation from the ranks of the white better class of the 1870s, who sought innovative ways to guarantee their prosperity as well as the fortune of their town.[16]

Charlotte's mills spawned a profusion of textile-related industries in which local businesspeople and professionals, as well as some northern capitalists, readily invested. Cottonseed oil mills, textile engineering firms, textile machinery and mill supply companies, cloth wholesalers and retailers, clothing factories, transportation companies, and warehouses all appeared in Charlotte in the 1880s and 1890s, transforming the town into the industrial and distributional hub of the Piedmont textile industry. Land development companies also followed in the wake of Charlotte's industrial growth. Many of them, like the Charlotte Consolidated Construction Company, the Belmont Springs Company,

Daniel Augustus Tompkins, New South industrialist.
(Courtesy of the North Carolina Division of Archives and History)

and the Highland Park Company, bought and developed property, erected homes and buildings, and promoted "manufacturing and other industrial enterprises" on the land that they owned.[17]

Daniel Augustus Tompkins played an integral role in the transformation of Charlotte into an industrial center. Although the town's cotton mill fever was under way long before he arrived in Charlotte in 1883, Tompkins was Charlotte's most articulate and relentless advocate of industrialization; he soon emerged as a national figure in the promotion of New South industry. Tompkins helped organize cotton mills and affiliated industries throughout the area.

A self-proclaimed "child of the Old South," Tompkins was born in 1851 in

Edgefield County, South Carolina, the son of a planter and physician. After attending the University of South Carolina, Tompkins transferred to New York's Rensselaer Polytechnic Institute in 1869, where he began to quench his thirst for industrial education. Upon graduation in 1873, he became an apprentice with the Bethlehem Iron Works in Pennsylvania. While at Bethlehem, according to his biographer, Tompkins "determined to devote his life to the development of the South, and he consistently aimed in that direction." Convinced that the South's future greatness lay in industrialization, Tompkins moved to Charlotte in March 1883 after making a careful survey of the region's budding industrial centers. Arriving with "a kit of machinists' tools," a missionary zeal to convert the South to an industrial economic order, and insatiable ambition, the young engineer hung out his shingle in Charlotte, declaring his profession as "Engineer, Machinist, and Contractor."[18]

Tompkins found evenings in Charlotte "intolerably dull," but as an agent of the Westinghouse Company, his days were filled with hard work as he sold engines throughout the state and South Carolina, serving as a traveling salesman, machinist, and mechanic for the company. Seeking to expand his business, Tompkins formed the D. A. Tompkins Company in 1884 with cotton merchants R. M. Miller and R. M. Miller, Jr. Realizing the potential profits to be made in the cottonseed oil business, Tompkins and his partners bought up all of the old mills of the American Cotton Oil Company, which had a near-monopoly on the cottonseed oil business, and promoted and built 250 cottonseed oil mills all over the South, including the Southern Cotton Oil Company in Charlotte. The Millers and Tompkins were also partners in the Piedmont Milling Company, which manufactured grain and cottonseed into products for market, as well as the Charlotte Oil Company, which specialized in manufacturing cottonseed oil.[19]

In 1889 the D. A. Tompkins Company expanded its facilities and entered the field of cotton mill construction by beginning work on the design of the Atherton Mills in Charlotte, one of three Tompkins-owned mills in the area. Tompkins claimed to have built more than a hundred cotton mills in the region. Not only did his firm design and construct mills, but Tompkins also helped finance mills, advocating installment plans to raise money locally. In addition, through his contacts with northern mill machine companies, he frequently interested northern investors in building southern mills. By the 1890s the D. A. Tompkins Company consisted of machine shops and a foundry. The firm specialized in designing, building, and equipping cotton mills, cottonseed oil mills, and fertilizer companies.[20]

In 1892, the same year he built Charlotte's Atherton Mills, Tompkins pur-

Southern Cotton Oil Company, Charlotte, 1910. (Courtesy of the
Robinson-Spangler Room, Public Library of Charlotte and Mecklenburg County)

chased the *Charlotte Observer* with J. P. Caldwell of Statesville and rejuvenated
the faltering newspaper. He fashioned the *Observer* into a powerful vehicle to
promote Charlotte and his gospel of the New South. As the *Atlanta Constitution*
had been for New South booster Henry Grady, the *Observer* became Tompkins's
pulpit. In innumerable columns, Tompkins reiterated his belief in laissez-faire
capitalism and the theory that the South's commercial, manufacturing, and
agricultural genius, evident in the early nineteenth century, had been obliterated
by slavery. Echoing Grady and other advocates of the New South creed, Tompkins insisted that the destruction of slavery had been a blessing because it paved
the way for the reemergence of the South's industrial genius. Not only did
Tompkins write hundreds of articles promoting industry and his vision of the
New South for the *Observer*, but he also frequently contributed to the *Manufacturers' Record*, the *Wall Street Journal* of mill owners. Small-town newspapers all
over the South reprinted his columns. Moreover, he spoke to countless clubs,
schools, boards of trade, and professional associations, advocating the redemp-
tive power of southern industry. By the mid-1890s Tompkins had emerged as
Charlotte's most influential and well-known citizen.[21]

As Tompkins and many of his lesser-known compatriots climbed the economic ladder from merchants and professionals to "mill men," as they called

themselves, they formed a new class in Charlotte, a manufacturing elite that self-consciously separated itself from less wealthy, less influential members of the town's white better class. Beginning in the 1890s, they began to organize select clubs and social organizations that formed the foundation of a distinctive social network and helped define them as the elite of the city. Their clubs replicated the "gentlemen's clubs" of the North, with which the "mill men" would have been well acquainted through business trips. Using northern society as a model, Charlotte's manufacturing elite coalesced rapidly as a class.[22]

The organization of the Southern Manufacturers' Club symbolized the emergence of a manufacturing elite in Charlotte and helped define its membership. Pointing out Charlotte's evolution into "a central point of the manufacturing interests of the South," Charlotte's mill men expressed "the need for some organization to which those connected with these interests and those who are commercially and professionally brought into relations with them may belong." The Southern Manufacturers' Club, organized in July 1894, aimed to "increase the intercourse of Southern manufacturers and business men with each other" as well as to promote southern industrial development. Moreover, the club would provide for its members "a pleasant place of common resort for entertainment," a "social club for businessmen." In addition to drawing membership from Charlotte and the surrounding area, the club expected to have "a large membership outside the city," as "it is desired that the club rooms shall be a meeting place for manufacturers South and their business agents North."[23]

The founding members of the club represented the economic elite of Charlotte and the surrounding area. The club attracted not only officers and directors of cotton mills and textile-related industries but also the heads of land development companies, a handful of bankers, a merchant, and a lawyer. Charter members included Tompkins as well as R. M. Miller, Jr., vice president of the Atherton Mills; Henry S. Chadwick, president of the Charlotte Machine Company; and Vinton Liddell, president of the Highland Park Manufacturing Company. Also joining as charter members were Edward Dilworth Latta, president of the Charlotte Consolidated Construction Company; Charlotte bankers Samuel Wittkowsky and M. A. Pegram; merchant E. M. Andrews; and lawyer Platt D. Walker. In addition, two mill owners from Spartanburg and Kings Mountain and two northern mill men, one from New York and the other from Providence, also signed on. Henry Chadwick—a native Vermonter who first came to Charlotte in 1887 as an agent of a northern machine company and later organized the Louise Mills—served as the club's first president. According to a club handbook, of the thirty-four original charter members who formed the club, only four had been born in Charlotte.[24]

Two months after its organization, the club moved into well-appointed quarters in the *Observer* building. Carpeted with Belgian rugs and paneled with dark wood, the club resembled the "gentlemen's clubs" found in northern cities and recently established in larger New South cities like Atlanta and Nashville. The Southern Manufacturers' Club featured a reception room, a writing room, a library, a billiard room, a veranda overlooking Tryon Street, and a complete staff of servants. The club also had a café where members could "entertain . . . club men of New York and other large cities . . . with pride born of the satisfaction that nowhere, North or South, is there to be found a more beautiful room than the cafe of the Manufacturers' Club of Charlotte." In 1910 the club built its own elegant four-story edifice on Poplar and West Trade streets.[25]

The Southern Manufacturers' Club, according to Tompkins, furnished "a perfect atmosphere" for informal business discourse. Tompkins estimated that "we get three or four times as many new enterprises as could be gotten if the proposals were formally brought up before an ordinary business men's meeting or board of trade." The general officers of the Southern Railway, Tompkins noted, for example, "cheerfully come to our club, cheerfully listen to suggestions from individual members . . . and are glad of the opportunity. There is nothing published and nothing has to be done immediately. . . . Discussions at the Manufacturers' Club require no formal answer."[26]

A year after the club organized, its members hosted the New England Manufacturers' Association, "the mill men of the North and East." Hosting their northern counterparts signified "new ties—social and business—between North and South: new and substantial friends for Charlotte, and who knows what new business schemes this visit may set on foot?" Charlotte mill men forged such strong ties with their Yankee counterparts that a few years later, Tompkins, while serving as president of the club, suggested that "Southern" be dropped from the club's name because it "provincializes the club." According to Tompkins, "The best loyalty to the South is to cosmopolitanize our institutions." Club members agreed with Tompkins and temporarily discarded the offending adjective from the club's name.[27]

As mill men rubbed shoulders in the exclusive chambers of the Manufacturers' Club, their spouses created an elite social network that further defined Charlotte's emerging manufacturing elite and separated them from less affluent townspeople. Like their spouses, women of the elite also seem to have used the example of their Gilded Age northern counterparts as a model. Elite women rejected the reforming impulse that had animated and helped define the better classes in the 1880s. Distancing themselves from the less fortunate, they replaced reform activities with purely social events, fashionable affairs that displayed their wealth. Moreover, the activities of women linked Charlotte's elite with their peers in both southern and northern cities. Just as women played a crucial role in defining the "better class" in the 1870s and 1880s, their activities helped to designate the town's elite in the 1890s.[28]

Around 1890 Charlotte's elite began to observe a "social season" similar to those in large northern cities as well as Atlanta and Nashville. The *Observer* reported such occasions with relish, referring to Charlotte "society" and "the elite," Charlotte's "one hundred and fifty" who sponsored and took part in an array of chic social events. The annual New Year's Open House in which the "smart set" opened their elegant homes to each other "in a merry exchange of good wishes for the coming year," served as the highlight of the season, while a series of theme parties punctuated elite social life. In 1895 Mrs. J. M. Smith hosted a "Mozart Party" at her North College Street home, "one of the sweetest affairs of the season," while Mrs. R. M. Miller's "déjeuner à la fourchette," a fancy French luncheon, was a feature of the 1897 season.[29]

Sumptuous dress balls formed the heart of Charlotte's social season. Sponsored by newly formed exclusive women's clubs, as well as individual women, a series of cotillions and germans bonded Charlotte's elite and provided a closed, controlled setting where their children could socialize with "their kind." In 1892 the Young Married Ladies' Club, headed by Mrs. R. L. Jones, opened the social season with a "Bal Poudre En Topis" for the "young, unmarried" elite, which was described by "one of the fresh young debutantes" as "novel, unique, delightful." In 1893 Charlotte's first annual cotillion was held at the Buford Hotel, and a year later the newly formed Cotillion Club sponsored the dance, attended by "the social world." Coming-out parties soon followed.[30]

Dances and coming-out parties not only served as exclusive social settings for the children of Charlotte's manufacturing elite but also linked them with their counterparts in other areas of the South. Charlotte hostesses often gave dances and parties in honor of visiting young ladies. In 1893 the "Misses Oates" hosted "a beautiful event" at their elegant North Tryon Street home for guests from Florida and Spartanburg. Honored guests at other affairs included visitors from Atlanta, Winston, Danville, Durham, and occasionally New York City. Thus, Charlotte's manufacturing elite and their children participated in an extralocal social network that tied them to their counterparts in other industrializing cities of the New South and in the North. Economic and social links forged in the paneled, smoke-filled rooms of the Manufacturers' Club were reinforced at cotillions and parties sponsored by elite women.[31]

Like elite women in northern cities in the Gilded Age, elite women in Charlotte generally confined their charitable work to serving on hospital boards or to sponsoring benefits, such as charity balls. In 1894, for example, elite women helped organize a "Great Charity Ball" held at the Buford Hotel "to replenish the depleted treasury of the poor." Later that year, members of the manufacturing elite frolicked at a lawn party benefit to aid orphan children. In general, women of the elite detached themselves from actual contact with the town's poor. Like other elite women at that time, Charlotte's society women found that by sponsoring charity events, they could augment their social standing by solidifying their position as a member of the elite in addition to fulfilling their duty to the less fortunate.[32]

While Charlotte's elite cavorted at chic parties and balls and set themselves apart from less affluent townspeople, a middle class, in turn, began to define itself against the elite. By the mid-1890s the white better class divided into two distinct social groups, a manufacturing elite and a middle class. Made up largely of small businesspeople, ministers, teachers, physicians, and their spouses, the white middle class continued to pursue many of the reform activities initiated by the better class in the 1870s and late 1880s. Indeed, the moralism and reforming impulse of middle-class men and women, fanned by the flames of evangelical religion, helped distinguish them from their social superiors, providing them with self-definition and purpose. As it had in the antebellum North, evangelical religion played a key role in defining the newly emergent white middle class in Charlotte in the 1890s.[33]

To some members of the middle class, the lavish social activities of Charlotte's elite men and women reflected their moral bankruptcy. Throughout the 1890s, the middle class became increasingly indignant about the drinking, dancing, and card playing of the elite. Evangelical revivalism, beginning with Charlotte's Great Awakening of 1887, continued to burn throughout much of the 1890s, ignited by both famous evangelists who conducted meetings in Charlotte as well as local ministers. Well-known evangelist Sam Jones, the "Moody of the South," helped focus middle-class sentiment against the town's elite during his 1890 Charlotte revival. Jones devoted nearly two sessions of his Charlotte meetings to an attack on local "society," accusing the town of "running 'society' pretty lively." Jones exhorted, "Society! There is no manhood, no womanhood, no religion in it." He contended in typically colorful language that society consisted of nothing but "the dude and the dudine," the dude "a wart on the devil's big toe," the dudine "a wart on his nose." Condemning the fashionable dances so popular among the elite, Jones exclaimed, "What's round dancing but square dancing with the corners cut off, and round dancing is nothing but hugging set to music." The evangelist saved his harshest condemnation for society women, whom he blamed for perpetuating the sins of their class: "God pity our women when they will be *particeps criminis* in the ruin of our boys. 'The demands of society'! Do I think more of society than my home?" Jones claimed that "for fifty years this town has been dominated by dry rot." He commanded Charlotte's preachers to "preach more on this subject" and to condemn church members who drank, danced, and played progressive euchre.[34]

One minister who boldly took up Jones's challenge was the Reverend R. C. Reed of the Second Presbyterian Church. In January 1891 the Young Ladies' Club of North Tryon Street, an association of young society women headed by banker's daughter Nan Dowd, made plans to sponsor a charity ball to benefit the Confederate soldiers' home in Raleigh. At a church service a few days before the event took place, Reed summoned his congregation to stand and sing a hymn of consecration signifying their commitment to living Christian lives. At the conclusion of the hymn, he asked the congregation whether "with that act of renewed consecration they could have anything to do, even most remotely, with the approaching Charity Ball." He cried, "Charity Ball! How would this combination sound in the ears of the Apostle Paul, who sang the praises of charity with an inspired tongue?" Balls were "hurtful to religion," and "many dear young people have been kept from the services" or "when here, have not been in a receptive mood" because of a ball. Reed exhorted his congregation, "Let all the Christians of Charlotte put their foot down on this thing and they can mash it into a sorry little affair."[35]

Likewise, a series of well-attended revival meetings held in Charlotte in the summer of 1895 revealed the growing differences between the town's middle class and the elite. In a sermon entitled "Who Is on the Lord's Side?," evangelist Dr. Wharton condemned "those church members who drank whiskey, played cards, attended theaters, and went to germans and dances." The next day, Wharton preached specifically to young women in the audience, "admonishing young ladies to care for their bodies, their minds, and their hearts," especially warning them "against associating with young men who drank, or ridiculed religion, or seemed to set their hearts upon being society men." A few months later, Sam Jones again visited Charlotte and reprised his attack on Charlotte society, condemning "progressive euchre parties along with the rest of fashionable life and frivolities."[36]

While the moral principles of members of the middle class helped to differentiate them from the elite—placing them "on the Lord's side"—members of the middle class also defined themselves by their activities among the class beneath them: the "mill people" employed in Charlotte's textile mills. By the mid-1890s, Charlotte, like many other textile towns of the Carolina Piedmont, found itself split between white "town people" and "mill people." Yet Charlotte's townspeople were also divided by class, between the manufacturing elite and a middle class. Whereas exclusive clubs and social networks distanced the elite from both the middle class and the mill workers, middle-class reformers—largely through the vehicle of evangelical religion—worked among the town's most marginal members, the mill people, in order to "uplift" them.[37]

Middle-class women played a key role in defining their class as separate from the elite and the mill people. At the same time that elite women distanced themselves from intimate encounters with the poor—forming clubs for purely social purposes and confining charity work to fashionable benefits—middle-class women continued to work among the poor to improve the lives of the less fortunate. The reforming activities of members of the middle class, like those of the better class of the 1870s and 1880s, defined them as a cohesive class and set them apart from both the elite and poorer members of the community.

Beginning in the mid-1890s, Charlotte's middle-class men and women, like their counterparts in the South Carolina Piedmont, discovered the "mill problem." By 1900, a string of mill villages encircled the town of Charlotte, most of them outside the city limits. In *Cotton Mills, Commercial Features* (1899), a handbook for aspiring cotton mill men, D. A. Tompkins spelled out the advantages of building mill villages beyond the city limits. Manufacturers could thereby not only avoid paying city taxes but also keep their operatives from the bad influence of lawyers, who might promote lawsuits that could prove costly to the mills. Moreover, residing outside of the city would insure "that employees go to bed at a reasonable hour and are therefore in better condition to work in day time."[38]

Although physically isolated from the town's middle class, who mostly lived in the central parts of the city as well as in Charlotte's first streetcar suburb, Dilworth, the mill people became an increasing cause for concern in the 1890s. The construction of four new mills in Charlotte between 1891 and 1897 greatly inflated the number of operatives. Rural families, squeezed by the agricultural crisis of the 1880s and 1890s, left their homes in the mountains and foothills in hopes that employment in Charlotte's cotton mills might give them the economic security they desperately sought. To many townspeople, mill people represented an unstable, potentially volatile element of the population. Propertyless and seemingly rootless, mill workers often migrated seasonally between the town and country as well as among Piedmont mills. Turnover in cotton mills at times exceeded 100 percent as families moved on in search of better opportunities. Also, although many local mill men boasted about the comfortable living conditions in their mill villages, slowdowns periodically shut down mills and epidemics ravaged villages, creating a tenuous existence for mill people. In 1896 the

Tompkins-owned *Observer*, in a rare moment of candor, appealed for aid to mill families stricken by a measles epidemic, as whole families "are down with the measles, and therefore all of their revenue is cut off," and "must either be relieved, or left to die of starvation." Middle-class reformers—headed by ministers J. A. Preston, L. R. Pruett, and J. F. Butt as well as bookkeeper T. S. Franklin, traveling salesman F. R. McNinch, grocer J. B. McLaughlin, and physician D. O'Donoghue—formed the Humane Society during the bitter winter of 1896 "to relieve all cases of need, but not to give indiscreetly," taking "great care . . . that the worthy poor may be properly relieved." McNinch was appointed head of the society, which remained active throughout the rest of the decade.[39]

Although middle-class townspeople occasionally aided sick and hungry mill people through poor relief, the bulk of their efforts focused on uplifting them through Sunday schools, revivals, and other evangelical organizations. Evangelical activity flourished in Charlotte in the 1890s, inspired by Sam Jones's visits as well as by a series of revival meetings in March 1893 held by world-famous evangelist Dwight Moody that drew thousands of listeners nightly. While Charlotte mill man R. M. Miller served as general chairman of the Charlotte Moody revival, and the city's leading businesspeople served on various promotional committees, the town's middle class became the bearers of Moody's message, carrying the evangelical banner to the peripheral parts of the city. Indeed, like Jones before him, Moody reinforced the moralism of the middle class by condemning the activities of the elite, as he attacked theater attendance, card parties, and whiskey drinking.[40]

Women, especially, served as ardent evangelical crusaders. Evangelicalism seems to have bonded women of Charlotte's middle class. Although middle-class women created competing networks of social activism in antebellum cities such as Rochester, evangelicalism bound women of the middle class in Charlotte, providing them with a common social vision and conveyance for reform. "The women of Charlotte are interested in missions, at home and abroad. The missionary spirit abounds most abundantly in this Christian city," noted the *Observer* in 1895, tellingly using the word "women" rather than "ladies," a designation used more commonly for elite females in the 1890s. Besides supporting Christian missions in far-flung places such as China, Charlotte's middle-class women centered most of their missionary fervor on Charlotte's mill people, particularly mill children. Charlotte's Presbyterian women were especially active in establishing Sunday schools in mill villages. In 1890 the Second Presbyterian Church founded a "prosperous mission" at the Alpha Mill and by 1892 had built up a flourishing Sunday school at the Ada Mill. The next year the church organized a Sunday school at Tompkins's Atherton Mills soon after it opened, in which Fannie Butt, daughter of an insurance agent, and Mrs. Edward Bell, a clerk's wife, played a particularly active role. By 1895 the Presbyterians had established the North Side Chapel for the operatives of the Ada Mill, and two years later the Methodists built a chapel at the Louise Mills. Women not only brought the gospel to mill children but also provided them with treats, such as ice cream parties and visits from Santa Claus.[41]

Revival meetings also targeted Charlotte's mill population. Dr. H. M. Pritchard of Charlotte's Tryon Street Baptist Church pitched his "Gospel Tent" in 1895 near the Gingham Mills as well as the Atherton Mills, even holding a special 8:00 A.M. service "in order to reach the night hands at the Atherton Mill." When mill owners extended the shifts of workers an extra hour, causing many of them to miss services, Pritchard requested mill managers "to so arrange the hours of work as to allow the operatives to attend these tent meetings," noting that "these meetings are designed to some extent to reach this class." The Gospel Tent crusade "stirred up the Baptists in that vicinity," and they soon established a Sunday school in the Atherton mill village. Presbyterians, Baptists, and Methodists also alternated Sundays preaching at the Atherton Lyceum, a facility built by Tompkins to house church services and a school.[42]

In 1896 reforming Protestant men and women introduced a popular youth organization to mill villages. The Christian Endeavor Society, a national interdenominational movement that aspired to incorporate youths into the Sunday school movement, established chapters at the Victor Mill and the North Side Chapel at the Ada Mill. The society proclaimed as its ultimate aim the "bringing of the world to Christ" and stressed missions, "strenuous loyalty to local church and denomination," "interdenominational spiritual fellowship," and "Christian citizenship."[43]

In only a few years, evangelical reformers had established numerous mill chapels and religious organizations for the town's mill people. The success of middle-class reformers suggests that many mill owners supported their efforts; it is likely that in Charlotte, as in other Piedmont textile towns, manufacturers encouraged mainstream Protestant mission work and probably backed it financially. Many mill owners believed that bringing mill people under the influence of Christianity made them better workers and citizens as well as more content with their lot.[44]

Although the church-related activities of ministers and Sunday school teachers may have bolstered the needs of mill owners, evangelical middle-class reformers were not simply hirelings of mill men. Instead, some of them used their bases in mill villages to challenge mill owners to improve the conditions of their workers. Focusing particularly on the long working hours of women and children, child labor, and education, the crusade of middle-class evangelical reformers often involved them in bitter public conflicts with manufacturers. Although reformers found their endeavors circumscribed by powerful mill men, they achieved concrete results in improving educational facilities for mill workers. At the very least, their well-publicized confrontations with mill men kept the problems of mill people before the public at a time when mill owners claimed that their workers lived comfortable, secure lives. Middle-class reforming men and women served as the conscience of the New South, their evangelicalism providing organizational vehicles, a language of protest, and a heart-felt mission to improve the lot of those less fortunate than themselves.

In 1895 the Reverend H. L. Atkins, pastor of the Church Street Methodist Church, wrote a letter to the *Observer* appealing to the state legislature to pass a labor law on behalf of "overworked poor white women and children in the State," who labored an average of seventy-two hours a week in cotton mills. Couching his argument in potent religious terms, Atkins asserted, "This oppression of women and children is not only a shame to the State but a burning sin against God and weak humanity."[45]

Charlotte mill man W. S. Mallory replied to Atkins's charges, scoffing at the minister's depiction of the "downtrodden." Mallory, treasurer of the Alpha Mill, portrayed Charlotte's mill workers as well paid, living in rent-free housing, and working "in a comfortable room." Mallory argued, "None of them are forced to work in a mill—they do it of their own free will. They know when they set in all about the hours of labor, etc." Child labor was the result of the greed of parents, not mill owners. "About one-half of the heads of families," claimed Mallory, "put their children in the mills and live on their wages. In their greed they force their little children to work when they should be at school." Reverend Atkins would do better, he suggested, to induce heads of families to go to work and send their children to school rather than to seek legislation. Mallory condescendingly reminded Atkins that "the mills are not run as charitable institutions, but to make money." Atkins should tend to those "outside of the mills, who are out of employment and suffering," before turning his attention to the " 'poor, downtrodden' factory hands."[46]

Mallory's patronizing attitude angered Reverend Atkins, who responded in a second letter to the *Observer*. Atkins attacked Mallory's depiction of "indolent" parents as "entirely off the subject," stressing that "the fact remains that in a few counties in North Carolina mill operatives are worked longer, by one or two hours in the day, than anywhere else in the State or nation," yet they were paid the same, or even less, than workers elsewhere. Atkins pleaded, "Will the good mill men . . . imagine for a moment that they are in the place of the operatives and the operatives in their places? Would you not then favor a reduction in time?" Atkins closed by quoting the Golden Rule: "As ye would that men should do unto you, do ye even so to them."[47]

Although North Carolina mill men successfully blocked any action by the state legislature to shorten working hours for women and children in 1895, the issue of child labor in southern textile mills grew into a national concern as the northern press, beginning in 1898, criticized the practices of southern mills. Local middle-class reformers reinforced the reports coming from the North. In late 1898 Methodist minister J. A. Baldwin, who worked among the operatives of the Atherton Mills, wrote an article entitled "Life in Southern Cotton Mills," a muckraking piece describing the conditions he encountered in Tompkins's model mill village. He focused on the brutal demands of mill work, particularly on women and children, mill workers who suffered from chronic illness, cruel overseers, and families kept in poverty by their need to move continually to find employment.[48]

Baldwin boldly sent the article to Tompkins to review, and Tompkins responded in the pages of his *Observer*. Baldwin's piece "is of chiefest interest," claimed Tompkins, "because of its pathos," yet Baldwin, he argued, had misplaced the blame for the problems of workers. Echoing his colleague Mallory, Tompkins contended that workers themselves were responsible for their condition, not the mill men. Work in cotton mills was not hard "but comparatively light and easy," maintained Tompkins, easier, in fact, than the work of a seamstress, secretary, or newspaper man—or, notably, even a Charlotte "gentlewoman." "A lot of gentlewomen would be delighted beyond expression" to receive the same compensation as cotton mill workers earned. If mill workers found themselves in trouble, it was because they were "of roving dispositions, are shiftless, and improvident."[49]

Tompkins's reply revealed the difference between his perception of the role of the minister and religion in the mill village and that of Baldwin. Rather than serving as an advocate of the mill people against the owners, Tompkins maintained, "preachers and teachers" needed to use their influence "to awaken in this class an interest in religion, in education and in the virtues of thrift and economy. . . . The work of the preacher, the teacher or the philanthropist cannot be done in legislative halls." Articulating the mill owners' vision of the utilitarian function of religious instruction, Tompkins argued that "it is for the preacher to tame the tramp family. It is for the preacher to fight ignorance, and these will have life-long jobs." Tompkins then proposed a labor bill for North Carolina limiting the employment of children under twelve years of age and restricting the work week to a maximum of sixty-six hours. The suggested legislation also required that "any man who should work his children for wages and himself remain in idleness wantonly" be sentenced to work on the public highway for ninety days per offense.[50]

Tompkins's proposal, although never submitted to the state legislature, temporarily deflected Baldwin's criticism, diverting attention from the issue at hand. The minister praised the bill and applauded Tompkins's efforts to improve the mills' surroundings and dwellings as well as his assistance "in improving the intellectual and moral conditions of the operatives." But although Baldwin momentarily acquiesced to Tompkins, he continued to fight for the rights of mill workers, extending his crusade to the arena of education. In 1902 Baldwin, appalled by the lack of educational opportunities available to mill children, initiated a movement to establish a school for Charlotte's textile workers. In a private letter to R. H. Edmonds of the *Manufacturers' Record*, Tompkins condemned Baldwin's plan, describing him as "one of these impatient fellows who is more or less intolerant of the irksome duties connected with the small church and wants to do something big at once." Baldwin, he claimed, "is undoubtedly very thirsty for some kind of fame." Like many mill men, Tompkins had little interest in educating mill children and did next to nothing to eliminate illiteracy among his workers. He believed that cotton mills themselves provided the only real education that operatives needed and that schools simply dragged "working young men and women" away from their daily work. If workers wanted an education, reasoned Tompkins, they could take correspondence courses.[51]

In spite of Tompkins's hostility, Baldwin and his plan prevailed. In 1903 the minister established the Southern Industrial Institute near the Hoskins Mill, supported by funds from the YMCA as well as gifts from some prominent Charlotteans. Taken over by the YMCA in 1908, the institute boasted 353 students by 1910, including 103 boarders from North and South Carolina mill villages, and offered an elementary and high school curriculum as well as courses in textiles, agriculture, domestic science, religion, and social work. In 1908 Tompkins allowed the institute to offer two classes at the Atherton mill village for children and older employees. Thus, the courageous challenges of middle-class reformers won some tangible improvements for the mill people, particularly in education. At the very least, they constantly kept the plight of mill workers in the public eye.[52]

As the white better class bifurcated in the 1890s into a manufacturing elite and a middle class, Charlotte's black better class continued to struggle to achieve economic advancement. Despite making some remarkable strides in small business and the professions in the 1890s, members of Charlotte's black better class nonetheless found their economic opportunities far more limited than those of their white counterparts. The town's flurry of mill building in the 1880s and 1890s bequeathed few benefits to the city's blacks, including both the black better class and the rest of the African American community. Despite their constant refrain that hard work and money would make them the equals of whites, Charlotte's black better class found that their race barred them from access to many of the economic benefits of the New South.

Throughout the 1880s, as Charlotte's mill fever began to rage, spokespersons for the black better class continually exhorted blacks to better themselves through education, property ownership, and the acquisition of wealth. In an appeal to the city's young black men, W. C. Smith argued in the *Charlotte Messenger* that if enough "intelligent young men" would aspire to "the higher order" rather than "the boot black and servant class . . . by their standing and general conduct [they] will force all men to respect them as gentlemen."[53]

In the pages of the *Messenger*, Smith publicized the success stories of Charlotte's black businesspeople. In 1882 he proudly noted that J. M. Goode ran "the most successful colored boarding house in the State" and that blacks owned "some of the best markets in the city, one of the best grocery stores, all the barber shops, and a newspaper." By 1888 Smith counted a dozen black-owned groceries in Charlotte as well as three butcher shops. Moreover, in 1886 J. T. Williams, formerly an assistant principal at the Myers Street Graded School, opened up practice as Charlotte's first black physician. Williams's presence not only helped improve the health of Charlotte's black community but also symbolized to many the possibilities open to hardworking blacks in the New South. "Yes, we are proud of him," wrote Smith, "because he is a negro, because he is a native North Carolinian, because he is an intelligent gentleman, because he is a regular M.D., [and] belongs to the same society with all our first-class doctors, because he is recognized by them and will do us good and honor our race."[54]

Despite these successes, Charlotte's African American community lacked many services available to the town's whites. "Right here in Charlotte," noted Smith, "a dollar in a black man's hands is not equal to a dollar in a white man's hands." Certain dry goods stores kept "different classes of goods for the two races," and drugstores "will not take a colored man's money for an innocent, refreshing drink." Although Charlotte's blacks faced discrimination in business dealings, Smith in 1887 referred to the city as an "open field" for enterprising blacks. He called for a black undertaker, photographer, drugstore, printing office, and lawyer. He promised "a rich harvest for every honest, earnest worker, who will exhibit a manly courage and patience."[55]

Only a few years after Smith appealed for more black enterprise, Charlotte's

Charlotte's black physicians, ca. 1895. *Standing, left to right*, A. A. Wyche,
N. B. Houser; *sitting, left to right*, J. T. Williams, W. H. Graves. (Courtesy of the
Robinson-Spangler Room, Public Library of Charlotte and Mecklenburg County)

Black businesspeople, Queen City Drug Store, ca. 1900.
(Courtesy of the Charlotte-Mecklenburg Historic Landmarks Commission)

blacks made considerable progress in small business and the professions, filling
many of the voids that Smith had publicized in the late 1880s. Charlotte got its
second black doctor in 1892 when M. T. Pope moved to the city from Henderson
and became an associate of Williams. That same year Pope, Williams, and R. B.
Tyler founded the Queen City Drug Company, the city's first black-owned and
-operated store, located on East Trade Street in the Second Ward. The drugstore featured "one of the finest soda fountains in the city," where, the *Star of
Zion* pointed out, "colored people suffer no disadvantage, either in the quality of
the drinks or the appearance of the place where they are served." Six years later,
Dr. J. L. Eagles, once a partner in the Queen City store, opened a second black-
owned drugstore on East Trade Street. By 1892 Charlotte also had two black
undertaking establishments owned and operated by Henry Boulware and Sydney A. Coles. Noting that "Charlotte's colored people are forging to the front as
artists in different lines," the *Observer* announced in 1896 that H. H. Hayden had
opened a "colored photograph gallery" on East Trade Street. In 1896 J. T.
Sanders opened a small bank and three years later, in partnership with W. F.
Thompson, opened the Charlotte Clothing Cleaning Company. By 1898 John S.
Leary, a native of Fayetteville, moved to Charlotte to become the city's first black
lawyer.[56]

The expansion of the black business and professional class in Charlotte in the

1880s and 1890s was part of a larger trend in the towns and cities of the Upper South. Although African American businesses tended to be small and the failure rate high, in cities such as Charlotte, Durham, Nashville, and Richmond, black businesses grew at a faster rate than they did in the Lower South. Black business seems to have been assisted by a growing number of professionals who helped provide capital for new black enterprises.[57]

One of the most significant economic developments for Charlotte's better class of blacks was the establishment of the AME Zion Publishing House in Charlotte in 1894. A stronghold of the denomination since the end of the Civil War, Charlotte secured the church's printing concern largely through the entrepreneurial skills of Bishop Thomas Henry Lomax. Lomax, a prominent prohibitionist in the 1880s, was a native of Cumberland County and had come to Charlotte in 1868. Eight years later, he was consecrated a bishop in the AMEZ church. He was a well-known figure in the community—among both blacks and whites—not only as a prominent cleric but also as a businessman who had accumulated a large amount of real estate in the area.[58]

In 1894 Lomax proposed to members of the Board of Bishops of the AMEZ church that they establish the church's publishing house in Charlotte. He then arranged for the purchase of a building through a united effort among the AMEZ churches of Charlotte and the community in general. The bishop organized a three-day fund-raising event in August 1894 that featured speakers— including two of Charlotte's white ministers—as well as vocal and instrumental music. The city's churches also took up special collections to raise money for the publishing house. On 15 August 1894 the Varick Memorial Publishing House, named after the denomination's founder, opened formally on College Street in a three-story brick building.[59]

The AME Zion Publishing House provided a potent symbol for Charlotte's better class of blacks in the 1890s; it signified black enterprise through education and hard work. Recalling the "strides and progress" made by blacks in the last hundred years, John C. Dancy, editor of the weekly denomination newspaper, the *Star of Zion*, noted at the publishing house's opening that it was "a credit to the church and the pride of the race." Producing all of the publications of the denomination, including the *Star of Zion*, Sunday school materials, and the *AME Zion Quarterly Review*, the publishing house drew the leading lights of the national church to Charlotte—writers, editors, and bishops—all of whom further articulated the vision of the black better class and, with their spouses, significantly augmented its ranks in Charlotte. Moreover, the publishing house provided employment and training for young black men. It was one of the few enterprises in the town where blacks could both learn a trade and find employment in white-collar occupations, such as clerks and managers. The publishing house teemed with activity and provided a new social center for the black community as it contained an auditorium and a large and spacious hall for social events. The *Observer* noted that "Printing, Preaching, and Prancing" often took place simultaneously at Varick Hall, with "preaching in full swing on the first floor; printing on the second, and dancing on the third."[60]

Despite the significant strides made in the 1890s, black business remained small business. In the decade when a manufacturing elite evolved among the white better class, the black better class continued to be engaged almost exclusively in small business and the professions. In 1898 Charlotte's blacks owned a dozen grocery stores, a meat market, a drugstore, two restaurants, an ice cream parlor, and fourteen barber shops. Yet only one black businessman had entered the realm of manufacturing: William H. Houser. A successful brickmason and contractor, Houser, who as a prohibitionist in 1881 had challenged John T. Schenck for his aldermanic seat, won contracts to erect cotton mills in and around Charlotte as well as churches and school buildings. He parlayed his wealth into a brick manufactory that opened in March 1898. Soon afterward, E. D. Latta of the Charlotte Consolidated Construction Company awarded him a contract to make 200,000 bricks for a gas plant in his suburb of Dilworth. By the turn of the century, Houser was one of the wealthiest blacks in the city.[61]

The fact that only a single African American was engaged in manufacturing by 1898 did not reflect a lack of interest for such ventures among the black better class. Like their white counterparts, Charlotte's black businesspeople had long been interested in industrialization, but they seem to have been discouraged from participating in Charlotte's mill building. Not only did the textile industry in the South bar black operatives, but black businesspeople, who could have invested small sums in subscription mills, appear to have been prohibited from doing so.

In 1887, as plans were being made for the opening of three new cotton mills in Charlotte—two of which were subscription mills—W. C. Smith intimated that blacks were barred from subscription investment, asking that "institutions of learning and industry" be opened to the African American "to give him an equal chance with the white man." The next year Smith noted that "factory fever seems to be raging in our city just now" and that "white capitalists have subscribed over a hundred thousand dollars to build them." Although installment buying appeared to be "for whites only," Smith supported industrialization in Charlotte, sounding like any other booster in writing about the mills: "Let 'em come. Anything to build up the city." Although blacks were barred from investing in and working at mills, Smith believed that cotton mills provided new opportunities for blacks, especially farmers. As white farmers left the countryside to work as operatives, he reasoned, black farmers could advance by buying their land, growing cotton for the factories, and raising "the corn and vegetables and the potatoes and cabbage to feed them while they spin."[62]

Despite the potential opportunities that industrialization offered African American farmers, Smith and other black businesspeople were far from sanguine about the color bar in the textile industry. For years, Smith and other spokespersons of the black better class had argued that blacks required only "a fair showing in the race of life." Given equal opportunity, blacks would "prove themselves as men." Yet the cotton mills, the quintessential symbols of progress in the New South, were not open to blacks. Smith and other members of the black better class denounced this discrimination. "Our city has organized nearly a dozen factories of one kind and another within the last two or three months," wrote Smith in 1888. "Hundreds of operatives are expected to be employed in these factories but no one thinks of seeing a black operative," he protested. Black grocer and entrepreneur A. W. Calvin tried to open the doors of industrialization to blacks, announcing plans in 1888 "to start a factory to be run by colored men." Yet nothing came of Calvin's plans, and the black entrepreneurs' dreams of becoming industrialists remained frustrated.[63]

With Charlotte's subscription cotton mills apparently off-limits to black investors, the black better class, like prosperous blacks in other southern cities, invested largely in real estate. They not only bought property for their personal use but also purchased lots and constructed rental units. In 1886 Eli Preston built six rental units, and a year later A. W. Calvin erected six rental houses on Mint Street in the Third Ward and also purchased a farm outside the city. Land in the Piedmont countryside, according to the *Messenger*, was inexpensive. "We see people around the city paying $4 to $6 per acre a year in rent," claimed editor Smith, "when [in] so many places land can be bought for the same or less." Many Charlotte blacks apparently heeded Smith's advice to "buy land and be men." In the 1890s J. T. Sanders purchased forty acres in Western Heights, a suburb being developed by white real estate man W. S. Alexander, and William Houser, Dr. J. T. Williams, and Bishop Thomas Lomax all accumulated valuable property both in and outside of the city.[64]

As the better class of whites organized mills and textile-related industries in the 1890s, fourteen African American entrepreneurs formed the Queen City Real Estate Agency, a development company. Representing Charlotte's wealthiest black citizens, the founders of the company included Dr. J. T. Williams;

AMEZ bishop and journalist George Wylie Clinton; the Reverend G. L. Black-well, manager of the AME Zion Publishing House; Biddle University president D. J. Sanders and four Biddle professors; and lawyer John S. Leary.[65]

Prominent members of the black better class also invested in expensive and stylish homes in the late 1880s and 1890s, much as their white counterparts had done in the 1870s. Bishop Clinton constructed a spacious home on North Myers Street in the First Ward, a street that became home to many prominent people associated with the AME Zion Publishing House. South Brevard Street, the heart of the "Brooklyn" neighborhood in the Second Ward, also became a fashionable address in the 1890s. Both J. T. Williams and W. W. Smith built large and fashionable homes on South Brevard in the 1890s, Williams's home costing $2,200. Similarly, Dr. N. B. Houser built a $2,000 residence nearby in 1897.[66]

Although many members of the black better class invested successfully in real estate—some of them accumulating considerable tracts of property in and around Charlotte—real estate investment did not generate the large profits reaped by white mill men through investment in industry. Nor did investment in real estate translate into economic or political power in either the black commu-nity or society at large. Moreover, real estate investment did little to generate jobs for the community's African Americans, most notably the white-collar positions that the black better class desired for their educated children.

In the 1890s Charlotte's black better class sent their sons and daughters to nearby black colleges and seminaries. Like their parents, the children of the black better class attended Biddle in Charlotte, Livingstone in Salisbury, Shaw and St. Augustine's in Raleigh, Bennett in Greensboro, and Scotia in Concord. The *Star of Zion* noted in 1899 that "Charlotte will send to College this year more students, both male and female, than in any year previous," a development that "speaks well for our city and her young men and women." Yet as they prepared their children for business and the professions, the black better class became increasingly aware that their progeny faced limited opportunities, given the dearth of large-scale black business and industry. It was enough for the better class in the 1880s—many of whom were only in their twenties and thirties—to own land and small businesses. But by the late 1890s, concerned with the future of their children, they began to demand more.[67]

In the column that he regularly penned for the *Observer*, the Reverend D. C. Covington, pastor of the Little Rock AME Zion Church, articulated a new, expanded economic vision of the black better class. "To become a strong race," declared Covington, blacks needed to do more than pursue education and "get property"; they also had to "build railroads and set up business for ourselves." Covington explicated the dilemma facing the mature black better class of the

1890s: "Hundreds of our boys and girls who are coming out of college and seminaries year by year have nothing to do from the fact that we are not set up in business as a race, so as to give them something to do." He called on "the married men among the race" to "organize stock companies of various kinds and thereby start up race enterprises everywhere."[68]

Similarly, Professor B. A. Johnson of nearby Livingstone College voiced the concern that the black better class and their children were denied access to economic opportunity because of the color bar embedded in the New South's economy. "The white boy of the present inherits his opportunity, the black boy of the present must make his opportunity." While repeating the refrain that blacks needed to be educated and save money, Johnson added another necessary ingredient: "For our boys we need capital. Capital to start a factory, capital to start a bank, capital to begin a business of any kind." Calling for black industrial enterprise, Johnson declared, "If the white man has built factories for his neighbors' boys and girls then we must concentrate here and there our savings and build factories for our boys and girls."[69]

In 1897 members of the black better class got the chance to pursue their dream of industrial development when Warren Coleman of nearby Concord announced his intention to establish a black-owned and -operated cotton mill. At the time of his announcement, Coleman may well have been the wealthiest African American in North Carolina. Born a slave in 1849, reputedly the son of Rufus Barringer and a slave woman, Coleman began his business career as a trader and peddler after the Civil War and established a successful grocery and confectionery business in Concord in the 1870s. After selling his business in order to attend Howard University in 1872, Coleman returned to Concord a year later, reestablishing his grocery store and investing in real estate in Cabarrus and surrounding counties. Coleman constructed dozens of rental houses and by 1890 had amassed a fortune of approximately $100,000. A member and trustee of the AMEZ church and active in the prohibition movement in the 1880s, Coleman epitomized the ideals of the black better class.[70]

Motivated by race pride and a desire to share in the seemingly limitless profits to be made in the textile industry, Coleman traveled across North Carolina in 1896 to stir up interest in his mill, proposing a subscription plan whereby even small investors could own shares in the mill. A black-owned and -operated mill would provide the chance "to win for us a name and place us before the world as industrious and enterprising citizens," proclaimed Coleman. "The watchword is onward and upward and if we ever expect to attain the heights of industrial usefulness, we must fall in line and march shoulder to shoulder in one solid phalanx along the road that leads to fortune and fame." Coleman not only spread his message among the state's black entrepreneurs but also publicized his plan in the *Manufacturers' Record*. "Negroes," he wrote, are "not idle and ignorant, as some of the readers may have heard, but on the contrary, are fairly educated, property-owning, self-respecting, industrious people."[71]

Initially receiving enthusiastic support for his plan, Coleman established the Coleman Manufacturing Company in 1897, listing twenty incorporators, among them some of the state's most prominent black citizens. AMEZ bishop J. W. Hood of Fayetteville headed the list, along with six other clergymen—two of them from the AMEZ church—from across the state. John C. Dancy of Salisbury, editor of the *AME Zion Quarterly Review*, served as an incorporator along with D. J. Sanders of Charlotte, president of Biddle University. The remainder of the incorporators included another black college president, two teachers, a doctor, an attorney, and six businesspeople, including M. J. Corl, a white businessman from Concord.[72]

Black women of the better class also lent their support to the Coleman Mill. Sarah Dudley Pettey, the wife of AMEZ minister and prohibitionist C. C. Pettey, penned a regular and influential "Woman's Column" for the *Star of Zion* in which she enthusiastically supported the enterprise. Declaring the mill "the closing event of the nineteenth century, and the crowning effort of Negro aspirations, capabilities and manhood," Pettey, like her male counterparts, saw both symbolic and practical meaning in the Coleman Mill. Not only would it represent full participation by her race in the New South's industrializing order, but also it might help provide economic security for the black community.[73]

In February 1897, as part of a fund-raising drive among North Carolina's urban black businesspeople and professionals, Coleman spent two days in Charlotte, assisted by banker J. T. Sanders. Canvassing the town's black better class, Coleman found an enthusiastic and willing group of contributors and raised $5,000 "among the leading colored people." A few days later, riding the crest of his success in Charlotte, Coleman held his first stockholders' meeting in Concord. Charlotte's S. B. Pride, a Biddle professor, was elected to the board of directors of the company. At the meeting, Coleman articulated the symbolic importance of the mill, comparing it to the Statue of Liberty. "It is high time we were doing something to help feed, clothe, and educate these vast numbers, and there is no better way of doing so than by organizing ourselves into business associations, utilizing our own talents and improving ourselves along all industrial lines." The fact that this duty fell to the better class was underscored by Professor R. A. Caldwell from eastern North Carolina, who asserted that "moral men and moral women are required to make success."[74]

In April 1897, when the AMEZ board of bishops met at the publishing house in Charlotte, Coleman and director John Dancy approached the board for support. Making "a strong plea" on behalf of the mill, Coleman and Dancy convinced the board to support the project. The board "unanimously voted its hearty endorsement of the enterprise," and most of the bishops bought stock in the company, subscribing a total of $1,600.[75]

Despite the enthusiasm of North Carolina's black better class for the project, Coleman soon realized that African Americans alone could not raise the capital needed to finance a mill. As a result, Coleman petitioned "white friends" about a month after the first stockholders' meeting. In the *Observer* and other newspapers, Coleman appealed to the paternalistic proclivities of some white industrialists, calling upon "the kind feelings of our white friends for fellowship in completing the work already begun." Among those who gave financial backing to Coleman's enterprise were tobacco and textile magnate Julian S. Carr and tobacco manufacturer Washington Duke.[76]

Despite having gained the support of the black better class, the AMEZ bishops, and two leading Tarheel industrialists, Coleman found it difficult to collect the subscriptions that had been pledged for the mill, leaving him plagued by a shortage of capital. Nevertheless, he went ahead with a cornerstone-laying ceremony, fearful that any additional delays would dampen enthusiasm for the project. On 8 February 1898 dignitaries, stockholders, and interested citizens gathered in Concord for the ceremony. Charlotte's representatives included the Reverend G. L. Blackwell and Bishop George Clinton. Reflecting the active interest and participation of black women of the better class in industrialization, Mrs. C. R. Harris, wife of an AMEZ bishop, and Mrs. H. A. Hunt, wife of a Biddle professor, also attended the ceremony.[77]

Bishop Clinton, along with several other speakers including black congressman George H. White and Julian Carr, addressed the assembly. Clinton called the cornerstone laying "one of the most sublime and significant events of this great progressive age." He took the opportunity to praise the South's racial progress and the aid of white patrons. Reflecting his class's bond with the white better class, Clinton argued that the black prospered in the South because "here he finds friends who know him best" and who offer "encouragement and protection." Reiterating the eternal theme of the black better class, Clinton claimed, "We only ask a man's chance in an unhampered race." Stressing the mutuality of black and white interests, he argued that "every negro that acquires a home of his own, or builds up a substantial business, thereby becomes a more worthy and helpful factor to the community as a whole."[78]

The cornerstone laying proved to be the emotional high point of the Coleman enterprise, a day that seemed to signal the triumph of the black better class and their full participation in the New South's industrial order. Financial problems soon overshadowed the glorious events of 8 February, as only a fraction of subscribers paid their pledges on the stock they had promised to buy. Although Coleman listed approximately 800 subscribers in 1898, only about 100 paid for their stock in full, at $100 per share. Rumors abounded concerning the imminent collapse of the black cotton mill, which the Reverend D. C. Covington vociferously denied in his *Observer* column. Covington claimed that some "newspapers and some mean enemies sent it out to the world that the cotton mill had gone under," but he assured his readers that the mill was nearly ready to resume operations.[79]

Covington's assurances, however, proved to be greatly exaggerated. Nearly a year and a half later, the mill had not yet opened. Strapped by unpaid subscriptions and the lack of additional stock sales, the company found itself entangled in debt. With a loan from Washington Duke, the Coleman Manufacturing Company began operations in the summer of 1901, with little publicity. Because of capital shortages, the mill operated only sporadically. By February 1902 Coleman claimed that the mill had 10,000 pounds of fine yarn for sale. Yet a year later hopes for the mill began to dwindle. The mill suffered not only from intense competition from well-established mills in the area but also from Coleman's managerial shortcomings and inexperience. Moreover, unable to meet payrolls consistently, the mill experienced a high turnover of operatives. When cotton prices rose significantly, Coleman shut down the mill. In March 1904 Warren Coleman died along with his dream of a black-owned and -operated cotton mill. Benjamin N. Duke foreclosed on the mill and eventually sold it to J. W. Cannon, who made it part of the Cannon Mills of Concord.[80]

The failure of the Coleman Mill was a bitter pill for the black better class to swallow. Imbued with symbolic meaning, the mill represented the aspirations of the black better class to become New South industrialists and to broaden the economic scope of all African Americans. In its failure, the Coleman Mill symbolized the problems facing entrepreneurs of the black better class. Not only did black entrepreneurs confront well-entrenched and experienced white competition, but also the black community lacked the economic base necessary to generate the large amounts of capital required to operate a textile mill successfully. Although members of the better class enthusiastically supported the idea of industrialization, they apparently did not have the resources to sustain such ventures. Although Charlotte's black better class had made significant progress by 1900, their economic base remained modest, limited to small businesses and real estate holdings; the fruits of New South industrialization remained "for whites only."

Despite the fact that no industrial elite emerged among Charlotte's black better class in the 1890s, the black better class took on many of the trappings of Charlotte "society." Charlotte's black better class replicated many of the fashionable social affairs of the white elite. They also likely modeled their activities on those of the "aristocrats of color" in older and larger American cities. Soon after Charlotte's white elite formed the Cotillion Club in 1894, blacks formed the Yale Cotillion, led by barber George Stevenson. "The colored dancing club," noted the *Observer*, "is not to be behind the white club in putting on style." The Brooklyn Elite Club sponsored germans and other entertainment, and the Elite Union, headed by teacher Carrie Coleman, produced dramatic presentations. The Athletic Club, "an organization composed of the best colored girls of the city," and the Pride of the South Club also sponsored dances. Literary clubs continued to flourish in the 1890s—the Dumas, Pierian, and Clariosophic among the most popular. Literary societies allowed the better class "to become familiar with current literature and the works of standard authors." The works of Shakespeare were particular favorites, as literary circles worked their way through *Julius Caesar, Hamlet,* and *Richard III.* While stressing "the advancement of the race," literary societies also hosted numerous social events, throwing receptions for newly married members of the black social set. In 1899 the Dumas Reading Circle, which, according to the *Star of Zion,* represented "the most cultured assembly known in Charlotte society," feted newlyweds Dr. and Mrs. A. A. Wyche with a "feast of gods and goddesses." Literary societies also held fund-raising events for local churches. In 1899 the Clariosophic Literary Society raised over $900 for Grace AME Zion Church by sponsoring an entertainment at Biddle University.[81]

Other social events among the black better class mirrored Charlotte's white "smart set." Professor H. A. Hunt of Biddle headed the Full Moon Carnival in April 1898, described by the *Observer* as "a high class affair" that "will attract the best element of colored people in the city." The local press, black and white, also featured news about black "society weddings," marriages "in colored high life" that were attended by the "elite of colored circles" and occasionally by some prominent white citizens. When Richard C. Graham, "one of the best and most popular waiters at the Buford Hotel," married Hattie L. Henderson at the Seventh Street Presbyterian Church, the *Observer* reported it as a "fashionable wedding in colored high life." Similarly, the marriage of Bishop Thomas Lomax's daughter, Isadore Lomax, "one of the most popular ladies in Charlotte, resplendent in the social circle and an accomplished pianist," to William B. Coles of Washington, D.C., "a brainy young man" with a U.S. government job in the capital, was "the most popular, largely attended and brilliant affair witnessed in the social circles for many years." Both prominent blacks and whites attended the event at Clinton Chapel.[82]

The social affairs of the black better class in the 1890s reflected those of Charlotte's industrial elite as well as the activities of the black elite in other American cities. But the accoutrements of elite life did not translate into economic power. Unlike members of the white elite who, as owners of mills and banks, emerged as powerful figures in Charlotte and the Piedmont in the 1890s, the black better class remained on the periphery as they had during the 1880s, with a circumscribed economic base and little influence, even in the black community. The political crises of the 1890s—the rise of populism, fusion politics, white-supremacy campaigns, and Jim Crow and disfranchisement—would test the strength of the black better class as well as their tenuous ties to powerful and influential whites.

5

FUSION POLITICS

As economic developments reshaped Charlotte's social classes in the 1890s, party politics underwent redefinition as well, a development that had significant implications for class and race relations. Issues of race, class, and politics, in part a legacy of the 1880s, intensified in the 1890s with a series of concomitant developments, each of which impinged upon the other. The cotton mill boom created new class divisions in Charlotte that not only complicated relations among the town's white citizenry but also threatened to divide whites politically. Although the white middle class and manufacturing elite overcame class differences and united in their allegiance to the Democratic party, "mill people," propertyless and poor, represented a political wild card, a potentially dangerous voting bloc that could help unseat the Democrats. As mill people threatened the unity of the white vote and the hegemony of the Democratic party, farmers in the countryside demanded that the Democrats take action to ameliorate their increasingly desperate economic condition. When cotton prices plummeted to staggeringly low levels, Mecklenburg farmers joined the Farmers' Alliance and insisted that Democratic politicians either respond to their plight or risk the organization of a third party that would sap the strength of the Democracy.

At the same time, Charlotte blacks, divided by class, reconsidered their political strategies. With the Republican party in shambles after the coalition experimentation of the 1880s, some black politicians hoped to reconstruct a party that would give blacks proper recognition. Other blacks, infuriated by their treatment at the hands of white party leaders, abandoned the Republican party altogether and cast their lot with the Democrats. Simultaneously, the better class of blacks, who had insisted throughout most of the 1880s that African Americans should spend less time on politics in their quest for recognition and full civic participation, soon saw possibilities for racial advancement in a newly constituted Republican party.

Both farmers and black Republicans attempted to work within the confines of the two-party system in the first few years of the 1890s, but they constantly found their aspirations crushed by intransigent party leaders. By 1892 many Alliance-men in Mecklenburg joined compatriots across the state in revolting against the Democratic party and forming the People's party. Two years later, Republicans and Populists joined forces and brought about a veritable revolution in North Carolina politics in a movement known as "fusion." Fusionists unseated the Democratic party and instituted a slate of reforms. Although the black better class initially rejected fusion, the success of the movement soon convinced them to support the coalition wholeheartedly.

Charlotte's white middle class and industrial elite viewed the fusion revolution with alarm. It not only threatened their snowballing economic advancement but also impeded their role in governing the state. As the fusion revolution seized North Carolina, a new generation of Democratic leaders emerged whose ambitions would be frustrated by fusion. These "Young Democrats" would fight tooth and nail to regain control of state politics; fusion would not only shape their style of politics but intensify their racial attitudes as well.

•   •   •   •   •   •   •

The people of Charlotte, black and white, entered the decade of the 1890s with boundless optimism. Four cotton mills, fondly referred to in the local press as "hummers," and a plethora of textile-related industries attested to the city's growth as the industrial center of the Carolina Piedmont. In 1890 J. L. Chambers, in a speech before the Chamber of Commerce, noted the industrial advances made by the city since he first arrived in 1878. Then Charlotte had consisted of "one machine shop and perhaps two planing mills," whereas "this morning," he bragged, "twenty-one black columns of smoke mark the spots where the stirring hum of almost as many different kinds of industries may be heard." By 1890 Charlotte had a population of well over 11,000 people; by 1900 the city would grow by 62 percent to over 18,000 inhabitants, making it one of the fastest-growing cities in the state (see table A.3).[1]

As white townspeople basked in the success of their briskly growing and increasingly wealthy town, black Charlotteans, particularly members of the better class, viewed the future auspiciously as well. In 1891 reporters for the *Star of Zion* wrote that "Charlotte is improving very rapidly" and that "the colored populace of the city seem to be contributing their share to the city's prosperity," citing "handsome and commodious residences and fine church edifices," a

Biddle University Class of 1894. (Courtesy of the Robinson-Spangler
Carolina Room, Public Library of Charlotte and Mecklenburg County)

"splendid core of teachers" and "an able set of ministers," as well as the "grand
work" of Biddle University. Biddle especially came to symbolize the progress
made by blacks since Reconstruction. In 1891 the trustees of the school, under
the auspices of the Northern Presbyterian church, appointed Biddle's first black
professors and its first black president, Dr. D. J. Sanders. Although some
southern white trustees resigned in protest over the firing of white professors to
make room for black appointees, the fact that blacks staffed the university
seemed to prove to many members of both races that African Americans had
indeed made great strides through education and hard work, methods long
espoused by the better class. Speaking at the 1896 Biddle commencement, black
congressman George H. White of North Carolina's Second District noted that
Biddle represented the advancement of the race "slowly but surely" from the
"foul valley" of slavery "to the top."[2]

The people of Charlotte also prided themselves on race relations in their
town. Charlotte's ubiquitous white boosters bragged about their progressive
black population just as they flaunted the city's cotton mills and enterprising
spirit. In 1895 the *Charlotte Observer*, hardly a beacon of liberal thinking under
the ownership of D. A. Tompkins, exclaimed that "Charlotte has the best
colored people in the State. . . . They are, upon the whole, aspiring and

ambitious." Similarly, H. M. Pritchard of Tryon Street Baptist Church, who penned a column for the *Observer*, praised Charlotte's black citizenry, citing "the general good conduct and character of the negroes of this city," especially "their enterprise and liberality in the direction of religious work."[3]

Indeed, the interaction of blacks and whites in the early 1890s, particularly among the better classes, reflected both fluid race lines and stable race relations. Despite the collapse of the prohibition movement in the late 1880s, the better class of blacks and whites remained well acquainted and still seemed to move easily within certain segments of each other's circles. Whites routinely attended musical and dramatic entertainments at black churches. "A large number of white people" attended a concert at the elite Seventh Street Presbyterian Church, the congregation of many Biddle faculty members, as well as the Colored Dramatic Club's play, "Jeptha's Daughter." Black camp meetings, held annually in Latta Park beginning in 1894, attracted "the best white and colored people," according to the *Star of Zion*. Sporting events, especially bicycle races at Latta Park, also drew biracial audiences.[4]

Interracial contact, however, followed clear-cut patterns within distinct boundaries and did not approach the degree of interaction experienced during the prohibition movement in the previous decade. Although the black better class encouraged the participation of members of the white elite in their religious and social events, the whites did not reciprocate; it is likely that even a Biddle professor would not have been welcome at First or Second Presbyterian Church. The black better class, constantly seeking respect and recognition in the New South, sought ties to prominent whites that whites, by contrast, did not require or feel compelled to offer in return.

Despite stable, and even friendly, associations between "respectable" blacks and whites, race-based conflict occasionally flared up in the early 1890s, betraying a subterranean volatility that periodically erupted in New South Charlotte. In October 1893 the *Observer* reported that a crowd of about "thirty Biddle beaux," only a few of whom allegedly had purchased tickets, took over the waiting room of the Richmond and Danville Railroad station and "possession of the first-class car," where they held "high carnival in there and white people could not or would not attempt to get in." The newspaper scolded the Biddle students, and blacks in general, for what it considered inappropriate social behavior. "There is a disposition among them," asserted the *Observer*, "when they are in superfluous numbers in public places—as railroad stations and cars, streetcars, etc.—particularly on gala occasions, to make themselves offensive to the whites about them by loud talking and such characters of misbehaving—good natured it may be."[5]

A few days later, Biddle president D. J. Sanders responded to the *Observer*'s charges. Sanders pointed out that six students, those who had gotten into trouble with the authorities, had obtained permission from railroad officials "to assist their sisters, cousins, and friends, on the way to Scotia Seminary, in changing cars, checking trunks, and giving them such attention as might be needed." The reason why it was necessary to aid the young women, noted Sanders, "is understood by those who know how roughly colored girls are treated on the roads and at the stations by the officials." Sanders went on to defend his students' behavior and the fact that his school taught "our boys to be law abiding," pointing out that none of the young men, despite reports of their disorderly behavior, had been arrested. The college president assured white townspeople "that Biddle has not lost its character and become a seat of rowdyism."[6]

Despite Sanders's assurances, the railroad station incident drew attention to the question of interracial mingling at Charlotte's railroad facilities. Only a few days after the Biddle episode, the *Observer* reported that "twenty-one negro women were counted seated in the 'ladies' waiting room at the Richmond and Danville station last night" and that all of them boarded the first-class car. The *Observer* argued that "the recent troubles at the Richmond and Danville depot may be the means of the railroad providing separate accommodations for whites and blacks at the depot."[7]

Following the advice of the *Observer*, Richmond and Danville Railroad officials established separate, allegedly equally appointed waiting rooms. Notably, the city's black better class did not protest this development. The *Star of Zion*, edited by Charlotte AMEZ minister George W. Clinton, declared its "regret . . . of the proposed action of the Richmond and Danville railroad authorities." But instead of chastising railroad officials for their actions, Clinton blamed blacks themselves and took the opportunity to instruct blacks on the importance of proper deportment in the New South. "Colored people must remember that this is a 'white man's country,' " wrote Clinton, "and in any controversy over waiting rooms or anything else under the control of the white man, the colored people are the surest ones to come out of the little end of the horn." When "our people at times . . . abuse their privileges," they "excite the wrath and disgust of their white friends and those abused privileges are taken away, and then you hear the hue and cry that you are oppressed and discriminated against when some thoughtless ignoramus is the cause of it all." Repeating the incessant refrain of the black better class, Clinton admonished his readers, "Be quiet, gentlemanly, attentive to your own business and you will find that you will get along much better than if you laugh loud, swagger, smoke cheap cigars and drink cheaper whiskey."[8]

Clinton's response to the first Jim Crow train station in Charlotte reflected a

Bishop George Wylie Clinton, ca. 1890. (Courtesy of the
Charlotte-Mecklenburg Historic Landmarks Commission)

problem embedded in the better class's philosophy of race progress, a difficulty that would be magnified as race relations worsened in the 1890s. Believing in self-help—that blacks themselves bore the responsibility for their own condition in the New South—members of the black better class blamed their own race, often the "lower sort," for hardening race lines rather than whites. Their faith in self-determination, that blacks needed to earn their rights, coupled with their belief in the inherent fairness of the social order and their white "friends" blunted overt protest as the shadow of Jim Crow began to darken their city in the early 1890s.

Summing up race relations in North Carolina after traveling across the state in 1892, northerner Albert Bushnell Hart wrote in *The Nation*, "Outward good nature there is, but almost no confidence." The confidence that still existed, particularly among the white and black better classes at the beginning of the decade, would be profoundly shaken by the political and economic turbulence of the next few years.[9]

.   .   .   .

In July 1888 black editor W. C. Smith commented on a new phenomenon taking place in the countryside surrounding Charlotte. "Pic-nics are held by the farmers in different localities to such an extent," he reported, "that it is said there is some political significance in them. Farmers' alliances . . . are having feasts in good eatings and big speeches." Smith noted the immediate consequences of the meetings: "The Democratic press is already scared into fits." In 1888 Mecklenburg farmers enthusiastically joined the Farmers' Alliance, a movement that would threaten the political, economic, and social status quo in Charlotte, North Carolina, and the South.[10]

In the late 1870s white farmers in Texas organized the Farmers' Alliance to improve their economic and social condition through cooperation. The Alliance believed that the only way for embattled farmers to successfully challenge the power of merchants and monopolies was to undertake cooperative endeavors, such as cooperative stores and cotton-buying houses, and to purchase cotton gins and warehouses. The Alliance drew on a rich tradition of farmer organization and protest in the South. Revitalizing the message of Greenbackers and Grangers, members of the Farmers' Alliance railed against merchants, railroads, and bankers, who, they believed, deprived them of the fruits of their labor.

In addition to bettering the economic condition of farmers, the Alliance also hoped to enrich the lives of its members, "mentally, morally, [and] socially." Stressing self-improvement, morality, and neighborliness, the Alliance provided a much-needed sense of community for isolated, embattled farm men and

women. In biweekly meetings of the sub-Alliances—local organizations under
the auspices of both county and state Alliances—farm men, women, and children gathered to hear lectures, enjoy short entertainment programs, and visit
with neighbors. Moreover, county Alliances often held picnics and occasionally
more long-term encampments.[11]

Beginning in 1887, Alliance organizers carried their message and their organization east to the cotton belt, and the Alliance, like the Grange before it, found
especially fertile soil in North Carolina. In the late 1870s and 1880s the plight of
the state's farmers worsened as they saw their economic independence evaporate
due to the lack of credit, the crop-lien system, plummeting cotton prices, and the
growth of large-scale tenancy. When Alliance organizers first arrived in North
Carolina in 1887, many of the state's farmers had already joined the North
Carolina Farmers' Association, an organization founded by Leonidas L. Polk,
founder and editor of the *Progressive Farmer* and a former state commissioner of
agriculture. Mecklenburg farmers responded enthusiastically to the Farmers'
Association. Native son Sydenham B. Alexander, former master of the state
Grange, served as president of the Farmers' Association.[12]

In January 1888 the Farmers' Association formally merged with the Farmers'
Alliance in North Carolina. Alexander was elected the first president of the state
Alliance, with Polk as secretary. According to Alexander, the purpose of the
Alliance was "to encourage education among the agricultural and laboring
classes, and elevate to higher manhood and womanhood those who bear the
burdens of productive industry." In 1888, only a year after the first Alliancemen
entered the state, there were 52 county Alliances and 1,018 sub-Alliances. By
1890 every county in the state had an Alliance, and 90,000 farmers belonged to
the organization.[13]

In Mecklenburg the Alliance enlisted many former Grangers and their
spouses who had risen up in indignation against "town people" in the 1870s.
Farmers Sydenham Alexander, T. L. Vail, E. C. Davidson, and J. B. Alexander—
all of whom had been prominent in the Grange movement—served as leaders of
the Alliance in Mecklenburg County. Townspeople and town interests, the
traditional bane of the Grangers, served as the targets of the Farmers' Alliance as
well. Alliancemen blamed merchants, bankers, and manufacturers for their
problems and resented the power and authority of the townspeople, which had
grown steadily since the Grange revolt of the 1870s. Mining a deep seam of
bitterness toward town merchants, the Alliance attracted an estimated 2,000
members in Mecklenburg by the summer of 1888 in its first few months of
existence.[14]

Indeed, many local farmers saw the Alliance as their last hope in challenging the all-powerful Charlotte merchants. In June 1888 a Mecklenburg Allianceman from Davidson appealed to his "brother farmers" to unite in the Alliance, "for if we fail this time, the farmer's doom is fixed, the merchants will then have us where they will hold us forever." In words seething with indignation, the writer pointed out that "when we farmers are in the fields working hard in the summer, with the drops of sweat falling from our brow . . . the merchants [are] sitting around the store doors with their linen shirts and black neckties on, waiting for us to bring in our first bale of cotton."[15]

The Alliance preached many of the same principles as the Grange—particularly economic cooperation. Soon after farmers established the Mecklenburg Alliance, they opened the Alliance Cotton Office, where members could have their cotton graded and bid upon, in an attempt to circumvent local cotton merchants. Located "in the center of Cottontown" on the corner of Trade and College streets, the Alliance buying house "greatly benefitted the market," according to the Alliance, since "Charlotte prices have been far above those of the surrounding towns and villages."[16]

Like the Grange, the Alliance also drew a large portion of its membership from farm women. Far more than church or temperance organizations, the Alliance gave women a chance to discuss crucial economic and political issues of the day on an equal footing with men. Women were elected to hold important positions in the Alliance, with some serving as lecturers and assistant lecturers. In North Carolina Leonidas Polk contended that women in the Alliance should enjoy equal rights in the order, which included participating in secret ritual and Alliance business. Although the Alliance fell short of endorsing woman suffrage, it expanded the traditional sphere of its female members, allowing them a much broader range of activity than that enjoyed by town-based sisters of the better classes.[17]

Even though the Alliance exhibited many features of the Grange, it departed significantly from the older farmers' movement in other ways. Whereas the Grange offered admission to anyone interested in agricultural pursuits, the Alliance limited its membership to the "farmer and farm laborer, mechanic, country schoolteacher, country physician or a minister of the gospel." Moreover, although both the Grange and the Alliance in the South limited their memberships to whites only, the Alliance helped generate the Colored Farmers' Alliance, a separate, parallel organization.[18]

Although barred from membership in the Farmers' Alliance, black farmers, injured by the same economic forces that oppressed their white counterparts, found the organization's program and cooperative strategy attractive. In the mid-1880s several black Alliances appeared in central and eastern Texas, and in 1888 enterprising black farmers organized the Colored Farmers' Alliance. Built on the same philosophy of self-help and race pride that motivated the town-based black better class in the 1880s, the Colored Farmers' Alliance hoped to help its members gain greater wealth and economic power through cooperation.[19]

In the summer of 1888, just as the white Alliance began to organize in the county, the Colored Farmers' Alliance commenced recruiting members in Mecklenburg. Fearing any movement that might unite blacks and whites based on their common class interests, the *Charlotte Democrat* noted this development with alarm. The *Democrat* asked the *Progressive Farmer*, the newspaper of the state Alliance, to explain its relationship to the Colored Alliance. Editor Leonidas Polk responded that only whites could join the Alliance but that black farmers had chartered an organization "somewhat similar." Fearing a backlash against the white Alliance—and reflecting the Alliance's adherence to southern racial mores—Polk reiterated that the black organization was "a separate and distinct organization." Nonetheless, he wished the black organization "God-speed" if "it shall make them more industrious, more frugal, more reliable, more thoughtful and a better people and better citizens." A few weeks later J. J. Rogers of Apex, North Carolina, the general superintendent of the Colored Alliance, responded to the *Charlotte Democrat*'s concerns about the black Alliance in Mecklenburg and North Carolina. Rogers noted that the Colored Alliance was "spreading rapidly" in North Carolina and the South. Like Polk, he stressed that the Colored Alliance was "a separate and distinct organization from the white Alliance" and that its "principal objects are: To educate the colored race, to make them more industrious, more frugal, more reliable, more thoughtful," and to better their economic condition.[20]

The size of the Colored Alliance in Mecklenburg as well as the identities of its members and details of their relationship with the white Alliance are unknown. It is likely that the black and white Alliances—like those in other parts of the South—had little interaction with each other, remaining separate, parallel organizations. By 1890 the national Colored Farmers' Alliance claimed two million members in twelve states. Although reports of the size of membership were probably exaggerated, the fact that black farmers were uniting in a large-scale organization sent chills up the spines of many white southerners. Moreover, as the white Alliance increasingly gravitated toward political action, the vision of an interracial farmers' party undoubtedly multiplied the fears of Democratic leaders.[21]

The white Farmers' Alliance—at first demanding nonpartisanship—soon came to realize its enormous political potential. Whereas the Grange had been avowedly nonpartisan, the Alliance did not hesitate to harness its organization for political purposes. As Leonidas Polk explained in 1888, "We don't want a farmers' party but we want to see the farmers of this country take sufficient interest in political matters and political action to keep a strict eye on all that their party does." Similarly, in 1889 Mecklenburg's Sydenham Alexander maintained that even though the Alliance did not contemplate forming its own party, "any party or any man who makes war upon its principles or who discriminates against the farmers' and laborers' interest is its enemy."[22]

The Alliance first attempted to shape Democratic politics in North Carolina in 1888, when it backed Alexander as the Democratic nominee for governor. Denied the nomination, the Alliance made Alexander their nominee for U.S. senator over Matt W. Ransom, a bid he also lost. But the disappointments of that year did little to dampen the enthusiasm of the Alliance for politics. Soon the subtreasury issue propelled the Alliance into the political vortex and became the litmus test for Alliance support.[23]

In 1889, at the St. Louis convention of the national Alliance, Charles W. Macune, a leading Allianceman from Texas, proposed a plan to help farmers protect themselves from the vagaries of the market. Macune suggested that the federal government establish warehouses and grain elevators where farmers could store imperishable commodities, such as cotton, until they chose to market their crops. Depositors would receive treasury notes equal to 80 percent of the crop's value and would pay 1 percent interest per month on the treasury notes as well as a minimal storage fee. They would then be free to withdraw their crops whenever they chose.[24]

The subtreasury plan soon became the focus of Democratic politics in Mecklenburg and North Carolina, as well as across the South. Many southern Democrats sympathized with a number of the Alliance's goals as articulated at the St. Louis convention, including the free coinage of silver to increase the money supply and curbing the power of the railroads and banks. But the subtreasury scheme stuck in the throats of many Democrats. Viewing the subtreasury plan as unconstitutional and antithetical to their philosophy of limited government, many southern Democrats resisted the plan, calling it "class legislation" and "paternalism." At the same time, southern Democrats realized that they could not afford to alienate Alliance members. If they withdrew their support, Alliance members could weaken the Democracy beyond repair and guarantee a return of Republican rule.[25]

Early in 1890 former governor and now U.S. senator Zebulon Vance of Charlotte found himself caught in the web of the subtreasury issue. The state Alliance began to pressure Vance to introduce the subtreasury bill in the Senate.

Although the senator privately opposed the bill, he faced reelection in the fall and feared the wrath of the state's farmers should he refuse. As a result, Vance introduced the bill in February 1890 with little enthusiasm, nevertheless receiving the warm accolades of the state's Alliancemen. By May 1890, however, as Vance appeared to waver in his support of the bill, the secretary of the state Alliance asked Vance to articulate in writing his position on the subtreasury plan and other Alliance proposals. Although Vance explained that he unequivocally favored some of the Alliance's demands—such as making silver equivalent to gold as a monetary standard—he clearly stated that he did not favor the elimination of the federal banking system or government ownership of railroads. Finally, on the crucial issue of the subtreasury, Vance wrote that he had not made up his mind but that he feared the plan was unconstitutional.[26]

By June 1890 Vance's misgivings about the subtreasury plan became public knowledge when the he wrote to state Alliance president Elias Carr that he could not support the subtreasury bill. Realizing the rift that his stance might cause among the state's Democratic voters, Vance appealed to Carr to maintain unity in the party and warned that a Democratic split would inevitably reintroduce the horrors of Radical Reconstruction.[27]

However, North Carolina's farmers were hardly in a conciliatory mood. Frustrated by Vance's apparent flip-flop on the subtreasury bill and weary of the Democratic party's insensitivity to their problems, many of the state's farmers vented their rage at Vance. Leonidas Polk and the *Progressive Farmer* led the attack on the North Carolina senator. Polk angrily denounced Vance in the pages of his influential journal, and he and other Alliance leaders began to wrestle with the fact that their organization might not be able to achieve its goals within the confines of the Democratic party.[28]

Despite his previous overwhelming popularity and his home ties to Mecklenburg, Vance lost the support of the county's farmers over the subtreasury issue, a development that spelled trouble for Mecklenburg Democrats. In July 1890 Clement Dowd, Vance's longtime Charlotte law partner, wrote to Vance about the situation in Mecklenburg. Serving as Vance's eyes and ears in the county, Dowd warned him that Polk's attacks in the *Progressive Farmer* "may be considered as voicing the sentiments of the Alliance people in this County & section of the State." Polk, wrote Dowd, "means mischief. . . . 'Good by, my party, good by' is the song he says he leaves the people singing wherever he goes—democrat or republican."[29]

The subtreasury plan and the growing power of the Alliance triggered a revival of animosity between town-based Democrats and their country counterparts. Members of Charlotte's white middle class and manufacturing elite wholeheartedly championed Vance and condemned what they believed were the outlandish demands of the Alliance. The Alliance's insistence on the subtreasury plan and other economic reforms threatened the prosperity that both the middle class and the manufacturing elite enjoyed.

Just as the *Charlotte Democrat* and the *Charlotte Observer* had defended town interests against the onslaught of the Grange in the 1870s, the *Charlotte Chronicle* served as the voice of townspeople against angry Alliance members in 1890. In fact, Dowd assured Vance during the subtreasury controversy that "the newspaper will attend to Polk" and that Vance should "rest easy" in the discharge of his "senatorial duties." As Dowd predicted, the *Chronicle* vociferously defended Vance's stance on the subtreasury bill, condemning Polk and the Alliance as a "political ring."[30]

Despite criticism in the local Democratic press, the county Alliance, at the request of the state Alliance, demanded that potential Democratic nominees pledge themselves, in writing, to support Alliance principles. North Carolina's Alliance leaders, like their counterparts across the South, maintained that the Alliance was nonpartisan but entered the political campaign of 1890 with the goal of electing legislators and county officials sympathetic to farmers' interests; in short, they hoped to take control of the Democratic party. In Mecklenburg the Alliance explained that the written pledge requirement was necessary because "politicians have so often deceived us by their verbal promises, which they break and then deny having made, that we have decided for the future to take their pledges in black and white."[31]

In June 1890 the county Alliance submitted a list of six demands to Hamilton C. Jones, a Charlotte lawyer and an aspiring Democratic nominee for the U.S. Congress. The demands, which reiterated the platform of the Alliance, included support for the abolition of national banks, the free and unlimited coinage of silver, and the subtreasury bill. Jones refused to sign the pledge, replying that his first loyalty lay with the Democratic party. The Alliance, he claimed, demanded "class legislation"; he concluded that the "white men of this State cannot afford to divide or to risk division" since "the Republican party has commenced a new crusade against the South in the shape of the Federal election law."[32]

The federal election law that Jones referred to added a heightened sense of risk to Democratic infighting. In 1890, as the Alliance began to assert itself in politics, the Republican-controlled Congress debated the Lodge Election Bill, known among southern Democrats as the Force Bill. The bill threatened to expand federal supervision of elections, imperiling the rampant fraud and capricious voter registration practices that cemented Democratic control in the

South. The Lodge Election Bill coupled with the Alliance revolt provided a double threat to Democrats in the South.

The *Chronicle* applauded Jones's feisty stance against the Alliance and once again attacked the farmers' foray into politics. The newspaper criticized Polk as a "little would-be political Moses, trying to array the farmers against all their neighbors who are not farmers." But of even graver consequence, the Alliance aimed "a blow at white supremacy in this State and section."[33]

Leonidas Polk, in the columns of the *Progressive Farmer*, defended himself and the Alliance against the furious attacks of the *Chronicle* and Charlotte's town-based interests that it represented. Charlotte's Democrats could no longer control the farmers, according to Polk, and their fears had elicited the attack on the Alliance. "The *Chronicle* is upset," maintained Polk, "because some of the farmers met in the Alliance store in Charlotte and refused to tell what they did." Defending the Alliance's venture into politics, Polk inquired, "Who has any more right to go into politics than the farmers?" He contended, "You say the majority should always rule. We are trying our best to rule and you won't let us." Polk sarcastically asked the *Chronicle*, which had previously downplayed the numerical strength of the Alliance, "Why let a few farmers with hayseed in their hair trouble you?"[34]

As Democrats and Alliancemen attempted to come to some settlement in order to maintain a united white political front, black Republicans, like many white Alliancemen, questioned whether they still had a place in their party. By 1890 the Republican party in North Carolina found itself in complete disarray. After a decade of division over coalition, prohibition, and the role of blacks, the party was nearly moribund, almost killed off by the 1888 "lily-white" debacle. That year, the party had found itself attacked by the Democracy in a virulent white-supremacy campaign that the Democrats hoped would keep the upstart Alliance from straying into the Republican fold. In response, Republicans implemented a new strategy, a "lily-white" movement, whereby the party attempted to disassociate itself from black voters. The strategy backfired, leaving the party in shambles and black voters alienated.[35]

Even before the 1888 disaster, W. C. Smith remarked on the estrangement of black voters from the party of emancipation. In the spring of that year, he noted that "the colored voter is not so very enthusiastic in politics as he once was." Granted few political offices and little patronage, many African American voters refused to support the party. Moreover, black Republicans in the South felt that they had been sold out by the policies of national party leaders in the post-Reconstruction era. From 1881 to 1885, President Chester Arthur's administration openly solicited the backing of antiblack independent political organizations in an effort to strengthen the party's flagging potency in the South. Furthermore, in 1883 a Republican-dominated U.S. Supreme Court struck down the 1875 Civil Rights Act as unconstitutional.[36]

Grover Cleveland's election to the presidency in 1884 also dampened enthusiasm for the Republican party among African Americans and challenged their party loyalty. After Cleveland became the first Democratic president since emancipation, many black voters realized that their freedom did not depend on a Republican president; they did not need to fear a return to slavery just because the Democrats occupied the White House. Politics simply did not seem as pressing to the South's blacks by the late 1880s as it once had been. "The colored man is no longer scared of slavery nor greedy for office," commented Smith. Moreover, Cleveland made a point of liberally bestowing political patronage on black supporters, a move not lost on black voters.[37]

Disaffection from the Republican party coupled with Democratic enticements to black voters forced national African American leaders to reassess their political strategies by 1890, a reevaluation of which members of Charlotte's black better class were well aware. From the mid-1880s on, influential black newspaper editors W. Calvin Chase of the *Washington Bee* and T. Thomas Fortune of the *New York Age* reminded blacks of their yet-unfulfilled political clout, arguing that it might best be realized by dividing their vote. The combination of growing black political independence and the upstart Farmers' Alliance seemed to portend tremendous political upheaval. Reflecting on this ominous sense of transition, W. C. Smith remarked with prescience, "North Carolina is ripe for change."[38]

Indeed, much of the change that Smith predicted originated with the state's black citizens. Black Republicans in the summer of 1890 called a convention of the state's African American voters "to consider the political situation" and "adopt such measures as may be deemed for the best interests of our people." A circular sent out from Raleigh by John H. Williamson described the reasons for calling the convention, all of which revealed deep-seated frustration and disaffection from the Republican party. The circular attacked "the National Administration," which "has discriminated against our race," and Republican leaders, who used blacks "as their servile tools," forcing them to "inquire whether we are now a part of the Republican party." Even Charlotte's preeminent black Republican politician, John T. Schenck, gave "his hearty endorsement" to the convention.[39]

On 27 August 1890 the black convention met in Raleigh, only a few days before the state Republican convention. Sixty counties sent 200 representatives to the meeting. Notably, delegates included Reconstruction-era politicians, such as Schenck and Raleigh's James H. Harris, as well as members of the better class, who in the 1880s had often been at odds with black politicians over prohibition and the place of politics in the black community. Sensing a chance to reshape the political system—with themselves in the lead—the black better class seized the opportunity to participate in the meeting, reentering the political arena in an attempt to facilitate a new, more effective political strategy for the 1890s.[40]

The press described the delegates as "the most intelligent men of the negro race." James H. Young, who called the convention to order, pointed out that the gathering included "lawyers, doctors, ministers, editors." Dr. J. C. Price of Livingstone College, one of the best-known black educators and orators in the South, gave one of two principal addresses to the assembly. With the party evidently in shambles, the time seemed propitious for the creation of a new Republican party, a party free from corruption and true to the traditional principles expounded during the Civil War and Reconstruction.[41]

After a number of speeches, the convention passed a series of resolutions articulating the dissatisfaction of blacks with the Republican party. The convention demanded "freedom of elections" and condemned "'bossism,' local and state." Finally, the delegates appointed a committee to meet with President Benjamin Harrison and his cabinet in order to present the resolutions of the convention and insist that national and state party officials "at once reconstruct their forces and give the negroes their full share of the offices under their control."[42]

The Democratic *Raleigh News and Observer* heralded the convention. Sensing deep division in the Republican party that could only help embattled Democrats, it suggested that the meeting "may mark a new departure in politics in North Carolina." But the white-controlled state convention of the Republican party soon submerged the demands of the black assembly in a typical display of tokenism. Although the convention placated blacks by appointing E. E. Smith, a black Republican from Wayne County, as the "temporary chairman," white Republicans continued to dominate party affairs, electing a white state chairman over black lawyer J. S. Leary of Fayetteville.[43]

With little change evident on the state level in August 1890, Mecklenburg's black Republicans, led by John Schenck, engineered their own revolt against county Republican leaders. Schenck and other black politicians declared "open war against the individuals who fatten on public office while the mass of Republican voters, the negroes, continue to draw the party water and hew the Republican cord wood." Meeting at Biddle University—a gesture that symbolized the support of Charlotte's black better class in the ensuing political struggle—the county's black Republicans expressed their "unbounded confidence in the Republican party," as "influenced and controlled by such men as Abraham Lincoln, Thad. Stevens, Charles Sumner and others." At the same time, the convention condemned local party leaders "for the unjust discrimination made against colored Republicans" through white patronage appointments. The convention also pledged not to support the candidates of the party "as at present organized."[44]

As disaffected farmers and black Republicans tried to maneuver within the confines of the two-party system in the summer of 1890, members of the Prohibition party in Mecklenburg County further complicated the political situation by holding a county convention and nominating a slate of candidates. In late September 1890 the county Republicans, badly split by race, agreed not to run their own candidates for the Senate, House, and constable races and instead support the Prohibitionist nominees—much to the chagrin of local Democrats who were already threatened by the Alliance. "Why will the Prohibitionists antagonize these friendly Democrats when they are engaged in a struggle for white supremacy, low taxes, and pure government, against a negro rabble?," asked the *Chronicle*.[45]

As the election drew near, county Democrats made a number of concessions to the county Alliance, although more militant Alliancemen remained unhappy with Vance and the party's position on the subtreasury plan. Sydenham Alexander won the Democratic nomination for Congress, and county Alliance president R. A. Grier received one of three Democratic nominations for the state House of Representatives. In addition, Democrats helped cement party unity by arguing that the preeminent issues in the election were the Lodge Election Bill and the tariff, both representing "home rule as against the centralization of government." As a result, most Alliance members stayed within the Democratic fold and the entire Democratic ticket swept the county, leaving the Republicans and Prohibitionists far behind. The low numbers of Republican votes recorded in the Second and Third wards suggest the frustration of many black voters, who simply stayed away from the polls.[46]

Despite the overwhelming Democratic victory in Mecklenburg and North Carolina, the election of 1890 represented an important watershed in the politics of the state. Legislative candidates supported by the Farmers' Alliance won big across the Tarheel State; after the election of 1890, North Carolina's legislature, like that of a number of other southern states, would be dominated by Alliancemen. The "farmers' legislature" of 1891, in which Alliancemen commanded the lower house, enacted a progressive agenda of legislation not seen since before the Civil War, including the establishment of a state railroad commission and an increase in school taxation. Moreover, the election showed that white Democratic farmers would no longer be distracted by white-supremacy arguments that diverted attention from severe economic problems. For the first time since Redemption in 1876, the party found itself seriously split over basic economic principles, with the subtreasury plan the focus of intraparty discord.[47]

Although Charlotte's black Republicans did not come close to accomplishing their goals in 1890, they had nonetheless voiced their disapproval of the party in the harshest terms to date. Their refusal to submit to white domination in the party and their willingness to seek alliances with the Prohibitionists suggested that the ties that once bound them to the GOP were badly frayed, if not broken. Moreover, 1890 marked the reentry of the better class into the political arena and foreshadowed the critical role they would play in refashioning North Carolina's politics.

The election of 1890 marked another significant development: it sparked more direct interaction between the white and black Farmers' Alliances in North Carolina. At the behest of the national organization in 1890, southern white Alliancemen began to foster a closer relationship with the Colored Alliance in an attempt to gain their support for their political agenda. In North Carolina the state Alliance, in the spring and summer of 1891, subsidized a campaign to expand the number of Colored Alliances in the state in the hopes of harnessing the political power of rural blacks for the agrarian crusade. Although the success of the campaign is unclear, the willingness of white Alliance leaders to cooperate with black farmers and seek their support presaged the biracial politics that would emerge in several years.[48]

Despite an obvious undercurrent of revolt, Democrats in North Carolina and Mecklenburg heaved a collective sigh of relief as they managed victory in the face of unprecedented dissension within the party. Yet subsequent events over the course of 1891 revealed the fragility of the truce between the Alliance and the Democratic party. In exchange for its support of Zebulon Vance in his bid for reelection to the Senate, the farmer-dominated state legislature demanded that Vance promise to work "to secure the objects of financial reforms as contemplated" in the platform of the Alliance, a bargain that Vance accepted. However, many of the state's Alliancemen wanted an outright pledge from Vance that he would support the subtreasury plan and denounced the Vance "deal" and the Alliance leadership that crafted it. The state's Alliancemen realized their worst fears when Vance, within three months of his reelection, declared that he felt no obligation to support the subtreasury bill. Vance's position, in the words of the *Chronicle*, created "a division as wide as the Gulf of Mexico" between the Democratic party and the Alliance.[49]

Stung by Vance and the Democratic party's resistance to their platform, many Mecklenburg Alliancemen, by August 1891, threw their support behind a third party: the People's party. Founded as a national party in Cincinnati in May 1891, the People's party appealed to disgruntled farmers in the West and South who were frustrated with the unresponsiveness of the two-party system. When Kansas Populist "Sockless" Jerry Simpson spoke to a massive gathering of Alliance members in Charlotte, the local press noted with trepidation that "whenever he alluded to the Third party or indirectly to Colonel Polk, the Alliancemen went wild with enthusiasm and joy." Prohibitionist T. L. Vail, president of the county Alliance, spoke out boldly at the Simpson rally as well, attacking those who "robbed" farmers, criticizing the current monetary system, and advocating the subtreasury plan as the remedy to the farmer's problems. "I am for a Third party!" he exclaimed. "I don't think a man ought to belong to a party, but the party to the man." Vail claimed that there was "little difference" between the two old parties since neither could accomplish anything for the farmer. "The Third Party is a limited express train bound for Washington," Vail shouted, as a thousand Alliance members jumped to their feet in a frenzy.[50]

In response, the *Chronicle* appealed to North Carolina's Democrats in the fall of 1891 to "commence to organize every city, town, hamlet, and township in the State" in order to "reach wayward Alliancemen." But the damaged relations between more radical Alliancemen and the Democratic party were already far beyond repair. Most observers viewed Polk as a third-party man by 1891, although he refrained from making any outright statement about supporting the third party. In the meantime, third-party sentiment grew in North Carolina and across the country throughout 1891. By the spring of 1892 three Mecklenburg sub-Alliances had endorsed the People's party.[51]

Democratic party leaders scrambled to keep North Carolina's Alliancemen within the fold. But Alliance demands—especially the subtreasury plan and the coinage of silver—conflicted directly with the interests of the white middle class and manufacturing elite, a significant and influential segment of the party, limiting the concessions that the Democrats were willing to make to the state's disgruntled farmers. Reflecting the frustrations of the white middle class and the industrial elite—who had the most to lose from the demands of the Alliance—a Winston lawyer warned Senator Vance that "the better class of voters such as the professional men—and town people are getting very sick of this eternal pandering to such like, and will stand it no longer—the farmer vote is not the only necessary element we must have to secure victory." Likewise, J. P. Caldwell, editor and copublisher with industrialist D. A. Tompkins of the *Observer*, described the political situation in the state as "more embarrassing than I have ever known." The Democratic party, he wrote to Vance, must take a "courageous stand" against the Alliance in order to "frighten them and block their game." Unless Democrats "show some nerve all is lost."[52]

In North Carolina Alliancemen took control of the Democratic convention in May 1892 and engineered the nomination of Elias Carr for governor over Bourbon candidate Thomas M. Holt. Although Polk and Alliance leader Marion Butler praised Carr's nomination as an Alliance victory, almost immediately both men bolted to the newly created People's party of North Carolina. The state People's party adopted the St. Louis platform—including the demand for the abolition of national banks and of speculation in futures, the unlimited coinage of silver, government ownership of transportation and communication facilities, and the establishment of subtreasuries—and endorsed Polk for the presidency of the United States.[53]

As the Polk-for-president movement grew dramatically, farmer-editor Polk died unexpectedly in June 1892, on the verge of the People's party convention in Omaha. Polk's death was a tremendous blow to the Populist movement in the South. In his place, the party nominated former Union general James B. Weaver, who had little support in the South. Despite Weaver's unpopularity and the death of Polk, the People's party continued to gain momentum in North Carolina and Mecklenburg. The continuation of hard times and the resistance of Democratic party leaders to farmers' entreaties practically assured the growth of the People's party in the South. Moreover, the nomination of Grover Cleveland as the Democratic candidate for president in June 1892 drove many more struggling farmers from the party into the arms of the Populists. Cleveland, a "goldbug," represented northeastern banking interests to many farmers. In addition, the Democratic party had flatly refused to adopt the Alliance's 1892 St. Louis platform, articulated several months earlier.[54]

In July 1892 an assembly of Alliancemen, disaffected Democrats, Prohibition-ists, and a handful of Republicans met first in Huntersville and then in Charlotte to form the People's party in Mecklenburg. Despite the diversity of their previous political affiliations, the Populists were bound by a common vision: the desire to create a more responsive political party that would address pressing economic and social problems. Reflecting the robust reforming impulse of the gathering, the assembly incorporated a prohibitionist plank in their platform and passed a resolution pledging themselves "to vote for no man who is profane, who gam-bles, or drinks, or who fails to pay his honest debts."[55]

Party organizers appealed to "every voter" in the county to be part of "the Reform movement that is sweeping over this State like a cyclone." Although confronted by Democrats wearing Cleveland hats and badges on Charlotte's streets, Populists resisted the "argument and reason" of the Democrats, according to the *Observer*. "There was no convincing the 'people' of the error of their way, nor no signs of repentance and tears on their part," mourned the newspaper. The assembly appointed delegates to the state People's party convention and passed a series of resolutions. Arguing that "reform should commence at home," they resolved to reduce the salaries of county officials and refused to vote for any county candidate who did not oppose the Force Bill.[56]

Notably, far from all Alliancemen joined the Populists. Most white southerners had deep attachments to the Democracy, the party of white supremacy and states' rights. To leave the party of their fathers and grandfathers was extremely painful for many, unthinkable for others. Mecklenburg's most prominent member of the Alliance, former state Alliance president Sydenham Alexander, refused to join the third party. Even though he publicly endorsed the St. Louis platform, Alexander maintained his loyalty to the Democracy and remained within the Democratic party to work for farmers' rights.[57]

The Tompkins-owned *Observer* castigated the People's party as a coalition without principle, willing to do "anything to beat the Democrats." The People's party was "composed of back-number Democrats, disappointed Republicans, Prohibitionists, brindletails, dyspeptics, soreheads and would-be-but-can't-be-bellwethers." The *Observer* attempted to paint the Populists as laughable extremists; not only did they support the subtreasury bill and government ownership of railroads but also, "we suspect, some . . . believe in woman suffrage and that the moon is made of green cheese."[58]

As the Democratic press railed against the third party, local Democratic leaders rallied their forces against the Populist threat. In Charlotte a new generation of "Young Democrats," as the local press called them, began to cut their teeth in local Democratic politics and provide leadership for the embattled party. They formed new political clubs, such as the Young Democrats Club, the Anti–Force Bill Club, and the Tammany Tigers, that served as the heart of local party activities.[59]

Most of the Young Democrats were middle-class professional men in their late twenties and early thirties who had been born during or immediately after the Civil War. Heriot Clarkson, who soon emerged as the leader of Charlotte's Young Democracy and who would play a prominent role in local and state politics well into the twentieth century, epitomized the Young Democrats. The son of a Civil War veteran, Clarkson was born in South Carolina in 1863 and ten years later moved with his family to Charlotte. After graduation from law school at the University of North Carolina at Chapel Hill in 1884, he returned to Charlotte and formed a law partnership with C. H. Duls. A lifelong prohibition-

Heriot Clarkson, ca. 1920. (Courtesy of the
North Carolina Division of Archives and History)

ist, Clarkson served as alderman in 1887–88 and was reelected to the Board of Aldermen in 1891.[60]

Clarkson and his compatriots served as the architects and executors of Democratic activism beginning in 1892. Shaping the Democratic response to the Populist threat, the Young Democrats organized dramatic public demonstrations in support of the Democracy. Torchlight processions and parades to rally party members in the city and the countryside became their hallmark.

The *Observer* noted this transition in party leadership in Charlotte and across the South, commenting on "the deep and thoughtful interest which the young men throughout the country are evincing in the success of the Democratic cause." The young men of the South "are almost universally Democratic." The *Observer* enthusiastically welcomed "the young clubs" and their vigorous zeal for the Democratic cause.[61]

As Democrats began to respond to the Populist threat in 1892, Republicans pondered their options and typically found themselves severely divided. The defection of white Democrats and Prohibitionists to the People's party presented the GOP with the greatest opportunity since the prohibition battles ten years earlier to oust the Democrats from power. But state Republican leaders disagreed over the best way to accomplish that goal. The Russell-Mott wing of the state Republican party, the same wing that supported the Liberal Antiprohibition coalition in 1882, opposed running a Republican ticket in 1892, fearing that a Republican slate would weaken the anti-Democratic forces. Republican leader Daniel L. Russell went so far as to suggest a coalition of Republicans and Populists. "Straight-out" Republicans, however, led by John B. Eaves, loathed the thought of another coalition and maintained instead that the Republican party should remain free of any alliances with the new third party. The Republican party should challenge the Democrats on every level, argued the Eaves faction, since the third party practically guaranteed Republican victory.[62]

During a chaotic state convention in September 1892, the Eaves strategy triumphed. But Republicans, black and white, remained badly divided. Although most black delegates, including Charlotte's John Schenck, supported running a Republican ticket, many prominent black politicians, such as Congressman George H. White, opposed it. Reporting on the convention, the *New York Times* commented that "the ticket is a weak one in many respects" and that "a large number of negroes will not vote for it because they feel they have been betrayed into the hands of the Bourbon Democrats." Moreover, the newspaper predicted that while an estimated 25,000 white Republicans had joined the People's party, "when the voting begins these men will go over to the Democratic party."[63]

Although Republicans tried to patch up their differences on the state level,

Mecklenburg Republicans remained divided over patronage issues and the role of blacks in the party. In March 1892 black Republicans, led by mail carrier J. W. Gordon, bolted against white party leadership in the most forceful action taken up to that time. Gordon called a meeting in March 1892 "to re-organize the party in Charlotte" as well as to denounce white Republican boss and postmaster Archibald Brady for his handling of patronage positions and for his treatment of black voters. Gordon claimed that Brady used "unfair and dishonorable means of controlling the negro vote" and was guilty "of bribing them and imposing upon their general ignorance." At a party meeting a few weeks later, "Gordonites" and "Bradyites" squared off in a heated session. Each faction eventually elected separate slates of delegates to the county and state conventions, which were subsequently contested, with the Bradyites receiving the nod of the state party bosses.[64]

By the fall of 1892, with their party deeply split and the local ticket in disarray, Brady and the county's Republican leadership, including John Schenck, endorsed local candidates of the People's party—much to the dismay of many black Republicans who hoped to reestablish pure, transcendent Republican principles and who deeply distrusted the Populists and their motives. The black better class, which had reentered the political arena in 1890 in an attempt to reform the Republican party, seemed especially disturbed and, as they had in the 1880s, attacked the leadership of unscrupulous black politicians. J. C. Cunningham wrote a letter to the *Observer* to criticize "the manner in which Brady and his colored servants are trying to deceive the poor ignorant class of colored people to vote for the Third Party." For years Brady and the Republicans had "been using the negroes as stepping stones to office," and they were now trying to exploit the black vote for the Populists. A few weeks later, Cunningham again attacked Brady for promising that "he would take the 'niggers' and lead them any way he chose." A boss like Brady would never command votes of "the decent colored voters." Cunningham warned, "Ah, Brady, when you go into your secret closet to sell the negroes, you must remember that the better class of colored people will not stand it." Abandoning the Republican party completely, Cunningham eventually sided with the Democrats in the election of 1892 and actively campaigned against the Republican-Populist coalition in Mecklenburg.[65]

With many blacks demonstrating their willingness to abandon the Republican party, the People's party openly vied for their vote. Although the extent of black populism in the county is unclear, the *Observer* reported that as the campaign heated up in October, third-party campaigners were "telling negroes that they have dropped the prohibition plank and will let them stand on a wet platform, if they will only join them." The Democratic newspaper called the Populist attempts "another little ruse to catch the poor ignorant nigger." The fact that the Populists downplayed the prohibitionist dimension of their party suggests that they vied for the votes of poorer blacks, not the better class.[66]

As the election drew near, Charlotte's Young Democrats organized parades and torchlight processions that reflected their bare-knuckle style of politics and foreshadowed the caustic public spectacles that they would hold later in the decade. Just six days before the election, 1,500 torchbearers marched through the streets of the city, followed by horsemen bearing signs denouncing local Republican leaders—black and white. Playing on the name of a popular patent medicine known as "S.S.S.," some Democrats brandished signs reading "S.S.S.—Schenck, Stir, Stench." According to the *Observer*, Charlotte had not witnessed such a scene "since the memorable Vance torchlight procession in '76."[67]

Division among Republicans insured an overwhelming Democratic victory in Mecklenburg. The newspaper celebrated by printing pictures of a crowing rooster, a traditional symbol of the Democratic party. The Democrats carried every office in Charlotte and Mecklenburg, and Sydenham Alexander was easily reelected to Congress. In state elections, Democrats triumphed as well, as voters elected Elias Carr as governor. But the Democratic victory did little to mask some fundamental political shifts taking place in North Carolina. Although the Democratic candidate for governor, Carr, defeated his Republican opponent, David Furches, by over 40,000 votes, the combined votes of Furches and Populist candidate Wyatt P. Exum would have defeated the Democratic nominee by a margin of 8,000 votes. In Mecklenburg a combined vote would have defeated Carr in the Clear Creek and Long Creek districts and nearly upset the Democratic candidate in Lemley, Paw Creek, and Providence. Despite the claims of one Mecklenburg ex-Allianceman that "at least 90 percent of the numbers of the Alliance in this co. withdrew from the organization when it became a partisan machine," Populists displayed impressive strength in Clear Creek, Long Creek, Lemley, Paw Creek, and Providence as well as the Huntersville and Deweese voting districts, while garnering a total of only 21 votes in the entire city of Charlotte in support of candidates for state office. Moreover, black voter participation declined markedly across North Carolina in 1892, falling to a post-Reconstruction low, with an estimated 36 percent of black adult males not voting and approximately 34 percent of participating black voters casting their ballots for the Democrats.[68]

Not only did the election of 1892 expose powerful new currents in North Carolina politics, but also the campaign and election loosed an avalanche of passions among Republicans, Populists, and Democrats alike that would inform political discourse for the rest of the decade. Every election in the next eight years would be loaded with the rhetoric of class and race as white and black, producer and consumer, "better class" and "masses," attempted to manipulate a wildly fluctuating party system to their own advantage.

In Charlotte's black community, shock waves from the events of 1892 reverberated throughout the course of the next year. The better class escalated their attack on black politicians and the Republican party. Influenced by national leaders such as T. Thomas Fortune, Calvin Chase, and J. C. Price, the black better class began to support the idea that blacks should leave the Republican party and divide their vote or suffer the consequences of second-class citizenship, an idea discussed since Reconstruction but cresting in popularity across the nation in the early 1890s. Charlotte's black better class likely took their cue from J. C. Price, president of nearby Livingstone College. One of the best-known African Americans of his day, Price had advocated since 1891 that blacks forsake the Republican party and divide their vote. An admirer of Grover Cleveland, Price argued that blacks should give their support to the party that best served their interests.[69]

In April 1893 Price addressed a large racially mixed audience at Charlotte's city hall concerning "the Southern race problem from the Negro's point of view," a speech he had recently presented to the Nineteenth Century Club in New York City. Price summarized the current condition of the southern African American. "He is denied equal accommodation for the money on railroad trains; he cannot get justice in the courts; he is lynched on slight provocation; he is denied equal participation with the white man in the affairs of government." Like other members of his class, Price contended that the "remedy for the race is education, refinement, industrial development." Price further delineated the traditional message of the black better class, contending that the best way for southern blacks to display their "manhood" was to divide their vote. "Division on racial lines is unwise and unfortunate," he maintained, "and until the colored vote divides, it will never be influential or respected." Noting that "the negro vote has already begun to divide," Price claimed that the time was now ripe for "the negro . . . at last to step in and settle the differences between whites."[70]

Price's comments received accolades from both the white and the black press. While the *Observer* praised the address as a harbinger of change, editor Clinton of the *Star of Zion* enthusiastically championed Price's position, arguing that the basic issue for the black voter was "that of thinking, choosing for himself." Clinton claimed that abandoning the Republican party was a dead issue since "it is hard to leave that which has already left you." Although he recognized that many blacks would disagree with Price, Clinton ventured that "the young, educated, thoughtful men of the race agree and endorse him."[71]

Similarly, black Democrat J. C. Cunningham, who fought Schenck and the city's Republicans in 1892, lauded Price's speech, taking his advice a step further by calling for a coalition of the better class of voters, black and white. "If the Negroes of the South will ever get better treatment in the future than we have in the past," he concluded, "we shall have to expect it through the majority of the best white people, who are Democrats, of course." A number of local black voters apparently agreed with Cunningham and participated in a conference of black Democrats held in Charlotte in late August 1893 "for the purpose of formulating plans of future success."[72]

A few months later, Clinton again attacked black politicians, much as W. C. Smith had done in the pages of the *Charlotte Messenger* ten years earlier. Displaying ambivalence about political involvement and stressing that politics should only play a secondary role in the black community, Clinton asserted, "Men who want to rise and have something that will be abiding will do well to think well before entering politics."[73]

The arguments of Charlotte's black better class that the black vote must be divided and their attack on black Republican politicians exacerbated tensions in the black community. The church again served as the playing field for community conflict as it had during the prohibition battles of the 1880s. In June 1893 J. C. Cunningham claimed that he had been "ejected" from the Republican "Third Party Sunday school" at Clinton Chapel for joining the Democrats and for criticizing the fusion coalition in Mecklenburg.[74]

Divisions within the black community severely crippled the already infirm Republican party, and the party could not muster any opposition to the Democratic slate in the 1893 municipal election. Even as Democrats swept to victory in Charlotte, however, the actions—and inaction—of the Democratic party on the state and national level helped pave the way for fusion between North Carolina's Populists and Republicans.

The year 1893 saw several developments that helped cement a coalition of Populists and Republicans. That year the Democratic state legislature further alienated many farmers by severely restricting the Alliance's business dealings. Moreover, the panic of 1893 plunged the nation into a severe depression, worsening the economic condition of long-embattled farmers, which did little to enhance Grover Cleveland's already limited popularity in the South. As Populist and Republican politicians geared up for the election of 1894, they began to discuss the idea of "fusion," of joining their tickets in order to end Democratic rule.[75]

Both Republican and Populist fusionists in North Carolina battled tenacious "straight-out" wings in their respective parties. Republicans found themselves divided along the same lines as they had been in 1892—between the Russell-Mott wing, which supported fusion, and the Eaves wing, which demanded a straight Republican ticket. Whereas the Eaves faction was convinced that Cleveland's unpopularity and disputes among local Democrats spelled sure victory for the state's Republicans, the Russell-Mott faction insisted that a victory could be guaranteed only by combining with the Populists. Populists also struggled with the strategy of fusion. Populist fusionists, led by Marion Butler, ultimately triumphed over the "straight-out" wing of the party; by late August 1894 fusionists in both parties prevailed, forming an alliance unique in the South.[76]

Stressing the common ground that Republicans and Populists shared, fusionists presented themselves as the party of reform, calling for changes in election laws enacted by the state legislature in 1889 that allowed Democratic registrars to disfranchise voters easily. Fusionists also emphasized their common abhorrence of the undemocratic county commissioner system and advocated larger appropriations for public schools. Following the lead of the state parties, Populists and Republicans fused in Mecklenburg as well, combining their tickets in hopes of breaking Democratic dominance in the county.[77]

The state's Democratic press ridiculed the coalition of Populists and Republicans, predicting that the "unholy alliance" meant "the beginning of the end of the Populists in North Carolina." In Charlotte the *Observer* sneered at the fusionists as representing the triumph of the "anything-for-office element" and haughtily remarked that "the combination is not one to concern Democrats" since it "cannot carry the state."[78]

Democratic party leaders felt far less sanguine, fully aware of the power of the biracial coalition. Only a few days after Populists and Republicans allied, the state Democratic leadership called for massive mobilization through the organization of new Democratic clubs all over the state. In Charlotte Young Democrats again played a key role in mobilizing the party. The Anti–Force Bill Club, headed by S. B. Waters, and the Young Men's Democratic Club, led by thirty-six-year-old lawyer Charles W. Tillett, organized rallies in Charlotte and in the county.[79]

Although fusion breathed new life into the Populist and Republican parties in the late summer of 1894, it raised some difficult issues for Charlotte's better class of blacks, most of whom opposed the coalition. Disaffected from the Republican party and believing that blacks would never be taken seriously until they practiced independent voting, some members of the better class envisioned an alliance with the better class of white Democrats, as suggested by J. C. Cunningham two years earlier. Moreover, the black better class continued to look down on lower-class black politicians and refused to cooperate with them. In March 1894 Clinton again hammered away at black politicians in the *Star of Zion*, calling them "a positive hindrance to our progress." He continued, "We candidly believe that were it not for the worthless, offensive Negro politician, one-half of this trouble—lynching and all—that we have had in the south would have been averted."[80]

Besides despising politicians of their own race, members of the black better class also remained deeply suspicious of the Populists. In April 1894, as the talk of fusion saturated political discussions, Clinton penned an extensive editorial in which he contended that blacks had nothing to gain by lending their support to the Populists. Notably, and typically, Clinton based much of his argument against fusion on the class differences that existed between the Populists and the better class of blacks while stressing the common ground shared by "progressive" Democrats and blacks. Populists, wrote Clinton, "are generally as much, if not more, opposed to giving fair play to the negro than are intelligent and progressive Democrats." They "are made up, as a rule, of the element of white people which has always been opposed to the progress and best interests of the negro." Clinton advised those of his readers who could no longer support the Republican party to "let politics alone or endeavor to make some sort of deal with their Democratic friends as will give them a chance to exercise the right of franchise in a manner that will promote the best interests of the country and State." Clinton preferred "straight out Democrats with all that the term implies" over Populists but also insinuated that if the Republican party would "return to the old landmarks, preach and practice Republican doctrine as it was in the days of Lincoln," the party might again have the undivided support of black voters.[81]

The *Messenger* concurred with Clinton that blacks had little to gain from fusion. In October 1894 the newspaper argued that the Populists had not treated the Republicans fairly in nominating candidates in 1892 or 1894. As a result, the *Messenger* refused to endorse the fusion ticket.[82]

Local fusionists, stunned at the rejection of the ticket by the local black press and the black better class, circulated a broadside in Charlotte entitled "Negro Slavery!," claiming that a Democratic victory meant the enactment of "a law Disfranchising all Non Property Holders. If You Don't Own Land You Can't Vote." Arguing that the poor—black and white—shared common interests, the fusionists urged blacks to "Vote the Populist Ticket and Save Your Liberty." Such tactics reflected the growing desperation of local fusionists as well as their lack of insight into class differences in the black community. Despite the dire predictions of the Populists, Clinton and his compatriots of the black better class believed that they had far more in common with "progressive" and "intelligent" white Democrats—people with similar interests and values—than with poor, uneducated white farmers.[83]

The cause of fusion, damaged by the denunciations of the black better class, was further weakened by the death of John Schenck, which left black Republicans without an established political leader. Charlotte's leading black politician died in March 1894 at the age of seventy. The *Observer* eulogized Schenck on its front page as "a natural-born politician" who for years had "carried the negro vote, almost as his own." In 1892, typically at odds with the black better class, Schenck had endorsed fusion and likely would have done so in 1894; his endorsement would probably have strengthened the coalition in Charlotte and in the county.[84]

As the 1894 election approached, the *Observer* warned that "this election is not to be carried without effort" and that the stakes in the election embraced "all that has been built up in North Carolina in twenty years." As they had two years before, Young Democrats in Charlotte organized dramatic political rallies. In a significant gesture, they dedicated the largest rally to the memory of Zebulon Vance, who had died the previous year. Vance was a hero to many of the Young Democrats; his dramatic campaign of 1876, which led to the "Redemption" of North Carolina from Republican rule, was one of the earliest political memories of their generation and a formative event. They saw their campaign against fusion as their tribute to Vance and the generation of their fathers, who had struggled to reestablish Democratic rule in North Carolina.[85]

The Vance rally began in Charlotte and ended in Sharon Township, symbolically uniting town and country Democrats. A procession of 2,000 Democrats—on horseback, in carriages, in wagons, and on foot—marched to the patriotic tunes of the Steele Creek Band, stopping at a speaker's platform erected on the spot where Vance had given his last speech in Mecklenburg. Along with Democratic candidates and party officials, several of Charlotte's most prominent businesspeople and industrialists, including mill man R. M. Oates, sat prominently on the platform. Three orators assailed the Populists and Republicans. Frank I. Osborne of Charlotte, the state's forty-one-year-old attorney general, referred to the third party as "born in Kansas, . . . the ugliest baby ever born" because "it is all mouth," while other speakers recounted the "horrors" of Republican rule during Reconstruction and attacked fusionists as "the biggest rascals in the world."[86]

After an emotionally charged campaign, Democrats again swept Mecklenburg County. As in 1892, fusionists showed little strength in Charlotte but carried the rural county voting districts of Crab Orchard, Huntersville, Lemley, and Paw

Creek. Although local Democrats initially exulted in their conquest, the state-wide results soon dampened their spirits as the fusionists claimed a resounding victory. The coalition captured six of North Carolina's nine congressional districts outright and gained another seat in a contested election. Fusionists also won all of the state and judicial offices. But most importantly, they now controlled both houses of the state legislature, which would allow them to choose the next U.S. senator as well as initiate many of the reforms they had championed during the campaign.[87]

A few days after the election, the *Observer* attempted to explain the stunning fusionist victory in North Carolina, contending that "hard times" and tight credit contributed to the defeat of the Democrats. "The people are unrestful and dissatisfied; they want something done—they do not know what—but nothing that is improving their condition very fast has been done and, being mad, they strike at the most prominent object in sight."[88]

With an impressive mandate from the people of North Carolina, the fusionist legislature of 1894 struck down the laws that had provided the framework for Democratic hegemony since 1876. Restoring the direct election of county commissioners, the legislature also enacted a new election law, probably the most liberal in the South. The new law provided for one judge from each party to be present when ballots were counted; eliminated the arbitrary ways in which voters could be disqualified under the old law; made partisan challenges of voter registration lists more difficult; and aided illiterate voters by providing for the use of colored ballots printed with party symbols. Moreover, the legislature increased state appropriations for public schools and other state institutions as well as setting legal interest rates at 6 percent. Finally, the legislature succeeded in electing Populist party head Marion Butler to the U.S. Senate for a full term and named Republican Jeter Pritchard to complete Zebulon Vance's unexpired Senate term. The achievements of the fusionist legislature of 1894 represented "a virtual revolution in North Carolina politics."[89]

The success of the fusionists caused a slight change of heart among Charlotte's better class of blacks, evident in the immediate aftermath of the fusionist victory. The *Star of Zion*, which had suggested cooperation with "progressive" and "educated" Democratic "friends" as a viable option only a few months earlier, cautiously praised the results of the election. The newspaper also anticipated, with relish, that "foul mouth, Negro hating and foxy Senator Ransom will be among the slain after next March," since he was sure to fall victim to the fusionist legislature. Although the black better class viewed fusionist achievements with optimism, they remained cautious about the role of blacks in politics and continued to counsel blacks to remain aloof of party affiliation. In April 1895

George Clinton wrote in the *Star of Zion* that "there never was a time or an occasion when the Negro needed to exercise more caution, wisdom, or true manhood than in casting his vote." He concluded, "Let the Negro acquit himself like a man. Stand up and vote for the right and God will take care of the rest."[90]

Whereas changes on the state level portended advancement for black voters in 1895, in Charlotte the Democracy reigned supreme. In the context of the unfolding fusion revolution, the municipal election in the spring of 1895 generated "more interest than any election since the last Presidential campaign." Charlotte Democrats charged aggressively into the campaign, firing "the first gun" in the election, meaning "to serve notice on the Democrats of the State that the Charlotte Democracy is on guard, and to suggest to the other brethren that they govern themselves accordingly." Republicans again could not manage to field a slate to oppose the Democrats. As a result, black voters in the Second Ward held their own convention and nominated brick manufacturer William H. Houser for alderman, calling for unanimous support from the ward's black voters. But without politician John Schenck to rally the city's black voters, most supported the white Democratic ticket instead, and Charlotte elected its first all-white aldermanic board since 1883.[91]

Democrats seemed firmly in control in Charlotte in 1896 as citizens there, as well as across the country, prepared for a crucial presidential election. Although presidential elections typically engendered massive excitement, the 1896 election was especially freighted with significance in the context of the nationwide Populist revolt and the fusionist coalition in North Carolina. After heated discussion and severe division in both the Democratic and Populist camps, William Jennings Bryan, the unabashed silverite from Nebraska, won the Democratic nomination, and the People's party threw its support behind the Democratic nominee, effecting Populist-Democratic fusion at the national level.

Bryan's nomination cast the Democratic party in Charlotte into temporary disarray. The industrial center of the Piedmont, Charlotte was also "the stronghold of gold-bugism in the State," according to local Democrats. Accepting Bryan as the nominee for president and swallowing the silverite planks in the Democratic platform of 1896 were nearly too much for Charlotte's white middle class and industrial elite to bear. Local Democrats wrote a number of concerned letters to the *Observer* decrying fusion with the Populists at the national level. One writer who signed himself as "Young Democrat" criticized his party's "unholy alliance with the party of Debs," which placed it in "the ranks of communists, anarchists and all those who are arrayed against capital." But at the same time, "Young Democrat" pointed out that political exigencies required even goldbugs to "stand by the party regardless of the currency question."[92]

Similarly, the *Observer*, despite its vigorous sound-money stance, supported Bryan's nomination and urged all local Democrats to do the same. "Sound money men," urged the press, "should not be unmindful of the fact that [Bryan] and they are in harmony upon all other points of doctrine, and should be willing for the moment to waive this objection." Bryan "stands against the protective principle and for fair play for the South."[93]

Even though Charlotte goldbugs coolly accepted Bryan's nomination and vowed to support the party, state and local fusion further complicated the upcoming election. As Democrats and Populists allied at the Democratic National Convention, North Carolina Populists again fused with the Republicans on the state and local levels in an attempt to replicate their astounding victory of 1894. After a great deal of debate over division of the ticket during the summer of 1896, the Republicans and Populists finally settled on a united slate for state offices and Congress but, confusingly, divided the ticket at the top. Both Populists and Republicans insisted on running their own candidates for governor. William A. Guthrie received the Populist nod, while Daniel L. Russell ran as the Republican candidate.[94]

On the county level, Populists and Republicans, after furious debate, also fused—much to the consternation of the Democrats. In Mecklenburg Populists and Republicans divided the ticket. Some Populists opposed the county fusion ticket, wishing instead for a pure Populist slate. But as one Mecklenburg Populist remarked, "It was half a loaf or nothing."[95]

Local Populists noted the growing strength of their party and fusion in Mecklenburg. J. P. Sossamon, editor of *The People's Paper*, Charlotte and Mecklenburg's Populist newspaper, and secretary of the executive committee of the Mecklenburg People's party, wrote hopefully to Populist senator and party chief Marion Butler that "we are determined to wipe modern democracy out of this county this year," even though Mecklenburg was "one of the worst Democratic holes in the State."[96]

The reforms enacted by the fusionist state legislature, as well as the interest generated by the Bryan versus McKinley showdown, not only breathed new life into the gravely ill Republican party but also eventually brought Charlotte's black better class back into the Republican fold. Their return gave the party and local fusion a much-needed boost. By 1896 the black better class enthusiastically embraced fusion, having witnessed the concrete reforms brought about by the state legislature. Spokespersons no longer suggested building coalitions with the better class of white Democrats. Moreover, the black better class benefited from fusion legislation in tangible ways as they began to take a prominent place in local politics, filling the void left by Schenck's death. By the fall of 1896, Mecklenburg had twenty-two black voting registrars, including seven in Charlotte alone. Among them were two members of the city's black better class, Dr. J. T. Williams and funeral director Sydney A. Coles. Black registrars were the direct result of the election reforms enacted by the 1894 legislature and the local Republican party's willingness to lure black voters back to their traditional party. The black better class also lent unprecedented support to both Republican and fusionist candidates during the 1896 campaign. They attended fusion rallies and even served as speakers. At a fusion rally chaired by Williams, lawyer John S. Leary addressed the audience, promising "that if the Republicans were successful that negroes would be put on juries." Even elite Grace AME Zion Church jumped on the political bandwagon by holding a "McKinley Fair."[97]

Although the black better class returned to the party of emancipation in 1896 and enthusiastically supported fusion, it is unclear to what extent black voters in Mecklenburg joined the People's party. Correspondence from Mecklenburg Populists to party chief Marion Butler makes no mention of black Populists. But since the Colored Farmers' Alliance had been active in the county and Populists two years earlier had made overtures to black voters, it is likely that some blacks played an active part in the People's party.

Local Democrats soon attacked the mingling of blacks and whites at fusionist political rallies. As they had in 1888, Democrats attempted to use race-baiting to whip up support for their party, a strategy adopted by Democrats across the state. Referring to a fusionist rally at Samaritan Hall where white fusionist candidates J. B. Alexander, J. P. Sossamon, and M. B. Williamson spoke to a predominately black audience, the *Observer* claimed that "such a mixture as was had at this meeting would have been very disgusting a few years ago to the men who participated in it." "A White Man" also wrote a letter attacking state Senate candidate Alexander for accepting an invitation to speak to a black audience instead of debating his opponent before a white crowd. He surmised that "when a fellow joins the Republicans he straightaway becomes desperately attached to the 'nigger.' "[98]

Charlotte Democrats also used racial issues in an attempt to guarantee the support of white mill workers. By 1896 the backing of mill workers had become increasingly critical to a Democratic victory in Mecklenburg, but they had shown signs of disaffection from the party. In 1890 Charlotte's mill people had supported Republican candidates, and their loyalty to the Democratic party remained suspect throughout the decade. Moreover, because of newly liberalized election laws enacted by the fusionist legislature, black registration increased significantly by 1896, making the white mill vote even more crucial. The *Observer* contended that "black convicts, aliens, and squatters" will "have the privilege . . . of killing the votes of honest men, bona fide citizens and taxpayers."[99]

In an attempt to offset this threat, the city's Young Democrats, led by Heriot Clarkson, organized Democratic Workingmen's Clubs in Charlotte's cotton mills. The year before, R. B. Davis of the state Democratic party wrote to Clarkson that Democrats should use the party's "attitude of pronounced hostility" toward blacks to rally the support of working-class voters. Davis advised Clarkson to "appeal directly to the laboring white men of the state, who, you are aware, are beginning to desert us, in great numbers, & only from despair & disgust." Davis warned that "there is no way we can be compensated for *their loss.*" By October 1896 Clarkson's Democratic mill clubs claimed over 300 members. At club meetings, mill workers listened to speeches by local party leaders warning that unless they voted Democratic, they would suffer under "Republican and negro supremacy." Every member of the Workingmen's Clubs also promised "to see that every white man who is out of employment" found a job. In addition, Clarkson organized courthouse rallies and torchlight processions in which mill workers displayed their support for the Democracy.[100]

Despite the work of the Young Democrats among the mill people, by election eve the fusionists had pulled ahead of the Democrats in Mecklenburg in their number of registered voters. In October 1896 Walter R. Henry, a Populist attorney in Charlotte, reported to Senator Butler the phenomenal progress of the fusionists in Mecklenburg by the fall of 1896—registration books in October reported "that we are seven or eight hundred ahead, Populists and Republicans."[101]

Faced with sure defeat, local Democrats, led by the Young Democratic firebrands, implemented far more extreme tactics than race-baiting rallies, speeches, and editorials. Feeling the ill effects of liberalized election laws, local Democratic authorities began jailing black voters in late October, just days before the election. They claimed that the voters had "failed to list their property or polls," a misdemeanor by state law. Since most of the blacks did not have the money to pay the fine for breaking the law, they would remain in jail long enough to prevent them from voting. The Democrats contended that 200 to 300 black voters had failed to list their property for their 1896 taxes. Jailing these voters, and intimidating countless other black voters, would erase the fusionist majority in the county. Attorney Henry noted that "this is undoubtedly intimidation under the Election Law, but it is not easy to establish."[102]

The fusionists soon fought back. Armed with the state election law, Henry at first threatened to have one Democrat arrested for voter intimidation for every black voter jailed. But, as Henry noted, "The trouble is, they can give bond. The negroes can't." Thus Henry played another card available to the fusionists. Because of the fusionist victory in 1894, many of the magistrates in the county were members of either the Republican or the Populist party. Henry plotted to use this advantage to beat the Democrats at their own game. The fusionists would issue warrants to tardy taxpayers "before our own Magistrates"; the sympathetic magistrates would then release them, pending appeal, on their own recognizance, allowing them to vote on election day. Securing the 300 black votes was crucial; if the Democrats succeeded in jailing black voters, Henry surmised, "it may lose us the county."[103]

Henry's plan worked. Outflanking Democratic intimidation tactics, fusionists scored startling victories in Mecklenburg, contributing to the statewide fusionist victory. In a surprising upset, Populist and fusionist J. B. Alexander defeated Young Democrat W. C. Dowd in the race for state senator. Moreover, Heriot Clarkson—architect of the Democratic party's intimidation tactics in Mecklenburg—suffered a humiliating defeat in his run for the North Carolina House when fusionists seized three of five seats, a development that would exacerbate Clarkson's hatred of fusionists.[104]

In state elections, fusionists triumphed again as well. Voters chose Daniel L. Russell as the first Republican governor since Reconstruction. In addition, they elected an overwhelmingly fusionist General Assembly made up of 72 Republicans, 64 Populists, 33 Democrats, and a single silverite.[105]

The day after the victory, a local Populist claimed that county fusionists had engaged in "a most tremendous fight against fraud and rascality" and had emerged victorious. Even though "the woods on the 3rd [election day] were full of the intimidated" and Democrats "unjustly erased" the names of many voters from the registration books—even stealing and destroying one ballot box—the fusionists had triumphed, a victory sealed by the courageous actions of Attorney Walter Henry. The Democrats "are cursing him bitterly."[106]

The bold deeds of Henry and other white Populists in defending jailed blacks must have helped overcome some of the mistrust that black voters—especially those of the better class—felt toward the Populists. The trials of the campaign and the election victory seemed to portend a lasting relationship among fusionists and an era of full-fledged reform. But within weeks of the election, the fusion alliance proved fragile. Even before the inauguration of Governor Russell, serious fissures appeared in the coalition as the two parties fought over whether to reelect Republican senator Jeter Pritchard, who, to the alarm of Populists, opposed free silver. Moreover, Populists and Republicans split over the issue of whether to maintain distinctly separate party organizations and over who should lead the fusion movement. Pritchard's reelection to the Senate, supported by Governor Russell, resulted in the withdrawal of the Populists from the fusion coalition. Consequently, Russell lost the Populist support that he needed in the legislature for the reforms he hoped to enact. At the same time, the governor lost the backing of his own party over his assault on the railroad lease of the North Carolina Railroad. Enacted in 1895 by Governor Carr without the confirmation of the fusionist legislature, the railroad lease had provoked many Populists who insisted that it sold the North Carolina Railroad to J. P. Morgan's Southern Railway without the approval of the people. Russell's attack on the lease reflected his increasingly radical stance, which disillusioned many of his Republican compatriots. As a result, the governor found himself isolated from both parties, neither of which deemed him trustworthy. In what could have been a stellar session of reform, the legislative agenda of the fusionists stagnated.[107]

In Charlotte and Mecklenburg the fusionist coalition proved to be short-lived as well, collapsing over the issue of patronage. Black voters, having enthusiastically supported fusion in 1896, anticipated the spoils of victory in 1897. They particularly coveted the postmastership of Charlotte, a position never held by an African American. J. W. Gordon, a lifelong Republican and veteran post office employee, seemed a logical and well-qualified candidate. Instead, white Republicans engineered the appointment of one of their own, J. W. Mullen, a move that deeply angered many black voters and seemed to signal business as usual. In October 1897 the black McKinley and Russell Club met at the courthouse and appointed a committee to go to Washington, D.C., to fight Mullen's appointment in Congress. "We intend to see whether the Republicans at headquarters will persist in continually and eternally turning the cold shoulder to we 'niggers,' who ·constitute the voting strength of the county," wrote "A Negro Voter" to the *Observer*. "If the 'nigger vote' were subtracted from the Republican strength in Mecklenburg County," he reminded readers, "there would not be enough Republicans left to tell the tale." The writer noted that the McKinley and Russell Club would meet every month "for the purpose of looking after the interests of the colored voters of the community" as well as "to foster a spirit of independence among our race" so that "when these white Republicans attempt to barter us off, we . . . get a small portion of the quid pro quo." A few weeks later, the club organized a series of monthly public demonstrations at Latta Park "for the purpose of insisting upon the recognition of the negro in the distribution of official patronage."[108]

Charlotte's black better class, ambivalent Republicans at best, seemed particularly infuriated by the reprehensible treatment they received at the hands of white Republicans. Undertaker Henry S. Boulware wrote two scathing letters to the *Observer* that graphically illustrated the injustice meted out to black Republicans by their white counterparts. Boulware explained that blacks "worked as we have never worked before and voted solid for the ticket from top to bottom," furnishing in Mecklenburg "about 3,800 votes to 150 cast by white Republicans." Yet of twelve patronage appointments held by Republicans in the county, blacks held only one: spittoon cleaner at the mint. "We colored Republicans are getting tired of this," wrote Boulware, "and we don't propose to stand it. . . . We will no longer be their tools." A few weeks later, Boulware threatened that "there must be fair division of the fodder or we will cease to pull the plow."[109]

While Charlotte's black better class viewed the fruits of fusion with disappointment, their white counterparts became increasingly frustrated with fusion's tenacious grip on state and local politics. As the black better class complained bitterly about the shortcomings of the coalition, white townspeople, led by the brash Young Democrats, began to prepare for the election of 1898, an election that would stand out for its viciousness in the annals of the state's often brutal political campaigns.

6

White Supremacy

In May 1899 Grace AME Zion Church, the prohibitionist congregation of the black better class, announced the start of a fund-raising drive to build a new and larger building. One of its members nostalgically recalled the contributions made by many "white friends" toward the building of the first Grace Church in 1887. He listed a group of prominent white citizens, including cotton factor John E. Oates, industrialist R. Y. McAden, politician and lawyer Rufus Barringer, and businessman John W. Wadsworth. These men, recollected the church member, had endorsed notes for the building's construction, helping make the first Grace Church building a reality.[1]

The memory of aid given by white friends must have been especially poignant to Grace's members in the spring of 1899. Only a few months earlier, Charlotte's blacks had witnessed the disintegration of race relations in their city and state with the onslaught of the brutal white-supremacy campaign of 1898 and a riot in Wilmington a few days after the election. That spring, as Grace Church planned to build a new facility, the newly elected Democratic legislature passed a Jim Crow railroad coach bill as well as a disfranchisement amendment that would strip the franchise from most of North Carolina's black voters.

Given the state of affairs in the spring of 1899, Charlotte's black better class probably longed for the cordial relations that they had once enjoyed with their white counterparts. But as the fund-raising announcement intimated, most of the white benefactors of Grace Church in the 1880s were now dead. R. Y. McAden had died in 1889, and both Rufus Barringer and J. W. Wadsworth had died in 1895. Many members of the white better class who had recognized the black better class and built coalitions with them during the prohibition campaigns and social reform movements of the 1880s had passed from the scene. They were being replaced by a younger generation of white leaders, Young

Democrats, who had established themselves earlier in the decade, a generation far less sympathetic to the black better class and blacks in general.[2]

During the crises of the late 1890s, Charlotte's black better class continually appealed to their white counterparts to come to their aid to defuse political race-baiting and race-based legislation. Revealing a class identity forged in the 1880s, the black better class called upon the better class of whites for calm, dispassionate, reasoned action against the white-supremacy onslaught as well as subsequent race-based legislation. Such appeals fell on the deaf ears of the new generation, men and women who came of age amid the disruption of populism and fusion politics, developments that had threatened both their economic advancement and their "rightful" place in the political order. Buttressed by Social Darwinism and "scientific" racial theories, the new generation led the attack against fusion and the state's blacks, nearly pushing North Carolina into a race war, and spearheaded both disfranchisement and Jim Crow legislation. Only too late did Charlotte's black better class learn the bitter lesson that they now had few friends in the white community.

· · · · · · ·

Black anger at the shortcomings of the fusionist coalition of 1897 spilled over into 1898, a crucial election year in which determined North Carolina Democrats would try to wrest power from the fusionists. Anticipating their pivotal role in the upcoming election, black Republicans met in the hall above the Queen City Drug Store in February 1898 and organized the Central Republican Club. Headed by Henry Boulware, who had led the revolt against white Republican leadership in 1897, club members declared that they were "tired of being made a cat's paw by the white Republicans" and demanded that they be recognized by both the Populists and the Republicans.[3]

Populists and Republicans, locked in internecine warfare and riddled by division, paid little attention to the demands of the black Republicans. People's party leader Senator Marion Butler, inspired by the national Democratic-Populist coalition effected by Bryan in 1896, launched a new strategy, hoping to fuse the state's Populists with Bryan Democrats in 1898 under the umbrella of reform and free silver. Endorsed by Governor Daniel Russell—a Republican in name only by 1898—the Butler-Russell strategy left the Republican party floundering, headless, and without direction.[4]

Butler's interest in building a coalition with the state's silver Democrats also badly sundered the People's party. In early May 1898, on the eve of the state Populist convention, Walter R. Henry, chairman of the executive committee of Mecklenburg's People's party, openly pronounced his disgust with Butler's strategy. Having played a key role in Mecklenburg's stunning fusionist victory of 1896 by defending incarcerated black voters, Henry had experienced Democratic intimidation and fraud firsthand. To fuse with his unscrupulous political nemeses was unthinkable. He warned Populists that they would "surrender all you have been laboring for" by embracing the Butler strategy, that cooperation was nothing less than "patent political dishonesty and hypocrisy" and "would prove a boomerang instead of political capital for the Populist Party."[5]

Despite the resistance of many Tarheel Populists, Butler carried the day at the state People's party convention in mid-May 1898. But, as Henry predicted, the plan boomeranged only a few weeks later. The state's Democrats, holding their own convention in late May, rejected the offer of the Populists. Fearing that they might alienate powerful, probusiness interests in the party, the Democracy opted instead to enter the campaign as a "pure" party, unadulterated by Populist influence.[6]

With the state's Populists and Republicans in even more disarray than usual, the Democrats took the lead in defining the terms of the 1898 campaign, designating it a battle for white supremacy. First suggested by Heriot Clarkson in 1897 and masterminded by forty-four-year-old state chairman Furnifold M. Simmons, the Democratic strategy placed the issues of white supremacy and "Negro domination" at the heart of the party's platform to rally the badly divided party and to dissolve the Populist-Republican alliance. Although the Democrats also recommended a strong railroad commission, improvements in the public schools, and the direct election of U.S. senators, their denunciation of the fusionist state legislatures of 1896 and 1897 and the cry of "Negro domination" served as the core of their campaign. Even though the number of black officeholders in North Carolina remained small, and hardly warranted the label "Negro rule," many Democrats, particularly from eastern North Carolina, feared a steady advance in black officeholding. As a result, the state Democratic party unleashed a brutally racist campaign that vilified black officeholders, exaggerated their numbers and influence, and asked white voters to redeem the state from black control.[7]

Caught off balance and immediately placed on the defensive, Populists and Republicans out of dire necessity again discussed fusion. Throughout the summer, the two parties debated whether they should once more repeat the fusionist strategy of 1894 and 1896. Both parties, however, were far weaker than they had been in the earlier campaigns. Mecklenburg's Populist party was a shadow of what it had been in 1896, a casualty of the aborted Butler strategy. Populist leader Walter Henry, for example, spent his time attacking Butler's leadership rather than rallying Populists and assailing his Democratic foes; county Democrats quickly seized the opportunity provided by Populist infighting. Davidson Populist W. A. Potts, describing total disorder in Mecklenburg's People's party, wrote, "I don't know one County that we need to carry worse than this one," but, he explained, "the deocrats [*sic*] are working my Township for all it is worth. . . . We need help and need it bad."[8]

Republicans also suffered from division and disaffection—mostly among angry blacks in their ranks. In July 1898 Henry Boulware warned both the Populists and the Republicans that "we will vote no fusion ticket this year unless there is a colored man on it. If white Republicans and Populists are too good to put a colored man on the ticket and vote for him, they are too good to get our votes this year."[9]

When the county Republican convention met in late August 1898—with the issue of Populist-Republican fusion still unresolved—black Republicans dominated the proceedings. Already intimidated by the Democrats' white-supremacy crusade, they divided over strategy. Notably, without the presence of politician Schenck or an influential successor, the black better class played a visible and influential role in the convention, filling the void left by the late Reconstruction leader. Professors S. B. Pride and H. A. Hunt of Biddle University attended as delegates, as well as minister D. D. Moore and businesspeople J. M. Goode and A. W. Calvin. Because of the vicious Democratic campaign well under way, the issue of proper decorum, always important to the black better class, became even more exaggerated. J. M. Goode, who served as secretary of the convention, demanded that the delegates display gentility because "the Democrats want you to 'cut up' and then they want to laugh at you for being ignorant." Goode then went on to demand patronage and officeholding for blacks since "the horse that pulls the plow ought to have the fodder." Calvin, on the other hand, well aware of the Democratic campaign strategy, argued that placing a black on the ticket would "give the Democrats a club with which to break your heads." Finally, the resolutions committee, made up entirely of African American delegates and headed by S. B. Pride, presented a series of proclamations that made no demands about nominating black candidates and simply endorsed fusion and a fusionist ticket "without reserve." As a result of the moderate approach of black Republicans, the party in Mecklenburg nominated an all-white slate.[10]

The temperate response of black Republicans and the divisions among the black better class reflected the dilemma that the white-supremacy campaign had created for them. With the elimination of "Negro rule" the designated goal of the Democratic campaign, black Republicans in Mecklenburg felt they could not risk running for office. To do so would only play into the hands of the race-baiting Democrats, who claimed that the state was controlled by blacks. Yet failing to place blacks on the ticket only reinforced their second-class status in the party, a position that they had loathed for years.

As Republicans and Populists debated their strategy in the summer of 1898, the white-supremacy campaign heated up in Charlotte and Mecklenburg. Local Democrats, led by Heriot Clarkson, enthusiastically embraced the party strategy and made white supremacy the singular campaign issue in Charlotte and Mecklenburg. The campaign had special, personal meaning for Clarkson. He had lost by only a handful of votes to fusionist candidates in the battle for a seat in the state legislature in the ruthlessly fought election of 1896. Two years later he again received the Democratic nomination, determined to capture the office that he believed was rightfully his. With thirty-six-year-old mayor and chairman of the county Democratic executive committee J. D. McCall, Clarkson and his Young Democratic compatriots executed the white-supremacy campaign with a vengeance, seeking to establish themselves as the heads of the political order.

The Young Democrats repeatedly unfurled the banner of race and white supremacy at local Democratic rallies. Clarkson attacked "negroes [who] had always allied themselves almost solidly against the whites," with the result that "the white voters were bound, in self-defense, to stand together." Party leaders again targeted Charlotte's white mill workers for sorely needed support. Mayor McCall and others spoke at the Atherton Mill on the issue of "white man's rule," appealing to the mill workers to unite in the cause of white supremacy.[11]

The *Charlotte Observer* aided the Young Democrats in saturating the local campaign with racial issues and stressing the importance of "rescuing" eastern North Carolinians from black rule. The paper claimed that although the party's campaign "strictly upon the color line . . . is not to our liking, for we are very fond of the colored race," blacks bore the responsibility for this development since they themselves had drawn the color line by voting as a solid bloc. White voters, the press contended, should follow suit. "Let the black people mend their ways and they will see the color line disappear quickly enough." Citing Wilmington, New Bern, and Tarboro as cities in peril, the *Observer* described the situation in the eastern portion of the state as "undoubtedly very bad" and warned that "people of the centre, the piedmont country and the west, know little or nothing about it."[12]

The *Observer* sent correspondent H. E. C. "Red Buck" Bryant to eastern North Carolina to report firsthand on the "horrors" of black domination. With titles such as "Negro Rule: Shall It Last Longer in North Carolina?" and "Human Devils in Command," Bryant's columns depicted black officeholders as depraved and ignorant creatures who held upright, intelligent white citizens hostage. Bryant also attacked local blacks as "trifling and lazy," a far cry from the praise that the *Observer* had heaped on Charlotte's black citizenry only a few years earlier. The newspaper even published a letter from "A Southern Woman" pleading for the "rescue" of the white race in the east and suggesting the predatory designs of black males upon white women. The existence of black postmasters made it unsafe "for any young lady to go to the office without a body guard." Warning of the possibility of bloodshed "unless there is a material alteration in political affairs in our extreme eastern counties," the writer appealed "to you, honest, faithful Christian men, both white and black, to help us."[13]

Young Democrats also drew on the popular theory of Social Darwinism to bolster their racist campaign. Describing the current state government as "the fusion abortion," one writer to the *Observer*, calling himself "Anglo-Saxon," asked, "Why should any man think that North Carolina is destined to prove an exception to Herbert Spencer's law of the 'Survival of the Fittest,' a law to which history has furnished no exception." Fusion represented an unnatural, "retrograde movement" that was "an offense unto God and man."[14]

Social Darwinism enamored Charlotte's white middle class in the 1890s, as it did their counterparts in other parts of the United States, and played a powerful role in shaping the rising generation's concepts of class and race. Not only did the theory provide a "scientific" basis for the concepts of white supremacy and black inferiority, but also it lumped all blacks into a single grouping. Social Darwinism replaced the paternalistic philosophy that guided the white better class in the 1880s. Having experienced the Old South and slavery, members of the white better class of the 1880s recognized both individuals and the existence of class differences in the black community and hoped to aid the black race by forming alliances with the better class of blacks, whom they deemed the natural leaders of the community. However, Social Darwinists grouped all blacks, regardless of their accomplishments, into a single, socially inferior category. As a result, for the white middle class of the 1890s, who were led by the Young Democrats, class identification across race lines all but ceased to exist. By contrast, the black better class, which had come of age in the 1880s, continued to maintain a strong identification with their white counterparts that would fashion their response in the aftermath of the election of 1898.

Whereas the cries of black domination and white supremacy resonated with voters in the eastern part of the state, in Charlotte the slogans simply did not make much sense, on one level. Despite the fusionist triumph in Mecklenburg in 1896, local blacks saw their political influence actually diminish during the 1890s. Although they served as voting registrars in 1896, blacks held no elective offices in the county in the 1890s and no black aldermen were elected after

1893—even though blacks had served on the board for all but two terms between 1868 and 1893. Moreover, despite the turbulence of North Carolina politics in the 1890s, race relations in Charlotte remained relatively stable throughout most of 1898. Members of Charlotte's black better class even bragged about
race relations in their city and state. In January 1898 the Reverend D. C.
Covington remarked in the *Observer* that "there is a growing feeling of goodwill
and pleasantness between the races here in good old North Carolina." A month
later Covington commented on "the friendly feeling that exists between the best
white people of our State and the blacks," asserting that "it is our duty to live
together in peace since the two races are here together."[15]

Despite the fact that Charlotte had not experienced anything approaching
black rule in 1898 and lacked severe indigenous racial tension, charges of black
rule rang true to the Young Democrats who had risen to the leadership of the
local Democratic party by the late 1890s. Threatened by the antibusiness rhetoric and legislation of fusionists and blocked from office by the success of the
Republican-Populist coalition in the county, the Young Democrats viewed white
supremacy as their birthright, an inheritance bequeathed to them by their fathers
that they were bound by honor to defend; the campaign of 1898 gave the Young
Democrats the chance to redeem the state from black rule, just as their hero
Zebulon Vance and their fathers had done in 1876. They could then take their
rightful place in state government, a place that had been denied them by fusion
and "Negro domination." Moreover, the campaign offered them a chance to
legitimize their place in the political order; victory in the battle of 1898 would
earn them a bona fide place in state politics.

Young Democrats and their battle for white supremacy dominated the campaign. The state's badly divided Populist and Republican parties did not agree to
fuse until September 1898, long after the white-supremacy campaign was well
under way. In Mecklenburg Populists and Republicans finally followed suit,
merging their tickets in mid-September, long after local Democrats had saturated the campaign with race-baiting.[16]

Fusion, however, hardly guaranteed the support of black voters, a necessary
element to repulse the Democrats. In the onslaught of the white-supremacy
campaign in Charlotte, some members of the black better class again entertained
the idea of dividing their votes as a way to escape the wrath of the white
supremacists. In late August 1898 the Reverend D. C. Covington wrote that he
believed, like the late J. C. Price, "that the diversity of the negro vote in this
country is the only thing that will bring about his political salvation." Black voters
should "drift to the party that will do the most for him in his struggle to rise. If
that party be the Democratic party, then certainly the negro will be found in it."[17]

J. W. Smith, editor of the *Star of Zion*, 1898. (Courtesy of the Robinson-Spangler Carolina Room, Public Library of Charlotte and Mecklenburg County)

The ugliness of the campaign soon forced Covington—and undoubtedly many other wavering blacks—to embrace the fusionists and to denounce the tactics of the Democrats. In September 1898 the *Observer* published a letter from white Rockingham minister Jesse Page describing black rule in eastern North Carolina. Livid at the cleric's gross misrepresentations, Covington wrote him an angry letter, published by the *Observer*, in which the black minister denounced "the malicious falsehoods and baseless rot that is being published by you and the corrupt party to which you belong." Page's "lying statements," he angrily predicted, "will serve to solidify the Populists and Republicans, especially the negro against you as never before."[18]

As a result of his wrathful letter, the *Observer* canceled Covington's column, "Afro-American Interests," which the minister had penned for two years. By originally sponsoring Covington's column, the *Observer* had demonstrated an interest in building bridges with Charlotte's black better class—as long as its members stayed in their place. The *Observer*'s reaction to Covington's outburst revealed the limits of its paternalism, and the newspaper exploited the incident to promote racial hostility in the city. The *Observer* condemned Covington's attack, claiming that "the better class of colored people of this city and State will not endorse this unwarranted assault upon such a man, but all intelligent people will see the spirit underlying it."[19]

The better class was hardly in the mood to defend a white supremicist or, for that matter, the Democratic party. As Covington predicted, the vicious nature of the white-supremacy campaign united Charlotte's blacks. Acting on the defensive, they overcame previous disagreements and combined to fight the Democrats. In September the Reverend J. W. Smith of Charlotte, editor of the *Star of Zion*, argued that despite all of its problems, the Republican party remained "the best party for the Negro." Quoting Frederick Douglass, Smith wrote, "The Republican party is the ship; all else is the sea." A month later, as racial attacks worsened, John C. Dancy, editor of the *AME Zion Quarterly Review* and customs collector at the port of Wilmington, spoke at a large rally of Republicans in Charlotte. Articulating the experience of many members of the black better class, Dancy explained that he "had thought at first not to enter this campaign but on account of the prejudices engendered by the raising of the race issue, I was forced to do so in justice to myself and my race, as well as to other classes." Dancy denounced the Democratic charge of "Negro rule" in the east, warning his listeners that a Democratic victory might mean the end of black voting rights in North Carolina. He advised blacks to register and "be prepared to vote against any man who had unfairly raised the negro issue in this campaign."[20]

While the white-supremacy campaign united blacks in self-defense, it simultaneously weakened the Populist party in Mecklenburg. As Democrats defined the campaign as a referendum on white rule and racial superiority, white Populists found themselves in a bind. Although many Populists continued to insist that class-related issues, not race, lay at the heart of the 1898 election, the campaign forced many previously loyal Populists to choose between "white supremacy" and "black domination."

Some Populists, such as newspaper editor J. P. Sossamon, resisted the Democrats' call for race loyalty, maintaining that the election was about conflicting class interests. Escalating his attack on the "Lawyercratic party otherwise known as the modern Democracy . . . the money power in North Carolina," Sossamon did his best to rally the fragmented and conflicted Populists. He exhorted his readers, "Don't vote with those money kings who are accumulating thousands while you are raising 5 cent cotton and other farm products at a loss." He scoffed at the "negro scarecrow" and wondered "why it is that this 'scarecrow' appears only in time of a campaign."[21]

Despite such pleas, many Populists succumbed to the race loyalty ultimatum of the Democrats. The Mecklenburg Populists suffered a shocking blow when Populist state senator J. B. Alexander, who had been elected to the legislature on the fusion ticket in 1896, abandoned fusion under the pressure of the campaign. He proclaimed his political independence, explaining, "I will vote for any of my friends that I choose and I will not vote for the fusion ticket," while noting that he did not intend to return to the Democratic party either. But neutrality on the part of former Populists meant certain defeat for fusion and dashed the hopes of fusionists who wished to salvage something from the election.[22]

Likewise, the issue of white supremacy also provoked some white Republicans to abandon their party or be labeled traitors to their race. The *Observer* noted in October 1898 that "one of the best signs we see is not only that Populists are flocking back to the Democratic party, but that many Republicans are announcing their purpose to vote with it, at least in this election." R. A. Christenbury, a self-described lifelong Republican, repudiated his party in a letter to the *Observer* because "fusion has saddled negro rule on my white brethren in the east and I am going to work and vote hereafter for their deliverance." Christenbury explained, "I am a white man and believe in a white man's government and for this reason, I hereby forever sever my connection with the Republican party, which is the negro party. . . . White men, get together!"[23]

Indeed, as the campaign drew to a close, neither Republicans nor Populists could muster an adequate response to the Democratic campaign. Fearing violence, fusionists shied away from political rallies and public speeches. Moreover, the fusionist cause lacked a forceful press. Across the state, many Republican and Populist newspapers acquiesced to white-supremacy arguments. Although Charlotte's *People's Paper* directly attacked the white-supremacy strategy of the Democrats, other newspapers, such as the *Progressive Farmer, Raleigh Caucasian*, and *Union Republican*, fell victim to Democratic tactics and published explicit "horror stories" about black domination. The state's Young Democrats had defined the terms of the campaign, and few white voters had the courage to challenge them.[24]

The better class of blacks in Charlotte, however, refused to cave in to racial demagoguery and assaulted the Democrats and their tactics. Placed on the defensive and no longer divided by strategy and ambivalence toward the GOP, the better class called for solidarity and obedience to the Republican party. In the *Star of Zion*, editor Smith pointed out that "the cry of 'nigger domination' " was "the last and only trump card that they can play in this diabolical campaign with any possible chance of winning"; it was a "scare-crow and false alarm." Blacks could never dominate North Carolina, he contended, "while there are three white men in North Carolina to one black man." Smith appealed to blacks to "go quietly to the polls and vote against every man that coughs up the race issue," warning black voters that if the Democrats regained control of the state, disfranchisement would not be far behind.[25]

In the final days of the campaign, the state bordered on race war. Violence flared in eastern North Carolina where Red Shirts, an organization resurrected from the Reconstruction era, allegedly killed two blacks and beat several others. In Mecklenburg Democratic officeseekers openly intimated their willingness to resort to bloodshed to win the election. *The People's Paper* reported that Democratic party chairman and Charlotte mayor J. D. McCall invited his followers to "turn their guns" on T. S. Cooper and W. R. Mullen, the heads of the county Populist and Republican parties. County Democrats also bragged that neighboring South Carolina Red Shirts would aid them at election time. Concerning the threat of Democratic violence, J. P. Sossamon warned, "There are hundreds of men in the Populist and Republican ranks that were in the confederate and union ranks that followed Lee and Grant . . . and red shirt toughs from S. C. don't scare some of us."[26]

Mecklenburg's Young Democrats supplemented threats of violence with dramatic parades and rallies in the name of white supremacy. The rallies aimed specifically at luring Populists back to the party while intimidating blacks. Organized by Clarkson, McCall, and twenty-four-year-old lawyer F. M. Shannonhouse, a massive parade in August snaked through Charlotte's streets. To demonstrate rural support for the Democracy, the parade featured members of township Democratic clubs, "the sturdy yeomanry of old Mecklenburg." Farmers marched and rode into Charlotte on horseback carrying banners inscribed with slogans such as "White Man's Supremacy" and "White Government." Teachers even dismissed school children from class to witness the parade, and they saw Tryon Street "full of horsemen from one end to the other" and joined the cheering throng. After the parade, several thousand spectators listened to a speech by South Carolina senator Benjamin R. Tillman, a longtime Alliance-man, who appealed for Populist support of the Democratic ticket. Tillman described fusion as "nothing but Republicanism" and argued that the Democrats must "invite Populists back as brothers and as white men who love North Carolina." Although not sparing Democrats criticism for their inattention to farmers, Tillman contended that "blood is thicker than water" and "if you Populists can't come back, stay at home on election day."[27]

The massive public displays engineered by the Democrats in Mecklenburg, along with threats of violence and racist rancor, paved the way for an overwhelming Democratic victory. Democratic tactics succeeded in neutralizing the fusionists. Not surprisingly, few blacks went to the polls. The drop in black voter participation, the desertion of many Populists from fusion, and the fact that "white Republicans also made themselves scarce" allowed Democrats in Mecklenburg to have "it all their way" as they took the county by over 1,700 votes, electing the entire Democratic slate. Heriot Clarkson won his long-coveted seat in the state House of Representatives, and his compatriot Frank I. Osborne landed the state Senate seat. Even the Second and Third wards, which, with their large black constituencies, had polled fusion majorities in 1896, fell to the Democrats in 1898. Fusion, always stronger in the county, broke down there as well. *The People's Paper* reported that Mecklenburg fusionists managed to salvage only a tax collector and constable "from the wreck."[28]

Voter fraud and violence helped guarantee the Democratic victory in Mecklenburg. Although the *Observer* claimed that election day passed quietly—even praising black voters for their good behavior—the Populist press reported mob violence. According to *The People's Paper*, a mob "composed of things who call themselves men and white Democrats" broke up a ballot box and assaulted a Populist registrar in the Providence district.[29]

Across the state, Democrats regained control of North Carolina, bringing an end to fusionist rule and bringing about the state's second "redemption." "The great tidal wave of Democracy has swept the State from Cherokee to Currituck," gloated the *Observer*, "and once more the white man's party will take possession of that which is its right by every law of birth, intelligence and principle." Democrats won majorities in both houses of the state legislature, electing five congressmen and their entire judicial ticket. In the wake of the victory, the

Observer admonished "our friends of eastern North Carolina" who "have been saved again by the Democratic party" to "stay with it hereafter. Don't run off after Farmers' Alliances and Populism."[30]

As white Democrats basked in their victory, a race riot in Wilmington attested to the fact that the campaign had stirred deep racial animosities not easily turned off at the end of the campaign. On 10 November, two days after the election, eleven blacks were killed and twenty-five wounded in a riot that also left three white men injured. In addition, a mob of about 400 whites destroyed the newspaper office and printing press of Alexander Manly, the editor of Wilmington's black newspaper and an outspoken advocate of fusion. As a result, a large number of blacks abandoned the city, including Wilmington's black mayor, and white Democrats took control of municipal politics.[31]

The outcome of the 1898 election and the horror of the Wilmington riot left Charlotte's black better class dazed. The events seemed to undo all the advances in "race progress" that the better class had been working toward for nearly two decades and to undercut their contention that blacks could indeed earn full equality in southern society. But rather than abandon their ideology of racial advancement, the black better class clung tenaciously to it. In the greatest crisis of their generation, spokespersons for the black better class insisted that blacks themselves carried their destiny in their own hands and could win back the respect of white citizens. Fearful of retribution, some leaders of the black better class called again for blacks to eschew politics. As they had done many times before in the wake of political defeat, the better class attempted to retreat from the political sphere. They again relegated politics to the background, emphasizing instead the importance of economic and moral advancement and gentility as the keys to race progress.

At the same time that they reiterated their philosophy of advancement, the black better class appealed to their "white friends" who had aided them in the past. In the crisis of 1898, the black better class continued to display a class-based identification with the better class of whites that had been forged in the 1880s. Moreover, they maintained faith in their white counterparts, believing they would somehow put an end to the racial hysteria that gripped North Carolina in 1898.

Finally, the black better class lashed out at blacks themselves as the cause of the hostility they faced in 1898. As in the past, their guiding principles of self-help and self-determination forced many members of the black better class to blame their race—especially black politicians and poorer blacks—for the violence and hatred that surrounded them rather than blaming white demagogues. In the minds of many, if southern blacks possessed the power to earn their rightful place in society, it followed that they in turn bore the responsibility for losing their foothold in the social and political order.

An ingratiating letter written by J. W. Smith of the *Star of Zion* to the *Observer* several days after the 1898 election and the Wilmington riot reflected the mind-set of Charlotte's black better class, who were reeling from the events of 1898. Smith wrote the letter in an attempt to ease racial tensions and assure the city's white citizens that blacks posed no threat to them. Only several weeks before, Smith had boldly castigated the Democrats and enthusiastically supported the Republican party as the one true hope for North Carolina's blacks. Now, he thanked the *Observer* for praising the behavior of Charlotte's black voters during the election and called for peace among the city's white and black citizens. "As long as the colored people of the city are respectful and law-abiding and merit the compliment paid by the *Observer*," Smith wrote, "they may rest assured that there will be plenty of good white friends who will see that the law is thrown between them and violence." He maintained that even in the face of injustice, "we must all be law-abiding and endeavor to make friends of the whites amongst whom we live and labor." Smith called upon both blacks and whites "to forget the bitter past . . . and agree to live in peace."[32]

While appealing for amity between the races, Smith wasted no time denouncing black and white politicians, "frenzied agitators," who "use them [blacks] as bones of social and political contention." Instead of engaging in politics, blacks should "work and be economical, rise on the rank of moral and religious worth, financial and intellectual respectability." Then, and only then, asserted Smith, "will the evils which now plague them fold their tents and silently commence to steal away."[33]

Other influential members of the state's black better class called for blacks to withdraw from politics in self-defense, viewing political activity and black politi-cians as the roots of their problems. In December 1898, in an address before a meeting of the Central North Carolina Conference, which included Charlotte, Bishop J. W. Hood of Fayetteville commented on the recent election and the Wilmington riot, placing the blame for the current state of affairs squarely on the shoulders of black politicians and the "poorer sort," who refused to follow the example of the better class. Notably, Hood traced the source of the troubles to the statewide prohibition election of 1881. In 1881 blacks, through the prohibition issue, "had the opportunity to divide the white vote so widely that it could never have been consolidated again." Recounting the events of 1881, the bishop remembered that "the best white people of the State, regardless of party, united with the best colored people in favor of Prohibition." If "the mass of our people could have been induced to vote for Prohibition and thus secured its adoption," Hood asserted, "the white people would have seen that we could be depended upon to support such measures as tended to be the best interest of the State, and what we have now passed through could never have occurred." Blacks "should have had an alliance with men worth standing with—men of intelligence and worth and character—who would not have forsaken us when they could no longer use us" rather than following "irreligious, ignorant and immoral political leaders."[34]

In a similar vein, Bishop C. R. Harris blamed Tarheel blacks for racial antagonism and marked the prohibition election of 1881 as the crucial turning point in race relations. In an address published in Charlotte's *Star of Zion*, Harris contended that in 1881 God sent the prohibition bill "upon the political arena," and a mighty battle ensued with "God and His preachers, white and black . . . allied with the best people of the State, Republicans as well as Democrats." If more blacks had followed the lead of the "best people," "the color line would forever be abolished." But "they let that tide pass, and its ebb drug back the Negro into well nigh irretrievable defeat." As a result, "righteousness was defeated without regard to color or party, and corruption has ruled politics since."[35]

The black better class's gloss on the events of 1898 shaped their response to the advent of Jim Crow and disfranchisement legislation in 1899. Their anger at the lower classes and their attempt to distance themselves from the "poorer sort" and black politicians, coupled with their faith in and continuing identification with the white better class, guided their reaction to the race-based legislation.

Throughout the 1890s, even through the darkest days of the white-supremacy campaign of 1898, the black better class believed in the exceptionalism of race relations in North Carolina. The Old North State, they insisted, would never succumb to Jim Crow statutes and voting restrictions like those that had already been passed in many southern states because North Carolina was blessed with an abundant and influential better class of whites and blacks. Commenting on the separate-car laws that existed in a number of southern states in 1897, D. C. Covington remarked that "it would have been a law in North Carolina long ago had it not been that the State is composed of some of the best white people that can be found anywhere." Even though fusionists had insisted that disfranchisement would be an inevitable consequence of Democratic victory—a charge vehemently denied in 1898 by Democratic chairman Furnifold Simmons—the black better class continued to have faith in North Carolina race relations. In December 1898, in the aftermath of the brutal campaign and the Wilmington riot, Bishop Harris contended in the *Star of Zion* that although blacks had been disfranchised in several states "one by one, . . . thank God, North Carolina is a better State than Mississippi. The colored people are too intelligent and the white people too fair, too just, to allow or demand disfranchisement of the Negro as a Negro."[36]

Yet less than a month later, in January 1899, when the Democratic state legislature convened, both a disfranchisement amendment and a Jim Crow railroad car bill topped the agenda. The legislature hoped to enact a program that would disassemble fusionist reforms over the course of the next two years and guarantee that fusion would never again occur. The legislature not only would overturn the liberal election laws passed by the fusionists and end county "home rule" but also took steps to guarantee the separation of the races both socially and politically. "The line of cleavage between the white and black races in North Carolina must be maintained," announced the *Raleigh News and Observer*. "This is the motto of the Democratic majority in the present legislature."[37]

On 18 February 1899 both houses of the state legislature approved a disfranchisement amendment, modeled on Louisiana's statute, to be placed before voters for approval in August 1900. The Mecklenburg delegation, headed by Heriot Clarkson and F. I. Osborne, supported the bill. As drafted, the amendment would disfranchise illiterate black voters while providing a "grandfather clause" to allow illiterate whites to retain their suffrage, thus annihilating the black electoral base that had made fusion possible.[38]

To the state's Young Democrats, many of whom were self-styled progressives, the amendment represented, in the words of Charles B. Aycock, "the final settlement of the negro problem as related to the politics of the state." Aycock, who in 1900 at the age of forty would be elected governor, came to epitomize southern progressivism. In a letter published in the *Observer* justifying the amendment, he asserted that disfranchisement marked "the beginning of a new era," since "a larger political freedom and a greater toleration of opinion will come to our people." Seemingly forgetting the fact that the Democrats themselves first made race the focus of politics in 1898, Aycock contended that through the amendment "the Democratic party will be set free from the trammels of the race issue and can enter upon a career of economic study and legislation." Moreover, "discussion of policies and principles will take the place of heated declamations and partisan abuse." The future governor noted that the amendment required that white boys who were then thirteen, and not "grandfathered" by the law, would have to learn to read and write in order to qualify as voters by 1908. He assured voters that this requirement would only be an incentive for education. The Democratic legislature, Aycock pointed out, had already increased the school fund by $100,000 for that purpose.[39]

Along with Aycock, Mecklenburg state representative Heriot Clarkson was one of the leading advocates of the constitutional amendment. "I was strongly in favor of the elimination of the negro in politics," he later recalled. "The constitutional amendment was agitated by me and I did all I could to have it enacted into law." Not only had fusionists defeated Clarkson for the state legislature in 1896, but he was also one of North Carolina's most zealous prohibitionists. For Clarkson, and many other budding young middle-class progressives, the elimination of black voters meant the almost certain passage of prohibition laws since black voters in Charlotte had consistently helped block local option in the 1880s. Prohibition, Clarkson believed, would be one of the first fruits of disfranchisement. "After the elimination to some extent of the negro in politics," Clarkson wrote an ally in Raleigh, "I feel it the solemn duty of every citizen who desires good government to throw themselves into the great fight of moral supremacy and enlist in the cause of temperance and righteousness." As early as 1897, Clarkson and members of his Charlotte law firm had been in touch with a Mississippi lawyer concerning the technicalities of that state's 1890 disfranchisement law and its consequences. They were assured that the law "deprived our elections of all features of bribery, bull dozing or counting out and is an intense relief to all the white people in this state. . . . You ought, by all means if the Democrats ever get a chance in North Carolina again, to adopt some such provision." Clarkson got his chance in 1899 and devoted much of his energy to the passage of the disfranchisement amendment. Thus, for Clarkson and his compatriots, issues of race and social reform became inextricably intertwined in the suffrage amendment. Young white middle-class reformers, weary of corrupt elections and the insidious influence of the saloon, seized upon the amendment as the vanguard of progress in North Carolina.[40]

The *Observer* concurred with Aycock, Clarkson, and other advocates of the amendment and threw its considerable weight behind promoting passage of the law. Disfranchisement "will put an end to much of the peanut politics with which the State has been cursed," argued the newspaper. Whites would no longer have to vote according to "the law of self-preservation" but could vote according to their views on "finances, tariffs, or other great questions."[41]

The discussion of the disfranchisement amendment and the impending referendum in August 1900 incited the better class of blacks to action. Given the tragedy of the Wilmington riot, their anger at black politicians and the lower classes, and their faith in their "white friends," spokespersons for the better class advocated moderation. J. W. Smith argued that black leaders should "do whatever they can to help their race in the South and temper the bitter feeling of prejudice against them." Good feeling could be maintained only by rejecting the appeals of angry black politicians, "by the Negro race sitting down hard and heavy on hot-headed speakers and writers whose indiscreet, hysterical babblings only excite the passions of the two races."[42]

In addition, the black better class again appealed to their counterparts, the better class of whites. Reflecting a class identification that would shape their actions in the crisis years of 1899 and 1900, the better class called for blacks "to hold on to the best element of the southern whites and by honorable and proper means find a basis of reconciliation." Charlotte merchant A. W. Calvin wrote to the *Observer* that "progressive, intelligent colored men largely get their ideas from progressive, intelligent white men."[43]

Calls for moderation soon evolved into explicit attacks on black politicians and more calls for the race to pull back from politics and concentrate instead on economic and educational advancement, a refrain played in crescendo in 1899 and 1900. In May 1899 J. W. Smith exhorted, "The Negro must learn that it is not enough to be a good politician." Instead, he argued, "ownership in the soil, identification with the industrial and commercial life of the State in the development of business is the great end of useful citizenship." Blacks must "get houses, land, money and education, and the question of . . . citizenship will be permanently settled." A few months later, Smith asserted that "industry, integrity, wealth, education and religion will command recognition everywhere"; if "Negroes as a mass get these things Anglo-Saxon prejudice will take a back seat."[44]

Despite his tone of moderation, Smith attacked apologists in the black community who allied themselves with white supremacists to the detriment of the race, those who would do the bidding of the white man at any cost or reject black civil rights outright. The focus of Smith's animus was most likely the Reverend R. H. Leake and his delegation of Tarheel blacks, who appeared before the General Assembly's Joint Commission on Constitutional Amendments in January 1899. Apologizing for blacks who demanded their political rights, in the style of Booker T. Washington, Leake and his delegation deferred completely to the Democratic lawmakers, encouraging them to do whatever they deemed best concerning disfranchisement. Contrasting himself with the apologists, Smith maintained that "one can be conservative without being apologetic." Race leaders must counsel "moderation, toleration and mutual concessions," but "let them not say anything that will detract one iota from the manhood of the race."[45]

Smith thus made it clear that he sought a middle way. He attempted to chart a course between Washingtonian-style apologists, who would trade off political rights for social harmony, and militant black politicians, who threatened to exacerbate already explosive race relations in the state. His course preserved race pride, decorum, and civil rights, all crucial elements in the philosophy of the black better class.

In addition to calling for upholding political rights and race pride, the black better class began to plot a course of action to defuse the disfranchisement crusade. In March 1899 Bishop J. W. Hood wrote a letter to the *Observer* outlining a strategy that would be enacted by the black better class over the course of the disfranchisement campaign. Hood's strategy, which he labeled "an appeal to reason," called for moderation, pleaded with the white better class to come to the aid of the state's blacks, and recommended a division of the black vote, a tactic long advocated but never effectively enacted. He suggested that "if the better class of white people think it would be a good thing to divide the negro vote, I assure them that it can be done." He then appealed to them to "come forward and oppose the ratification of this amendment, which will assure its defeat."[46]

Hood also sketched the divisions that fractured the black community in 1899 and weakened its defense of civil rights. "There never has been a time when negroes were so much divided as now," he lamented. Some believed in "protection," while others advocated free trade. "Some believe in Prohibition, some in high license, while others believe in free whiskey." Moreover, "some radical negro politicians are fighting the negro ministers, because they have advised a conservative course in political matters." Yet division provided a rare opportunity to the white better class to secure the goodwill of the state's blacks by coming to their aid: "There has not been a time since the reconstruction period in which the better class of white people have had a better opportunity to secure the confidence of the negro in politics as they now have."[47]

Charlotte's black better class praised Bishop Hood's comments and strongly championed his position. J. W. Smith commented that the "article has produced a deep impression and put both races to serious thinking." The influential *AME Zion Quarterly Review*, edited by John Dancy, also applauded Hood's letter, calling it "one of the calmest, most dispassionate and unanswerable pleas from the Negro standpoint in favor of justice and fair play that has yet appeared." He hopefully predicted that "it will no doubt serve its purpose, of awakening the better class of whites to a sense of their duty, to a class of people who have served them better than any class ever served another in the history of the world." Charlotte's *Africo-American Presbyterian* concurred, asserting that the bishop's letter "hit the nail on the head" and that he "put the case straight. It should be read by our white fellow citizens."[48]

Although the better class of blacks optimistically waited for their white counterparts to come to their aid to defeat the amendment, the white middle class demonstrated no willingness to do so. They had heard the black better class call for the division of the vote periodically through the 1890s but had seen little concrete change. In a letter to the *Observer*, "Northern Democrat" from nearby Iredell County scoffed at Bishop Hood's suggestions and described incidents of violence and intimidation perpetrated by black Republicans against blacks who dared vote the Democratic ticket. "I suppose this is the easy road which the bishop proposes for the colored man to travel in enjoying the privilege of voting the Democratic ticket and this is about the way the average one would be treated if he dares leave the Republican party," he jeered. As to Hood's suggestion that blacks be invited to participate in the Democratic party and have a say in its affairs, the writer contended that "the mere mention of it under past experience is enough to turn one's stomach."[49]

Even more importantly, many of the "white friends" of Charlotte's black better class, who had aided them in the 1880s and early 1890s, had passed from the scene to be replaced by their far less sympathetic sons and daughters. The younger generation had experienced the frustrations of fusionist rule and had in 1898 "redeemed" the state in the name of their fathers. Many of the new generation that came of age in the 1890s had not participated in the class-based interracial movements of the 1880s. Moreover, they were well versed in the new theories of Social Darwinism and convinced of the scientific irrefutability of white supremacy. As a result, they dismissed the entire black race as inferior; unlike their parents' generation, they failed to recognize class distinctions in the black community. Finally, the white middle class viewed disfranchisement as the key to political and social reform and, as a result, threw its weight behind the amendment.

As the black better class formulated a strategy to defuse disfranchisement, the state legislature began to discuss a separate railroad car law for North Carolina. Although the railroads fought Jim Crow legislation, contending that "there was neither necessity or demand for separate cars," the *Raleigh News and Observer* insisted that "almost unanimous public sentiment" favored Jim Crow legislation. Also, despite the fact that the impending bill seems to have sparked little debate among Charlotte's white citizenry, the *Observer* concurred that "the popular demand for separate car legislation is unanimous."[50]

As the Democratic legislature fought over the details of the bill, the black better class denounced the legislation. Rather than oppose it on the basis of racial discrimination, they condemned the bill chiefly on the grounds that it did not take into account class differences among blacks. Bishop George W. Clinton explained his opposition to the bill in a letter to Mecklenburg state senator Frank I. Osborne and Representative Heriot Clarkson. Clinton wrote that "my chief objections to it . . . are that it puts all Negroes on the same level, regardless of behavior and other considerations," and that it "is founded on an unjust as well as unreasonable prejudice." Similarly, the Reverend L. S. Flag of Asheville wrote to the *Observer*, "What inducement can the mental and moral educators of our race hold out to our youth when the culture and refinement of the State treat us all alike? . . . I know that the men who represent the great state of North Carolina can enact a law without discriminating against a lady or gentleman on account of color." Moreover, like Bishop Hood and his supporters in their strategy to prevent disfranchisement, the minister appealed to the white better class to come to the aid of their black counterparts. "Surely the men who have befriended us in the past will not, because of the conduct of irresponsible persons, enact a law that will have a tendency to crush the self-respect of those among us who are endeavoring to rise to genteel manhood and true womanhood." Despite these appeals, the state Senate passed the Jim Crow railroad bill on 1 March 1899, a few weeks after the House approved the measure; the bill went into effect that spring.[51]

The Jim Crow railroad law dealt a hard blow to the black better class and reflected how far their concepts of class and those of their white counterparts had diverged by the late 1890s. The black better class had believed that class status, once earned, could not be denied, that achievement would secure their status. As the children of Reconstruction, they had absorbed aphorisms about hard work, success, and respect from their Freedmen's Bureau teachers. Their experiences in the 1880s and 1890s had led them to believe that they could achieve the respect of their white counterparts, who had sought them out—and had granted them recognition—to work in tandem with them for prohibition and other social reforms. Convinced that education, moral propriety, and property ownership would win them the respect of white society, the black better class learned instead that few whites in 1899, even the better class with whom they still identified, made distinctions among blacks, that the current generation would never grant them equality—regardless of their accomplishments.

The black better class lashed out in anger and frustration at the Jim Crow legislation, particularly because it lumped all blacks, regardless of class, into a single category. J. W. Smith denounced the Jim Crow cars as an attempt "to humiliate the Negroes, especially the educated ones." The promise to give equal accommodations to black passengers "is the most consummate sham and hypocritical subterfuge ever practiced upon a wronged people." Smith explained that "we have no objection to being separated from white people if they will place colored ladies and gentlemen in a coach where they can be protected against white and black roughs alike, but we do protest, and will never be content to be forced to mingle and compelled to ride among and next door to the lowest element of both races while fare is exacted for first class accommodations."[52]

Stung by the Jim Crow law, the black better class continued their battle against disfranchisement. The strategy to divide the black vote to circumvent disfranchisement received a boost when AMEZ bishop Alexander Walters of New Jersey, president of the National Afro-American Council, advocated the tactic. The National Afro-American Council had succeeded the National Afro-American League, founded in 1890 by newspaper editor T. Thomas Fortune. Fortune originally conceived the league as a vehicle for black organization and agitation for the protection of blacks' rights. Fortune even insisted that blacks be prepared to participate in revolution, if necessary, to safeguard their rights. The league disintegrated only a few years after its founding, but Bishop Walters resurrected it as the National Afro-American Council in 1898, in the wake of the Wilmington riot, to address degenerating race relations in the United States.[53]

Several members of Charlotte's black better class belonged to the council, including George Clinton and J. W. Smith, and they heeded Walters's advice. In the aftermath of Wilmington and threatened disfranchisement legislation, Walters advised conciliation between blacks and whites in the South—a far cry from the more militant stance taken by Fortune in 1890. Yet, unlike Booker T. Washington, Walters insisted that blacks exercise their right to vote and play an active part in the political process—even as Democrats if necessary; they should "make friends with the ruling classes of the South by voting the Democratic ticket, especially where they are invited to do so." Charlotte's J. W. Smith wholeheartedly agreed with Walters's advice, claiming, "Southern state after Southern state is rapidly disfranchising the Negroes because they won't divide their vote, and unless the Negroes soon see the advantage it will be to them from a division of their forces and vote they will soon have no vote to divide."[54]

Advocates of disfranchisement, however, ridiculed the strategy of the black better class. The *Observer* asserted that although the advice was "eminently true and sensible," it "comes now too late" since "Southern whites have become thoroughly tired of their biennial contests with this solid mass of ignorance." The newspaper concluded that "the case of the negro as a voter is now irremediable, except as by education he qualifies for the franchise."[55]

In response, Walters assured Charlotte's white skeptics that "the enlightened negro stands at the threshold of the door offering his aid to the dominant party of the South, which means future peace and prosperity for the Southland." Unconvinced, the *Observer* replied, "The negro has voted uniformly for bad government and the conditions which he has brought are intolerable. There is nothing left the white man but to disfranchise him or move out."[56]

In addition to calling for a division of the vote, the black better class insisted that even if the disfranchisement amendment passed, it would be struck down by the Supreme Court. Their confidence in the federal government was rooted in their generational experience as the children of Reconstruction. Even though the national Republican party had abandoned the cause of southern blacks after 1877, the black better class remained adamant in their faith in the inviolability of the Fourteenth and Fifteenth amendments; the federal courts, they believed, would surely defend the sanctity of the Constitution. Moreover, in 1900 southern blacks seemed to have a more sympathetic president than they had had for some time. William McKinley had been elected to the presidency in 1896 with the general support of black voters, who believed he represented, in the words of one black newspaper, a return to "an old time, rock-ribbed, dyed in the wool Republican administration." Soon after taking office, McKinley demonstrated his support for blacks by naming African Americans to several highly visible posts in the federal government. He had even appointed Charlotte's Dr. J. T. Williams as consul to Sierra Leone in 1898, concrete proof to Charlotte's black citizenry that McKinley was a friend of the race.[57]

Charlotte lawyer J. S. Leary articulated his faith in the federal government in an appeal to his concerned compatriots. Admitting that he had "little doubt" that the amendment would be ratified by the state's voters, he nonetheless called upon black North Carolinians in the *Star of Zion* to "not give up hope. The end is not yet. The Supreme Court of the United States will be the final arbiter in this matter." The Fourteenth and Fifteenth amendments protected the rights of black voters, Leary insisted. "The Negro's hope is in the paramount organic law of the land, and his vindication will be in his having the manliness to bring the matter to the attention of the courts."[58]

Although some members of the black better class appeared confident that justice would prevail, a committee of the National Afro-American Council, which included George Clinton and J. W. Smith, called upon "every member of our race, man, woman and child," to observe a day of fasting and prayer on 2 June 1899. The council summoned all ministers "to crowd their churches in sunrise devotion on the following Sabbath (June 4th) for special song, prayer and remarks in keeping with the occasion" and asked ministers to "deliver a sermon upon the duties of the hour."[59]

Despite appeals for divine intervention, tension between the races worsened as Democrats officially launched the campaign for the ratification of the disfranchisement amendment in February 1900. Charles Aycock officially opened the crusade in Mecklenburg with a speech at the courthouse on 19 February 1900. He reiterated the dire need for the amendment, claiming that fusionists had "inflamed decent public sentiment" and had "forced law-abiding citizens to depend on rifles for protection." He also assured his listeners of the constitutionality of the amendment. As Charlotte mayor J. D. McCall distributed "white-supremacy" buttons, Aycock "was told by the many people that crowded around him to shake his hand that he had made one of the best political speeches ever heard in this county."[60]

Local Democrats wasted little time in organizing for the upcoming August election in which voters would also be asked to elect state officers and representatives, including governor. A few days after Aycock's speech, local party leaders announced that Democratic clubs would be formed in every township in the county. "The general sentiment in Mecklenburg," the *Observer* remarked, "seems to be that the coming election means the greatest political struggle ever known in this State and that it is in white men to stand by white supremacy."[61]

The next month Democrats formed the Mecklenburg White Supremacy Club, whose executive committee consisted of Mayor McCall, W. C. Dowd, and Heriot Clarkson. The club's charter, drenched in Social Darwinism, referred to "our sturdy ancestors" who had fought for "the liberty and freedom of this country" while "the ancestors of the negro were in the state of savagery in the wilds of Africa." Although blacks had been "Christianized and civilized to some extent by the Southern white men," they had obtained the ballot "by force of arms and the misfortune of war . . . contrary to nature." The club, "believing that it is best for both races, whom Providence created, not equal, that the white man shall rule this land," adopted a constitution that declared its aim and object "to aid in maintaining white supremacy and white labor in North Carolina and to carry the constitutional amendment."[62]

The club's vow to uphold the sanctity of white labor in the South was likely aimed at gaining the support of Charlotte's cotton mill workers, a significant and unpredictable voting bloc. Given the high stakes in the election of 1900, Democratic officials did all they could to insure that mill workers would vote for their party. By July 1900 Democratic leaders had formed white-supremacy clubs at the Victor, Atherton, and Gingham mills, at which prominent Charlotte citizens exhorted mill workers to be loyal to their race. Typical was Robert Gadd's address to the workers at the Atherton Mill in April 1900. Gadd told the workers that "any white man who votes against the amendment makes a candid acknowledgement that he prefers the African to the Anglo-Saxon and makes it apparent that he is no better than a negro." He appealed to "every iota of manhood and maternal love" to rid the state of the threat of black domination, "this desperate and hideous monster." Likewise, thirty-year-old lawyer Brevard Nixon presented Social Darwinism to workers at the Louise Mill, claiming that "white supremacy is as old as history" and "founded on the native superiority of the white race." Nixon argued that "science, history, and the common observation of mankind prove the illimitable inferiority of the negro race."[63]

While Young Democrats organized white-supremacy clubs and targeted mill workers for support, they also enlisted their spouses in the fight for the disfranchisement amendment. In the spring and summer of 1900, middle-class women, as well as a handful of their elite sisters, substituted disfranchisement for the more traditional causes they had pursued during the decade. Putting aside their religious work among the town's poor and their hosting of fashionable parties, women of both the middle class and the elite promoted the disfranchisement crusade. In April 1900 the White Supremacy Club asked "the ladies" to "contribute to the success" of a Democratic rally by donating decorations and arranging for children from the graded school to sing at the gathering. The club assured the women that "the speeches will be interesting and quite clean." Among the women who responded to the appeal were middle-class women such as Mrs. F. M. Shannonhouse and Mrs. I. W. Faison, a physician's spouse, as well as a few members of the industrial elite, such as the wife of merchant and mill investor H. Baruch.[64]

White women remained active throughout the course of the amendment campaign—albeit in a supporting role. In August 1900 the ladies prepared barbecue for 5,000 people at a massive Democratic rally held just days before the election. In addition to the culinary labor that they supplied, their presence endorsed the Democrats' claims that the disfranchisement amendment would help protect white womanhood from the threat of blacks. By their attendance at disfranchisement rallies, white women of the middle class and the elite gave their blessing to the racial politics of their men.[65]

Although cautioning Democratic speakers against inciting "unnecessary violence" in their discussion of the amendment, the *Observer* played a key role in promulgating racial tension in Charlotte to aid the passage of the amendment. Throughout the spring and summer of 1900, the *Observer* printed articles that allegedly proved the scientific basis of white supremacy and the inferiority of the black race. Especially popular was an address by Charlotte native Dr. Paul Barringer of the University of Virginia, who contended that scientific observation confirmed that the black race was degenerating, both physically and morally. "In every part of the South," he claimed, "it is the opinion of every man of unbiased mind that the second generation is infinitely worse than the first."[66]

Barringer's "scientific opinion" demonstrated dramatically the chasm separating his generation from that of his father. Barringer's father, Civil War general Rufus Barringer, had been a longtime advocate of the freedpeople of Charlotte and Mecklenburg, a tenacious Republican who helped found the party in the county and relentlessly fought for black civil rights during Reconstruction (see chapter 2).

The Republican and Populist parties offered little opposition to the campaign conducted by the *Observer*, although the black press denounced the race-baiting of the newspaper. "The Democratic editorials in the daily and weekly news-papers," noted the *Star of Zion*, "might be condensed into this shape without any injustice to the editors: We got along very well with the Negro as a servant and an inferior being, but we have no use for him as voter and office holder."[67]

It was soon clear that blacks could not count on much help from either local Republicans or Populists since both parties were nearly decimated by the 1898 white-supremacy debacle. In April 1900 the county Republican convention was "lily-white," without a single black delegate, the result of both the disillusion-ment of black voters with the party and the conscious effort of Republican leaders to shed their party's image as the "Negro party." Although it denounced the proposed amendment "as a high-handed outrage," the Republican party was without black support and therefore helplessly impaired. Although Republicans and Populists fused for a fourth time in 1900, presenting a combined slate of state and local candidates, fusion, in the view of the *Observer*, was "practically an admission of the hopelessness of the fight against the amendment." The *Observer* noted, "The Republicans simply find they cannot hold the Populists in line against the wave of white supremacy."[68]

As the disfranchisement campaign got into gear, Charlotte's black better class braced for the onslaught. Responding to Bishop Hood's warning in February that "when you disfranchise a man you reduce him to slavery of the worst type," a number of the state's black leaders, including Charlotte ministers G. L. Blackwell and George C. Clement of the AME Zion Publishing House, orga-nized a conference in nearby Salisbury. The participants called for a return to harmonious race relations in the state and appealed "to the thinking element of the white race of the State, irrespective of past or present party affiliation to unite with those who oppose the proposed constitutional amendment, and use their best influence to defeat this unjust measure." While calling for the defeat of the amendment, the conference implored blacks to maintain standards of decorum, "to excite no animosities or bitter prejudices, which would redound to our utter discomfiture."[69]

Others reiterated the call for moderation and decorum while attacking un-scrupulous politicians and their followers, summoning the black better class to provide leadership in the time of crisis through moral suasion. In the *Star of Zion*, J. W. Smith echoed sentiments about politics that the black better class first articulated in the 1880s. He argued that in order to free citizens from the grasp of "unscrupulous politicians," the "first great thing to be done is to create a non-partisan public sentiment which will condemn wrong." He continued, "Then we shall be ready for statutes and constitutional amendments which will prove effective remedies against these evils." The law "would then become, as it should be, the mighty weapon with which the loyal and upright citizen is armed for the enforcement of his own rights and security of government."[70]

Although the black better class attempted to take the moral high ground to deflect the amendment, no such sentiment existed among their white counterparts. Instead, white Democrats escalated their white-supremacy tactics, appealing to the lowest common denominator among whites of all classes, papering over class differences through appeals to white solidarity. Immediately preceding the election, Democrats held an immense rally and parade in the streets of Charlotte, organized by Heriot Clarkson as chief marshal. A large contingent of Young Democrats served as assistant marshals, representing in a vivid way the ascension of a new generation of political leadership with a strikingly different attitude toward blacks than their parents had displayed. J. Frank Wilkes, the son of social reformer Jane Wilkes, who had founded Charlotte's black Good Samaritan Hospital in the late 1880s, served as an assistant to Clarkson. Osmond Barringer, the son of Republican and black patron Rufus Barringer, also assisted Clarkson.[71]

According to the *Observer*, the rally "represented the gathering and unity in principle of the white Democracy in Mecklenburg." The Young Democrats paid homage to well-known older politicians. Former Populist senator J. B. Alexander, former Allianceman and Democratic representative Sydenham Alexander, and lawyer Hamilton Jones led the parade. As in the 1898 white-supremacy campaign, the Young Democrats identified the disfranchisement campaign with the Redemption battles of their fathers. Wearing the symbol of white supremacy that harkened back to the days of Reconstruction, contingents of Red Shirts, representing "the best men" from each voting district, followed the local dignitaries and carried white-supremacy banners; the Pineville unit's standard read "Down with Nigger Rule." The parade wound its way to Latta Park, where thousands of listeners heard former Confederate general and race-baiting senator Matt Ransom give a speech in which he claimed that the election came down to "whether ignorant, black people, or the fathers and heads of families—the men who followed Lee at Gettysburg, Cold Harbor— . . . shall rule." After several more speeches, the crowd adjourned for barbecue prepared by the ladies. Ransom's reference to the Civil War undoubtedly stirred the hearts of the Young Democrats, who saw in the disfranchisement campaign their chance to fight a war in the name of white southern honor.[72]

The next day, voters in Mecklenburg, along with their counterparts across North Carolina, overwhelmingly approved the disfranchisement amendment. In addition, Democrats in Mecklenburg won by the largest majority since fusion and helped elect Democrat Charles B. Aycock governor, along with a Democratic state legislature. According to the *Observer*, Republicans and Populists "recognized the hopelessness of the contest and made no fight to speak of." Despite J. W. Smith's urgings in the *Star of Zion* that "the Negro who neglects his political duty at this crisis in history deserves to be disfranchised," the black turnout "was exceedingly light in all precincts," according to the *Observer*. The Red Shirt rally the day before the election undoubtedly helped keep blacks at home on election day.[73]

The *Observer* hailed the election as "one of the greatest days that ever dawned upon North Carolina." Not only would the disfranchisement amendment "be a stimulus to education," but also "disfranchised negroes will be better treated by the white people and better protected than ever before." As Charlotte's white citizens reveled in victory, blacks attempted to make sense of the devastating blow. J. W. Smith pleaded with his disheartened compatriots: "Let the Negro race of North Carolina not grow discouraged. God is still on the throne; and if we will draw nigh to Him, he will draw nigh to us and make 'all things work together for good to them that love the Lord.'" The black character would be tempered by the fire of disfranchisement, he suggested. "Every race of people that amounts to any thing to-day came up through severe conflict and much oppression," contended Smith. "As black people we have seen darker days than we see today."[74]

Similarly, John Dancy sounded a note of optimism in the grim aftermath of the passage of the disfranchisement amendment. In the *AME Zion Quarterly Review*, Dancy wrote that "the Negro feels relieved after the severe tension to which he has been subjected for many months." Moreover, "he feels that his friends are still in possession of the National Government." Again reflecting the faith of his generation in the federal government, forged in the years of Reconstruction and encouraged by the McKinley administration, Dancy called for federal authorities to intervene and settle the question of the franchise "definitely once for all." The black community should also circumvent the amendment by "turning every church room, social hall, and gathering place, of whatever character, into a school room for young people in the day, and the fathers at night, to be taught to read, write, and spell." He concluded that "the only hope for our future is along the lines of wise counsel and conservatism."[75]

The events of 1900 would force the black better class to reconsider their philosophy of race progress. As blacks struggled to make sense of the new state of affairs, the white middle class, no longer distracted by race-based politics and the threat of fusion, would fashion its own new ethos that centered around progressive politics and social reform. The Jim Crow world of the early twentieth century again forced the races into separate spheres, and the fluidity of race and class relations evidenced in the 1880s and early 1890s would not be replicated for many years to come.

IN THE WAKE OF
DISFRANCHISEMENT
AND JIM CROW

In the spring of 1905, Dr. J. T. Williams of Charlotte wrote his close friend, journalist W. C. Smith, from Sierra Leone. Williams, appointed in 1898 by President William McKinley as consul to the West African nation, anxiously kept in close contact with Smith about the worsening race relations in his hometown and state. Five years after the passage of the disfranchisement amendment, Williams offered advice to his colleague in Charlotte—and other members of the black better class—as they attempted to regroup in the face of the loss of their civil rights and persistent racial animosity. He remarked that his post in Sierra Leone had offered him the opportunity to learn more about commerce and observed that "the more I see of it the more thoroughly I am convinced that it is what we in the States need to give us power." He continued, "It appears that though late, we as a race are beginning to learn the fact from a bitter past experience that money will accomplish what legislation will not."[1]

Many of Williams's friends and acquaintances in Charlotte had reached the same conclusion by 1905. Legislation, even in the form of the Fourteenth and Fifteenth amendments to the Constitution, had not been enough to guarantee full citizenship rights to African Americans in North Carolina or the South. With black political participation repressed by the 1900 voting amendment in North Carolina, Williams and other members of the black better class once again shifted their strategy of promoting race progress, downplaying the importance of politics and stressing economic advancement instead, much as they had in the

1880s. The shift came, however, only after white politicians pushed them out of the political sphere entirely.

As the black better class and the white middle class restructured their activities and redefined their relationship in the years following disfranchisement, race relations in Charlotte worsened. Although disfranchisement defused the volatility of New South politics, race relations after 1900 remained explosive as many whites responded with alarm to what they saw as the hopeless regression of the black race. Some white Charlotteans began to demand more segregation of blacks, including in recreational facilities and streetcars. Consequently, the years from 1900 to 1910 saw the institution of a rigid Jim Crow system of racial segregation that would stand firm for the next half century.

• • • • • • •

In the immediate aftermath of the passage of North Carolina's disfranchisement amendment, J. W. Smith filled the columns of the *Star of Zion* with aphorisms and examples of race progress intended to provide encouragement to his readers and place the most recent crises in a larger historical and theological context. "The Lord is faithful," insisted Smith. "At times when it seems that He has deserted us He has simply gone before to prepare the way for us." Smith also published a weekly column, entitled "The Negro Is Rising," that provided examples of race progress from across the country. Two months after the passage of the disfranchisement amendment, Smith proudly drew on a local example of black economic advancement. "Despite the disfranchisement of Negroes," he wrote, "Mr. E. D. Latta, owner of houses, the electric lights and streetcars of Charlotte, North Carolina, has 25 or 30 Negroes in said city erecting four large wholesale brick stores, two stories high . . . and not a white man bossing them. It is a beautiful sight," asserted Smith, "and shows Negro efficiency."[2]

Smith's attempt to rally the black better class in the wake of disfranchisement seemed especially urgent given the climate of race relations in North Carolina after 1900. Disfranchisement did little to ease tensions between the races; instead, the poisonous atmosphere generated by the race-baiting political campaigns of 1898 and 1900 persisted throughout the first decade of the century. Concerned white citizens incessantly discussed the "Negro Problem" as "scientific" theories purporting the degeneration of the black race, introduced during the political campaigns of the late 1890s, gained wide popular acceptance. "Look where you may," a worried resident of Charlotte wrote to the *Charlotte Observer* in 1903, "you cannot avoid facing the race question. The negro as an unsolved problem faces us daily." Local courtrooms brimmed with black defendants, creating "a small sea of black faces" as "the colored man seems to be literally breaking loose from his former moorings." White residents feared that many blacks were "running amuck," causing local men to purchase "revolvers for their women folks" and forcing husbands to "no longer stay away from home at night."[3]

Not only did whites perceive blacks as increasingly criminal, but they also mourned the passing of the docile "old-time Negro." A letter to the *Observer* lamented the decline of the "old-time Negro preacher," the uneducated minister "of the days befo' de war," as the *Observer* put it, who was "rapidly passing away." The newspaper reported the death of a well-known "black Mammy" who had been born a slave of the Carson family and had remained in their employment after the war. The *Observer* praised her simplicity and devotion and commented sadly and nostalgically that the "aged negro who was both servant and friend of the white man is seen infrequently."[4]

Replacing the "old-time Negro" was the "new Negro." According to white critics, "new Negroes" did not know their place and constantly challenged the social mores of New South society. One white townsman penned a letter concerning what he considered the irritating habit of younger blacks to "mister" themselves. "A young colored woman speaks of her husband as 'mister' and the younger generation of the race now use the term in introductions," he complained. "Ten years from now there will not be any negro 'Uncles'" since "the antebellum type colored man" will have passed from the scene. H. E. C. Bryant, whose race-baiting articles in the *Observer* during the 1898 white-supremacy campaign made him a minor celebrity in North Carolina, contended that "the young negro is indifferent, unreliable, untrained, and indolent."[5]

White citizens of Charlotte cited the alleged indolence of blacks as the reason for a growing shortage of black labor in their town. J. W. Wadsworth, owner of the city's premier livery stable, complained that "you've just got to scour the town to get servants. And then they will refuse to work for less than fifteen cents an hour." Moreover, black workers "quit because of a cross look," resulting in "almost an entirely new force of negroes every week." Wadsworth griped, "Never in all our experience have we had such an experience with negroes."[6]

In the wake of disfranchisement, emigration from North Carolina became an increasingly attractive course of action for many of the state's blacks. Not only did the Tarheel State lose prominent black residents, such as former congressman George H. White, who left the state permanently in 1900, but North Carolina and Mecklenburg also lost numerous artisans and laborers. Although out-migration was not new in 1900, to white observers in Charlotte it seemed especially acute. Between 1900 and 1910, as Charlotte's population more than doubled, the city's black population continued to grow significantly, by 64 percent. But Mecklenburg's black population stagnated even as the county's overall population grew by over 20 percent. Between 1890 and 1900, the county's black population increased by 22 percent, but it grew by only 7 percent between 1900 and 1910 and in the next decade increased by only 5 percent.[7]

Soon after the passage of the disfranchisement amendment in August 1900, the *Observer* noted the black exodus with concern. "The Negro is a failure as a voter," the *Observer* argued, "but he has his uses as a farm laborer," concluding that for economic reasons alone "it is suicidal to drive them, by bad treatment, out of the State." Despite this warning, by 1903 the newspaper reported that white farmers in the county were suffering severe labor shortages and that the black exodus was "beginning to effect the people in the city," who had to pay a hefty increase in wages. The press also criticized "good colored people who were doing well here" but "who had listened to the stories of big wages and easy life in the North and took the bait." Despite their seeming hatred for the "degenerate" black race, white citizens of Charlotte decried the loss of cheap black labor, claiming that the South was the "natural home of the Negro" and that out-migrating blacks were "leaving the best friends they ever had to locate among a people of whom they know nothing and who know nothing of them."[8]

Amazed by the assertions in the white press, J. W. Smith pointed out that it was no mystery to the state's blacks why many felt the need to flee North Carolina. "When Negroes leave a place by the wholesale, there must be some reasons for it," he explained in the *Star of Zion*. "The bitter race feelings which the politicians worked up in the campaigns of 1898 and 1900 has [*sic*] much to do with the exodus." Although Smith agreed that the South "is naturally the home of the black man," he pointed out that southern states had deprived "him of his suffrage, thrust upon him jim crow cars and lynch him without giving him a chance to face a judge and jury to disprove his guilt." As a result, blacks relocated to "sections of this country where at least citizens' and God given rights are not wholly deprived them." Smith concluded, "The world is wide; trains are running in every direction, and there are places where the honest and industrious Negro can and will go to be a man and not a beast of burden."[9]

Despite encouraging blacks to migrate in the wake of disfranchisement, Smith and many members of the black better class did not passively acquiesce to the political and racial climate of North Carolina. Instead, they sought ways to challenge the voting amendment, to retain some semblance of a political voice, and to improve race relations. The strategy of Charlotte's black better class in the immediate aftermath of disfranchisement placed them in a broad middle ground between Booker T. Washington and the militant "anti-Bookerites" who challenged Washington's strategy. Rejecting both extremes—quiescence and overt agitation—leaders of the black better class called on blacks simply to work within existing political and legal channels to challenge disfranchisement.[10]

Since the amendment did not go into effect until 1902, Smith urged his readers in the fall of 1900 to exercise their right to vote and to support Republican McKinley's bid for reelection against Democrat William Jennings Bryan. McKinley had proven himself a friend of the race by appointing many blacks to government positions, he argued, and deserved the support of black voters. In addition, the editor confidently contended, "Before the close of President McKinley's second administration, those States that don't care to obey the fifteenth amendment of the United States Constitution but have disfranchised thousands of illiterate black voters but not a single white voter will either have to make their amendment apply to both races alike or have their representation cut down in Congress."[11]

Bishop George W. Clinton, who had in the past only ambivalently supported black political participation, joined Smith in urging support for McKinley. The future of black citizenship, he contended, depended on McKinley's election. Clinton argued that the 1900 presidential election "is one of the most important since the election of Lincoln." Although Lincoln's election "gave us the amended constitution, the emancipation and citizenship for the American Negro . . . upon the election of McKinley depends the maintenance of the amended constitution and the citizenship of the Negro." A vote for Bryan, argued Clinton, was a vote for racial demagoguery, "a vote for Tillmanism, for North Carolina's, South Carolina's, Mississippi's and Louisiana's nullification of the three sacred amendments to the federal constitution and the continued degradation of the Negro, to say nothing about the turning back of the hands on the dial plate of American progress for years to come."[12]

Besides counseling blacks to vote, leaders of the black better class championed the fight against disfranchisement through legal channels. In the fall of 1900 Bishop Alexander Walters of the National Afro-American Council, of which Bishop Clinton served on the advisory council, promised that his organization would contest southern disfranchisement amendments all the way to the U.S. Supreme Court if necessary. J. W. Smith appealed to his readers to back the legal efforts of the council. He implored, "Let every Negro man, woman and child in this country and especially in those states where their race is disfranchised contribute a dollar, more or less, for the maintenance of our political rights." The editor warned with foreboding of the high stakes involved. "If the fifteenth amendment can be trampled under foot with impunity, so can the thirteenth and fourteenth amendments," he cautioned. "If we as a race do not wake up and contend for our rights we will soon be in slavery again, or we will have no rights that a white man is bound to respect."[13]

Despite the hopes that Charlotte's black better class placed in the McKinley administration, neither McKinley nor his successor, Theodore Roosevelt, demonstrated interest in aiding the plight of the South's disfranchised voters. More concerned with maintaining sectional goodwill and encouraging the fledgling "lily-white" Republican party in the South, McKinley and Roosevelt turned a deaf ear to the appeals of disfranchised southern blacks. Without the support of the Republican administration, legal challenges to the amendment faltered. Ignored by the federal government, blacks were also increasingly pushed to the periphery of political affairs in Charlotte and North Carolina—all in the name of "progress."[14]

Beginning in 1901, Charlotte's Young Democrats, led by Heriot Clarkson, began a campaign to weaken black political influence even before the disfranchisement amendment dealt its death blow in 1902. Clarkson organized a 1901 campaign to elect forty-two-year-old land developer Peter Marshall Brown as mayor on a platform of social reform. Brown's supporters were confident that their candidate's program would appeal to many white voters but feared that black voters, who had demonstrated a hostility to reform issues in the past—such as prohibition—might jeopardize a Brown victory.

As a result, Clarkson drafted two bills, each of which aimed at eliminating the black vote and political influence a full year before the state disfranchisement amendment went into effect. The first bill, known as the Charlotte Election Bill, was a hefty package of election "reforms"—containing thirty-four sections— that required a secret Australian ballot system. To eliminate illiterate black voters—but not white—the bill allowed an election judge to "prepare" the ballots of those who could not read or write. Since election judges were all Democrats after 1898, the law virtually guaranteed that no black Republican voters would be aided in using the secret ballot. To dilute black representation on the Board of Aldermen, the bill increased the number of aldermen from the First and Fourth wards from three to five, "owing to the increase in white population in those wards," while maintaining three aldermen in the Second and Third wards, "the Negro wards." The second bill called for a "registered primary" in Mecklenburg County. Touted by southern progressives such as Clarkson as a democratic improvement over party conventions to nominate candidates, the white primary limited participation to white voters only. The bill was drafted, in Clarkson's words, so that "white voters can have a free ballot and a fair count."[15]

The voting bills epitomized white southern progressivism and signaled a new era in municipal politics, which had been gestating throughout the 1890s.

Notably, white supremacy informed—and limited—progressive reform initiated by whites in the South. Advocates of the bills stressed their democratic features, contending that they would reduce fraud in elections, guarantee white supremacy, and generally improve social harmony in their city. The secret ballot, Clarkson assured white voters, would guarantee the rule of "the descendants of the patriots of the Revolution—the Anglo-Saxon," rather than "the descendants of men, many of whom were savages in the wilds of Africa when the Revolution was in progress." The bills were "fair to the white man and not unfair to the negro" and were "in the interest of all the people in the city of Charlotte."[16]

In the spring of 1901 Clarkson, accompanied by five prominent local citizens, went to Raleigh to urge passage of the bills in the state legislature, maintaining that the secret ballot and the white primary prevented "designing men" from "colonizing negroes" and prohibited "buying an election." He concluded, "I believe it will save us from bitterness and strife, and bring peace, harmony and good feeling." The state legislature agreed and approved the Charlotte Election Law and the primary bill, the first of their kind in North Carolina.[17]

The election legislation, sponsored by Charlotte's Young Democrats, set off a flurry of controversy in the Democratic party during the mayoral primary. Brown's opponent, Dr. R. J. Brevard, criticized the legislation and what he viewed as the excessive tactics of the Young Democrats. Brevard, who at age fifty-three was older than his opponents, had been elected mayor in 1891 and left office in 1895, just as the Young Democrats began to assert themselves in the party. Brevard represented the older, passing generation of political leadership in Charlotte, a generation far more moderate than the fiery Young Democrat progressives.[18]

Brevard explained that he agreed with Brown and the Young Democrats on the importance of maintaining white supremacy. Yet he feared that the secret ballot system would "operate to disfranchise all unlettered white men who did not want to ask the judges to mark their ballots" and would keep "numbers of good men" from going to the polls because "they would not admit in public their inability to read." Brevard also charged that Clarkson and his compatriots had railroaded the laws through the legislature "without due notice to the citizens of Charlotte."[19]

Brown repudiated Brevard's claims and stated bluntly that the election law would not hurt white voters but aimed to "keep out the negroes who have no right to vote. No white man will lose his vote," Brown promised. He even offered "$100 to any white man who is deprived of his right to vote on account of the fact that he cannot read or write" under the Charlotte Election Law. Brown also defended the election law as a necessary means to enforce white supremacy before the disfranchisement amendment went into effect. Since "the people of North Carolina cannot possibly reap the benefits of the constitutional amendment before the 1st day of January, 1902 . . . the negro vote is calculated to play as important a part in deciding the next municipal contest as it has in times past." Without the election law, white supremacy could easily be threatened.[20]

Despite the controversy of the election law, Brown and the Young Democrats prevailed. Charlotte held its first white primary on 9 April 1901, which effectively eliminated black influence in municipal elections, guaranteeing the white supremacy that the Young Democrats so rabidly sought. Moreover, it introduced the secret ballot to city elections, undoubtedly disfranchising many illiterate white voters, as R. J. Brevard had predicted. Finally, P. M. Brown triumphed over his older, more experienced opponent, guaranteeing that the Young Democrats would shape Charlotte's political agenda in the first years of the century.[21]

As Charlotte's election law disfranchised most of the city's black voters in 1901, North Carolina's Republican party took steps the next year to further weaken any black political influence that remained after disfranchisement. In an attempt to expunge, once and for all, its reputation as the "black man's party," Republican leaders launched another "lily-white" crusade, as they had during the campaign for ratification of the suffrage amendment in 1900. In September 1902, at the state convention in Greensboro, Republican leaders refused to seat any black delegates, including former congressmen Henry P. Cheatham and James O'Hara. In a humiliating display, white delegates expelled their black counterparts to the tune of a song that included the lyrics, "It's better to be a white man, Than a coon, coon, coon." In the *Star of Zion*, J. W. Smith condemned the white delegates' actions as "flagrant and outrageous; and he who does not know this is an ignoramus, and he who cannot see it is a blind ass."[22]

The party's actions, Smith pointed out, were ominous. Refusal to recognize black delegates "means that the white Republicans of North Carolina are willing to accept as constitutional, without testing it in court, the infamous amendment which disfranchises illiterate Negro votes, but not illiterate white voters." Moreover, the party demonstrated its willingness to sacrifice the remaining eligible black voters as a ploy to draw recruits from the Democratic party. Smith charged that the Republican leadership had cynically and irrevocably turned "its back upon the principles advocated by Lincoln, Grant, Sumner, Reed and others." He angrily predicted that when the Republicans realized that few Democrats would abandon their party for the GOP, the Republican party "will, with bland smiles and honeymouths, return like a dog to its vomit." When they do, he claimed, "they will meet with a cold wave; for they will not meet the illiterate Negro voters who will never vote again . . . but 65,000 thinking Negro voters in

North Carolina who can read and write and who, grossly indignant at the perfidy and treachery practiced upon the Negro delegates, will never again until mules shake hands be a slave to any party."[23]

Charlotte and Mecklenburg Republicans also fashioned a new image for their party that had no room for blacks. Mill man George B. Hiss emerged as the new spokesperson for a reinvented Republican party and issued a statement bluntly proclaiming that "there is no negro" in the local party. By the late summer of 1902, at the county convention, the local party pledged its allegiance—with no apparent sense of irony—"to principles of the great Republican party, as taught by Lincoln, Grant, Garfield and McKinley" and endorsed Theodore Roosevelt's domestic and foreign policies. Through the fall of 1902, the Republicans displayed a newfound energy that even surprised their Democratic opponents as they pitched their party on the strength of the nation's prosperous economy.[24]

Some members of the black better class angrily challenged their exclusion from the party of emancipation. J. W. Smith called for the state's remaining eligible black voters to organize and assert their independence from the Republicans. When irate black voters in nearby Salisbury formed the Colored Voters' League of North Carolina and pledged allegiance to no particular party but only to the best interests of their race, Smith praised their efforts and called for the "65,000 intelligent Negro voters in North Carolina who can vote" to form similar leagues in every town in the state. If blacks stood together, they would control "the balance of power" and "command the respectful recognition of all parties in this State." With both the Democratic and Republican parties hostile to black voters, Smith contended, "we must now 'hang together or hang separately.'" The editor concluded, "Knifed by the recent Republican convention, if the Negroes do not show political independence now, but are willing to hang after white Republicans that do not want them, they are a set of fools that ought to be driven to the bottom of the Cape Fear river."[25]

Despite such appeals, the apparent permanence of the disfranchisement amendment and the actions of the state and local Republican parties provoked a rift among blacks over strategy. Like their counterparts across the South and the nation, Charlotte's black better class by 1902 suffered a "divided mind" over the approach African Americans should take regarding the loss of their political rights. With hopes for a peaceful solution rapidly evaporating, the moderate middle ground began to recede; black Americans found themselves choosing between Washington's accommodationist strategy, which would put off political rights well into the future, and the approach of anti-Bookerites, who stressed the non-negotiable nature of political and civil rights and demanded agitation to restore them.[26]

Beginning in 1902, some members of Charlotte's black better class embraced the Washington position, calling on blacks to spurn politics entirely and devote themselves to business instead. Editor Smith noted this shift in October 1902, remarking that "some of our Negro leaders since the enactment of the disfranchisement law and the turning down of the Negroes by lilly [*sic*] white Republicans are advising the Negroes to get out of politics and enter business." Among those who took such a position was Charlotte businessman J. T. Sanders. Echoing Washington, Sanders contended in a letter to the *Star of Zion*, "You may talk about the Negro problem and say all sorts of things about him, but his condition will remain just as it is now until we shall master the principles of business as other business men have done." He continued, "No race in the world has ever succeeded without first learning business and how to do business economically."[27]

Growing support for Washington's strategy provoked an angry response from editor Smith, who vehemently denounced the Washingtonian position and those, like Sanders, who would downplay the importance of political rights. Basic constitutional rights, such as voting, he maintained, could not be bargained away without dire consequences. "It is bad advice," he wrote, "for it means to give up on our rights as citizens." Again, he warned ominously that if blacks "give up the fifteenth amendment to the Constitution of the United States, which gives us the ballot, our political enemies will attempt to force us to give up the thirteenth amendment which sets us free, and the fourteenth which makes us citizens." He exhorted his readers to "not grow indifferent or discouraged to any of our rights" but to "agitate in the newspapers, on the platform, in the pulpit, in the legislative and congressional halls and, if necessary, contend for them in the highest courts of the land until they are granted."[28]

Despite Smith's confidence in the ultimate triumph of justice, his newspaper reported the obstacles faced by even the most conscientious black voters. In October 1902 Smith remarked that "the unconstitutional amendment is working lovely." Not only had it "politically killed the illiterate Negro," but also "some of the registrars acting under its influence are so anxious to disfranchise the Negroes who can read and write that they do not want to register them." Voting officials in Raleigh, he reported, refused to register some blacks who failed to use a hyphen in a compound word. Also, a Rutherford County registrar denied registration to an aspiring black voter who misspelled the word "divided."[29]

The tactics of Democratic registrars, the "lily-white" movement in the Republican party, and black ambivalence about political activity all combined to dampen the enthusiasm of eligible black voters. Moreover, despite appeals from black leaders like Smith who asked the Roosevelt administration to denounce

the Republican "lily-white" movement in the South, by March 1903 the president supported the party strategy. Smith estimated that only 10,000 blacks
registered to vote in the entire state in the election of 1902. And in the municipal
election of 1903, only 51 black voters out of an estimated 300 eligible black
voters, compared to a total of 2,411 white voters, registered to vote in Charlotte.
Local Democrats took delight in the shrinking numbers of black voters. The
Observer smugly remarked in 1902 that " 'beware the colored vote!' "—the cry of
white supremacists and disfranchisers only a few years before—was now "the
funniest statement and the most subtle irony that has ever been heard in this
community." The newspaper claimed that "the negro in Charlotte is the most
maimed, ineffectual voting element in a body politic that has ever existed since
the grant of the magna charta." Even editor Smith, who had heroically attempted
to rally shell-shocked black voters in the wake of disfranchisement and white
primary laws, wearily admitted in the fall of 1903, "The Negro is convinced now
that he must work out his own salvation and not depend upon the white man or
any political party to do it."[30]

No longer a viable political force after 1902, the black better class repeated the
refrain that they had sung since the 1880s, downplaying the importance of
politics while asserting the significance of education, property ownership, morality, and economic advancement as the keys to race progress in the South. In
November 1903 the Reverend C. C. Somerville, pastor of Charlotte's black First
Baptist Church, published a pamphlet entitled "My Brothers" that reiterated the
long-held beliefs of the black better class, advising blacks that they must first
prove themselves to whites before any progress could be made. "When the race
has demonstrated beyond cavil its power to think, its ability to purchase and hold
property, its rights to the highest citizenship, its hatred for crime, its belief in
justice and fair play, its disapproval of vagrancy, its high respect for womanhood,
its ambition to be educated," proclaimed Somerville, "and not until then, let the
impartial historian write its epitaph." Similarly, Biddle student J. A. Thomas
Hazell condemned indolence and stressed the importance of "never-ceasing,
ever-pursuing hard work and unbroken honesty," spelling out twelve rules for
success, including independence, punctuality, politeness, frugality, generosity,
and the conscientious pursuit of a business or trade.[31]

In addition to stressing the traditional values of the black better class, spokespersons continued to emphasize that their class played a critical role in promoting race progress, in "uplifting" the race as a whole. In December 1903 the
Reverend R. S. Rives argued in the *Star of Zion* that southern blacks could
overcome the obstacles of race prejudice if the better class did its best to uplift
the rest of the race. "The world's standard of Negro intelligence and moral

worth is based upon the lowest and most vile of our race," he contended, and "until we recognize the task of lifting up that class to the plains of Christian civilization, we will be held down."[32]

Likewise, in his 1904 Emancipation Day address given before a packed auditorium at Grace Church, Bishop George Clinton argued that "the educated Negro is the balance wheel, yea, the safety valve of the whole situation." Clinton called for blacks to face "the untoward conditions which confront him" with "character, culture, credit, concentration, and courage."[33]

Yet Clinton and likely many other members of the black better class—despite their moderate tone—never advocated Washington's strategy. Although by the time of his Emancipation Day address, Clinton had publicly defended Booker T. Washington against growing attacks by his opponents, his defense of Washington was less an endorsement of the Tuskegean's strategy than a criticism of the harshness of the growing anti-Washington crusade. In 1903, in an essay in *The Souls of Black Folk*, W. E. B. Du Bois spearheaded a severe attack on Washington, criticizing his acceptance of a subordinate position for blacks in the South's political, social, and economic order for the sake of racial harmony. Du Bois's assault helped focus long-standing sentiment against Washington's strategy and represented a resurgence of anti-Bookerite sentiment.[34]

Long active in the national arena, Clinton was well aware of the antagonism that existed toward Washington since his rise to national prominence in 1895. "That men have differed with Mr. Washington in some of his views" came as no surprise to Clinton. But Clinton criticized "a crusade of criticism" perpetrated against Washington by "a few men of the race, some would be leaders." Although Clinton claimed that Washington "believed in his race," he implied that Washington's strategy was only one of a variety of viable approaches to "the Negro question." Washington, argued Clinton, "has done more along *certain lines* to elevate the race than any single man now living." He concluded, "Race discord and opposition to those who are endeavoring in their particular way to strengthen the race do more to hinder race progress than outside influences."[35]

Rather than fully endorse Washington, the black better class retreated to the maxims of an earlier time. Yet spokespersons for the black better class found it necessary to recast some of their ideas to fit the harsh realities of the Jim Crow South. Some suggested that blacks must conceive of rights and even freedom in new ways. Moreover, they placed greater emphasis on preparing the next generation for full civic participation, a shift that indicated that they held little hope of recovering lost civil rights in their own lifetimes.

In November 1903 Dr. J. E. Shepard of Durham, secretary of the International Sunday School Association, addressed a gathering of Charlotte's black

citizens and offered a new definition of citizenship. "To you who are discouraged," he proclaimed, "citizenship is not in constitutions but in the mind.
That man is free and has liberty who can curb passions and evil desires. My
mind, my soul, and my virtue are ever free." Shepard exhorted his listeners, "Let
us teach our children lessons of sobriety and truth, let us live at peace with all
mankind, let us stay in the Southland and work out our destiny. Let the world see
that the negro has recognized the opportunities and responsibilities . . . , that he
has stopped whining and gone to work, that he has stopped suckling and is trying
to eat meat and all will be well."[36]

Similarly, Bishop Clinton intimated that blacks' exercise of political rights
might well be postponed far into the future. It was thus crucial that members of
the black better class prepare their children for the challenges that lay ahead. In
February 1903 Clinton argued that blacks "must exercise much prudence, great
patience, unceasing perseverance and a firm faith in God. If these things be done
and he continues to educate his children, acquire homes and land, improve his
morals and realizes that to be a good Negro is far better than being a bad . . . , his
course will be ever onward and upward. Time will tell what place he shall occupy
as a citizen of this country regardless of section."[37]

· · · · · · ·

As Charlotte's black better class attempted to settle for future rewards, white
Democrats and Republicans vied for control of the city and state. In the first few
years of the decade, the state Democratic party divided when powerful manufacturers and businesspeople within the party ranks, known as Independents—a
group that included Charlotte's D. A. Tompkins—revolted against the party.
Disgusted with the remnants of populism that persisted in the party, particularly
free silver policies, which were embodied in the renomination of Bryan for the
presidency in 1900, Independents ran their own ticket against the Democratic
party in 1902. They had little success, however, and the party ultimately brought
the mavericks back into the fold. Democrats continued to dominate both local
and state elections, despite the Republican party's attempts to refurbish its
image. Racked by internal discord, which weakened its appeal to business
interests, the Republican party remained an anemic challenger to Democratic
rule. By 1902 Democratic hegemony was so entrenched that the *Observer* remarked that "in North Carolina the Republican party is but a memory."[38]

In Charlotte, P. M. Brown's election as mayor in 1901 reflected the continued
dominance of the Democratic party in local affairs. Although the election law
served as the premier progressive reform of the Young Democrats following
disfranchisement, Brown and his compatriots soon turned their attention toward

improving Charlotte's moral climate, one of the chief components of their progressive agenda.

The Young Democrats took their cue for their social reform platform from the city's ministers and middle-class women, who continued to be effective catalysts for social reform in Charlotte. Continuing the fight for moral improvement that they had begun in the 1890s, some of Charlotte's ministers began to attack what they viewed as the city's unhealthy moral condition. In February 1901, as Brown and the Young Democrats geared up for the white Democratic primary, the Reverend J. W. Stagg preached a sermon at Second Presbyterian Church in which he assailed city officials for failing to suppress Charlotte's many gambling dens. "The present rottenness must be stopped," he fumed. "Young men here, like everywhere are being tempted and tried and going wrong." Mayor J. D. McCall replied defensively that there had been more gambling arrests during his administration than during any other and intimated that Charlotte's saloons were the root cause of the gambling evil. "Let Dr. Stagg turn his guns on the bar-room hells," raged McCall, "and I will do all I can to help him." The Reverend Alexander J. McKelway, editor of the *Presbyterian Standard*, agreed with McCall that saloons, in most cases, harbored gambling dens as well as prostitution rings. McKelway made an impassioned plea to "every man who loves decency and hates impurity . . . to merge other differences and unite in the effort to destroy the triple monster of evil by piercing the saloon."[39]

Other townspeople joined in the call to purge Charlotte of immoral influences. Real estate man F. C. Abbott pointed out that corruption in Charlotte tarnished the city's image and ultimately hampered its economic development. The Reverend H. F. Chreitzenberg, minister of Tryon Street Methodist Church, turned the debate about Charlotte's morality into an attack on Charlotte "society," a favorite ploy of local clergy since the early 1890s. Progressive euchre, he contended, played by society ladies, was just as bad as poker played in a smoke-filled saloon. "When we have shown the Christian women of the city that prize card-playing is wrong," the minister concluded, "then we can bring combined Christian pressure to bear upon the gambling rooms of Charlotte."[40]

As concerned citizens decried Charlotte's iniquity in the spring of 1901, P. M. Brown and his Young Democratic supporters constructed a platform that addressed the concerns of many of the town's troubled middle-class voters, promising to "use all the police power for the suppression of gambling and other kindred vices." Furthermore, he promised to abolish saloon screens as well as back and side entrances in order to eliminate "the security afforded by the cover of darkness and screened doors" and to limit the operating hours of the city's bars.[41]

Brown's reform program overshadowed his opponent's criticism of the Charlotte Election Law and ushered in the Young Democrats' era of progressive
reform. In the opinion of Clarkson, as well as other middle-class reformers, "the
fight was a great one for morality" and Brown's election "was the greatest in
years." Brown immediately initiated many reforms he had promised in the
primary. In June the Board of Aldermen, at Brown's behest, announced that
Charlotte's saloons must close at 9:00 P.M. instead of 1:00 A.M. In addition, to
make drinking as public as possible, the city eliminated obstructions "to hide the
man who crooks his arm; nor may thirsty individuals enter a saloon through a
side or rear door, trap door or an elevator or a back stairway."[42]

Reformers soon demanded more than social pressure to terminate the pernicious influence of the saloon. They began to sketch a strategy to abolish the
liquor trade once and for all, resuming the fight to eradicate alcohol that had
been inaugurated in the 1880s by their parents' generation. After the failure of
local-option elections in the 1880s, prohibitionists attempted to squelch the
saloon through state and local legislation. In 1891 Mecklenburg County commissioners forced thirteen Charlotte saloons to close by refusing to issue licenses
for operation. Although challenged by Charlotte's Board of Aldermen, the
commissioners managed to keep the saloons closed for fifteen months.[43]

Beginning in the 1890s, opponents of alcohol also attempted to control liquor
through the dispensary movement. Popular in neighboring South Carolina,
dispensaries were early versions of state liquor stores and afforded the state the
right to control liquor sales. In February 1899, as the newly elected Democratic
state legislature drafted Jim Crow and disfranchisement laws, Charlotte found
itself in the middle of "the most spectacular fight regarding a dispensary bill."
Despite the protests of liquor dealers, a dispensary bill for the city passed in the
House after Charlotte prohibitionists sent a delegation of its most prominent
citizens, including lawyers George E. Wilson and Charles W. Tillett, bearing a
petition of 3,000 names in support of the bill. Lawyer E. T. Cansler, a member of
the dispensary delegation, claimed that the movement had the support of "nine
of ten people of Mecklenburg, four-fifths of the taxpayers," and that the petition
included the names of twelve of the city's eighteen lawyers, six aldermen, all of
Charlotte's ministers, "and a majority of its manufacturers." But when the bill
came up for consideration in the state Senate, Mecklenburg senator Frank I.
Osborne refused to back the legislation since he had previously promised local
liquor dealers that he would not interfere with their business. Osborne's response precipitated a violent reaction in Charlotte. "Such an uprising of the
people has not been known in fifty years," reported the *Raleigh News and
Observer*. Even though 100 townspeople chartered a special train to Raleigh to

plead with Osborne and the committee considering the bill, it was defeated. The *News and Observer* claimed that no other issue of the legislative session—which included votes on the disfranchisement amendment—"had attracted half the crowd of spectators or evoked half the interest."[44]

Although dispensary legislation failed in 1899, middle-class social reformers continued to carry the torch for liquor control. Women especially played a key role in keeping the issue of prohibition alive. Although barred from voting, women, through temperance organizations such as the WCTU, guaranteed that the liquor question remained before the public and continued to have a prominent place on the progressive political agenda. Throughout the 1890s, the women of the WCTU pursued their temperance goals largely through educational efforts. In 1894 the organization placed tracts in hotels and held temperance rallies at which speakers, often local ministers, lectured on various anti-alcohol topics. In 1895 the Charlotte WCTU participated in a nationwide petition campaign, sponsored by the national WCTU, in which 4 million women signed petitions presented to Congress asking for an end to the liquor traffic. Women temperance advocates also held a variety of entertainments throughout the decade to publicize their cause in dramatic ways. In February 1897 Mrs. R. N. Littlejohn hosted a "Hatchet Party," at which guests planned "to strike some blows with their little hatchets at the great intemperance tree," and "white ribbon teas" were popular. On 20 May 1900, as townspeople celebrated Mecklenburg Declaration of Independence Day, the WCTU offered "plenty of cool water free" to thirsty visitors near the town square. By 1901 the WCTU's activities had expanded to include ministry to prisoners and narcotics abusers as well as "scientific temperance instruction" in the local schools.[45]

Temperance activity was not limited to middle-class white women. The enthusiastic activities of the better class of black women throughout the 1890s, in their own chapter of the WCTU, reflected the spirit of progressivism in the black community as well. Like their white counterparts, black women emphasized education as a means of achieving a liquor-free society. In 1895 the Colored WCTU opened an ice cream parlor in the AME Zion Publishing House to raise funds for a reading room. Members also held mass meetings where they distributed pledge cards.[46]

Although they lacked even indirect political influence once their spouses were barred from politics in 1901, black women continued to work for temperance in their own community as they had in the 1880s. Mary Lynch, a member of Grace AME Zion Church, a teacher at Livingstone College, and a veteran of the prohibition wars of the 1880s, emerged as "perhaps the most enthusiastic temperance advocate in the State." Lynch attended meetings across the country and, the *Star of Zion* claimed, "organized hundreds of Temperance Unions." She served as state president of the Colored WCTU, founded in 1895. The organization held its statewide meeting in Charlotte in the summer of 1901. Like their white counterparts, members of the Colored WCTU stressed the importance of temperance education in bringing "sunshine to many a cloudy home, joy in place of sorrows, smiles and happy laughter in place of grief and streams of tears." It seems likely that the Colored WCTU's mission to save the domestic circle, "the sacred shrine of home," took on special meaning after disfranchisement and Jim Crow. Although black women temperance workers had made the same pleas in the 1880s, the black better class's new emphasis on preparing the next generation for full civic participation gave their message additional force.[47]

Through the temperance agitation of women, antiliquor sentiment seems to have grown by the turn of the century, boosted by drunken Christmas revelry in 1899. Even "the old drinkers, and drunkards, stood aside in disgust and saw the young men and boys reeling on the sidewalks, taking in the town." As a result, Charlotte's ministers pledged to pursue a new crusade against the saloon. A temperance advocate called upon "mothers, sisters and wives to join the crusade, help our noble preachers and save the boys."[48]

Sentiment against the saloon did not derive solely from ministers and concerned women. In March 1902 the *Observer* printed a revealing conversation with a Charlotte businessman who articulated the antialcohol attitude of the commercial community, an attitude that paralleled temperance arguments made by businesspeople in the antebellum United States. "It is apparent," he claimed, "that a man can't drink liquor and keep up with the procession." The drinking man "gradually lags behind and then he is shelved," noted the businessman. "Ten years ago it might have been said that all young men in Charlotte drank, and the business world forgave occasional intoxication," but "now the heads of commercial houses in this city . . . divide the sober men from those who drink." Summing up the antiliquor attitude of the business community, and the Social Darwinist worldview embedded in it, he contended, "The creed of the business world demands the survival of the fittest, and no drinking man is fit for the fight."[49]

The practical concerns of businesspeople and the moral considerations of middle-class ministers and women fused by 1904 and invigorated the prohibition movement with a burst of energy unseen since the 1880s. Disfranchisement also vitalized the prohibition forces, allowing reformers once again the chance to close the saloon through a local-option election. With blacks removed from politics, local-option elections no longer threatened to divide the community into warring factions that vied for black votes; black voters, who cast the deciding votes in the local-option elections of the 1880s, had been eliminated. Furthermore, the removal of black voters abolished the concern that prohibition would divide the Democratic party and reintroduce Republican rule. After 1902, Democrats had nothing to fear. That year the *Biblical Recorder*, a North Carolina Baptist newspaper, remarked, "As long hoped, the first fruits of disfranchisement of the negroes bids fair to be progress in legislation prohibiting the saloon."[50]

Middle-class ministers, who had worked in tandem with the Charlotte WCTU throughout the entire decade of the 1890s, led the way in reviving the local-option election in Charlotte. Since it was socially unacceptable for women to inaugurate a political movement publicly, they likely influenced their clergy to do so for them. In December 1903 clerics from Charlotte's Second Presbyterian Church, East Avenue Associated Reformed Presbyterian Church, Tryon Street Methodist Church, and Tenth Avenue Baptist Church formed a committee to circulate a petition for a municipal prohibition election. The clerics indicated "that they will accept no compromise in their fight" and would battle for nothing less than total prohibition. Although led by the ministers of Charlotte's middle-class congregations, the prohibition movement also attracted the city's lone Catholic priest, Father Francis of St. Peter's Roman Catholic Church.[51]

The Charlotte Anti-Saloon League, founded in September 1903 and headed by Heriot Clarkson, joined Charlotte's ministers in calling for a local-option election. The executive committee of the league, which included Clarkson, former Charlotte mayor J. D. McCall, and the Reverend Alexander McKelway, prepared a platform for the prohibition campaign that they published in January 1904. The arguments for prohibition made in the 1904 platform mirrored those of the campaigns of the 1880s. Prohibitionists claimed that alcohol was "the canker worm that has eaten into the heart of the body politic." But the all-white Anti-Saloon League, unlike the interracial prohibition clubs of the 1880s, singled out the pernicious influence of alcohol on the black race. Although arguing that "no race is exempt" from the evil of the saloon, the league claimed that alcohol was "especially injurious to the child race, the negro race." The special emphasis on blacks reflected both the hardening of race lines since the 1880s and the acceptance of theories of race regression among the new generation of prohibitionists. As their parents' generation had argued in the 1880s, the prohibitionists of 1904 contended that the abolition of alcohol "is above party, above creeds, above nationalities; it is a matter of conscience."[52]

Compared to the bitter and explosive local-option elections of the 1880s that became hopelessly entangled in issues of politics, class, and race, the 1904 campaign against the saloon proceeded smoothly and with little conflict. In July 1904

Charlotte's prohibitionists finally reaped their long-awaited harvest. Waging a smooth, efficient campaign, which was headed by Clarkson, the drys handily won, carrying all four of Charlotte's wards. Prohibition went into effect in Charlotte in January 1905. In the next four years, Clarkson, who headed the state Anti-Saloon League, and other local prohibitionists worked fervently for statewide prohibition, effected after a successful statewide referendum in 1908.[53]

In the first few years following the successful local-option election, Charlotte prohibitionists maintained that the elimination of the saloon had proved to be the panacea they had promised. In a 1908 pamphlet, published to support the statewide referendum on prohibition, they claimed that prohibition had halved the number of crimes in Charlotte and decreased drunkenness by 75 percent. Moreover, prohibition "purified the general atmosphere of the city morally" and "has caused a deeper interest in spiritual things," reflected in "record-breaking memberships" in local churches.[54]

Although prohibition served as the fundamental reform for members of the white middle class, reformers attacked a whole range of social problems in the first decade of the twentieth century. By 1900 many middle-class white women had become increasingly concerned with the problems of working women, first targeted in the late 1880s, and they channeled much of their reforming impulse into helping their less-fortunate sisters. Like their activities in the 1890s, the reforms of middle-class women in the period from 1900 to 1910 reinforced class differences between Charlotte's middle and working classes. In the spring of 1901, just as the Young Democrats initiated P. M. Brown's reformist campaign, middle-class women, headed by Mrs. W. G. Rogers, established two day nurseries in Charlotte. The nurseries, located on South Church and South Tryon streets, were established "to lift some of the burden from the shoulder of the toiling mothers" and to lend "comfort and cheer to the little ones," who were "placed under the tender care of sympathetic and Christian women." A few months later, the Charlotte Woman's Club, organized in 1901, announced plans to build a club for working women that would offer "cheap board and lodging to working girls and others." To fulfill their objective, the Woman's Club organized the Charlotte YWCA in February 1901. Led by Mrs. W. S. Liddell, the YWCA hoped to "provide an attractive and comfortable home at minimum cost" to working women as well as to "provide seemly diversion and pleasure and to throw a moral and religious safeguard around the lives of working women." A month later, the YWCA opened in a six-bedroom flat in the Southern Real Estate Loan and Trust Company building, located on Fifth Street.[55]

Despite a continuity of concerns, the reforming women of 1902 asserted an independence unknown in their mothers' generation. Although women reformers of the 1870s and 1880s relied heavily on public appeals for support of poor relief and hospitals, the officers of the YWCA declared that they did not "propose to cry charity and beg." Reflecting a confidence in their own organizational skills and independence that was built on the experience of their mothers, the YWCA women explained that the minimal fees they charged boarders made their organizations self-sustaining. The *Observer* commented on the accomplishments of Charlotte's female reformers. "These Charlotte women fail in nothing," commented the newspaper. "In this town they manage hospitals and are back of all charity. They are foremost in all kindness, all giving, all thoughtfulness for the unfortunate."[56]

While the Woman's Club engendered reform activity in the first decades of the century, evangelical religion continued to stimulate reform activities for the white middle class, as it had in the 1890s. In 1903 reforming women, ministers, and political progressives all joined forces to establish a Florence Crittenton Rescue Home after hearing an inspirational sermon by evangelist Charles N. Crittenton on his work among "fallen women" in New York City and his establishment of the Florence Crittenton Rescue Mission, where expectant unwed mothers received both physical and spiritual care while learning a trade. By early February an all-male board of directors, which included minister J. W. Stagg, Heriot Clarkson, and Mayor P. M. Brown, had been organized. Although men served on the board, women formed the Crittenton Circle to support the work of the home. The home began operations in February 1903 and by October had aided twenty-four "unfortunate, misguided girls."[57]

In addition to focusing on the plight of women, middle-class reformers also persisted in their fight to better the lot of the mill people, particularly children. Around 1900, young men and women of the middle class helped organize night schools for mill operatives and volunteered as teachers. In 1902 the *Observer* remarked that "night schools in this city now do much to better the condition of young mill operatives." Although mill men generally tolerated the educational activities of the middle class, they looked with less favor on agitation for child labor laws, a concern that grew stronger after the turn of the century.[58]

As in the 1890s, the actions of middle-class reformers on behalf of mill children often placed them in conflict with powerful mill owners. The Reverend Alexander McKelway emerged as the leading spokesperson in favor of a child labor law for North Carolina's textile industry. In 1898 he had taken over the editorship of the *Presbyterian Standard*, published in Charlotte, and turned the denominational newspaper into an outspoken opponent of child labor. For McKelway, and other white progressives like him, child labor laws were part of a package of progressive reform that also included disfranchisement, prohibition, and white supremacy. McKelway feared that child labor resulted in the "race degeneracy" of southern Anglo-Saxons, "the purest American stock on the continent." He inveighed against the southern textile industry for its abuse of children since "the child is the savior of the race."[59]

While McKelway railed against child labor in the *Presbyterian Standard*, others assailed the system in letters to the Tompkins-owned *Observer*. "Now that the leaf of politics pure and simple is turned down," wrote a concerned citizen in December 1902, "no question is of more absorbing interest to the public mind . . . than that of the employment of children in the cotton and other textile mills of North Carolina." Appealing to mill owners to cooperate in the reform efforts, the writer described "the awful grind . . . a wearisome treadmill . . . an irksome routine of bare existence. . . . Where is the escape from it?" he asked. "Where are the hours for play, the days for study, the opportunities for the development of a life that might have its generous ambitions, its material successes, its intellectual advancement, its moral elevation?"[60]

The *Observer*, not surprisingly, defended the employment policies of the mill men. "The cotton mill owners of the South are undoubtedly giving more attention to the betterment of the working people than the factory operators in any other part of the United States," the newspaper contended. Nevertheless, the newspaper noted that "the mill men recognize that civilization is against child labor" and came out in favor of a conservative child labor law that limited the employment of children under twelve years of age.[61]

In 1903 North Carolina instituted the state's first child labor law. The law prohibited the employment of children under twelve and limited the hours of children under eighteen to no more than sixty-six per week. Notably, the law included no provisions for enforcement, which was left to the discretion of employers.[62]

Although the mill men hoped that the weak child labor law would silence critics like McKelway, the anemic legislation only fanned the flames of reform. In 1904 McKelway became secretary for the southern states in the newly formed National Child Labor Commission and headed the campaign to introduce more stringent laws in the state. Conducting a number of investigations into conditions in North Carolina mills and publicizing the results, McKelway and his fellow reformers outraged mill owners, who charged that the reformers were actually agents of New England textile interests bent on crippling southern industry.[63]

Despite the attempts of McKelway and others to abolish child labor, legislation languished. A 1905 bill that prohibited the employment of girls under fourteen and banned night work for children under sixteen went down in defeat when mill operators lobbied against its passage. In 1907, as the cry for child labor restriction grew even more acute, manufacturers introduced their own bill, passed by the legislature. The bill included a provision that banned the employment of children under thirteen unless they were apprenticed. The law, however, allowed twelve- and thirteen-year-olds to work for four months if they went to school for six months. Not until 1913 did the state legislature pass a law with any teeth, prohibiting night work for children under sixteen and mandating county school superintendents to inspect mills for violations of the law.[64]

Middle-class reformers also confronted mill owners on issues of public health. In 1909 a controversy over hookworm pitted middle-class public health advocates, led by Dr. William Allan, against mill owners. Allan and his compatriots attempted to publicize a hookworm epidemic raging in the town's mill villages and blamed mill owners for allowing unsanitary conditions among their workers. In response, D. A. Tompkins attacked Allan in the pages of the *Charlotte Evening Chronicle*, which he owned, calling the hookworm problem "largely suppositional." Public officials refused to back up Allan's claims, hesitating to challenge Tompkins and other powerful mill owners, and nothing was done to alleviate the problem.[65]

Allan's showdown with Tompkins demonstrated the limitations faced by middle-class reformers in their attempts to better the lot of mill people. Mill men such as Tompkins wielded a tremendous amount of power in Charlotte and the Piedmont, and they could often easily crush any perceived threats to the status quo. Nevertheless, the activities of middle-class reformers kept issues of social welfare in the public eye and cast doubts on the claims of mill men.

Progressive reform in postdisfranchisement Charlotte also included legal segregation. Alarmed by what they perceived as the regression of the black race, some white citizens contended that regulating interaction between the races would reduce conflict and enhance social harmony. Thus, they demanded rigid barriers in public facilities to separate the races. In May 1903 the Charlotte Consolidated Construction Company, which owned the streetcar system and Latta Park in Dilworth, announced plans to erect a separate "new pavilion for colored people at Biddleville" and to bar blacks from the Latta Park pavilion. Charlotte's blacks had used the facility since it had opened in 1892. "The new pavilion," explained the *Observer*, "is made necessary by the fact that Latta Park will no longer reasonably hold both races, and the negroes need a meeting place and a place of recreation." Moreover, "it would have been unpleasant, to say the least, for the white people of the community to mingle with, even to the slightest extent, the negroes at Latta Park another summer." Edward Dilworth Latta, president of the Charlotte Consolidated Construction Company, justified the separate facility by contending that "the object of the new pavilion" was to give blacks their own meeting place similar to the white facility. "The negro imitates the white man and it is well that he should do this socially as well as in other respects," explained Latta condescendingly. "A dance or colored play at their pavilion would be a good thing for them."[66]

By 1906 distressed white citizens had abandoned Latta's language of paternalism. In September 1906 a four-day race riot in Atlanta sparked demands in Charlotte for segregated streetcars. A concerned white townsman wrote to the *Observer*, "The feeling between whites and negroes is undoubtedly growing more acute and it behooves us to use every reasonable precaution to prevent trouble such as they are having in Atlanta." The writer suggested that "one thing which might lessen the danger of trouble would be to have separate compartments for the races in the street cars." As a "constant patron of the street cars," the writer had "observed lately that the negroes are making themselves more and more objectionable to the white passengers by their insolent behavior." Only recently in nearby Salisbury "a white man was shot and killed . . . just for reproving an insolent negro."[67]

Sentiment for segregated streetcars grew over the next few months in Charlotte and across the state. In March 1907, with little fanfare, the state legislature passed a law requiring the separation of blacks and whites in the state's streetcars. As a result, the Tarheel State became one of seven southern states to implement statewide streetcar segregation between 1902 and 1907. On 1 April 1907 streetcar systems in North Carolina's cities—including Charlotte, Durham, and Asheville—complied with the order. In Charlotte the *Observer* published a brief and inconspicuous notice that the Charlotte Consolidated Construction Company would observe the state law. The press explained that black passengers, beginning on 1 April, should sit in the rear of the streetcars.[68]

Some black citizens protested their second-class treatment. The *Observer* reported that Joe Robertson, "a young negro man," was arrested for disorderly conduct after he "swore fluently" at the conductor of the Tryon Street car, who had "told him to go back and sit." The black better class took a different approach to the new law. Like black businesspeople and professionals in other southern cities, Charlotte's black better class protested Jim Crow streetcars by organizing a boycott. Streetcar boycotts occurred in every state of the former Confederacy between 1900 and 1907. Although the *Observer* reported a boycott in Wilmington and threats of a similar action in Asheville, the newspaper never acknowledged Charlotte's streetcar boycott. Ministers organized the movement in Charlotte as they had in Montgomery and Columbia. Bishop Clinton and the Reverend W. R. Douglas, pastor of Little Rock AME Zion Church in Charlotte's

First Ward, led the protest. Floretta Douglas Gunn, Reverend Douglas's daughter, recalled that "Bishop Clinton and my father got together and said they would not ride the streetcar." Clinton and Douglas "talked to the people" in Charlotte and attempted to rally support for the boycott.[69]

The streetcar boycott, although an overt protest against the second-rate treatment of blacks, fit the moderate philosophy of the black better class. Never directly confrontational, the black better class organized a temperate protest, one that endeavored to challenge new Jim Crow legislation without angering white citizens and allowed the better class to maintain standards of decorum and gentility. The lack of an alternative form of transportation for many blacks, however, hampered the protest. Although "Bishop Clinton had horses" and could continue to go about his duties, according to Gunn, less wealthy black citizens depended on the streetcar. "The people had to go to work," she recollected. "My father had to visit members." Consequently, the boycott collapsed in Charlotte as it did in all other southern cities.[70]

The failure of the streetcar boycott marked the political swan song of Charlotte's black better class. Driven out of the political sphere by discriminatory election laws and unable to mount an effective protest against Jim Crow streetcar legislation, members of the black better class withdrew into their own community. They channeled their energy into pursuing economic advancement while reiterating their constant theme of individual improvement as the key to racial progress. Despite setbacks early in the century, however, the subsequent history of Charlotte's black better class vindicated J. T. Williams's claim that "money will accomplish what legislation will not."

EPILOGUE

. . . .

In spite of the frustrations and aching disappointments experienced by Charlotte's black better class, in 1915 they celebrated the fiftieth anniversary of emancipation. Publishing a booklet entitled *Colored Charlotte*, the better class commemorated the accomplishments of the city's black citizenry since the Civil War. The publication contained photographs of many of Charlotte's most prominent black residents, stately homes, and handsome churches. Scores of advertisements for black businesses attested to "race progress"; undertakers, barbers, druggists, grocers, tailors, dentists, and contractors proudly publicized their businesses in *Colored Charlotte*.

Despite the optimistic tone of the publication, the year 1915 was hardly hopeful for African Americans in Charlotte and across the nation. The federal government seemed even less concerned than ever about the plight of black Americans. Virginia-born Woodrow Wilson occupied the White House and had expanded segregation in federal offices, a practice instituted by his predecessor, William Howard Taft. National African American leaders remained severely divided over the best course of action to attain civil equality for black Americans. W. E. B. Du Bois and adherents of his Niagara movement had supported Wilson's presidency in 1912 over Taft and Roosevelt, only to have their hopes dashed. Booker T. Washington, Du Bois's nemesis, died in 1915 with no clear successor to promulgate the accommodationist strategy. Just before Washington's death, D. W. Griffith's blockbuster film, *The Birth of a Nation*, based on Thomas Dixon's white-supremacy novel, *The Clansman*, opened in 1915, portraying blacks as either beastly or hopelessly subservient. In North Carolina the Republican party continued to rebuff eligible black voters, despite sporadic attempts by loyal black Republicans to regain a place in their party. Moreover, schemes for severe segregation of the races received great publicity. In 1913 Clarence H. Poe, editor of the *Progressive Farmer* and a resident of Raleigh, conceived of a plan approximating apartheid whereby rural blacks would be segregated by regulating land sales and tenantry by race. Pushed out of the state by racial hostility and pulled to the North by new job opportunities, blacks continued a steady out-migration. Between 1900 and 1920 Charlotte's black population grew moderately but shrank significantly in relation to the white population. In 1900 blacks in Charlotte made up nearly 40 percent of the population; by 1920 they made up only 31 percent.[1]

In spite of the overwhelming obstacles faced by the black citizenry in 1915, *Colored Charlotte* attempted to demonstrate to whites just how far the black race had come since the days of slavery and to encourage even greater advancement among blacks. In an introduction to the booklet, Bishop George Clinton emphasized that while *Colored Charlotte* illustrated progress "for our own encouragement and inspiration," at the same time, "the people of other races should know what we are doing in the way of proving ourselves substantial citizens and valuable members of the community in which we live." Once again maintaining that blacks could earn full participation in southern society, he asserted that property ownership, exemplary citizenship, and "the moral, social, religious and general development of the community" would prove that blacks indeed were "entitled to the same just and impartial treatment and favorable consideration accorded to other good citizens." Moreover, it was up to the "thoughtful and enterprising members of the race" to "stimulate and inspire" the rest of the black community, to "make them more anxious to attain success and move forward along every line that will make the race strong and useful."[2]

Clinton's words and the *Colored Charlotte* booklet attested to the persistence of the black better class's philosophy of race progress. Clinton's 1915 introduction could just as well have been written thirty-five years earlier, in the 1880s. The bishop's message to the people of Charlotte still stressed the importance of uplift and self-help. He continued to place the responsibility for full civic participation on the shoulders of blacks themselves and to insist that through hard work, proper decorum, education, and property ownership, they could achieve justice.

In light of the events at the turn of the century, Bishop Clinton's words must have seemed bittersweet to his black readers. The black better class's philosophy of self-help and individual responsibility had not generated, in their lifetime, the respect from the white community for which they longed, nor had their achievement secured the equality they so desired. Despite their education, diligence, wealth, and morality, their civil rights had only diminished, their status had only shrunk.

Given the tragic story of race relations in Charlotte and North Carolina that unfolded in the prime of Clinton's life, his words may seem hopelessly anachronistic at best, sickeningly ingratiating at worst. In light of disfranchisement and Jim Crow, the horror of the Wilmington riot, and the heartless abandonment of blacks by the Republican party in North Carolina and the South, it seems difficult to fathom how Clinton and his listeners could cling so tenaciously to their philosophy of race progress. Yet fifty years after emancipation, Clinton and other men and women of the better class could look with pride at their accomplishments—particularly in business—and discern a glimmer of hope for the future. *Colored Charlotte* included a table of black businesses, trades, and professions in Charlotte and Mecklenburg. The table listed 3 real estate companies, 31 restaurants, 20 shoe-making shops, and 24 grocery stores. Moreover, the city and county in 1915 boasted 12 black physicians, 2 lawyers, 20 professors, and 103 schoolteachers.[3]

In publicizing the mushrooming of black businesses, *Colored Charlotte* pointed to an unintended consequence of Jim Crow segregation. Ironically, the Jim Crow world of the twentieth century provided a broader economic base for black merchants and professionals than they had experienced in the 1880s and 1890s. In the harsh climate of the legally segregated South, black business opportunity had actually improved; as race lines hardened, members of the black community patronized black businesses in an unprecedented manner, benefiting the better class. Between 1898 and 1915, for example, the number of black grocery stores in Charlotte doubled, the number of restaurants tripled, and the number of black doctors quadrupled. In 1915 Charlotte boasted 144 black-owned businesses, including 10 boardinghouses, 3 hotels, 5 drugstores, and 3 insurance companies. By the early 1920s black businesses had grown to such an extent that several members of the better class, including Dr. J. T. Williams and barber Thad Tate, helped found the Mecklenburg Investment Company in 1921. The company erected a handsome three-story red-brick office building on the corner of Third and Brevard streets, a symbol of black enterprise, which housed offices of black professionals and businesses.[4]

Visible economic progress in the early twentieth century probably helped take some of the sting out of disfranchisement and Jim Crow. Yet for Bishop Clinton and other men and women of his class, tangible material advancement did not quench their desire to regain full citizenship rights. In spite of Bishop Clinton's conservative words in *Colored Charlotte*, he and other men and women of his generation devoted the rest of their lives to resisting white supremacy in a variety of ways.

Bishop Clinton remained active in the political arena despite disfranchisement, white primary laws, and the policies of the "lily-white" Republicans of the state. In 1920 the General Council of the AMEZ church appointed Clinton to write an open letter to Republican presidential nominee Warren G. Harding. He informed the future president that blacks who could still exercise the franchise in the South would not blindly vote for him because he was a Republican. He called

Christmas reception at the home of Bishop and Mrs. George Clinton,
ca. 1918. (Courtesy of the Robinson-Spangler Carolina
Room, Public Library of Charlotte and Mecklenburg County)

upon Harding to regain the support of southern black voters by assuring them
that he would strike down discriminatory legislation.[5]

Bishop Clinton's wife, Marie Louise Clay Clinton, attempted to make her
mark in politics as well, but her hopes were thwarted by white-supremacist
voting registrars. A graduate of Atlanta's Clark University and a well-known
vocalist and church leader, Marie Clinton tried to register to vote in 1920 in
Charlotte, soon after women won the franchise. Despite her education and
gentility, voting registrars in Charlotte rejected her application.[6]

The activities of the Clintons attest to the fact that members of the black better
class did not give up their dream of full civic participation. Although thwarted by
callous political leaders and racist voting registrars, they continued to assert
themselves in the political sphere. They never retreated into silent accommoda-
tionism.

Bishop Clinton and his wife, and other members of their generation, would
never see the restoration of the civil rights that they had lost. Bishop Clinton
died in 1921, the year that Charlotte native Cameron Morrison, a Young Democrat at the turn of the century, became governor of North Carolina. Only three
years later, his compatriot, Heriot Clarkson—the originator of the 1898 white-
supremacy campaign and the Charlotte Election Law of 1901—won a seat on

the North Carolina Supreme Court. The ascendancy of Morrison and Clarkson to the highest offices in the state guaranteed that the aspirations of the black better class would be postponed for some time to come; the Tarheel State was safely in the grip of the now-mature Young Democrats. The interracial class cooperation and the fluidity of class and race lines that the black better class had experienced in the 1880s receded in memory, overshadowed by the harsher racial climate of the twentieth century.

Yet the philosophy of Clinton and other members of the black better class lived on, absorbed by their children and grandchildren, the men and women who would lead the fight to restore civil rights lost at the turn of the century. Although obstructed in their attempts to exercise political power, Clinton and his generation created both the ideals and the institutions that would sustain their vision of race progress through the next several generations.

Churches established in the first years of emancipation and lovingly celebrated in the pages of *Colored Charlotte* served both as a shelter against the indignities of the Jim Crow South and a propagator of the values of the black better class. The Reverend Curtis Kearns, who grew up in the elite Seventh Street Presbyterian Church in the 1920s and 1930s, remembered that "the main contribution of the church was to tell young people, 'You *are* somebody, you *can* be somebody.'" The church "challenged young people to develop to their highest potential," resulting in "all the young ministers that came out of Seventh Street . . . all the school teachers, the lawyers, the dentists and the Ph.Ds."[7]

The black better class continued to place a high premium on education during the dark days of Jim Crow. Throughout the 1910s, 1920s, and 1930s, they sent their children to local colleges and seminaries, perpetuating the business and professional class that had first emerged in the 1880s. Rejecting Washington's appeal for industrial education, the better class of blacks continued to furnish their children with liberal arts educations at Biddle (later Johnson C. Smith), Scotia, and Livingstone. Aurelia Tate Henderson, whose barber father Thad Tate had helped found Grace AME Zion Church during the prohibition battles of the 1880s, pointed out that the absence of a black high school in Charlotte before 1923 did not deter the better class from educating their children. Upon completion of the eighth grade in city schools, boys continued in the high school department at Biddle, and girls finished at Scotia Seminary in Concord.[8]

In addition, some members of Charlotte's black better class worked assiduously to better the state's educational facilities for black pupils. Dr. George E. Davis, a Biddle professor, served in North Carolina's Division of Negro Education, established in 1921. Davis rallied poor, rural black North Carolinians to contribute their scant funds to help build schools for their children, with the aid of the Julius Rosenwald Fund, which provided matching funds for building rural schools. Through Davis's efforts, hundreds of Rosenwald schools appeared across the state, greatly improving educational opportunities for Tarheel blacks.[9]

Other members of Charlotte's black better class combined political pressure and personal contacts with powerful whites to enhance public services available to blacks. Aurelia Tate Henderson recalled that her father, Thad Tate, parlayed his relationship with Governor Cameron Morrison into a training school for black juvenile offenders. Concerned with the large number of black youths consigned to chain gangs for committing crimes, Tate broached the subject with Morrison, a longtime client, who was then running for governor. The barber offered to rally black support for Morrison's candidacy in return for Morrison's promise to establish a training school for young black men in trouble with the law. After Morrison won the governor's seat in 1920, he established the Morrison Training School in Hoffman, North Carolina.[10]

While schools and churches helped keep the dream of full civic participation alive, black businesses and professions proudly publicized in *Colored Charlotte* in 1915 ultimately provided the economic base that would later allow Charlotte's blacks to challenge segregation and disfranchisement through legal channels. By the mid-twentieth century, the children and grandchildren of the black better class began to contest the Jim Crow world that had isolated their forebears. Black businesspeople and professionals—men and women with a firm economic footing in their community and with the know-how and monetary resources to pursue their fight through legal channels—would lead the civil rights movement in Charlotte. They vindicated the vision of the black better class and J. T. Williams's assertion in 1905 that "money will accomplish what legislation will not."

In 1940 Charlotte undertaker Kelly Alexander, Sr., founded a chapter of the National Association for the Advancement of Colored People (NAACP), which served as the nucleus of a movement that would contest local segregation. Born in 1915, the year that *Colored Charlotte* was published, Alexander was the son of Zechariah Alexander, who had established a highly successful undertaking business just as Jim Crow and disfranchisement came crashing down on the black better class. Zechariah Alexander taught his children self-respect and self-help and placed a high premium on education. His son Kelly graduated from college and, after a stint in New York City, returned to Charlotte in 1939 to work in the family business. After founding Charlotte's branch of the NAACP, Alexander helped establish a civil rights coalition in Charlotte that ultimately broke down the walls of Jim Crow in the city.[11]

In 1957, in the premier challenge to segregated schools in Charlotte, which

was mounted by Alexander and other civil rights leaders, fifteen-year-old Dorothy Counts integrated Charlotte's Harding High School. Counts was the daughter of Presbyterian minister Herman Counts, an associate of Alexander's in
Charlotte's fledgling civil rights movement, and her grandfather had taught at
Johnson C. Smith University. On the morning of 4 September 1957, as a mob of
screaming, jeering whites nearly enveloped her, Dorothy Counts walked into the
school, her head held high, launching integration in Charlotte's public school
system.[12]

In 1964 minister Darius Swann, a graduate of Johnson C. Smith University
and a longtime friend of the Counts family, filed a lawsuit against the Charlotte
school system challenging the city's failure to move beyond token integration of
local schools. Ruling on *Swann v. Charlotte-Mecklenburg*, Judge James McMillan
ordered the local school system to bus children in order to achieve racial balance
in the public schools. *Swann* ultimately became the national test case for the
busing issue. In 1971 the U.S. Supreme Court upheld *Swann* in a landmark decision that reconfigured the racial makeup of schools across the United States.[13]

By the mid-twentieth century, then, the heirs of the black better class led the
way in breaking down the barriers of Jim Crow, regaining what their forebears
had lost. Notably, sympathetic white middle-class liberals aided them in their
efforts. Among them was Pete McKnight, editor of the *Charlotte Observer*, which
at the turn of the century, under the ownership of D. A. Tompkins, had lent its
powerful voice to white supremacy and disfranchisement. White business and
civic leaders also aided the process of dismantling Jim Crow, sensing the inev-
itability of change and fearing the consequences of violent resistance. A year
before the 1964 Civil Rights Act mandated desegregation, Charlotte had, for the
most part, desegregated the city's public accommodations through the cooperative efforts of white businesspeople, city officials, and civil rights leaders. Also,
when the school-busing order divided the city into angry factions, Maggie Ray, a
white middle-class woman who headed the Citizens Advisory Group, which
advised the school board, managed to formulate a school integration plan that
satisfied both the community and federal officials.[14]

Like the prohibition crusade of the 1880s, the civil rights movement joined
men and women of the same class across race lines. Although probably not aware
of it, the black and white men and women who labored together in Charlotte's
civil rights movement worked within an innovative tradition of social reform first
devised by the better classes of New South Charlotte seventy years earlier.
Although shattered by the racial politics of the late nineteenth century, interracial cooperation surfaced once again as members of a later generation fought
tenaciously for what they deemed the fundamental reform of their day.

APPENDIX

. . . .

Table A.1
North Carolina Towns, 1850–1860

	Total Population (% increase)	Slave (%)	Free Black (%)
		1850	
Wilmington	7,264	3,031 (41.7)	652 (8.9)
New Bern	4,681	1,927 (41.2)	800 (17.1)
Fayetteville	4,646	1,542 (33.1)	576 (12.4)
Raleigh	4,518	1,809 (40.0)	456 (10.1)
Washington	2,015	840 (41.6)	219 (10.9)
Morganton	1,978	298 (15.0)	5 (0.3)
Edenton	1,607	1,008 (62.7)	67 (4.2)
Warrenton	1,242	602 (48.5)	28 (2.3)
Charlotte*	1,065	456 (43.6)	36 (3.4)
		1860	
Wilmington	9,552 (31.5)	3,777 (39.5)	573 (6.0)
New Bern	5,432 (16.0)	2,383 (43.9)	689 (12.7)
Fayetteville	4,790 (3.1)	1,519 (31.7)	465 (9.7)
Raleigh	4,780 (5.8)	1,621 (33.9)	466 (9.7)
Salisbury	2,420	1,073 (44.3)	80 (3.3)
Charlotte	2,265 (112.7)	825 (36.4)	139 (6.1)
Henderson	1,961	1,225 (62.4)	22 (1.1)
Elizabeth City	1,798	620 (34.5)	217 (1.1)

Sources: U.S. Bureau of the Census, *Seventh Census of the United States, 1850*, and *Population of the United States in 1860, Eighth Census.*
*Charlotte was not listed in the "Population of Cities and Towns" table of the 1850 census but probably ranked around ninth.

Table A.2
Occupational Breakdown, Charlotte, 1850 and 1860

	1850	1860
White-collar/professionals	97 (43.7%)	246 (28.7%)
Skilled laborers/artisans	114 (51.4)	340 (39.6)
Unskilled laborers	8 (3.6)	254 (29.6)
Farmers	3 (1.4)	18 (2.1)
Total	222 (100.1)	858 (100.0)

Source: U.S. Bureau of the Census, Manuscript census schedules, Mecklenburg County, North Carolina, 1850 and 1860.

Table A.3

North Carolina Towns: Population, 1850–1910, and Racial Composition, 1850–1880

	1850	1860	1870	1880	1890	1900	1910
Charlotte	1,065	2,265	4,473	7,094	11,557	18,091	34,014
Wilmington	7,264	9,552	13,446	17,350	20,056	20,976	25,748
Fayetteville	4,646	4,790	4,660	3,485	4,222	4,670	—
Raleigh	4,518	4,780	7,790	9,265	12,678	13,643	19,218
Durham	—	—	—	2,041	5,485	6,679	18,241
Greensboro	—	—	280	1,373	3,317	10,035	15,895
Winston	—	—	—	—	8,018	10,008	17,167

% Increase

	1850–60	1860–70	1870–80	1880–90	1890–1900	1900–1910
Charlotte	112.7	97.5	58.6	62.3	56.5	88.0
Wilmington	31.5	40.8	29.0	15.6	4.6	22.7
Fayetteville	3.1	−2.7	−2.5	21.1	10.6	—
Raleigh	5.8	62.9	18.9	36.8	7.6	40.9
Durham	—	—	—	168.7	21.8	173.1
Greensboro	—	—	—	390.4	202.5	58.4
Winston	—	—	—	—	24.8	71.5

Racial Composition

	1850		1860		1870		1880	
	b	w	b	w	b	w	b	w
Charlotte	47%	53%	40%	60%	42%	58%	47%	53%
Raleigh	50	50	43	57	53	47	47	53
Wilmington	51	49	46	54	59	41	60	40

Sources: U.S. Bureau of the Census, *Seventh Census of the United States, 1850*; *Population of the United States in 1860, Eighth Census*; *Statistics of the Population of the United States, 1870*; *Statistics of the Population of the United States, 1880*; *Compendium of the Eleventh Census, 1890: Population, Part 1*; *Census Reports*, vol. 1, *Twelfth Census of the United States, 1900: Population, Part 1*; and *Census Reports*, vol. 1, *Thirteenth Census of the United States, 1910: Population, Part 1*.

Table A.4
Average Wealth, Charlotte, 1870

	Real	Personal	Total
Lawyers	$4,379	$6,721	$11,100
Merchants/dealers	5,108	5,545	10,653
Physicians	4,362	1,408	5,770
Machinists	1,363	681	2,044
Carpenters	532	137	669
Tailors	428	97	525
Brickmasons	240	81	321

Source: U.S. Bureau of the Census, Manuscript census schedules, Mecklenburg County, North Carolina, 1870.

Table A.5
Charlotte's Ten Wealthiest Black and White Residents, 1870

	Occupation	Real/personal property	Total
Black Residents			
John Schenck	carpenter	$1,800/700	$2,500
Burwell Johnston	butcher	2,000/450	2,450
Burt Schenck	clerk	1,000/50	1,050
Thomas Holly	housepainter	500/500	1,000
Jefferson Hagler	butcher	600/150	750
Robert Hayes	railroad hand	600/50	650
George Andrews	miner	500/100	600
Robert (?)	shoemaker	500/100	600
Frank Alexander	drayman	550/40	590
Nancy Jones	laborer	500/25	525
White Residents			
William Johnston	railroad president	$190,000/95,000	$285,000
John Means	farmer	150,000/4,000	154,000
R. Y. McAden	banker	95,000/30,000	125,000
William Sloan	railroad president	45,000/80,000	125,000
W. R. Myers	farmer	25,000/75,000	100,000
John Morehead	gentleman	65,000/25,000	90,000
H. G. Springs	real estate broker	33,000/50,000	83,000
Joseph A. Wilson	lawyer	25,000/55,000	80,000
John Y. Bryce	commercial merchant	65,000/2,000	67,000
J. H. Carson	grocer	35,000/30,000	65,000

Source: U.S. Bureau of the Census, Manuscript census schedules, Mecklenburg County, North Carolina, 1870.

Table A.6
Cotton Mill Investors, Charlotte, 1880–1900

Professionals		
Attorneys	11	
Physicians	1	
Engineers	1	
Ministers	1	
Bankers	2	
Bank cashiers	1	
Clerks of court	1	
Subtotal		18
Merchants		
Cotton merchants/brokers	5	
Dry goods merchants	6	
Grocers	3	
Hardware merchants	1	
Grain merchants	1	
Subtotal		16
Other commercial occupations		
Confectioners/bakers	1	
Insurance agents	1	
Real estate brokers	1	
Photographers	1	
Manufacturers	1	
Machinery agents	1	
Subtotal		6
Farmers	1	
Total		41

Sources: Data was compiled from lists of investors in the Charlotte Cotton Mill (1880) and the Victor (1888), Ada (1888), Alpha (1888), Highland Park (1891), Atherton (1892), Louise (1896), Gold Crown Hosiery (1897), and Chadwick (1900) mills in the Records of Corporation, Mecklenburg County Courthouse, Charlotte, North Carolina. Of 56 mill investors listed, 41 were identified in the 1880 census, *Branson's Business Directory*, or the Charlotte City Directory.

Table A.7

Production of Cotton, Corn, and Wheat, Mecklenburg and Adjacent Counties,
1860–1880

| | Mecklenburg | | Adjacent Counties (N.C.) and Districts (S.C.) | |
	1860	1880	1860	1880
Cotton (bales)	6,112	19,129	32,519	82,641
Corn (bushels)	550,235	539,385	2,699,358	3,183,102
Wheat (bushels)	641,202	66,767	554,432	439,634

Sources: U.S. Bureau of the Census, *Agriculture of the United States in 1860, Eighth Census*, and *Report on the Products of Agriculture, General Statistics, Tenth Census*, vol. 3.

Table A.8

Occupational Breakdown by Race, Charlotte, 1880

	White	Black
White-collar/professionals	49.2%	4.5%
Manufacturers	.8	0
Skilled laborers/artisans	36.9	14.7
Unskilled laborers	11.9	77.7
Farmers	1.3	3.0

Source: U.S. Bureau of the Census, Manuscipt census schedules, Mecklenburg County, North Carolina, 1880.

NOTES

· · · · · · · · · ·

ABBREVIATIONS

The following abbreviations are used throughout the notes.

CCO   City Clerk's Office, Charlotte, North Carolina.

NCC   North Carolina Collection, University of North Carolina, Chapel Hill, North Carolina.

NCDAH   North Carolina Division of Archives and History, Raleigh, North Carolina.

RBRFAL   Records of the Bureau of Refugees, Freedmen, and Abandoned Lands, Record Group 105, National Archives, Washington, D.C.

SHC   Southern Historical Collection, University of North Carolina, Chapel Hill, North Carolina.

INTRODUCTION

1. For studies of middle-class formation in the antebellum North, see Paul E. Johnson, *A Shopkeeper's Millennium*; Ryan, *Cradle of the Middle Class*; Gilkeson, *Middle-Class Providence*; and Blumin, *Emergence of the Middle Class*. Whereas Johnson stresses the importance of evangelical religion as the "moral imperative" around which the middle class formed, Ryan argues for the centrality of domestic values as the key to middle-class formation. Gilkeson emphasizes the importance of "collective organizations" in generating a middle class. Synthesizing and adding to these studies, Blumin documents the convergence of social and economic forces critical to the formation of a middle class. Moreover, he, unlike the others, rejects a linear model of class formation, arguing that lines between the middle and working classes blurred in the early twentieth century.

In the stimulating epilogue of *Emergence of the Middle Class*, Blumin begins to develop a typology of middle-class formation, suggesting that the class development that occurred in the large cities of the Northeast was not necessarily characteristic of the entire nation. Charlotte may, indeed, represent another type of class formation, representative of new cities of the New South. See ibid., 298–310.

2. Woodward, *Strange Career of Jim Crow*, 31–65, and *Origins of the New South*, 142–74, 130–32. Woodward's emphasis on the "newness" of the New South has spawned numerous challenges to his thesis. Among the most sweeping of Woodward's revisers is Jonathan M. Wiener, who posited in *Social Origins of the New South* that in Alabama the planter elite retained power in the decades following the Civil War and that in terms of power and class relations the New South duplicated the Old South. Although historians of North Carolina have noted that the Tarheel State did not resemble Wiener's Alabama in that it did not have an entrenched, powerful planter class, most recent scholarship has come down firmly in the continuity camp. Taking their cue from Dwight Billings's 1979

examination of power and politics in New South North Carolina, Robert C. Kenzer, Gail Williams O'Brien, and Paul D. Escott all emphasize continuity in class relations in the Old and New South, stressing the persistence of antebellum elites in the New South era and the stability of the power that they exercised. See Billings, *Planters and the Making of a "New South"*; Kenzer, *Kinship and Neighborhood*; O'Brien, *Legal Fraternity*; and Escott, *Many Excellent People*; see also O'Brien, "Power and Influence." Two notable exceptions to North Carolina's continuity school are found in dissertations by James M. Shirley and Samuel M. Kipp III. Shirley's study of Winston-Salem, "From Congregational Town to Industrial City," stresses the emergence of a "new elite" after the Civil War. Similarly, Kipp argues in "Urban Growth and Social Change" that Greensboro's industrialization "was the product of indigenous efforts" but was "initiated primarily by newcomers to the community" (208, 210). David L. Carlton's study of class relations in Piedmont South Carolina's mill towns, *Mill and Town*, also supports Woodward's interpretation of the significance of a "new middle class," as does Don H. Doyle's *New Men, New Cities, New South*.

3. Willard Gatewood's *Aristocrats of Color* explores the development of an American black elite in the nineteenth century and traces its origins to an antebellum free black community and privileged slaves, many of whom were light-skinned. Although there are many parallels between Gatewood's "aristocrats of color" and Charlotte's black "better class"—especially the values they shared—the better class had different origins than their aristocratic counterparts and were far less exclusive on the issue of skin color.

4. Carlton's study of Piedmont South Carolina mill towns, *Mill and Town*, depicts an often bitter struggle between middle-class "town people" and the "mill people" who worked as factory operatives. Charlotte appears even more complex, however, as "town people" divided into competing factions.

CHAPTER I

1. "Rail Road Celebration at Charlotte," *North Carolina Whig*, 3 November 1852; "Cotton Trade in Charlotte," ibid., 17 November 1852.

2. Tompkins, *History of Mecklenburg*, 68; Henderson, *Washington's Southern Tour*, 5.

3. For more on the discovery of gold in the Carolina Piedmont, see Roberts, *Carolina Gold Rush*; Brown and Hoffman, "Gold Mining," 18–35; and Blythe and Brockmann, *Hornet's Nest*, 267.

4. The *Catawba Journal* regularly reported market prices in Cheraw, Charleston, and Fayetteville, and merchants from each of these markets advertised heavily in the Charlotte paper. The 1810 census reported that Mecklenburg cotton generally sold for $25 per bale and was "all sent to Market principally Charleston, South Carolina." See U.S. Bureau of the Census, Manuscript census schedules, Mecklenburg County, North Carolina, 1810, 1830, and 1850, and Blythe and Brockmann, *Hornet's Nest*, 111. Between 1830 and 1840, thirty-two of North Carolina's sixty-eight counties lost population and the state's population increased by only 2.5 percent. See Powell, *North Carolina through Four Centuries*, 250.

5. Of twenty-nine promoters of the Charlotte and South Carolina Railroad listed in the local press, ten were well-to-do farmers, nine of whom resided in the county; seven were merchants; four were lawyers; two were physicians; one was a manufacturer; and two were hotelkeepers. A mail contractor, a coiner, and a clerk of the court rounded out the list. Since local, private subscriptions financed the Charlotte and South Carolina Railroad rather than governmental funds, Fox and other Democrats may have felt no conflict

between their party loyalty and support for the railroad. Moreover, by the late 1840s, when the benefits of railroads were obvious, the issue no longer polarized Whigs and Democrats as it had in the 1830s. According to Harry Watson's study of Cumberland County, North Carolina, railroad building in the 1830s divided town and county people over questions of political economy and helped define the Whig and Democratic parties, with the largely town-based Whigs supporting internal improvements and the Democrats in the county opposing them. But by the 1840s, Watson notes, the "anticommercial ethos" of Cumberland's isolated farmers was waning, and by the 1850s, Whigs "had won the argument for economic development, and an increasing number of Democrats had begun to see things their way." See Watson, *Jacksonian Politics*, 14, 41–59, 198, 282–83. For more on the cooperation between town and country interests in building railroads across the South, see Goldfield, "Pursuing the American Urban Dream," 54; see also Thornton, *Politics and Power*, 275–76, on the often bitter struggle for railroads.

6. "Rail Road Meeting," *Charlotte Journal*, 4 March 1847; "Charlotte and South Carolina Railroad," ibid., 1 January 1847.

7. "Rail Road Convention," ibid., 11 March 1847; "Rail Road Convention," ibid., 6 May 1847.

8. "Rail Road Subscription," ibid., 10 June 1847; "Our Railroad," ibid., 24 June 1847; "The Rail Road," ibid., 19 August 1847. Cabarrus County was the most enthusiastic of the adjoining counties, subscribing $15,000. Rowan subscribed $2,000; Iredell, $4,000; Lincoln and Gaston, $7,000 each.

9. Blythe and Brockmann, *Hornet's Nest*, 261; Trelease, *North Carolina Railroad*, 82, 38; "Rail Road Meeting," *North Carolina Whig*, 23 May 1854; "An Act to Incorporate the Wilmington and Charlotte Rail Road," ibid., 28 March 1855.

10. Powell, *North Carolina through Four Centuries*, 282; Trelease, *North Carolina Railroad*, xii; Stover, *Railroads of the South*; Black, *Railroads of the Confederacy*, 2. The census figures used by both Stover and Black to determine the increase in railroad mileage between 1850 and 1860 do not include the approximately thirty miles of track built in North Carolina as part of the Charlotte and South Carolina Railroad.

11. "To Whom It May Concern," *North Carolina Whig*, 8 December 1852; Connor, *North Carolina*, 55. It is difficult to compare the growth of North Carolina towns between 1850 and 1860 because only a few of the same towns are listed in population tables for both census years. But available statistics suggest that inland towns with rail connections outstripped older coastal towns in population growth during the decade. See table A.1.

12. "Important Rail Road Meeting," *North Carolina Whig*, 14 June 1854; "Our Fall Business," ibid., 24 October 1854; "Our Produce and Grocery Market," 23 November 1854. Noting the powerful impact of railroads on North Carolina's economy in the 1850s, Trelease contends in *North Carolina Railroad*, "In general, the early railroads commercialized existing local economies and broadened them into regional economies" (327).

13. "To Our Mountain Friends," *North Carolina Whig*, 6 September 1853; "Our Fall Trade," ibid., 16 August 1854; Elias and Cohen advertisement, ibid., 11 October 1853; "More Like a City Than Ever," ibid., 20 December 1859; "Charlotte v. Salisbury," ibid., 3 October 1854. For examples, see various advertisements, ibid., 1858–60.

14. Ibid., 6 September 1853; "Our Produce and Grocery Market," ibid., 23 November 1854. The following people served on the first Board of Directors of the Bank of Charlotte in 1853: merchants T. H. Brem, David Parks, S. P. Alexander, A. C. Steele, and H. B. Williams and lawyers J. H. Wilson and W. R. Myers.

15. Ibid., 14 June 1854, 30 January 1855, 27 January 1857. Shore posits in *Southern Capitalists* that antebellum leaders were never reactionary "pre-capitalists" but espoused

capitalism even as they held slaves (xii). Russell argues in *Atlanta*, however, that although Atlanta's urban promoters were "not explicitly anti-industrial," they were "lukewarm rather than hostile to industrialization" (39–49). By contrast, Charlotte's town leaders enthusiastically embraced small industry and made it a selling point for the railroad as early as 1847.

16. "Local Improvements," *North Carolina Whig*, 15 June 1853; "Charlotte and Her Destiny," ibid., 22 September 1852; "Town Improvements," ibid., 3 August 1854.

17. "Town Improvements," ibid., 3 August 1854; "The Time to Subscribe," ibid., 28 November 1854; "Street Notes," ibid., 17 October 1854; "The Condition of Our Streets," ibid., 21 February 1854; "The Central Rail Road and Town Bridges," ibid., 21 March 1854. Professionals and small businesspeople dominated the town commission between 1853 and 1865. Of 49 men who served as town intendants (mayors) and commissioners during that period, 39 appeared in the censuses of 1850 and 1860. A total of 28 were businesspeople or professionals, 10 were skilled tradesmen, and 1 was a planter. David Goldfield notes that antebellum civic leaders in the South "formed an interlocking directorate permeating every aspect of city life that counted in guiding their city toward prosperity and recognition." Civic leaders served on the boards of railroads and other industries as well as in town government. See Goldfield, "Pursuing the American Urban Dream," 60.

18. "Female Academy," *North Carolina Whig*, 16 February 1853; "Our Female Academy," ibid., 17 October 1854; Charlotte Board of Aldermen Minutes, 3 May 1858, CCO. For more on the cultural aspects of civic boosterism, see Doyle, *Social Order of a Frontier Community*.

19. "Our Mechanics and Their Works," *North Carolina Whig*, 20 July 1853; "The Prosperous Condition of Charlotte," ibid., 14 June 1854.

20. "Fashion," ibid., 7 November 1854.

21. "Thespian Club," ibid., 10 January 1864; "Christian Association," ibid., 5 May 1857.

22. See Friedman, *Enclosed Garden*, xi–xiii, 19, and Lebsock, *Free Women of Petersburg*, 193–236.

23. See, for example, "Ladies Fair," *North Carolina Whig*, 17 November 1857, and "A Party," ibid., 25 October 1859. Lebsock in *Free Women of Petersburg* contends that the church "offered a respectable space in which women could indulge in new kinds of assertion" (216).

24. Charlotte Presbyterian Church Minutes, 4 August 1858, Drury Lacy Papers, SHC.

25. Ibid. Lebsock argues that in antebellum Petersburg the creation of a female orphan asylum was "not so much a rejection of woman's sphere as it was an attempt to give institutional form and public importance to its most positive features" and that the organization of the asylum "clearly heightened the women's sense of their own significance." Antebellum women's organizations and the women's culture they helped create and sustain "went hand in glove with nineteenth-century stereotypes." See Lebsock, *Free Women of Petersburg*, 210, 224.

26. The common entrepreneurial outlook of Charlotte's businesspeople and county planters supports DeCredico's depiction of the common interests of planters and town businesspeople in Civil War–era Georgia and challenges Genovese's portrayal of the anticommercial attitudes of antebellum planters and their power to retard southern economic development. See DeCredico, *Patriotism for Profit*, 16–19, and Genovese, *Political Economy of Slavery*. In addition, the large real estate and slave holdings of many of Charlotte's merchants suggest that they owned farms in the county. See U.S. Bureau of

the Census, Manuscript census schedules, Mecklenburg County, North Carolina, 1850 and 1860.

27. "Whiggery and Democracy Contrasted," *North Carolina Whig*, 8 November 1853. Howe in *Political Culture of the American Whigs* notes that Whigs propagated "self-culture," stressing "self-denial, self-help, and self-control" (16–37).

28. "Election Returns," *Charlotte Journal*, 10 November 1848; "The Result," *North Carolina Whig*, 18 August 1853; Thomas W. Dewey to Bessie Dewey, 4 August 1854, Drury Lacy Papers, SHC. According to Williams in "Foundations of the Whig Party," the Whig party in North Carolina defied any simple explanation in terms of its geographic base, especially after 1840. The Piedmont counties of Mecklenburg and Lincoln, he notes, "voted overwhelmingly Democratic" in every gubernatorial election from 1836 to 1850. But O'Brien in *Legal Fraternity* points out that in Guilford County, Whiggery dominated and the Democracy was always weak (30). Watson in *Jacksonian Politics* notes, however, that Whig strength grew in the state's towns and villages after 1839. By 1842 "a large majority of town dwellers were voting Whig while a smaller majority of countrymen were voting Democratic." Watson argues that "a division between rural and village communities was evidently a pattern of primary-group rivalries which was relevant to the shape of the second party system in almost every North Carolina community" (313).

29. For more on the Whig party as a vehicle for the emerging middle class in the antebellum period, see Paul E. Johnson, *A Shopkeeper's Millennium*, 138. Howe argues that the decline of the Whig party in the South "is a measure of the declining appeal of its bourgeois value system and the corresponding success of the premodern value system of the Southern Democrats." But instead of middle-class Whigs being eclipsed by the planter mystique in the 1850s, the Charlotte example suggests that a nascent business and professional class was gaining strength in the South during the 1850s but was considerably weakened by the collapse of Whiggery and the lack of a viable successor to the Whig party. See Howe, *Political Culture of the American Whigs*, 259.

30. Overdyke, *Know-Nothing Party*, v; Thornton, *Politics and Power*, 354; "The American Party," *North Carolina Whig*, 29 May 1855; "American Mass Meeting," ibid., 10 July 1855; ibid., 3 July 1855; "Election," ibid., 31 July 1855; ibid., 11 November 1856; "Old Line Whigs," ibid., 9 September 1856; "The Whig Convention," ibid., 26 April 1859. The American party fared badly in elections in 1855 and 1856.

Overdyke in *Know-Nothing Party* notes that in North Carolina, one of the states in the South with the lowest percentage of foreign-born inhabitants, "little grounds for nativism existed" (33). According to the 1850 census, Charlotte had twenty foreign-born inhabitants in the work force. Of these, all but one, a German, came from the British Isles, and nearly all were professionals or skilled craftsmen, hardly the "foreign dregs" that the Know-Nothing party railed against. See U.S. Bureau of the Census, Manuscript census schedules, Mecklenburg County, North Carolina, 1850.

31. For studies of the temperance movement in antebellum towns, see Paul E. Johnson, *A Shopkeeper's Millennium*, 55–61; Ryan, *Cradle of the Middle Class*, 132–44; Doyle, *Social Order of a Frontier Community*, 226; and Gilkeson, *Middle-Class Providence*. See also Rorabaugh, "Sons of Temperance," and "Temperance Meeting," *Miner's and Farmer's Journal*, 9 March 1833.

32. Bessie Dewey to Mary Rice Lacy, 15 February 1855, Drury Lacy Papers, SHC; "Communications," *North Carolina Whig*, 5 January 1853. Doyle in *Social Order of a Frontier Community* notes that the temperance issue "dominated local politics after the mid-1850s" and "tapped the community's social divisions at their deepest level" (217–26).

33. *North Carolina Whig*, 8 December 1852.

34. "Town Election," ibid., 21 January 1853.

35. "A Word for the Gentlemen," ibid., 26 March 1853. For more on women and the temperance issue, see Bordin, *Woman and Temperance*.

36. "Grog or No Grog," *North Carolina Whig*, 11 December 1855; "Democratic Anti–Know Nothing Meeting," ibid., 18 December 1855; Overdyke, *Know-Nothing Party*, 85; *Western Democrat*, quoted in *North Carolina Whig*, 21 December 1855.

37. "Public Meeting," *North Carolina Whig*, 3 January 1856; "Municipal Election," ibid., 22 January 1856.

38. Gusfield in *Symbolic Crusade* argues that temperance served as the "symbolic crusade" for the middle class to secure their social status, abstinence being "a mark of middle class membership" (25). Paul E. Johnson in *A Shopkeeper's Millennium* calls the temperance issue in antebellum Rochester, New York, "a middle-class obsession" (55–61). For Ryan in *Cradle of the Middle Class*, temperance represents "the apotheosis of associations" crucial to the development of a middle class (132–44). Echoing Gusfield, Doyle in *Social Order of a Frontier Community* argues that in Jacksonville, Illinois, temperance served as the symbolic crusade that "rallied the middle class around an ethos of respectability, hard work, and self-improvement" and served as the instrument to project the values of the middle class on the entire community (226). In antebellum Providence, Rhode Island, temperance became the means by which many members of the community "began to view themselves as members of the stable, industrious, sober middle class, defined less by occupation or wealth . . . than by the values they cultivated" (Gilkeson, *Middle-Class Providence*, 32). Tyrell in "Drink and Temperance" argues that the temperance movement in the antebellum South won its strongest support "from small-town middle class people, from professionals, merchants, skilled tradesmen, and entrepreneurs engaged in manufacturing" (496). But events in Charlotte suggest that such a characterization may be oversimplistic. Tyrell also proposes that ethnic and religious divisions may explain temperance allegiances better than social class, yet Charlotte's wets and drys were almost exclusively native-born Protestants.

39. "Temperance Meeting," *North Carolina Whig*, 18 March 1856.

40. U.S. Bureau of the Census, Manuscript census schedules, Mecklenburg County, North Carolina, 1850 and 1860; Franklin, *Free Negro in North Carolina*, 15. Wade in *Slavery in the Cities* notes that by 1860, "slavery was disintegrating in Southern cities" because of problems in maintaining discipline and control in an urban setting (4, 244). Although the 1860 census compendium listed 74 free blacks in Charlotte, the manuscript census listed 139.

41. U.S. Bureau of the Census, Manuscript census schedules, Mecklenburg County, North Carolina, 1850 and 1860. On the "hiring out" system and the flexibility of slavery in southern towns, see Wade, *Slavery in the Cities*, 26, 38–39.

42. "Ordinances of the Town of Charlotte," *Western Democrat*, 26 January 1864. On slave and free black restrictions in southern cities, see Goldfield, "Pursuing the American Urban Dream," 65. Many of these ordinances were in effect in the 1850s.

43. Franklin, *Free Negro in North Carolina*, 58–120.

44. "Ordinances of the Town of Charlotte," *Western Democrat*, 26 January 1864.

45. U.S. Bureau of the Census, Manuscript census schedules, Mecklenburg County, North Carolina, 1860; Franklin, *Free Negro in North Carolina*, 228–29; Michael Johnson and Roark, *Black Masters*, 37, 66.

46. Several outstanding works trace the emergence of a free black elite in the Old South. See, for example, Gatewood, *Aristocrats of Color*, 12–29; Berlin, *Slaves without Masters*; and Michael Johnson and Roark, *Black Masters*.

47. U.S. Bureau of the Census, Manuscript census schedules, Mecklenburg County, North Carolina, 1860. For more on free black institutions in the Old South, see Berlin, *Slaves without Masters*, 296.

48. Franklin, *Free Negro in North Carolina*, 211–12; "Our Colored Population," *North Carolina Whig*, 29 September 1852.

49. *North Carolina Whig*, 14 February 1854; "The New England Clergy," ibid., 28 March 1854; ibid., 23 November 1854.

50. "Take Care of Him," ibid., 28 June 1854; "An Abolitionist Done For," ibid., 24 March 1857.

51. "The Affair at Harpers Ferry," ibid., 1 November 1859; "Be on Your Guard," ibid., 29 November 1859; "Charlotte Light Infantry," ibid., 20 December 1859; "Meeting of the Cavalry," ibid., 3 January 1860; "Mecklenburg Dragoons," ibid., 24 January 1860.

52. Historians have long cited the war as a stimulus to the development of class consciousness and conflict in the South. See, for example, Escott, *After Secession*, esp. 94–134, and Tatum, *Disloyalty in the Confederacy*. For class conflict in North Carolina, see Escott, *After Secession*, 99–103, and *Many Excellent People*, 39–84; Paludan, *Victims*; Scarboro, "North Carolina and the Confederacy"; and Auman, "Neighbor against Neighbor." William C. Harris offers an especially subtle interpretation of class conflict and politics in North Carolina, arguing that Holden's peace movement "heightened class consciousness among yeomen whites," who increasingly viewed the war as "a rich man's war and a poor man's fight." But "class divisions never reached the point where they threatened the traditional political order" as Holden "kept the discontent channeled into the regular party current that reflected the old political experiences and ideologies and cut across class lines." See William C. Harris, *William Woods Holden*, 130.

53. *North Carolina Whig*, 19 July 1859, 29 May 1860.

54. The *North Carolina Whig* endorsed Bell, while the *Western Democrat* supported Breckinridge. See *North Carolina Whig*, 22 May, 28 August 1860.

55. "Union Men to the Polls," *North Carolina Whig*, 21 October 1860; "Watchman, What of the Night?," ibid., 27 November 1860.

56. Barrett, *Civil War in North Carolina*, 3–4.

57. "Public Meeting," *Western Democrat*, 4 December 1860; "Public Meeting," *North Carolina Whig*, 4 December 1860. The villagers of Morrow's Turn Out expressed bitterness toward the federal government for having "failed to promote the welfare of Southern States," while citizens at a meeting at Wallis's Steam Mill confirmed their faith in the Constitution, arguing that the South "should acquiesce, so long as he [Lincoln] remains a *constitutional* President." See "Meeting of Citizens of Morrow's Turn Out," *Western Democrat*, 18 December 1860, and "Union Meeting in Mecklenburg," *North Carolina Whig*, 15 January 1861.

58. For more on the American Revolution as an inspiration for Confederates, see Thomas, *The Confederacy as a Revolutionary Experience*.

59. *Western Democrat*, 26 February, 5 March 1861; Tatum, *Disloyalty in the Confederacy*, 10.

60. *Western Democrat*, 16 April 1861; Tatum, *Disloyalty in the Confederacy*, 10; "Surrender of Anderson," *North Carolina Whig*, 16 April 1861.

61. *Western Democrat*, 22, 30 April 1861.

62. Rable, *Civil Wars*, 47; "The Address of Miss Sadler," *North Carolina Whig*, 23 April 1861; "Flag Presentations," ibid., 30 April 1861. Rable argues that women served as "silent participants" in the flag-presentation ceremonies. But Lebsock in *Free Women of*

Petersburg notes that even in the antebellum period flag-presentation ceremonies for militia units presented one of the "few occasions in which women spoke in public before mixed audiences" (231). Recent studies of southern women stress the limited long-term impact of the war in transforming gender roles, which seems to be the case in Charlotte as well. Rable argues that while the war temporarily expanded the role of many southern women, it provided no "long-lasting consequences" since "women still performed largely auxiliary tasks in the economy" and since both southern men and women believed "that peace would return women to the domestic circle." Although the "war had opened doors for these women," he argues, the end of the conflict "closed them just as quickly, and traditional notions about femininity survived more or less intact." See Rable, *Civil Wars*, 112. Similarly, in *The Enclosed Garden*, Friedman contends that although the Civil War provided "an alternate experience for women and new responsibilities" that "raised expectations about changes in women's roles, the southern community obstructed any radical shift in women's status" (92).

63. *Western Democrat*, 30 July, 10 September 1861.

64. Ibid., 30 July 1861, 15 July 1862.

65. Rable, *Civil Wars*, 137–38; "Ladies' Aid Society," *North Carolina Whig*, 17 September 1861.

66. Soldiers' Aid Society Minutes, 1861, Drury Lacy Papers, SHC; "Ladies' Aid Society," *North Carolina Whig*, 17 September 1861; *Western Democrat*, 1 October 1861.

67. Soldiers' Aid Society Minutes, 1861, Drury Lacy Papers, SHC; "Acknowledgement," *North Carolina Whig*, 12 November 1861.

68. In their study of the prominent free black Ellison family in South Carolina, *Black Masters*, Johnson and Roark note the family's support of the Confederacy as a means to help secure their precarious freedom in wartime South Carolina (301–7).

69. *Western Democrat*, 1 July 1862; "Effects of the War on the South," ibid., 15 October 1861.

70. For more on how the Civil War stimulated entrepreneurship in the South, see DeCredico, *Patriotism for Profit*. DeCredico argues that "Georgia's entrepreneurial revolution of the antebellum years was catalyzed anew by the demands of Civil War mobilization" and "accelerated trends that had been afoot for nearly twenty years before the first shots were fired" (ibid., 152). See also Russell, *Atlanta*, 91–92.

71. DeCredico, *Patriotism for Profit*, 28; *Western Democrat*, 7 January 1862; "Public Meeting," *North Carolina Whig*, 25 February 1862; "Manufacture of Arms," ibid., 25 February 1862; "Stockholder's Meeting," *Western Democrat*, 30 April 1862.

72. Greenwood, *On the Homefront*, 10.

73. Ibid.

74. Ibid., 11.

75. In *Patriotism for Profit*, DeCredico argues that the Confederate war machine helped diversify the economy in Georgia while transforming backwater towns into urban and industrial centers (42–47, 70).

76. *Western Democrat*, 13 May 1862.

77. Dandridge S. Burwell to Edmund S. Burwell, 3 March 1863, Edmund S. Burwell Papers, SHC.

78. Mrs. Robert Burwell to Edmund S. Burwell, 8 August 1863, Edmund S. Burwell Papers, SHC.

79. "Hard Times," *North Carolina Whig*, 10 December 1861; *Western Democrat*, 13 May 1862.

80. *North Carolina Whig*, 7 October 1862; *Western Democrat*, 2 December 1861.

81. Barrett, *Civil War in North Carolina*, 184; Auman, "Neighbor against Neighbor," 59–92; William C. Harris, *William Woods Holden*, 115; Tatum, *Disloyalty in the Confederacy*, 111.

82. William C. Harris, *William Woods Holden*, 112–19; *North Carolina Weekly Standard*, 30 July 1862.

83. William C. Harris, *William Woods Holden*, 115–19; *North Carolina Weekly Standard*, 9 July 1862.

84. "The 'Standard' versus Colonel Johnston," *North Carolina Whig*, 18 March 1862; *North Carolina Weekly Standard*, 6 August 1862.

85. Cheney, *North Carolina Government*, 1401; Tatum, *Disloyalty in the Confederacy*, 113. Johnston carried only ten counties other than Mecklenburg: Bladen, Cleveland, Columbus, Duplin, Edgecombe, Gaston, Halifax, New Hanover, Warren, and Wilson.

86. William C. Harris, *William Woods Holden*, 125; Barrett, *Civil War in North Carolina*, 183; Scarboro, "North Carolina and the Confederacy," 144.

87. William C. Harris, *William Woods Holden*, 125, 127–29, 132; "Public Meeting in Mecklenburg County," *North Carolina Weekly Standard*, 19 August 1863.

88. William C. Harris, *William Woods Holden*, 132; "Dr. J. G. Ramsay," *North Carolina Weekly Standard*, 21 October 1863.

89. *Charlotte Bulletin*, quoted in *North Carolina Weekly Standard*, 21 October 1863; *Western Democrat*, 20 October 1863.

90. "Meeting of the Citizens of Mecklenburg County," *Western Democrat*, 1 September 1863.

91. Ibid., 10 November 1863; Cheney, *North Carolina Government*, 393.

92. William C. Harris, *William Woods Holden*, 137.

93. *North Carolina Weekly Standard*, 24 October 1864.

94. "Town Ordinances," *North Carolina Whig*, 11 June 1861.

95. "Runaways," *Western Democrat*, 16 June 1863; "The Negroes," ibid., 7 March 1865.

96. Greenwood, *On the Homefront*, 14; Mrs. Robert Burwell to Edmund S. Burwell, 16 February 1865, Edmund S. Burwell Papers, SHC.

CHAPTER 2

1. D. H. Hill, "Education," *The Land We Love*, May 1866, 1.

2. *Western Democrat*, 3 July 1865.

3. Greenwood, *On the Homefront*, 17; *Western Democrat*, 3, 25 July 1865.

4. William C. Harris, *William Woods Holden*, 168–69; Charlotte Board of Aldermen Minutes, 23 June, 17 July 1865, CCO.

5. Trelease, *North Carolina Railroad*, 155; "Business in Charlotte," *Western Democrat*, 29 August 1865.

6. *Western Democrat*, 15 May 1866, 20 November 1868, 11 August 1866.

7. "Death of Maj. Clement Dowd," *Daily Charlotte Observer*, 15 April 1898; "Rufus Yancey McAden," in *Cyclopedia of Eminent and Representative Men*, 199–200. My profile of Charlotte's business leaders from 1865 to 1880 is based on a list of individuals who were officers in trade organizations, delegates to commercial conventions, and directors and officers of banks and railroads. Of fifty-nine names generated, biographical information—including origin and date of birth—for twenty-nine could be found. My study parallels Doyle's profile of business leaders in both Nashville and Atlanta in 1880. Doyle found that most of these leaders had been born in the 1820s and that "a surprisingly large

number had arrived in Atlanta and Nashville before the war broke out." In addition, most of them had been "born in modest circumstances in the rural South, had migrated to cities in their youth, and had built their fortunes there." Many had "transcended individual success in one line of business to engage in a variety of entrepreneurial ventures" with other businesspeople. Doyle concludes that although the economic leaders of Nashville and Atlanta were "by no means all 'new men' who emerged untouched by the war," they "entered the postwar era with the economic wind at their backs." See Doyle, *New Men, New Cities, New South*, 87–110.

8. *Western Democrat*, 29 August, 26 September 1865, 6 November, 18 December 1866; the Reverend Robert Burwell to Edmund S. Burwell, 24 November 1866, Edmund S. Burwell Papers, SHC.

9. *Western Democrat*, 22 December 1868, 4 June 1867.

10. Ibid., 20 April 1869.

11. John C. Barnett to E. Whittlesey, 29 June 1865, quoted in Roberta Sue Alexander, *North Carolina Faces the Freedman*, 7. Noting the fact that freedpeople sought opportunity, escape from violence in the countryside, and services such as schools, Rabinowitz in *Race Relations* comments that "both push and pull factors were at work" in the migration of freedpeople from the country to the city (22–24).

12. "The Crops," *Western Democrat*, 20 June 1865; "A Bad Sign," ibid., 14 November 1865; ibid., 16 October, 18 September 1866, 14 November 1865, 17 April 1866; "Leaving," ibid., 25 December 1866. For black and white relations in other southern towns during Reconstruction, see Rabinowitz, *Race Relations*.

13. Captain John C. Barnett, assistant superintendent of the Freedmen's Bureau, "Circular to the Freedmen of Western North Carolina," 1 October 1865, Mint Museum of History, Charlotte, North Carolina.

14. Hannibal D. Norton, "Monthly Report," 26, 31 December 1866, RBRFAL.

15. A. W. Shaffer, "Annual Report," 1867, Hannibal D. Norton, "Monthly Report," January 1867, and Thomas McAlpine to Brevet Lieutenant Colonel Jacob F. Chur, 25 May 1868, all in RBRFAL. The Freedmen's Bureau furnished transportation from Charlotte to ex-slaves who made contracts to work for planters in Mississippi, Georgia, Alabama, Florida, and Texas.

16. "Reports of Outrages," 1–15 July 1866, and "Complaints and Dispositions," October 1867–September 1868, both in RBRFAL.

17. U.S. Bureau of the Census, Manuscript census schedules, Mecklenburg County, North Carolina, 1860 and 1870.

18. Berlin in *Slaves without Masters* contends that "blacks who had enjoyed freedom before the war generally remained at the top of the new black society. Throughout the postbellum South they controlled a disproportionate share of black wealth, skill, political power, and social leadership" and continued to hold high social status well into the twentieth century. Calling themselves "old issue free," they "stood scornfully aloof from the mass of former bondsmen" (ibid., 386–90). Gatewood in *Aristocrats of Color* also argues that the "colored aristocracy" of the late nineteenth and early twentieth century had its roots in the antebellum free black community (7–29).

19. Walls, *African Methodist Episcopal Zion Church*, 190; J. W. Smith, "Early History of Seventh Street Presbyterian Church, U.S.A, Now First United Presbyterian Church, U.S.A., Charlotte, North Carolina," 1976, Vertical Files, Robinson-Spangler Carolina Room, Public Library of Charlotte and Mecklenburg County, Charlotte, North Carolina.

20. "Biddle Memorial Institute," *Western Democrat*, 8 October 1867; T. D. McAlpine to Jacob Chur, 10 January 1868, and "Special Requisition for the Students of Biddle

Memorial Institute at Charlotte," which includes a request for 11 woolen blankets, 40 bed sacks, 50 great coats, 60 pairs of trousers, 60 shirts, 60 pairs of shoes, and 60 pairs of flannel drawers, both in RBRFAL.

21. A. W. Shaffer, "Annual Report," 22 September 1867, and T. D. McAlpine to H. C. Vogell, superintendent of education, Raleigh, "School Report," 18 November 1868, both in RBRFAL.

22. Plotting the areas of residence of different races and classes in Charlotte based on the 1875–76 *Charlotte City Directory*, Thomas Hanchett in "White-Collar, Blue-Collar, and Blacks" found that in the First Ward, for example, blacks resided on twenty-eight blocks, only three of which were all black. According to Hanchett, "people of color fitted into the physical fabric of the city just as whites did. Poorer laborers tended to live in low-lying areas or close to the edge of town—areas that held whites as well as blacks. More fortunate souls lived closer to the city center, either as renters or owners" (ibid., 10–11). In his study of five postbellum southern cities, *Race Relations*, Rabinowitz found a similar pattern, noting that a "house-by-house examination reveals a certain amount of racial intermixture within city blocks" (98).

23. "Report of Schools," March–December 1868, and the Reverend Willis L. Miller to the subassistant commissioner, "School Report," 26 May 1868, all in RBRFAL.

24. Roberta Sue Alexander, "Hostility and Hope," 115–16; Jones, *Soldiers of Light*, 3; Abbott, *Republican Party and the South*, 100; "Editorial," *The Land We Love*, August 1867, 353.

25. Roberta Sue Alexander, *North Carolina Faces the Freedman*, 25–29, and "Hostility and Hope," 114; *North Carolina Weekly Standard*, 12 September, 10, 17 October 1866. Schenck may also have been a delegate to the above-mentioned first statewide freedmen's convention held in Raleigh in September 1865. Although the Charlotte newspapers did not report the convention, the *New Berne Daily Times* listed the names of the delegates, citing "—— Shanks of Charlotte." See "The Colored Convention," *New Berne Daily Times*, 2 October 1865.

26. "John Schenck Is Dead," *Daily Charlotte Observer*, 31 March 1894. In his study of black political leadership in Reconstruction South Carolina, *Black over White*, Thomas Holt found that a free black in 1860 had "better than ten times the chances of his enslaved brother to become one of the leadership group" (43). Armstead Robinson in "Plans Dat Comed from God" found that many black politicians in Reconstruction Memphis came from the ranks of the "upper-status group" of the black community and that many were free before the war (71–102). Similarly, John Blassingame in *Black New Orleans* found a connection between "social class and political preferment," although, he notes, it is unclear whether "certain Negroes were selected to high important political posts because of their social prestige" or whether "social prestige was based on political standing" (159).

27. For more on the role of black veterans in Reconstruction politics, see Berlin et al., *Freedom*, 769–70, and Williamson, *After Slavery*, 369.

28. William C. Harris, *William Woods Holden*, 170, 214.

29. Ibid., 220–22.

30. Hoffman, "Republican Party in North Carolina," 21, 26; Abbott, *Republican Party and the South*, 159.

31. "The Republican Meeting in Charlotte," *Western Democrat*, 28 May 1867; William C. Harris, *William Woods Holden*, 223.

32. "The Republican Meeting in Charlotte," *Western Democrat*, 28 May 1867; "The Column Moving—Republican Meeting in Charlotte," *North Carolina Weekly Standard*, 4 September 1867; "Rufus Barringer," in Ashe, *Biographical History*, 116–24. In a long and

fascinating letter to the *North Carolina Weekly Standard* on 30 September 1868, Barringer gave a detailed explanation for his affiliation with the Republican party. He cited his love for the Union, his opposition to the war, and the fact that he believed "moral causes" triumphed in the Civil War. Moreover, his experience in the war "dispelled in some measure prejudices I had against the masses, and especially colored people." Barringer also displayed a great deal of anger toward "the politicians and the upper class," who he believed had failed to carry their weight during the war. He likened southern Republicans to the "new men" who emerged as leaders after the American Revolution to lead the new nation.

33. "The Column Moving—Republican Meeting in Charlotte," *North Carolina Weekly Standard*, 4 September 1867; "Republican Convention," ibid., 20 November 1867.

34. William C. Harris, *William Woods Holden*, 231–32.

35. "The Reconstruction Prospect," *Western Democrat*, 12 November 1867; "The Conservative Meeting in Mecklenburg," ibid., 19 November 1867.

36. "Advice Gratis," ibid., 7 May 1867.

37. Only 13 Conservatives were elected to the convention, held from 14 January to 17 March 1868, compared with 107 Republicans. See Lefler and Newsome, *North Carolina*, 489.

38. "The Result," *Western Democrat*, 26 November 1867. As partisan politics grew in intensity, Yates exhorted townspeople to "do whatever we can to encourage the South to pay more attention to rebuilding their shattered fortunes and restoring the waste places, and less to party and party politics." See "State Convention," ibid., 14 January 1868. Powell in *North Carolina through Four Centuries* notes that many whites across the state, although "disgusted with the Reconstruction programs of Congress . . . remained aloof" and did not bother to register to vote (392).

39. "Meeting of Union Leagues at Charlotte," *North Carolina Weekly Standard*, 12 February 1868.

40. William C. Harris, *William Woods Holden*, 237, 240.

41. "Republican Meetings in Charlotte, Salisbury, Lexington, High Point," *North Carolina Weekly Standard*, 25 March 1868; "Governor Holden in Charlotte," ibid., 25 March 1868.

42. William C. Harris, *William Woods Holden*, 242; T. D. McAlpine to Colonel J. F. Branford, 30 March 1868, RBRFAL; *North Carolina Weekly Standard*, 22 April 1868; Lefler and Newsome, *North Carolina*, 491; "Election in North Carolina," *Western Democrat*, 5 May 1868.

43. T. D. McAlpine to Lieutenant Colonel Jacob F. Chur, 26 May 1868, RBRFAL.

44. *North Carolina Weekly Standard*, 29 April 1868.

45. William C. Harris, *William Woods Holden*, 248–49; *North Carolina Weekly Standard*, 22 July 1868; T. D. McAlpine to Brevet Major D. Wells, 15 January 1868, RBRFAL; "City Authorities," *Western Democrat*, 4 August 1868.

46. "Editorial," *The Land We Love*, December 1868; "Letter from Gen. Rufus Barringer," *North Carolina Weekly Standard*, 30 September 1868.

47. William C. Harris, *William Woods Holden*, 251; T. D. McAlpine to J. F. Chur, 11 October 1868, and J. F. Chur to T. D. McAlpine, 15 October 1868, both in RBRFAL; "A Serious Charge," *Western Democrat*, 17 October 1868.

48. "The Result," *Western Democrat*, 10 November 1868; Lefler and Newsome, *North Carolina*, 492–93.

49. "The Result," *Western Democrat*, 10 November 1868.

50. Republican strength in Charlotte politics closely resembled that in Richmond and

Nashville, where, according to Rabinowitz, Republicans dominated from 1868 to 1870 only as part of the provisional government. By contrast, Republicans in Atlanta, while never a majority on the city council, managed to elect one mayor. See Rabinowitz, *Race Relations*, 8–17.

51. Ibid., 270–71. In addition to Schenck, who was elected in 1870, 1871, 1872, and 1879, the following African Americans served as aldermen between 1865 and 1879: John C. Davidson (1868–69); J. N. Hunter (1868–69); Jefferson Hagler (1873, 1874, 1875, 1877); Burwell Johnston (1874, 1876); Frank Alexander (1875); and J. W. Gordon (1875, 1877, 1879).

52. "Letter from Charlotte," *North Carolina Weekly Standard*, 20 July 1870.

53. "Charlotte and the North-West," *Western Democrat*, 8 February 1870.

54. Hahn, *Roots of Southern Populism*, 137–69; Wright, *Old South, New South*, 34; "Farming Prospects," *Western Democrat*, 2 February 1869; ibid., 11 October 1870. For details on cotton, corn, and wheat cultivation, see table A.7.

55. "The Railroad Meeting," *Western Democrat*, 19 April 1870; "Objections to the Proposed County Subscriptions to Our Railroads," ibid., 10 May 1870; "The Railroad Subscription," 24 May 1870, *Charlotte Democrat*, 11 April 1871.

56. Hahn, *Roots of Southern Populism*, 145–46; Charlotte Board of Aldermen Minutes, 22 May 1871, CCO; U.S. Bureau of the Census, *Report on the Cotton Production*, 22. The guano trade also had grown to such an extent that in 1874 the city taxed the sale of guano by the ton. See Charlotte Board of Aldermen Minutes, 30 May 1874, CCO.

57. "The Railroad Picnic," *Charlotte Democrat*, 23 July 1872; "The Connection," ibid., 18 March 1873; "Charlotte to Greenville," ibid., 29 April 1873; "The Carolina Central Railway," ibid., 17 March 1874; Charlotte Board of Aldermen Minutes, 19 December 1870, 14 April 1874, CCO.

58. "Charlotte, Columbia, and Augusta Railroad," *Western Democrat*, 26 April 1870; "A T and O RR," ibid., 26 July 1870; "A T and O Railroad," *Charlotte Democrat*, 1 August 1871; "Air Line," ibid., 8 August 1871. For more on the emergence and role of the furnishing merchant, see Woodman, *King Cotton*, 296–314. See also Hahn, *Roots of Southern Populism*, 170–203. In an examination of power holding in Mecklenburg County from 1850 to 1880, Gail Williams O'Brien constructs an elaborate "power index" in order to test theories about continuity and change through the watershed of the Civil War. O'Brien concludes that nonfarmers held the reins of power in Mecklenburg both before and after the Civil War and "a single elite, as opposed to a pluralist system, existed in Mecklenburg County, 1850–1880." Moreover, "no wholesale replacement of an elite occurred during this thirty-year period, but, rather, members were gradually replaced as they grew old, died, or, in a few rare instances, moved away." Although O'Brien's power index is compelling, her study attempts to be "an analysis of power and not a study of socioeconomic structure upon which inferences about power were based." Therefore, it does not take into account the fundamental transformations in Mecklenburg's economy in the 1870s—particularly the growth of cotton culture—that redefined the distribution of power after the Civil War, greatly expanding the economic power of town merchants at the expense of county farmers. Although many of the same people may have held political office before and after the Civil War, many newcomers who came to Charlotte as merchants and cotton buyers in the late 1860s and 1870s wielded economic power in the county during the 1870s, which marked change rather than continuity in New South Charlotte. See O'Brien, "Power and Influence," 120–37.

59. "Cotton," *Western Democrat*, 1 March 1870; ibid., 10 October 1870.

60. "The Farmer's Mutual Aid Association," *Charlotte Democrat*, 23 December 1871;

"Proceedings of the Farmer's Mutual Aid Society of Mecklenburg County," ibid., 28 November 1871.

61. "To Cotton Sellers—An Important Arrangement," ibid., 11 March 1873.

62. "Public Meeting in Mallard Creek Township," ibid., 6 May 1873; "Public Meeting," ibid., 20 May 1873; "Public Meeting," ibid., 10 June 1873.

63. Nordin, *Rich Harvest*, 22; Buck, *Granger Movement*, 58; "Patrons of Husbandry," *Southern Home*, 16 June 1873. For more on the history of the Grange in North Carolina, see Noblin, *Leonidas Lafayette Polk*, 98–99.

64. Buck, *Granger Movement*, 280–81.

65. For more on the Torrance family, see J. B. Alexander, *History of Mecklenburg County*. James H. Davis reported $75,000 in real estate and $150,000 in personal property in 1860; in 1870, M. L. Davis, his son, reported a total of $7,800 in wealth. The first six Granges founded in Mecklenburg were at Long Creek, Mallard Creek, Steele Creek, Providence, Lemley, and Charlotte. See "Col. Aiken's Work," *Daily Charlotte Observer*, 12 June 1873; "Organization of the State Grange of the Patrons of Husbandry," ibid., 13 July 1873; and ibid., 20 July 1873, 20 January 1874. County Grangers also participated in the state Grange. E. C. Davidson, Mrs. E. C. Davidson, and Thomas L. Vail all served on the executive committee of the state Grange.

66. "The Matter Settled," *Charlotte Democrat*, 29 July 1873; "Cotton," ibid., 29 July 1873.

67. See, for example, "The Class Combination," ibid., 16 September 1873; "Letter to the Editor," ibid., 12 November 1874; "Leaving Out the Middle-men," ibid., 27 January 1874; and ibid., 14 April 1874. The *Charlotte Democrat* constantly stressed the common interests of town and country people, arguing that "the country people prosper just in proportion to the prosperity of businessmen and people of Charlotte," yet at the same time it helped inflame passions between town and country people by attacking the Grange and defending business interests. See, for example, ibid., 4 September 1876; "Grangers," *Southern Home*, 1 June 1874; and *Charlotte Democrat*, 13 September 1875.

68. "The Grangers and Their Business Agents," *Daily Charlotte Observer*, 12 June 1874; Nordin, *Rich Harvest*, 155; "Important to Grangers," *Daily Charlotte Observer*, 12 November 1874; "Direct Trade Movement," ibid., 11 November 1874; "That Proposition," *Charlotte Democrat*, 9 November 1874; *Charlotte Democrat*, quoted in "The Cotton Question," *Daily Charlotte Observer*, 17 November 1874. See also "The Unfortunate Movement," *Charlotte Democrat*, 18 October 1875; "Direct Trade Union," ibid., 7 May 1875; and "Cotton," *Southern Home*, 25 January 1875.

The *Charlotte Democrat* took such a virulent stance against the Grange that the *State Agricultural Journal* asked Grangers not to patronize the newspaper. See *Charlotte Democrat*, 31 March 1874. The Graham Grange of Mecklenburg promised not "to patronize any merchant or tradesman who withdraws his patronage from the *Southern Home* on the ground that it advocates the cause of the Patrons of Husbandry" and promised to increase subscriptions to the *Southern Home*. See "Grange Meetings," *Southern Home*, 4 January 1875; "Resolutions of Mallard Creek Grange," ibid., 30 November 1874; and ibid., 14 December 1874. Charlotte's third newspaper, the *Daily Charlotte Observer*, published and edited by Charles R. Jones, originally sympathized with the Grange movement. Jones heartily supported the Direct Trade Union in the fall of 1874, but his stance probably got him in trouble with local merchants whom he relied on for advertising revenue. Soon after he endorsed the union, he inexplicably moderated his stance, causing James F. Johnston, the head of the Direct Trade Union, to question whether Jones had "rather gone back on the Grangers." Although Jones insisted that he had not abandoned the Grange, the

Observer never again voiced strong sentiments in favor of the farmers' movement and instead placated the town's businesspeople, arguing that "a certain number of middle men or merchants are necessary." This shift suggests that local merchants also threatened to pull their advertising from the *Observer* and that Jones, unlike Hill, succumbed to the pressure and moderated his position. See "Off Grangering," *Daily Charlotte Observer*, 19 September 1874; *Charlotte Democrat*, 31 August 1874; and "A Question Answered," *Daily Charlotte Observer*, 19 November 1874.

69. "Mecklenburg County Convention," *Daily Charlotte Observer*, 6 July 1875; "The City and County—Etiquette and Justice," ibid., 3 July 1875; "The County Convention Monday," ibid., 3 July 1875; "Anti-Convention Democrats," ibid., 22 July 1875.

70. "The Anti-Conventionists," ibid., 21 July 1875. Republicans appealed to "men who earn their bread by honest toil, and who have the backbone in the face of party displeasure, to come out and express their sentiments in opposition to the Convention." The *Daily Charlotte Observer* denied that many farmers crossed party lines to attend the convention. See ibid., 24 July 1875.

71. "White Men of Mecklenburg," ibid., 1 August 1875; "The Election," ibid., 6 August 1875; ibid., 7 August 1875; "Election in Mecklenburg," ibid., 7 August 1875.

72. County Democrats rejoined the party fold in 1876 as every county precinct except Pineville supported Vance in the election. The only precincts to vote for Republican candidate Settle were in the Second and Third wards, which each had a black majority. See "Vote of Mecklenburg," *Charlotte Democrat*, 9 November 1876.

73. Ibid., 1 October, 17 December 1872. For example, merchants Graham and Williams moved their entire business from Fayetteville to Charlotte in 1871, and W. P. Bynum, an established lawyer, moved to Charlotte from Lincolnton in 1872. See ibid., 1 October, 23 January 1872.

74. See, for example, "Musical Entertainment," ibid., 3 December 1872; "Charlotte Opera House," ibid., 27 September 1875; ibid., 14 September 1874; and "Fun and Exercise," ibid., 16 May 1871.

75. "A Mistake," ibid., 21 June 1875; "Costly Experience," ibid., 1 July 1873.

76. "Leaving Out the Middle Man," ibid., 27 January 1874.

77. "Meeting of the Merchants and Business Men," *Western Democrat*, 26 July 1870; "Board of Trade," ibid., 2 August 1870; "Mechanical Association," ibid., 8 March 1870; "Meeting of Mechanics," *Charlotte Democrat*, 17 January 1871; "City Improvements," ibid., 14 May 1872; "City Improvements," ibid., 4 June 1867; "Trip to Charlotte, North Carolina, from the Augusta Chronicle and Sentinel," ibid., 12 March 1872. In his examination of the emergence of a middle class in the antebellum North, Stuart Blumin points to the significance of the "divergence of economic circumstances between men who 'worked with their heads' and men who 'worked with their hands'" in the Jacksonian period. Nonmanual businesspeople made more money than manual workers, allowing them to accumulate more property and engage in entrepreneurship, which helped define them as "middle class" as opposed to "working class" manual laborers. See Blumin, *Emergence of the Middle Class*, 107–21.

78. "Excursion to Cleaveland Springs," *Daily Charlotte Observer*, 16 July 1876; Bessie Dewey to Thomas Dewey, 12 July 1869, Drury Lacy Papers, SHC; *Charlotte Democrat*, 23 July 1880.

79. "Fun and Exercise," *Charlotte Democrat*, 16 May 1871; "Skating Rink," ibid., 31 October 1871. See, for example, "Opera House," ibid., 10 May 1875, and ibid., 17 May 1875.

80. See "Mecklenburg Historical Society," *Charlotte Observer*, 3 May 1875; "The

Ladies Memorial Association," ibid., 4 June 1872; and Rip Van Winkle Book Club Minutes, Drury Lacy Papers, SHC. Several studies of middle-class formation in antebellum northern towns focus on the importance of voluntary organizations in helping define an emerging middle class. See especially Gilkeson, *Middle-Class Providence*, and Blumin, *Emergence of the Middle Class*, 192–229.

81. Hanchett, "White-Collar, Blue-Collar, and Blacks," 5; "A Stroll through the Outskirts," *Daily Charlotte Observer*, 9 January 1876.

82. Charlotte Board of Aldermen Minutes, 30 January 1871, CCO.

83. Ibid.; "Home and Hospital—A Praiseworthy Enterprise," *Daily Charlotte Observer*, 29 January 1876. The Charlotte Home and Hospital was renamed St. Peter's Hospital in 1898.

84. Lebsock, *Free Women of Petersburg*, 195–210; Hewitt, *Women's Activism and Social Change*, 70; McCarthy, *Noblesse Oblige*, 6–11, 23.

85. McCarthy, *Noblesse Oblige*, 23. McCarthy contends that for women in antebellum Chicago, "institution building afforded a sense of purpose and identity, increased their mobility, and won a good deal of public approval. It allowed them to escape the narrow confines of the home without openly challenging the dictates of the cult of domesticity" (ibid.).

86. *Charlotte Democrat*, 17 January 1879. The relief committee consisted of Wilkes, Jones, and VanLandingham, founders of the Church Aid Society, as well as Mrs. Charles J. Fox, Mrs. Whitsett, Mrs. Owens, Mrs. B. R. Smith, and Mrs. Powers.

87. Hewitt contends in *Women's Activism and Social Change* that in antebellum Rochester, "affluence and its female applications to benevolence were products, pillars, and public signs of membership in Rochester's emerging elite" (50).

88. "Mike Lipman's Great Combination Show," *Western Democrat*, 26 March 1867; "Civil Rights at the Opera House," *Daily Charlotte Observer*, 3 April 1875; "The Graded School," *Charlotte Observer*, 2 November 1873; "Public Schools in Mecklenburg," ibid., 20 July 1874; Charlotte Board of Aldermen Minutes, 24 April 1871, 27 June 1868, 12 May 1873, CCO.

89. "Civil Rights at the Opera House," *Daily Charlotte Observer*, 3 April 1875; "Civil Rights in the Theatre," ibid., 15 May 1875. Rabinowitz in *Race Relations* also found that challenges to segregation "were most pronounced after passage of the 1875 Civil Rights Act" but that most failed (195).

90. Rabinowitz, *Race Relations*, 62; U.S. Bureau of the Census, Manuscript census schedules, Mecklenburg County, North Carolina, 1870.

91. U.S. Bureau of the Census, Manuscript census schedules, Mecklenburg County, North Carolina, 1870; A. W. Shaffer to Lieutenant Colonel Jacob F. Chur, 27 August 1867, and T. D. McAlpine to Lieutenant Colonel Thomas P. Johnston, 22 March 1868, both in RBRFAL.

92. "Festival," *Daily Charlotte Observer*, 5 June 1873; "A New Colored Organization," ibid., 9 February 1876; *Charlotte Democrat*, 17 April 1876, 2 November 1877, 28 July 1878, 22 August 1879; Charlotte Board of Aldermen Minutes, 5 June 1871, CCO; "Fourth of July," *Charlotte Democrat*, 10 July 1876.

93. "Idleness," *Charlotte Democrat*, 2 May 1871; Foner, *Reconstruction*, 296; *Charlotte Democrat*, 30 May 1879; Charlotte Board of Aldermen Minutes, 22 May 1871, CCO.

94. "Arrested," *Charlotte Democrat*, 18 June 1872. Schenck resigned his seat on the Board of Aldermen but was reelected in 1879.

95. "The Future Prosperity of the Colored People," *Daily Charlotte Observer*, 25 March 1876.

96. "A Significant Movement of the Colored People," ibid., 18 March 1876; "Letter from the Reverend Garland H. White, President of the Colored People's New Movement," ibid., 18 March 1876.

97. Rabinowitz in *Race Relations* also found protests from black Republicans in Richmond and Atlanta in the Reconstruction era concerning their shabby treatment in the party (284–303). By contrast, Foner in *Reconstruction* depicts Reconstruction blacks as maintaining a "remarkable political unity" (398). Similarly, Bess Beatty, in her study of blacks and national politics, *Revolution Gone Backward*, traces black disillusionment with the Republican party during the post-Reconstruction era, neglecting divisions that existed during late Reconstruction.

98. "Republicans Caucusing," *Daily Charlotte Observer*, 12 April 1876; "Pandemonium Broke Loose!," ibid., 26 June 1876. The Democratic *Daily Charlotte Observer* reveled in Schenck's humiliation of white Republicans, noting that "it was a sight that made the Democratic heart leap for joy." The paper continued, "John rose upon the floor, cool as a cucumber; he threw shot and shell into the camp of his white brethren with such marked effect as to make them livid with rage, and cause them to almost foam at the mouth, while not so much as a bead of perspiration stood upon his brow. . . . Schenck was the master of the situation." See "The Late Radical Convention," ibid., 27 June 1876.

99. William C. Harris, *William Woods Holden*, 286, 296.

100. "Hatred of White Republicans to the Colored Race," *Southern Home*, 18 September 1876; "Colored Men Behold," *Daily Charlotte Observer*, 15 July 1876.

101. "The Colored Vote," *Daily Charlotte Observer*, 10 August 1876; "Radical Mob-law and Violence in Mecklenburg," ibid., 22 August 1876; "Another Assault upon a Colored Democrat," ibid., 22 August 1876.

102. "Vance Colored Democratic Club," ibid., 4 November 1876; "The Colored Club Meeting," ibid., 11 November 1876; "To the Colored People," ibid., 29 October 1876; "To the Colored Voters of Charlotte," ibid., 29 October 1876, the signers of which included John A. Young, R. M. Miller, Stenhouse and Macauley, John L. Morehead, and A. B. Davidson; "The Colored Tilden and Vance Club," ibid., 31 October 1876.

103. "Intimidation!," ibid., 4 November 1876.

104. "Vote of Mecklenburg," ibid., 9 November 1876; "The Colored Men," ibid., 9 November 1876.

CHAPTER 3

1. "Prominent Colored Men," *Charlotte Messenger*, 1 January 1887; "What Shall We Do to Be Saved?," ibid., 4 June 1887.

2. Ibid., 12 February 1887.

3. Whitener, *Prohibition in North Carolina*, 59.

4. Previous examinations of prohibition in the New South have generally ignored the aspect of class. Whereas historians of the antebellum North, such as Paul Johnson and Mary Ryan, have associated temperance societies with middle-class formation and middle-class ideology, southern historians have failed to make such a connection, instead emphasizing social control and evangelical religion. Carl Harris describes the basic thrust of prohibition as the attempt "to place the blacks more firmly and efficiently under the discipline of economically powerful white groups." He also finds a relationship between evangelical religion and prohibition. Don Doyle's discussion of prohibition in Nashville also emphasizes evangelicalism. Paul Isaac, in his study of prohibition and politics in Tennessee, contends that prohibitionists viewed their reform as a way to uplift the lower

classes, both black and white, but that prohibitionists also sought a sober, docile work force. Harris, Isaac, Doyle, and John Moore, who examined the prohibition movement in Atlanta, all portray black involvement in prohibition as instigated by whites. Moore addresses the issue of black involvement most thoroughly, tracing the role of blacks in Atlanta's successful prohibition campaign of 1885. But although he documents interracial cooperation and the black community's role, he never explores why some blacks were "dry" and others "wet," disregarding the class dimension of the prohibition movement. See Paul E. Johnson, *A Shopkeeper's Millennium*; Ryan, *Cradle of the Middle Class*; Carl V. Harris, *Political Power*; Doyle, *Nashville*; Isaac, *Prohibition and Politics*; and Moore, "The Negro and Prohibition in Atlanta."

5. *Charlotte Democrat*, 9 July, 10 September 1880; "The Question of the Day," *Charlotte Observer*, 1 February 1881.

6. "The Question of the Day," *Charlotte Observer*, 1 February 1881; *Charlotte City Directory*, 1879–80; Charlotte Board of Aldermen Minutes, 10 June 1880, CCO.

7. "Prohibition Meeting Tonight," *Charlotte Observer*, 27 January 1881; "Prohibition Meeting Last Night," ibid., 28 January 1881.

8. "Prohibition Meeting Last Night," ibid., 28 January 1881; "The Movement Begun," ibid., 1 April 1901. In her study of women's reform movements in Memphis, Marsha Wedell notes that prohibition organizations, particularly the Woman's Christian Temperance Union, provided a significant outlet "for women to develop their capabilities, expand female networks, and exercise authority in the public sphere." Prohibition activities "offered Southern women a respectable forum from which they could both perform their duty as a defender of the nineteenth century home and family, and simultaneously exercise their growing desire to widen that very 'sphere' to which they had been assigned." See Wedell, "Memphis Women and Social Reform," 80, 92. See also Bordin, *Woman and Temperance*, 5–8.

9. *Charlotte Observer*, 28 January 1881; "The Question of the Day," ibid., 1 February 1881. Of 202 names of prohibitionists mentioned in the local black and white press, 146 could be traced to the census of 1880 or the *Charlotte City Directory* of 1879–80. A total of 105 were white residents of Charlotte, 89 (85 percent) of whom were white-collar professionals or their spouses, 11 (11 percent) of whom were skilled artisans or spouses, and 5 of whom were farmers.

10. "The Question of the Day," *Charlotte Observer*, 1 February 1881.

11. "The Movement Begun," ibid., 1 April 1881.

12. Whitener, *Prohibition in North Carolina*, 60, 67.

13. "The Movement Begun," *Charlotte Observer*, 1 April 1881.

14. Williamson, *Crucible of Race*, 86. Liberals, argues Williamson, "possessed a sanguine faith, an optimistic adventurousness, [and] a willingness to experiment in search of progress" (ibid., 5–6). See also ibid., 85–107, for an extended discussion of racial liberalism.

15. Of 146 prohibitionists mentioned in the press that could be traced to censuses and city directories, 41 were African Americans. Seventeen (40 percent) of these were white-collar professionals or their spouses, 18 (45 percent) were skilled artisans or their spouses, and 6 (14 percent) were unskilled workers. For a breakdown of the occupations of black and white Charlotte residents in 1880, see table A.8.

16. Penn, *Afro-American Press*; Rosa Smith, interview with author, 15 March 1984; Parker, *Biddle–Johnson C. Smith University Story*, 7; *Charlotte Messenger*, 17 March 1883; Parker, *Biddle–Johnson C. Smith University Story*, 95; Walls, *African Methodist Episcopal Zion Church*, 580. Calvin occasionally penned a column for the *Charlotte Messenger* in

which he stressed the values of education, hard work, and economic advancement. See, for example, *Charlotte Messenger*, 17 February 1887.

17. "What Is a Negro?," *Charlotte Messenger*, 22 January 1887.

18. "Education," ibid., 29 July 1882; "Our Young Men," ibid., 16 September 1882; ibid., 8 July 1882. In her study of northern missionary teachers in Reconstruction Georgia, Jacqueline Jones describes the moral, intellectual, and civic values that teachers instilled in their pupils and their emphasis on the importance of self-determination. She comments, "Like most middle-class northerners of the time, the teachers assumed that a free man was the master of his own destiny. The strength of personal character and determination went a long way in explaining who was successful in life and who was not." See Jones, *Soldiers of Light*, 109–10.

19. "Colored Class at Work," *Charlotte Messenger*, 15 January 1887; "Prominent Colored Men," ibid., 1 January 1887; "What Is a Negro?," ibid., 22 January 1887.

20. Ibid., 15 July 1882. August Meier points out in *Negro Thought in America* that "the entire complex of race pride and solidarity, of economic development and self-help . . . was necessarily held to the exclusion of interest in agitation for civil rights and political activity" (55).

21. See, for example, "Colored Men on the Jury," *Charlotte Messenger*, 7 August 1886; "Women on the Chain Gang," ibid., 14 August 1886; and ibid., 23 October 1886. Meier describes the strategy embraced by Charlotte's black better class as a tradition of "protest and accommodation." Although this description embraces both poles of action that existed within the scope of the strategy, "accommodation" seems too strong a word to portray the philosophy and actions of the black better class. Even though they were far from militant in their outlook, they constantly drew attention to racial injustices in their society. See Meier, *Negro Thought in America*, 69–82.

22. Meier, *Negro Thought in America*, 42–58; *Charlotte Messenger*, 22 January 1887.

23. "Public Baptizing," *Charlotte Messenger*, 19 May 1883; "A Sickening Scene," ibid., 24 February 1883.

24. "A Sickening Scene," ibid., 24 February 1883; "Moral Guides," ibid., 2 October 1886. Gatewood in *Aristocrats of Color* also notes the importance of what he calls "the genteel performance" for the "colored aristocracy" and the tension between the impulse to uplift the masses and the need to be distinguished from them: "Some aristocrats of color alternated between the uplift approach and the stratagem of placing distance between themselves and the ill-mannered masses" (189).

25. Gatewood traces a national network of black elites and argues that a "colored aristocracy" in cities such as Washington, D.C., Baltimore, Charleston, and New Orleans derived "from the ranks of the elite free black society and privileged bondsmen," who "viewed themselves as natural leaders, superior in culture, sophistication, and wealth to the parvenu free." Light skin often served as a prerequisite for admission to the elite. Charlotte's black "better class" was probably more like Atlanta's "aristocracy," as described by Gatewood. He argues that in newer southern cities, such as Atlanta, which lacked a significant free black community, the "colored aristocracy" consisted of many non-natives who traced their origins to the "house-servant group," and skin color was a less important factor for membership in the elite. See Gatewood, *Aristocrats of Color*, 27, 69–92. Of 33 African American male and female prohibitionists mentioned in the local press who could be found in the census, 21 were listed as mulatto and 12 as black. Of 9 African American antiprohibitionists who could be traced to the census, 5 were black and 4 mulatto.

26. *Charlotte Messenger*, 31 July, 27 November 1886, 19 March 1887, 23 October 1886,

22 January, 26 February 1887. Gatewood in *Aristocrats of Color* also notes the importance of clubs and voluntary associations in defining membership in the black "upper class" of larger towns and cities (210–46).

27. See, for example, *Charlotte Messenger*, 31 July, 27 November 1886, 22 January 1887.

28. "Kissing Parties," ibid., 6 January 1883; Annie Blackwell, "Woman as a Religious Factor in the Home," *AME Zion Quarterly Review*, October–January 1899–1900, 18; "Women in the Court House," *Charlotte Messenger*, 3 March 1883. Of fifteen black women prohibitionists mentioned in the local press who could be located in the census, twelve were listed as "keeping house." For an exploration of a feminist sensibility among the black better class, see Gilmore, "Gender and Jim Crow."

29. "Our Opera House," *Charlotte Messenger*, 2 March 1883; ibid., 16 September 1882.

30. "Wet or Dry?," *Charlotte Observer*, 17 April 1881.

31. See, for example, "Nearing the End," ibid., 30 April 1881, and "Grand Rally Last Night," ibid., 26 April 1881.

32. "Make the Issue," ibid., 8 April 1881; "Progress of Prohibition," ibid., 8 April 1881; "Wet or Dry?," ibid., 17 April 1881; ibid., 30 April 1881.

33. "Progress of Prohibition," ibid., 8 April 1881.

34. "A Prohibition Sermon," ibid., 28 April 1881; "Nearing the End," ibid., 30 April 1881; "A Final Appeal from a Colored Man," ibid., 30 April 1881.

35. "Whiskey versus Reform," ibid., 27 April 1881.

36. "The Movement Begun," ibid., 8 April 1881.

37. "Prohibition," ibid., 27 January 1881.

38. See, for example, ibid., 1, 12 April 1881; "Wet or Dry?," ibid., 17 April 1881; and ibid., 1 February, 3 May 1881.

39. Of thirty-two names of antiprohibitionists appearing in the local press, twenty-four were listed in the 1880 census or city directories. Unskilled laborers accounted for 28 percent of the antiprohibitionists, and skilled artisans 24 percent. White-collar professionals constituted 42 percent of the antiprohibitionists, but half of them were saloon-keepers and grocers.

40. "Antiprohibition," *Charlotte Observer*, 22 April 1881; "Wet or Dry?," ibid., 17 April 1881.

41. Whitener, *Prohibition in North Carolina*, 71–74.

42. "A Prohibition Sermon," *Charlotte Observer*, 26 April 1881; "The Election Today," ibid., 4 August 1881.

43. "The Antiprohibitionists," ibid., 1 May 1881.

44. "The Question of the Day," ibid., 24 April 1881.

45. Ibid., 26, 14, 24 April 1881.

46. "The Prohibition Triumph," ibid., 3 May 1881.

47. Ibid.; "Gratitude after Victory," ibid., 4 May 1881.

48. Charlotte Board of Aldermen Minutes, 4 May 1881, CCO; "The Prohibition Triumph," *Charlotte Observer*, 5 May 1881.

49. "The Ladies Buckling on Armor," *Charlotte Observer*, 24 May 1881; "Colored Prohibition," ibid., 15 July 1881.

50. "Men of Mecklenburg," ibid., 2 August 1881.

51. "Colored Prohibition," ibid., 15 July 1881.

52. See, for example, "Meeting of the Ladies' Prohibitory Society," ibid., 30 June 1881, and "Men of Mecklenburg," ibid., 2 August 1881.

53. Ibid., 5 August 1881; "Men of Mecklenburg," 2 August 1881.

54. "Decidedly Moist," ibid., 5 August 1881; Whitener, *Prohibition in North Carolina*, 73, and "North Carolina Prohibition Election of 1881," 86.

55. Charlotte Board of Aldermen Minutes, 15 August 1881, CCO.

56. Whitener, "North Carolina Prohibition Election of 1881," 71–93; Bromberg, "'Pure Democracy and White Supremacy,'" 69–72.

57. Whitener, "North Carolina Prohibition Election of 1881," 88.

58. Ibid., 89; "The Liberal Convention and the Nominees," *Charlotte Observer*, 27 August 1882; ibid., 3 September 1882.

59. "The Liberal Party," ibid., 9 September 1882.

60. Ibid.; "Our Position," ibid., 3 September 1882. Bromberg in "'Pure Democracy and White Supremacy'" points out that Jones's attacks on the county government system in June 1882 brought him "a torrent of abuse" from Democrats in eastern counties who viewed him as heretical but that the *Observer*'s stance "did embolden some other western Democratic papers to raise objections to the system, and a furious controversy raged" (73–74).

61. "The Messenger," *Charlotte Messenger*, 1 July 1882; ibid., 15 July 1882.

62. Ibid., 15 July 1882; "Coalition," ibid., 5 August 1882.

63. "To Liberals and Coalitionists," ibid., 12 August 1882; "Liberal Party Convention," ibid., 19 August 1882.

64. Ibid., 2, 16 September 1882.

65. "How Should We Vote?," ibid., 30 September 1882; ibid., 28 October 1882.

66. "On the Eve of Battle," *Charlotte Observer*, 4 October 1882; "Red Shirts and Mounted Men," *Charlotte Messenger*, 7 October 1882.

67. "County Election," *Charlotte Observer*, 9 November 1882; Whitener, "North Carolina Prohibition Election of 1881," 91.

68. "Hear Ye! Hear Ye!," *Charlotte Messenger*, 2 June 1883; "What It Teaches," ibid., 11 November 1882; "The Negro Politician," ibid., 16 December 1882.

69. Whitener, *Prohibition in North Carolina*, 59, 90.

70. "The Prohibition Club," *Charlotte Observer*, 22 April 1886; "Prohibition Club," ibid., 28 April 1886.

71. "The Colored Prohibitionists," ibid., 30 April 1886.

72. Whitener, *Prohibition in North Carolina*, 106; *Charlotte Observer*, 14 April, 14 May, 1 June 1886, 15 August 1887; "The Demorest Contest," *Charlotte Chronicle*, 8 May 1889.

73. "Both Sides Holding Forth," *Charlotte Observer*, 26 May 1886.

74. "State Prohibition Platform," *North Carolina Prohibitionist*, 28 June 1887.

75. *North Carolina Prohibitionist*, 1886–87; "The Prohibition Question," *Charlotte Observer*, 14 April 1886. Although Vail headed the state Prohibition party, Mecklenburg County did not hold a Prohibition party convention or run Prohibition party candidates in local elections, which suggests that the party had little support in Charlotte or the county.

76. "Charlotte Goes Wet," *Charlotte Observer*, 30 June 1886.

77. "The Election Yesterday," ibid., 8 June 1886.

78. "A Congregation Divided on Prohibition," ibid., 22 May 1886.

79. "A New Church," *Charlotte Messenger*, 1 January 1887.

80. "That New Church," ibid., 9 April 1887. See also "Trouble in the Colored Churches," *Charlotte Observer*, 6 March 1887.

81. "That New Church," *Charlotte Messenger*, 9 April 1887. Of the forty-odd charter members, twenty-one were listed in the 1880 census or the city directory.

82. "Peace in Zion," *Charlotte Messenger*, 15 January 1887.

83. "Observations in the Far South," *Star of Zion*, 28 September 1893.

84. "Settled At Last," *Charlotte Chronicle*, 10 May 1888.

85. "Charlotte Goes Wet," ibid., 5 June 1888.

86. "Bribing Voters," ibid., 13 January 1889; "Election Bribery," ibid., 15 January 1889.

87. "Objections to Communion Wine," ibid., 3 February 1889.

88. "Another Prohibition Election," ibid., 17 March 1889; "The Prohibition Petition," ibid., 7 May 1889.

89. "Dick Morse's Scheme," ibid., 7 May 1889; "Prohibition Petition," ibid., 7 May 1889.

90. Whitener, *Prohibition in North Carolina*, 94; WCTU minutes, quoted in ibid.

91. "Wise Words on Prohibition," *Charlotte Chronicle*, 15 June 1889; Charlotte Board of Aldermen Minutes, 17 June 1889, CCO.

92. "A Commendable Charity," *Charlotte Chronicle*, 21 November 1886; "Need of a Hospital," *Charlotte Messenger*, 11 December 1886.

93. "The Colored Hospital," *Charlotte Chronicle*, 29 July 1888.

94. "The Hospital for Colored People," ibid., 13 March 1887; "Art Exhibit," ibid., 12 December 1886. Dr. Brevard, a white physician, and Dr. J. T. Williams, a black physician, "promised medical attendance without charge" for blacks. Most of the town's druggists also "agreed to make marked reductions in their prescriptions and medicines." See "A Commendable Charity," ibid., 21 November 1886.

95. "House of the Good Samaritan," *Charlotte Messenger*, 19 May 1888; ibid., 22 December 1888; "Good Samaritan Hospital," *Charlotte Chronicle*, 10 July 1891.

96. "The Evangelist at Work," *Charlotte Chronicle*, 8 February 1887; "The Evangelistic Meetings of the Rev. R. G. Pearson," ibid., 12 February 1887; "A Great Awakening," ibid., 26 February 1887; "The Great Revival," ibid., 3 March 1887; "The Great Revival," ibid., 15 February 1887; "The Evangelistic Meetings," ibid., 17 February 1887; "Pearson's Farewell," ibid., 3 March 1887.

97. "A House of Refuge," ibid., 3 March 1887; "Invading the House of Ill Fame," ibid., 27 February 1887; "The House of Refuge," ibid., 6 March 1887; "The House of Refuge," ibid., 16 March 1887; "Sent to Baltimore," ibid., 29 March 1887.

98. Lockman, *A Century's Child*, 23–29; "Humane: Thompson Orphanage and Training School," *Charlotte News*, 26 May 1914; "Founding Monuments of Charity," *Charlotte Chronicle*, 5 February 1888; "The Presbyterian Home and Hospital," ibid., 9 February 1888; "Opening of the Presbyterian Home," ibid., 3 May 1888; "Presbyterian Home and Hospital Formally Opened in Interesting Exercises," ibid., 5 May 1888; Claiborne, *Unto the Least of These*, 3–6; "The Day Nursery," *Charlotte Chronicle*, 8 February 1888; "The Day Nursery—Building Selected," ibid., 10 February 1888; "The Nursery Opened," ibid., 21 February 1888.

CHAPTER 4

1. Tompkins, *History of Mecklenburg*, 183.

2. "Rail Road Meeting," *Charlotte Journal*, 4 March 1847; Standard and Griffin, "Cotton Textile Industry," 150–51.

3. Standard and Griffin, "Cotton Textile Industry," 159; "Rock Island Woolen Mills," *Western Democrat*, 15 January 1867; "Rock Island Manufacturing Company," *Raleigh Register*, reprinted in *Western Democrat*, 3 December 1867.

4. "Cotton Factory," *Western Democrat*, 6 October 1869; "Cotton Manufacturing," ibid., 16 February 1869; "Important Sale," ibid., 21 June 1870.

5. "Our Mining Interests," *Charlotte Democrat*, 8 October 1872; "Spoke and Handle Factory," ibid., 20 August 1872; "Shoe Factory," ibid., 2 September 1873; ibid., 14 June 1875. For more on the revival of gold mining and the role of northern investment in the 1870s, see, for example, "Mining Operations," *Western Democrat*, 8 November 1870, and *Charlotte Democrat*, 23 October, 23 December 1876, 7 November 1879. On the symbolic meaning of cotton mills, see Woodward, *Origins of the New South*, 131, and Carlton, *Mill and Town*, 67–75.

6. "Cotton Factories and Machine Shops," *Daily Charlotte Observer*, 21 August 1873; "Labor and Capital," *Charlotte Democrat*, 19 March 1872.

7. "Cotton Factories North and South," *Charlotte Democrat*, 18 March 1873. Griffin in "Reconstruction of the North Carolina Textile Industry" notes that in North Carolina, "in the promotion of cotton factories, the editors of Charlotte and Wilmington were the most outspoken, and their columns provided busy country editors with a constant flow of ammunition for local promotion" (41).

8. "The Cotton Factory," *Daily Charlotte Observer*, 14 October 1873.

9. "Charlotte Cotton Factory Company," *Charlotte Democrat*, 28 September 1874; "Cotton Factory," ibid., 26 October 1874; ibid., 4 May, 13 April 1877, 20 June 1879. The *Charlotte Democrat* blamed speculation in cotton futures for the demise of some cotton-buying houses. See ibid., 22 June 1877. Charlotte's banking houses, with the exception of the Bank of Mecklenburg, appear to have weathered the depression. The *Democrat* noted in January 1877 that "there are $1,112,321.02 on deposit in the Banks of this city. . . . Charlotte is the money-centre and will be the trading centre of the South." See "Bank of Mecklenburg," ibid., 9 August 1875; ibid., 23 August 1875; and "Money," ibid., 26 January 1877.

10. *Southern Home*, 11 October 1875; "Cotton Manufacture," ibid., 12 July 1875; ibid., 19 July 1875; "That Cotton Factory," ibid., 11 October 1875. In 1874 local Grange chapters also recommended the establishment of a farming implements factory in Charlotte, although there is no evidence that such a factory was ever opened in the town. See "Catawba River Council Patrons of Husbandry," *Daily Charlotte Observer*, 7 October 1874.

11. "A Communist Correspondent," *Charlotte Observer*, 22 July 1875; *Southern Home*, 26 July, 16, 23 August 1875.

12. Charlotte Board of Aldermen Minutes, 30 December 1879, CCO; *Charlotte Democrat*, 9, 16, 23 January 1880. Woodward in *Origins of the New South* notes that toward the end of the 1870s, the "decade of despair," a "sudden quickening of life in commerce and investment" occurred in some parts of the South (111–12).

13. Woodward, *Origins of the New South*, 132; Records of Corporation, Mecklenburg County Courthouse, Charlotte, North Carolina.

14. "Robert M. Oates, Esq.," in Dowd, *Sketches of Prominent Living North Carolinians*, 283–84; "Rufus Yancey McAden" and "Dr. John H. McAden," in *Cyclopedia of Eminent and Representative Men*, 2:199–200, 257–58; "Death of Mr. E. K. P. Osborne," *Daily Charlotte Observer*, 15 May 1894.

15. Dan M. Lacy in "Beginning of Industrialism in North Carolina" claims that there is no evidence of any cotton mill established by northern interests before 1895 in North Carolina and that there was no significant influx of northern capital into the state's textile industry until the depression that began in 1893 (74). It appears, however, that at least one of Charlotte's mills, the Atherton Mills, relied in part on northern capital. Although Tompkins, R. M. Miller, Jr., and E. A. Smith incorporated the mill in 1892, the *Observer* announced that the mill represented a combination of "Charlotte and Northern Capital"

and that Tompkins had interested "parties from New York and New England" in the venture. Also, the mill was "named for one of the Northern projectors." See "A 'Sixth' Hummer on the List," *Daily Charlotte Observer*, 15 July 1892. Since Charlotte's mills were incorporated by local citizens, it is difficult to determine the extent of northern investment in mills built in the 1890s from the Records of Corporation.

The origin and background of New South industrialists have been a source of controversy in southern historiography. In *Origins of the New South*, Woodward argues that the "new men" of the New South, merchants and professionals, were the driving force behind industrialization. A series of revisionist works have questioned Woodward's assertion. Wiener, in *Social Origins of the New South*, claims that planters continued to dominate in the New South and blocked efforts at industrialization. In *Planters and the Making of a "New South,"* Billings argues that in late nineteenth-century North Carolina, cotton mills were built not by the commercial middle class, "new men with new principles," but instead by planters; the "New South" merely represented a continuation of the Old South, with the persistent domination of the planter class. Billings estimates that "over half (57 percent) of the mills operating in North Carolina during this period were owned completely or partly by agrarians" (ibid., 64). Escott draws heavily on both Wiener and Billings in *Many Excellent People*, arguing for "continuity in power relationships" over two centuries of North Carolina history. In examining the origins of New South industrialists, he attempts to refine Billings's thesis, arguing that although new men gained influence in the state, North Carolina's power relationships remained undemocratic, as they had been before the war. Examining investors in seventy Piedmont textile mills from 1885 to 1900, he contends that investors fell into two categories. First were "men who had already established themselves in the textile industry" and continued to reinvest—prominent textile families such as the Holts, Cones, and Odells (216). The second group consisted of "significant numbers of merchants, businessmen, and professionals, large and small." Merchants, bankers, and professionals, notes Escott, "were especially important in the towns, such as Charlotte" (217). Although recognizing the significance of merchants and professionals "and broad participation by smaller businessmen" (216), Escott nevertheless refers to them as part of the "elite," which seems to assign them to the same class as the antebellum planters who, he argues, continued to dominate the state, thus conflating the two different social groups—the old planter class and the new merchant and professional class. Escott's table of mill investors suggests that farmers played an insignificant role in mill building, making up less than 5 percent of all mill investors, while merchants, professionals, and bankers made up a third of all investors (218). In *Mill and Town*, Carlton supports Woodward's thesis, asserting that "the town-dwelling middle class" was responsible for the industrialization of the South Carolina Piedmont and that "the entrepreneurial energy" for building mills "was chiefly generated in the neighborhoods in which they were built." Carlton found that most mill investors in the South Carolina Piedmont, like those in Charlotte, were involved in commercial enterprises. A fifth of the investors came from the professional ranks, while farmers played "distinctly minor roles in mill development." See Carlton, *Mill and Town*, 40–81. Kipp in "Urban Growth and Social Change" also found that "the industrialization of Greensboro in the period from 1870 to 1920 was the product of indigenous efforts" and came largely from the middle class (210).

16. Sitterson and Griffin both stress the continuity of family ownership of textile mills in North Carolina before and after the Civil War. See Sitterson, "Business Leaders in Post–Civil War North Carolina," 111–21, and Griffin, "Reconstruction of the North Carolina Textile Industry." See also Escott, *Many Excellent People*, 198–99, for a more

recent reiteration of this thesis. Carlton in *Mill and Town* notes that "dependence on agriculture fostered chronic uncertainty and high credit costs," while "the cotton mill with its constant turnover seemed to offer a measure of stability" (67). See also Perry, "Middle-Class Townsmen," 191.

17. Records of Corporation, Mecklenburg County Courthouse, Charlotte, North Carolina.

18. Winston, *Builder of the New South*, 22–26, 69–76.

19. Tompkins, quoted in Tullos, *Habits of Industry*, 156; Clay, "Daniel Augustus Tompkins," 31–32; Records of Corporation, Mecklenburg County Courthouse, Charlotte, North Carolina.

20. Clay, "Daniel Augustus Tompkins," 34–37; Winston, *Builder of the New South*, 132. Tompkins also owned the Edgefield Manufacturing Company in his hometown of Edgefield, South Carolina, and the High Shoals Company in Gaston County (Tullos, *Habits of Industry*, p. 157). For more on the links created between the northern and southern textile industries through northern machine companies and their agents, see Beatty, "Lowells of the South," 37–62.

21. For more on Tompkins's ownership of the *Charlotte Observer*, see Claiborne, *Charlotte Observer*, 85–139.

22. Doyle in *New Men, New Cities, New South* examines the role of exclusive social clubs and networks in the formation of a New South business elite (189–225). However, he seems to conflate the "business elite" of the 1880s with that of later decades and does not make a distinction between an emerging industrial elite and a middle class. For an examination of the role of exclusive organizations in the creation of an elite class in a northern city, see Baltzell, *Philadelphia Gentlemen*, 340–42.

23. "A Manufacturers' Club," *Charlotte Observer*, 24 July 1894; *Southern Manufacturers Club—By Laws and House Rules*, NCC. According to Baltzell in *Philadelphia Gentlemen*, "The circulation of elites in America and the assimilation of new men of power and influence into the upper class take place primarily through the medium of urban clubdom" (340). Doyle in *New Men, New Cities, New South* notes the importance of metropolitan men's clubs in creating a business elite in Atlanta and Nashville (208–9).

24. "A Manufacturers' Club," *Charlotte Observer*, 24 July 1894; "Bullet through His Brain," ibid., 3 March 1899; *Southern Manufacturers Club—By Laws and House Rules*, NCC. According to the club handbook, as late as 1909, only 15 percent of resident members were natives of Charlotte.

25. "The Manufacturers' Club," *Daily Charlotte Observer*, 20 September 1894.

26. Tompkins, letter to the *Manufacturers' Record*, 28 June 1901, quoted in Winston, *Builder of the New South*, 356–58.

27. "New Englanders, Welcome," *Daily Charlotte Observer*, 23 October 1895; "Welcome, Manufacturers," ibid., 31 October 1895; Tompkins, quoted in Winston, *Builder of the New South*, 356. By the time the club built its new quarters in 1910, it again used the name Southern Manufacturers' Club.

28. Doyle in *New Men, New Cities, New South* also notes the importance of society women in defining the elite class in Atlanta and Nashville: "Their clubs, parties, debutante balls, and other social events acted as screening devices that allowed the wives of the elite businessmen to act as gatekeepers who passed approval on the newcomers and newly rich seeking entry into the intimate social world of the local upper class" (213–14).

29. For more on the social season in Atlanta and Nashville, which also featured New Year's receptions, debutante parties, and dances, see Doyle, *New Men, New Cities, New South*, 213–14. The *Charlotte Chronicle* reported the start of Charlotte's "social season" in

January 1890, and the *Charlotte Observer*, which succeeded the *Chronicle* as the city's leading newspaper in 1892, especially publicized the activities of Charlotte "society." See, for example, "Social Season," *Charlotte Chronicle*, 16 November 1890. Hosts for the 1893 New Year's Open House included textile manufacturers J. H. McAden and R. M. Oates, textile engineer S. W. Cramer, and Mecklenburg Iron Works owner Captain John Wilkes. See "Ushered in Splendor," *Daily Charlotte Observer*, 3 January 1893; "Mozart Party," ibid., 14 December 1895; and "A Stylish Affair," ibid., 7 February 1897.

30. "Society Dots—The Season Opens," *Daily Charlotte Observer*, 11 October 1892; "The 'Girls' Cotillion,'" ibid., 13 May 1893; "The First Cotillion," ibid., 9 September 1893. See also "Miss Hutchison's Debut," ibid., 22 May 1895, on the coming-out party of the daughter of banker D. P. Hutchison. In his study of Philadelphia's elite, *Philadelphia Gentlemen*, Baltzell points out that "the debutante ritual . . . serves the latent function of containing family wealth and power within a small select circle; the democratic whims of romantic love often play havoc with class solidarity" (12). Doyle in *New Men, New Cities, New South* also notes that "society events in Atlanta and Nashville provided a forum within which the sons and daughters of the upper class could find suitable marriage partners" (212–18).

31. "The Season's Debut," *Daily Charlotte Observer*, 2 September 1893; "The German," ibid., 22 September 1893. See also, for example, "A Theatre Party," ibid., 18 December 1895, and "The German," ibid., 28 August 1895. Social contacts with northerners sometimes led to marriage. In 1895 Mary Moore Young of Charlotte married Lawrence Dodsworth of New York City, a member of the Manufacturers' Club. See "A Brilliant Social Event," ibid., 24 September 1895.

32. "The Great Charity Ball," ibid., 6 February 1894; "The Lawn Party," ibid., 21 June 1894; McCarthy, *Noblesse Oblige*, 30.

33. Evangelical religion and the social reform movements that it engendered have been cited by several historians as crucial to the self-definition of an emerging middle class in the antebellum North. See especially Paul E. Johnson, *A Shopkeeper's Millennium*, and Ryan, *Cradle of the Middle Class*. See also Blumin, *Emergence of the Middle Class*, esp. 193–206.

34. "Shelling the Woods," *Charlotte Chronicle*, 27 April 1890; "The Night Service," ibid., 30 April 1890.

35. "Charity Ball," ibid., 23 January 1891. Despite Reed's condemnation, the Young Ladies' Club raised $200 and declared the affair "financially and socially a brilliant success." See "The Benefit Ball," ibid., 28 January 1891.

36. "The Auditorium Services," *Daily Charlotte Observer*, 6 July 1895; ibid., 7 July 1895; "Sam Jones in Charlotte," 2 October 1895.

37. Carlton in *Mill and Town* traces the emergence of "town people" and "mill people" in South Carolina. See also Hall et al., *Like a Family*. Carlton argues that "reformers and mill men alike were 'town people'" with close personal and familial ties and that reformers and mill owners were bound by "class affinity and solidarity." Moreover, he found that in Piedmont South Carolina, like Charlotte, "the bulk of the reformer's approbrium was directed . . . at the operatives, above all the mill family," rather than the mill owners. Reformers refused to attack the mills and the mill system, he asserts, because they feared the power of the mill men. See Carlton, *Mill and Town*, 193–94, 174. But by merging "town people" into a single class, united against the "mill people," Carlton overlooks the significant class differences that had emerged among white "town people" by the mid-1890s. Although Carlton is undoubtedly correct in stressing the inhibitions of

reformers, the example of Charlotte suggests that at least a handful of middle-class reformers courageously criticized powerful mill owners.

38. Tompkins, *Cotton Mills, Commercial Features*, 34–35.

39. "A Cry for Help," *Daily Charlotte Observer*, 17 January 1896; "Humane Society Organized," ibid., 8 January 1896. For more on the economic reasons for the migration of families from the countryside to the factory, see Hall et al., *Like a Family*, 31–33, and Tullos, *Habits of Industry*, 134–71. By 1907 the annual turnover rate among laborers in the southern textile industry was 176 percent (Hall, *Like a Family*, 107). For an extensive examination of the discovery of the "mill problem" by middle-class townspeople in the South Carolina Piedmont, see Carlton, *Mill and Town*, 129–70. In 1893 a local mill man, in a letter to the *Daily Charlotte Observer*, asserted, "Manufacturers, as a class, are not hard-hearted or tyrannical toward their operatives. Not only are the operatives living in comfort, but as a class they are contented and happy." See "The Mill Built Last Year," *Daily Charlotte Observer*, 11 February 1893.

40. "Moody's First Sermon," *Daily Charlotte Observer*, 9 March 1893; "Making Ready for Moody," ibid., 2 February 1893; "The Interest Is Increasing," ibid., 10 March 1893.

41. "Prosperous Mission," *Charlotte Chronicle*, 15 May 1890; "A Lecture and Reception," *Daily Charlotte Observer*, 20 November 1895; "Ice Cream Treat—The Ada Mission," ibid., 12 July 1892; "The Victor Lawn Party," ibid., 28 June 1896; "The Atherton Mission," ibid., 27 January 1893; "North Side Chapel," ibid., 24 December 1895; "New Chapel Opened," ibid., 12 October 1897. In her path-breaking study of antebellum Rochester, *Women's Activism and Social Change*, Hewitt found "multiple forms of public action" among middle-class women reformers "that often placed them in competition" rather than creating a common "female solidarity" (40).

42. "The Gospel Tent Meetings," *Daily Charlotte Observer*, 8 October 1895; "The Tent Meeting Last Night," ibid., 9 October 1895; "The Gospel Tent Meeting," ibid., 22 October 1895; "A New Baptist Sunday School," ibid., 26 October 1895; "Preaching at the Lyceum," ibid., 17 January 1896.

43. Ahlstrom, *Religious History*, 858; "Christian Endeavor Column," *Daily Charlotte Observer*, 27 September 1896. The Christian Endeavor movement became so strong in Charlotte that the *Observer* devoted a regular column to its activities. See, for example, "Christian Endeavor Column," ibid., 4 February 1900.

44. "Epworth League Chapel," *Daily Charlotte Observer*, 4 August 1896; Hall et al., *Like a Family*, 124–26.

45. "Overworked Factory Workers," *Daily Charlotte Observer*, 8 January 1895.

46. "Reply to Mr. Atkins," ibid., 9 January 1895.

47. "Reply to Mr. Mallory," ibid., 11 January 1895.

48. "Labor in the Cotton Mills," ibid., 18 January 1899.

49. Clay, "Daniel Augustus Tompkins," 180; "Labor in the Cotton Mills," *Daily Charlotte Observer*, 18 January 1899.

50. "Labor in the Cotton Mills," *Daily Charlotte Observer*, 18 January 1899.

51. Clay, "Daniel Augustus Tompkins," 107; D. A. Tompkins to R. H. Edmonds, 25 July 1902, Daniel Augustus Tompkins Papers, SHC. Although Tompkins set up a night school at the Atherton Lyceum, it was short-lived.

52. Clay, "Daniel Augustus Tompkins," 108.

53. "Our Young Men," *Charlotte Messenger*, 16 September 1882.

54. Ibid.; "Colored Business Men," ibid., 14 January 1888; ibid., 24 July 1886. A year after Williams set up his practice in Charlotte, Smith noted that "the death rate among the

colored people has greatly decreased since we have a colored doctor," citing a city report showing death rates of blacks and whites as "nearly equal." See ibid., 19 March 1887.

55. Ibid., 2 July 1887; "The Open Field," ibid., 20 August 1887.

56. "A New Colored Physician," *Daily Charlotte Observer*, 27 April 1892; ibid., 5 November, 23 April 1892; Records of Corporation, Mecklenburg County Courthouse, Charlotte, North Carolina; *Star of Zion*, 18 August 1895; "Afro-American Interests," *Daily Charlotte Observer*, 30 January 1898; "Colored Artists," ibid., 26 April 1896; "Banker Sanders in New York," ibid., 7 July 1896; "The Charlotte Clothing Cleaning Company," *Charlotte Observer*, 28 January 1899; *Daily Charlotte Observer*, 16 March 1898; *Charlotte City Directory*, 1897–98. Charlotte got a third black physician when Dr. W. H. Graves moved to the city from Reidsville. See *Daily Charlotte Observer*, 23 September 1898.

57. Schweninger, *Black Property Owners*, 178.

58. "Death of Bishop Lomax," *Daily Charlotte Observer*, 1 April 1908.

59. "Varick Memorial Day at Charlotte, N.C.," *Star of Zion*, 15 July 1894; "The Varick Memorial," ibid., 16 August 1894.

60. "The AME Zion Publication House," ibid., 23 August 1894; "Printing, Preaching, and Prancing," *Daily Charlotte Observer*, 6 September 1895.

61. *Charlotte City Directory*, 1897–98; *Daily Charlotte Observer*, 19 October 1894; "Order Given for Bricks," ibid., 31 July 1898. Besides building an addition onto the Atherton Mill, Houser constructed cotton mills at Henrietta, Concord, High Point, and Mount Holly and by 1888 had built nine mills. See "W. C. Houser," *Charlotte Messenger*, 21 January 1888. According to a township income tax list printed in the *Observer* in 1902, Houser paid $200 in taxes, second only to D. J. Sanders, president of Biddle University, who paid $500. See "Local Income Tax-Payers," *Daily Charlotte Observer*, 20 August 1902.

62. "What Is a Negro?," *Charlotte Messenger*, 22 January 1887; ibid., 14 January 1888; "Buy Land," ibid., 18 February 1888.

63. See, for example, "The Chronicle and the Negro," ibid., 14 January 1888.

64. Ibid., 21 August 1886, 12 November, 27 August 1887; "Buy Land," 18 February 1888; "Afro-American Interests," *Daily Charlotte Observer*, 5 December 1897; "Afro-American Interests," ibid., 7 November 1897; "Death of Bishop Lomax," ibid., 1 April 1908. According to Lomax's obituary, at the time of his death, he had accumulated approximately $70,000 in real estate and personal property, owning many houses in the Second Ward and a farm north of the city. Schweninger notes that wealthier blacks "rarely invested in 'liquid assets'—stocks, bonds, silver, gold, jewelry, cash, bank savings," but instead, like their antebellum counterparts, they invested most of their profits in real estate. He argues that this approach reflected "an investment strategy" rather than the fact that blacks may have been barred from certain types of investment, such as subscription stockholding in white-owned mills. See Schweninger, *Black Property Owners*, 222.

65. Records of Corporation, Mecklenburg County Courthouse, Charlotte, North Carolina. Besides those listed in the text, the following men incorporated the Queen City Real Estate Agency: H. J. Green, a notary public and agent of the Royal Benefit Society of New York; J. D. Martin, H. A. Hunt, P. G. Drayton, and S. B. Pride, all professors at Biddle University; brickmason W. E. Hill; barber Thad L. Tate; money broker J. T. Sanders; and J. R. Kirkpatrick.

66. "Afro-American Interests," *Daily Charlotte Observer*, 7 November 1897; ibid., 15 July 1897.

67. *Star of Zion*, 21 September 1899. The *Star* regularly reported on the comings and goings of Charlotte's black college students. See, for example, ibid., 13 May, 3 June 1897, 18 May, 5 October 1899.

68. "Afro-American Interests," *Daily Charlotte Observer*, 7 November 1897.

69. "Our Boys and Their Opportunities," *AME Zion Quarterly Review*, January/February 1899.

70. Burgess, "Tar Heel Blacks," 96–136. Burgess argues that Coleman's father was "a white man whose identity is not known" but who was described as being "distinguished by military and financial ability." However, Powell, *Dictionary of North Carolina Biography*, states that Coleman's father was General Rufus Barringer (401).

71. Coleman, quoted in Burgess, "Tar Heel Blacks," 168; *Manufacturers' Record*, 8 July 1896, quoted in ibid., 173.

72. Burgess, "Tar Heel Blacks," 181–238. Burgess includes detailed biographical information about each of the mill's incorporators.

73. Quoted in Gilmore, "Gender and Jim Crow," 279.

74. "The Colored Mill," *Daily Charlotte Observer*, 20 February 1897; ibid., 21 February 1897; "The Colored Cotton Mill," ibid., 23 February 1897; Coleman, quoted in Burgess, "Tar Heel Blacks," 266–67; R. A. Caldwell, quoted in ibid., 269.

75. "Colored Bishops' Meeting," *Daily Charlotte Observer*, 2 April 1897.

76. "Colored People's Cotton Mill," ibid., 30 March 1897; Burgess, "Tar Heel Blacks," 284.

77. Burgess, "Tar Heel Blacks," 301–11.

78. "A Red Letter Day for Negroes," *Daily Charlotte Observer*, 10 February 1898.

79. Burgess, "Tar Heel Blacks," 325–40; "Afro-American Interests," *Daily Charlotte Observer*, 14 August 1898.

80. Burgess, "Tar Heel Blacks," 366–83.

81. "The Yale Cotillion," *Daily Charlotte Observer*, 16 January 1894; ibid., 30 December 1893; "She Stoops to Conquer," ibid., 12 April 1894; ibid., 24 January 1896, 22 October 1892; *Star of Zion*, 20 July 1899, 18 May, 9 November 1899. Gatewood in *Aristocrats of Color* describes debut parties, weddings, and balls sponsored by the black elite in various American cities (202–9).

82. "Full Moon Carnival," *Daily Charlotte Observer*, 24 April 1898; *Star of Zion*, 29 September 1898; "Fashionable Wedding in Colored High Life," *Daily Charlotte Observer*, 1 March 1894. See also, for example, "A Colored Marriage," ibid., 20 November 1894; "Two Colored Events of Interest," ibid., 29 February 1896; and *Star of Zion*, 15 November 1894.

CHAPTER 5

1. "Charlotte!: The Fair 'Queen City,'" *Daily Charlotte Observer*, 20 May 1892.

2. "The Queen City," *Star of Zion*, 8 October 1891; "From Somerville to Charlotte," ibid., 16 April 1891; "Biddle University Trustees," *Charlotte Chronicle*, 18 June 1891; "The Biddle Commencement," *Daily Charlotte Observer*, 4 June 1896.

3. "Jeptha's Daughter," *Daily Charlotte Observer*, 31 August 1895; "Liberality of Our Negroes," ibid., 15 April 1894.

4. "The Concert Last Evening," ibid., 30 April 1892; "Jeptha's Daughter," ibid., 4 September 1895; *Star of Zion*, 22 July 1897; *Daily Charlotte Observer*, 30 June 1895.

5. *Daily Charlotte Observer*, 15 October 1893; "The Occurrence on Wednesday Night—Some Precepts," ibid., 13 October 1893.

6. Ibid., 15 October 1893.

7. Ibid., 17 October 1893; "Something Should Be Done," ibid., 19 October 1893.

8. *Star of Zion*, 26 October 1893.

9. Hart, "Cross-Section through North Carolina."

10. *Charlotte Messenger*, 14 July 1888.

11. McMath, *Populist Vanguard*, 64–76.

12. Ibid., 35–40; Noblin, *Leonidas Lafayette Polk*, 204.

13. Sydenham Alexander, quoted in Jeffrey, "Women in the Southern Farmers' Alliance," 352; Hicks, "Farmers' Alliances," 171.

14. "A Nigger in the Woodpile," *Progressive Farmer*, 10 July 1888. The *Observer* listed the names of "prominent Alliance men" who attended a speech in Charlotte in March 1891. See "Senator Terrell's Speech," *Daily Charlotte Observer*, 21 March 1891.

15. "Notes from Alliances," *Progressive Farmer*, 5 June 1888.

16. *Charlotte Democrat*, 31 August 1888; *Progressive Farmer*, 26 October 1888; Hicks, "Farmers' Alliances," 172–73.

17. Jeffrey, "Women in the Southern Farmers' Alliance," 349–65.

18. Constitution of the Farmers' Alliance, quoted in *Progressive Farmer*, 10 July 1888.

19. McMath, *Populist Vanguard*, 44–45; Gaither, *Blacks and the Populist Revolt*, 3–4.

20. "A Nigger in the Woodpile," *Progressive Farmer*, 10 July 1888; "The Colored Alliance," ibid., 31 July 1888.

21. Gaither, *Blacks and the Populist Revolt*, 11. McMath in *Populist Vanguard* notes that "formal contact between the black and white Alliances was slight before 1890" (46).

22. Leonidas Polk, quoted in Noblin, *Leonidas Lafayette Polk*, 209; "The Farmers' Alliance and Politics," *Progressive Farmer*, 26 March 1889.

23. Noblin, *Leonidas Lafayette Polk*, 209.

24. McMath, *Populist Vanguard*, 60.

25. Ibid., 91; Bromberg, "'The Worst Muddle Ever Seen,'" 21.

26. Bromberg, "'The Worst Muddle Ever Seen,'" 24–25.

27. Ibid., 25–26.

28. McMath, *Populist Vanguard*, 95.

29. Clement Dowd to Zebulon Vance, 24 July 1890, Zebulon Vance Papers, SHC.

30. Clement Dowd to Zebulon Vance, 4 September 1890, Zebulon Vance Papers, SHC; *Chronicle*, quoted in *Progressive Farmer*, 19 August 1890. Noblin in *Leonidas Lafayette Polk* notes that the state election of 1890 pitted "organized farmers and their friends" on the left against "business and professional classes of the towns, led by corporate executives and lawyer-politicians," and "conservative farmers" on the right (231).

31. "The Alliance in Politics," *Charlotte Chronicle*, 17 June 1890.

32. Ibid.; Noblin, *Leonidas Lafayette Polk*, 220–26.

33. "Party Intolerance," *Charlotte Chronicle*, 3 July 1890; "The Times, the Democrat, and the Chronicle," ibid., 6 July 1890.

34. "The Alliance in Politics," ibid., 10 July 1890; *Chronicle*, quoted in *Progressive Farmer*, 19 August 1890; "The Chronicle and the Alliance," ibid., 19 August 1890.

35. Bromberg, "'Pure Democracy and White Supremacy,'" 426–27; Anderson, *Race and Politics*, 145.

36. "North Carolina Politics," *Charlotte Messenger*, 7 April 1888; Meier, *Negro Thought in America*, 22.

37. "North Carolina Politics," *Charlotte Messenger*, 7 April 1888; Meier, *Negro Thought in America*, 32.

38. Quoted in Meier, *Negro Thought in America*, 29–31, 36; "North Carolina Politics," *Charlotte Messenger*, 7 April 1888.

39. "A Race Convention," *Charlotte Chronicle*, 10 July 1890.

40. "Negroes in Convention," *New York Times*, 27 August 1890; "The Colored Convention," *Raleigh News and Observer*, 27 August 1890.

41. "The Colored Convention," *Raleigh News and Observer*, 27 August 1890.

42. Ibid.; "Negroes in Convention," *New York Times*, 27 August 1890.

43. *Raleigh News and Observer*, 28 August 1890; "Radicals Have Their Day," ibid., 29 August 1890.

44. "A Negro Revolt," *Charlotte Chronicle*, 20 August 1890.

45. "Prohibition Primary," ibid., 2 August 1890; "Don't Overlook This," ibid., 1 October 1890; "A Warning to Prohibitionists," ibid., 1 October 1890.

46. "Let's Get Together," ibid., 31 October 1890; "Old Mecklenburg," ibid., 5 November 1890. In the race for Congress, for example, Republican nominee R. M. Norment received only 58 votes in the Second Ward and 68 in the Third Ward.

47. Noblin, *Leonidas Lafayette Polk*, 246–51; Bromberg, "'The Worst Muddle Ever Seen,'" 40, 38.

48. McMath, *Populist Vanguard*, 124–25.

49. Bromberg, "'The Worst Muddle Ever Seen,'" 39–40; *Charlotte Chronicle*, 2 July 1891, quoted in Bromberg, "'The Worst Muddle Ever Seen,'" 40.

50. "'Sockless' Jerry Simpson," *Charlotte Chronicle*, 27 August 1891.

51. "Democrats Should Organize," ibid., 6 September 1891; Noblin, *Leonidas Lafayette Polk*, 251.

52. Thomas H. Sutton to Zebulon Vance, 4 March 1892, and J. P. Caldwell to Zebulon Vance, 13 April 1892, both in Zebulon Vance Papers, SHC.

53. Noblin, *Leonidas Lafayette Polk*, 276–81.

54. McMath, *Populist Vanguard*, 140.

55. "A Third Party," *Daily Charlotte Observer*, 24 March 1892; "The People's Party Formed," ibid., 17 July 1892.

56. "The People's Party Formed," ibid., 17 July 1892; "Preparing for the 28th," ibid., 24 July 1892.

57. "Capt. Alexander Answers," *Progressive Farmer*, 5 June 1892; "The Political Rubicon," *Daily Charlotte Observer*, 29 July 1893.

58. "The Proposed Union of Forces against the Democracy," *Daily Charlotte Observer*, 27 July 1892; "A Ticket Which Invites Defeat," ibid., 21 August 1892.

59. "Anti–Force Bill Club," ibid., 5 July 1892; "Tammany Tigers," ibid., 12 November 1892.

60. "Heriot Clarkson," ibid., 28 January 1942. Other leading Young Democrats included lawyer E. T. Cansler, born in 1866; hosiery manufacturer R. M. Oates, Jr., born in 1869; bank teller W. C. Wilkinson, born in 1866; and lawyer Charles W. Tillett, born in 1857.

61. "The Club Means Business," ibid., 20 July 1892; "The Young Men in Line," ibid., 26 July 1892.

62. Crow and Durden, *Maverick Republican*, 46–48; Anderson, *Race and Politics*, 191–97.

63. "Named a State Ticket," *New York Times*, 8 September 1892. Chairman Eaves named John Schenck temporary chairman of the second day of the convention and earlier had appointed him to the Committee on Credentials, which suggests that Schenck endorsed Eaves's strategy.

64. "The Republican Mass Meeting—Postmaster Brady Denounced," *Daily Charlotte Observer*, 20 March 1892; "Bradyites vs. Gordonites," ibid., 27 March 1892; ibid., 14 June 1892.

65. "Do Not Be Delivered," ibid., 30 October 1892; "Cunningham's Parting Blast," ibid., 7 November 1892; "Timely Words to Colored Voters," ibid., 2 November 1892.

66. Ibid., 29 October 1892.

67. "Bright Lights to Victory," ibid., 1 November 1892; "Charlotte Ablaze with Light," ibid., 2 November 1892.

68. "Landslide in Mecklenburg," ibid., 9 November 1892; Anderson, *Race and Politics*, 203; L. M. McAlister to Zebulon Vance, 20 September 1893, Zebulon Vance Papers, SHC; Crow and Durden, *Maverick Republican*, 48.

69. For more on Price's advocacy of dividing the black vote, see Price, "The Negro in the Last Decade."

70. "The Rev. Dr. J. C. Price," *Daily Charlotte Observer*, 25 April 1893.

71. Ibid.; *Star of Zion*, 11 May 1893.

72. "Charlotte (N.C.) Items," *Star of Zion*, 18 May 1893; ibid., 3 August 1893.

73. Ibid., 13 July 1893.

74. "The Post Office Janitorship," *Daily Charlotte Observer*, 17 June 1893.

75. Kousser, *Shaping of Southern Politics*, 184.

76. Crow and Durden, *Maverick Republican*, 48–49.

77. Ibid.

78. "It Has Come True," *Raleigh News and Observer*, 31 August 1894; "The End of the Party," ibid., 31 August 1894; *Daily Charlotte Observer*, 31 August 1894.

79. "Charlotte Has Two Democratic Clubs," *Daily Charlotte Observer*, 20 September 1894.

80. *Star of Zion*, 29 March 1894.

81. "Nothing in It for the Negro," ibid., 10 April 1894.

82. "Not Ready for Delivery Just Yet," *Daily Charlotte Observer*, 17 October 1894.

83. "A Very Stupid Populist Fable," ibid., 6 November 1894.

84. "John Schenck Is Dead," ibid., 31 March 1894.

85. "Col. J. S. Carr's Address," ibid., 5 September 1894; "To Work! To Work!," ibid., 28 September 1894; "Charlotte Has Two Democratic Clubs," ibid., 20 September 1894.

86. "Col. J. S. Carr's Address," ibid., 5 September 1894.

87. "Mecklenburg Democracy," ibid., 7 November 1894; Anderson, *Race and Politics*, 222–23.

88. "What Caused It?," *Daily Charlotte Observer*, 11 November 1894.

89. Crow and Durden, *Maverick Republican*, 50. Kousser in *Shaping of Southern Politics* describes the new election law as "probably the fairest and most democratic election law in the post-Reconstruction South" (187).

90. "Election Opinions," *Star of Zion*, 15 November 1894; ibid., 11 April 1895.

91. "Charlotte News," ibid., 18 April 1895; *Daily Charlotte Observer*, 20 March 1895; "Ward 2 Nominations," ibid., 3 April 1895.

92. "Charlotte Hears Watson," *Daily Charlotte Observer*, 4 August 1896; "Fusion Is Dishonorable," ibid., 14 August 1896.

93. "For President, William J. Bryan," ibid., 11 July 1896.

94. Crow and Durden, *Maverick Republican*, 66–67.

95. "County Fusion Effected," *Daily Charlotte Observer*, 27 August 1896; J. P. Sossamon to Marion Butler, 21 September 1896, Marion Butler Papers, SHC.

96. J. P. Sossamon to Marion Butler, 21 September, 19 October 1896, both in Marion Butler Papers, SHC.

97. "Colored Gentlemen Judges," *Daily Charlotte Observer*, 3 October 1896; "Meeting at Samaritan Hall," ibid., 1 October 1896; ibid., 31 October 1896.

98. "Meeting at Samaritan Hall," *Daily Charlotte Observer*, 1 October 1896; ibid., 1 October 1896. For more on Democratic race-baiting tactics in North Carolina during the 1896 election, see Crow and Durden, *Maverick Republican*, 72.

99. "Registration Ends—Voting Next," *Daily Charlotte Observer*, 18 October 1896. The *Daily Charlotte Observer* reported on 7 October 1892 that "a canvass of the vote at the Charlotte Cotton Mill was taken yesterday, and of all the hands employed, there are only two who will vote the Republican ticket. At the last election it was just the other way, only two voted the Democratic ticket."

100. R. B. Davis to Heriot Clarkson, 16 May 1895, Heriot Clarkson Papers, SHC; "Working Men Organize," *Daily Charlotte Observer*, 8 October 1896; "Young Democracy at Work," *Daily Charlotte Observer*, 14 October 1896.

101. Walter R. Henry to Marion Butler, 20 October 1896, Marion Butler Papers, SHC.

102. Ibid.

103. Ibid.

104. "The Great Battle Is Over," *Daily Charlotte Observer*, 4 November 1896; "The Official Vote of Mecklenburg," ibid., 6 November 1896.

105. Crow and Durden, *Maverick Republican*, 73.

106. Joseph H. Wilson to Marion Butler, 4 November 1896, Marion Butler Papers, SHC.

107. Crow and Durden, *Maverick Republican*, 75–90.

108. "To Fight Mullen," *Daily Charlotte Observer*, 14 October 1897; "A Card," ibid., 29 October 1897.

109. "The Colored Republicans," ibid., 13 November 1897; "It Gets Worse and Worse," ibid., 28 November 1897.

CHAPTER 6

1. "Grace AME Zion Church," *Daily Charlotte Observer*, 3 May 1899.

2. Several other historians have noted the significance of a generational shift in explaining the growth in racial hostility in the late nineteenth-century South, but with different emphases. In his essay "A Generation of Defeat," David H. Donald argues that in the 1890s the Civil War generation reached middle-adulthood and that segregation and disfranchisement "should be viewed as the final public acts, the last bequests, of the Civil War generation." In Charlotte, however, members of the Civil War generation formed the core of the town's better class in the 1870s and 1880s and displayed paternalistic feelings toward the black better class. Moreover, most members of the Civil War generation were deceased by the mid-to-late 1890s—before Jim Crow and disfranchisement legislation. Instead, white-supremacy campaigns, Jim Crow, and disfranchisement were all initiated by the next generation, men and women shaped by a vastly different set of experiences from those of their parents. See Donald, "A Generation of Defeat," 7–18.

By contrast, Joel Williamson in *Crucible of Race* posits a shift in "mentalities" concerning race in the 1890s and suggests a generational basis for this change. "Radicalism" emerged in the 1890s—overshadowing both "conservative" and "liberal" mind-sets of the 1880s—and reflected a fear of the "new Negro," who seemed to be "retrogressing" toward a "natural state of bestiality" (111). Dominating in the 1890s, radicals "profoundly altered public and private institutions to effect real reductions in the quality of life for black people" (6). Notably, Williamson describes the radicals of the 1890s as a generational cohort, the "children of Reconstruction" (180), emphasizing the formative childhood experiences of this generation. In particular, he argues, they were shaped by a sense of powerlessness as their fathers left to fight the Civil War. The radicals of the 1890s, he argues, hoped to regain "a power over their lives and persons that their fathers and mothers lost" (ibid., 181).

Williamson's argument concerning the ascendance of a new generation of "radicals" seems to fit the Charlotte experience. But his dependence on psychosexual explanations for the emergence of radicalism obscures simpler reasons for the attitudes of the new generation of southern leaders in the 1890s. Although the new generation may have been the "children of Reconstruction," they were also, importantly, the children of "Redemption." In Charlotte most of the new generation of political leaders were born during the Civil War or soon afterward; few had any firsthand knowledge of the war. Instead, their first formative political experience was probably Zebulon Vance's Redemption campaign in 1876, which they re-created in the white-supremacy campaigns of the 1890s.

3. "Colored Republicans Organize," *Daily Charlotte Observer*, 3 February 1898.

4. Crow and Durden, *Maverick Republican*, 119.

5. "To the Populists of Mecklenburg County," *People's Paper*, 13 May 1898. Populist newspaper editor J. P. Sossamon sided with Henry, maintaining that the Butler plan had no support in Mecklenburg and that he could not uncover a single Populist "who has decided to return to the Democratic party." See *People's Paper*, 13 May 1898.

6. Crow and Durden, *Maverick Republican*, 122–23.

7. Ibid., 139; Edmonds, *The Negro and Fusion Politics*, 138. Williamson in *Crucible of Race* also cites Furnifold Simmons as a representative of the new generation of "radicals" that dominated in the 1890s (177). For a discussion of the extent of black officeholding in North Carolina, see Edmonds, *The Negro and Fusion Politics*, 84–134. Edmonds points out that during North Carolina's fusion years, black voters elected a single congressman, ten state legislators, and only a handful of county commissioners and officers and did not dominate on the federal, state, or county level. Based on this data, Edmonds concludes that Democrats concocted the cry of "Negro domination" to unseat the fusionists. By contrast, Anderson maintains that although blacks did not dominate anywhere in the state, "Democrats recognized a substantial increase in Negro influence, of which black officeholding was but one aspect, and that fusion rule meant a reversal of the trend of the early 1890s." He argues that "it would be a mistake to conclude that white supremacy was a contrived issue, that Democratic leaders were not genuinely concerned about increasing black political influence." See Anderson, *Race and Politics*, 251–54.

8. W. A. Potts to Marion Butler, 20 July 1898, Marion Butler Papers, SHC.

9. "Henry Boulware's Threat," *Daily Charlotte Observer*, 29 July 1898.

10. "The Republican Convention," ibid., 28 August 1898.

11. "Champions of Democracy," ibid., 15 October 1898; "Barkley to Democrats," ibid., 28 October 1898.

12. "The Color Line," ibid., 28 August 1898.

13. Claiborne, *Charlotte Observer*, 105; "Negro Rule: Shall It Last Longer in North Carolina?," *Daily Charlotte Observer*, 10 September 1898; "Human Devils in Command," ibid., 10 September 1898; "Negroes Trifling and Lazy," ibid., 23 July 1898; "Wilmington's Negro Rule," ibid., 7 September 1898; "New Bern's Fearful Plight—Negro Magis-

trates Running Mad," ibid., 9 September 1898; "Negroes in the East Arming," ibid., 9 October 1898; "A Cry for Rescue," ibid., 22 October 1898.

14. "It Offends Decency," *Daily Charlotte Observer*, 30 October 1898.

15. "Afro-American Interests," ibid., 23 January 1898; ibid., 2 February 1898.

16. Crow and Durden, *Maverick Republican*, 125. For the debate over county fusion, see "There Will Be No Fusion," *Daily Charlotte Observer*, 17 August 1898; "The Vacillating Populists," ibid., 6 September 1898; and "Fusion on in Mecklenburg," ibid., 17 September 1898.

17. "Afro-American Interests," *Daily Charlotte Observer*, 28 August 1898.

18. "Vicious Attack upon a Beloved Minister," ibid., 14 October 1898.

19. Ibid.

20. "John C. Dancy Speaks Here," ibid., 13 October 1898; "Best Party for the Negro," *Star of Zion*, 22 September 1898.

21. *People's Paper*, 29 July, 13 May, 28, 14 October, 2 September 1898. See also "An Appeal to the Voters of Mecklenburg," ibid., 4 November 1898.

22. "Dr. Alexander Will Not Support the Fusion Ticket," *Daily Charlotte Observer*, 6 November 1898.

23. "Good Men to the Rescue," ibid., 15 October 1898; "Leaves the Republican Party," ibid., 12 October 1898.

24. Crow and Durden, *Maverick Republican*, 128; Muller, "New South Populism," 143.

25. "A Race Issue Campaign," *Star of Zion*, 27 October 1898.

26. Crow and Durden, *Maverick Republican*, 133; "Editorial Comment," *People's Paper*, 2 September 1898; ibid., 28 October 1898.

27. "'Democracy Is Immortal,'" *Daily Charlotte Observer*, 5 November 1898.

28. "Mecklenburg Did Her Best," ibid., 9 November 1898; "Returns Are Now All In," ibid., 10 November 1898; *People's Paper*, 11 November 1898. Although Crab Orchard, Mallard Creek, Lemley, and Huntersville maintained slight fusion majorities, Democrats won back the Berryhill, Providence, Paw Creek, and Long Creek districts.

29. "The Election," *People's Paper*, 11 November 1898.

30. "Mecklenburg Did Her Best," *Daily Charlotte Observer*, 9 November 1898; ibid., 10 November 1898.

31. For a thorough account of the Wilmington riot, see Prather, *We Have Taken a City*.

32. "Some Good Advice by a Negro," *Daily Charlotte Observer*, 15 November 1898.

33. Ibid.

34. "Race Disturbances," *Star of Zion*, 15 December 1898.

35. "Bishop's Address: The Negro Leaves God—God Leaves the Negro," ibid., 22 December 1898.

36. "Afro-American Interests," *Daily Charlotte Observer*, 24 October 1897; "Bishop's Address: The Negro Leaves God—God Leaves the Negro," *Star of Zion*, 22 December 1898.

37. "The Two Races Must Live Forever Apart," *Raleigh News and Observer*, 29 January 1899.

38. Crow and Durden, *Maverick Republican*, 138–41; "The Senate's Vote 41 to 6," *Daily Charlotte Observer*, 19 February 1899. The amendment required that in order to register to vote, a person must "be able to read and write any section of the Constitution in the English language" and must have paid a poll tax for the previous year. The law did not deny the franchise to anyone who "was on January 1, 1867, or at any time prior thereto, entitled to vote under the laws of any State in the United States wherein he then resided, and no lineal descendent of any such person, shall be denied the right to register and vote

at any election in this State by reason of his failure to possess the educational qualifications herein prescribed, provided he shall have registered in accordance with the terms of this section prior to December 1, 1908."

39. "The Amendment Defended," *Daily Charlotte Observer*, 18 September 1899. Despite the fact that throughout 1899 and 1900 Democrats insisted that the disfranchisement amendment was constitutional, Charlotte lawyer W. A. Guthrie also pointed out "that the U.S. government had its hands full taking care of its wars in Porto Rico, Cuba, the Philippines and Hawaii. We will probably not be interfered with here. The sentimentality that formerly interfered with us is rapidly dying out." See ibid., 22 August 1899.

40. Heriot Clarkson, "Important Events of My Life," n.d., Heriot Clarkson to J. W. Bailey, 12 July 1903, and Murray F. Smith to Thomas W. Alexander and Clarkson and Duls, 23 November 1897, all in Heriot Clarkson Papers, SHC.

41. "One Reason Why the Amendment Should Be Adopted," *Daily Charlotte Observer*, 16 December 1899.

42. "What Must Be Done," *Star of Zion*, 5 January 1899.

43. Ibid., 26 January 1899; "Negro Characteristics," *Daily Charlotte Observer*, 13 August 1899.

44. "Useful Citizenship," *Star of Zion*, 11 May 1899; ibid., 17 August 1899.

45. Haley, *Charles N. Hunter*, 122–23; *Star of Zion*, 19 January 1899.

46. "Constitutional Amendment," *Daily Charlotte Observer*, 12 March 1899.

47. Ibid.

48. "Bishop Hood's Article," *Star of Zion*, 16 March 1899; *AME Zion Quarterly Review*, January/February 1899; *Africo-American Presbyterian*, quoted in *Star of Zion*, 23 March 1899.

49. "Views of a Northern Democrat," *Daily Charlotte Observer*, 16 March 1899.

50. "Laying the Track for Separate Cars," *Raleigh News and Observer*, 1 February 1899; "The Railroad Attitude toward a Separate Car Law," *Daily Charlotte Observer*, 2 December 1898.

51. "Appeal for Justice," *Star of Zion*, 2 March 1899; "The Separate Car Law," *Daily Charlotte Observer*, 10 January 1899; "Jim Crow Car Bill Passed," *Raleigh News and Observer*, 22 February 1899; "Separate Car Law Passes the Senate," ibid., 2 March 1899.

52. "Whites Not Shouting over It," *Star of Zion*, 22 June 1899; ibid., 2 March 1893. The *Observer* printed a number of reports claiming that many of the state's white citizens were unhappy with the Jim Crow law because of overcrowded white cars and blaming the railroads, who fought the legislation, for intentionally making conditions miserable in separate and divided cars. See, for example, "The Jim Crow Law," *Daily Charlotte Observer*, 21 June 1899. Despite the fact that the *Observer* had reported near unanimity of white support for the bill in late 1898, the newspaper admitted that the bill was not "received with any jubilation whatever by the North Carolina public." See "No Enthusiasm over the Separate Car Law," ibid., 15 June 1899. For a contrasting point of view, see "The Separate Car Law," ibid., 16 June 1899.

53. Meier, *Negro Thought in America*, 129–30; "Of Race Interest," *Star of Zion*, 22 September 1898; "Divide Your Votes," ibid., 2 November 1899. For more on the National Afro-American League and the National Afro-American Council, see Thornburgh, *T. Thomas Fortune*; "National Afro-American Council," *Star of Zion*, 23 September 1898; and "Be a Slave to No Party," ibid., 9 November 1899.

54. "Divide Your Votes," *Star of Zion*, 2 November 1899.

55. "Good Counsel, but Over-Due," *Daily Charlotte Observer*, 11 November 1899.

56. "A Plea for the Negroes," ibid., 22 November 1899; "The Negro and His Vote," ibid., 22 November 1899.

57. *Washington Bee*, quoted in Gould, *Presidency of William McKinley*, 28, 154.

58. "The End Is Not Yet," *Star of Zion*, 2 March 1899.

59. "Fast—Pray to God," ibid., 4 May 1899.

60. "Aycock on the Amendment," *Daily Charlotte Observer*, 20 February 1900.

61. "White Supremacy," ibid., 23 February 1900.

62. "A White Supremacy Club," ibid., 2 March 1900.

63. "Democrats Speaking," ibid., 4 July 1900; "White Supremacy Meeting," ibid., 22 April 1900; "Spoke for the Amendment," ibid., 3 June 1900; "The White Man Must Rule," ibid., 20 May 1900.

64. "To the Ladies," ibid., 27 April 1900.

65. "A Brand New Fusion Ticket," ibid., 28 February 1900.

66. Ibid., 13 April 1900; "Dr. Barringer's Paper," ibid., 1 May 1900.

67. *Star of Zion*, 5 July 1900.

68. "A Lily White Convention," *Daily Charlotte Observer*, 29 April 1900; "A Brand New Fusion Ticket," ibid., 28 July 1900; "Populists and the Amendment," ibid., 24 April 1900.

69. "Annual Address," *Star of Zion*, 1 February 1900; "The Negroes in Council," *Daily Charlotte Observer*, 13 February 1900. The resolutions committee included John C. Dancy, Congressman George H. White, W. M. Provinder, Jesse B. Colbert, William A. Peggins, G. L. Blackwell, George C. Clement, E. Moore, Frank M. Noble, R. B. Bruce, P. A. Stevenson, B. A. Johnson, W. H. Goler, and D. C. Suggs.

70. "Create Public Sentiment," *Daily Charlotte Observer*, 7 June 1900.

71. "A Big Democratic Rally," ibid., 19 July 1900; "The Rally of the Democrats," ibid., 1 August 1900. Wilkes, employed at the family-owned Mecklenburg Iron Works, was thirty-six years old, while Barringer, a publisher, was only twenty-four.

72. "The Rally of the Democrats," ibid., 1 August 1900.

73. "3,500 Democratic Majority," ibid., 3 August 1900; "Last Chance to Register," *Star of Zion*, 19 July 1900.

74. *Star of Zion*, 9 August 1900.

75. *AME Zion Quarterly Review*, October 1900; "Editorial Briefs," ibid., September 1900.

CHAPTER 7

1. J. T. Williams to W. C. Smith, 11 April 1905, in the private collection of Rosa Smith, Charlotte, North Carolina.

2. *Star of Zion*, 25 October 1900; "The Negro Is Rising," ibid., 11 October 1900.

3. "The Negro and the Future," *Daily Charlotte Observer*, 25 October 1903.

4. "The Old-Time Negro Preacher," ibid., 30 December 1902; "Passing of a Black Mammy," ibid., 10 February 1904.

5. "A Variety of Idle Comment," ibid., 22 December 1902; "The Negro as a Laborer," ibid., 27 January 1901. In his examination of the establishment of Jim Crow laws in five southern cities, Rabinowitz also found considerable complaint about upstart "new Negroes," whom he defines as a younger, educated generation "born in freedom" and having "no fond memories of slavery or attachments to the past as did some of their older relatives." Concern with the "new Negro" appears much earlier in the cities of Rabino-

witz's study than in Charlotte, as he cites examples as early as the mid-1870s. The "new Negroes" in Charlotte probably included the offspring of the city's black better class who emerged in the 1880s. See Rabinowitz, *Race Relations*, 333–39.

6. "Negroes Refuse to Work," *Daily Charlotte Observer*, 23 October 1903.

7. U.S. Bureau of the Census, Census of the United States, 1890, 1900, 1910, and 1920. The census would not have reflected seasonal migrations that may have accounted for the labor shortage as well.

8. Anderson, *Race and Politics*, 308; *Charlotte Observer* editorial, reprinted in the *Star of Zion*, 27 September 1900; "Negroes Still Leaving," *Daily Charlotte Observer*, 23 June 1903; "Movement of the Colored Cooks North," ibid., 19 July 1903; "The Future of the Negro," ibid., 7 October 1901.

9. *Star of Zion*, 13 March 1902; "A Negro Exodus," ibid., 3 March 1902. See also "Negro Exodus—The Causes," ibid., 27 September 1900.

10. Meier in *Negro Thought in America* discusses a "large middle ground of opinion that held to a broad spectrum of ideologies" in existence at the turn of the century that "employed a judicious combination of militance and accommodation" between the strategic poles articulated by Washington and his critics (172).

11. *Star of Zion*, 11 October 1900; "Victory and What It Means," ibid., 15 November 1900.

12. "A Bishop's View—How Can Any Thoughtful Negro Support Mr. Bryan?," ibid., 18 October 1900.

13. "He Will Test the Amendments," ibid., 22 November 1900.

14. Gould, *Presidency of William McKinley*, 29, 159–60; Meier, *Negro Thought in America*, 168.

15. Heriot Clarkson, "Important Events of My Life," n.d., Heriot Clarkson Papers, SHC.

16. Grantham, *Southern Progressivism*, xvi–xviii; "Speech of Heriot Clarkson at Presbyterian College," 22 February 1900, Heriot Clarkson Papers, SHC; "Election Act for Charlotte," *Daily Charlotte Observer*, 2 March 1901.

17. "Charlotte Election Law," Heriot Clarkson Papers, NCDAH. In an excellent overview exploring the problems of defining progressivism, Daniel T. Rodgers argues that progressives "did not share a common creed or a string of common values" but instead "possessed an ability to draw on three distinctive clusters of ideas—three distinct social languages—to articulate their discontents and their social visions." Rodgers defines these languages as antimonopolism, an emphasis on social bonds, and social efficiency. See Rodgers, "In Search of Progressivism," 113–32.

18. "Our New Mayor," *Daily Charlotte Observer*, 6 May 1891.

19. "Brevard and Others Talk," ibid., 9 April 1901; "And Dr. R. J. Brevard Replies," ibid., 6 March 1901.

20. "Speeches for Mr. P. M. Brown," ibid., 9 April 1901; ibid., 29 March 1901; "The Mayoralty," ibid., 5 March 1901.

21. "P. M. Brown Is Nominated," ibid., 10 April 1901.

22. Song quoted in Haley, *Charles N. Hunter*, 142; "Stabbed by False Friends," *Star of Zion*, 18 September 1902. For more on the "lily-white" movement of 1900, see Steelman, "Progressive Era," 399–400.

23. "Stabbed by False Friends," *Star of Zion*, 18 September 1902.

24. "Political Gossip," *Daily Charlotte Observer*, 19 August 1902; "Will Nominate a Ticket," ibid., 26 August 1902; "Republicans Energetic," ibid., 21 September 1902.

25. "Negroes Aroused," *Star of Zion*, 25 September 1902; "Organization Our Salvation," ibid., 25 September 1902.

26. On the "divided mind" of African Americans in the wake of disfranchisement, see Meier, *Negro Thought in America*, 161–89. Gatewood in *Aristocrats of Color* also notes that "aristocrats of color" divided over racial strategy, with members of the elite splitting into both the accommodationist and militant camps (300–322).

27. *Star of Zion*, 2 October 1902; "Business Principles," ibid., 20 March 1902.

28. Ibid., 2 October 1902.

29. Ibid., 23 October 1902.

30. Baily, *Liberalism in the New South*, 84; *Star of Zion*, 6 November 1902; *Daily Charlotte Observer*, 27 April 1903; "2,217 Persons Registered," ibid., 24 April 1903; *Star of Zion*, 20 August 1903.

31. "Pamphlet by a Colored Minister of Charlotte," *Daily Charlotte Observer*, 29 November 1903; "How to Get On in the World," *Star of Zion*, 12 February 1903.

32. "The Race Question," *Star of Zion*, 24 December 1903.

33. "Thoughts for the Occasion," ibid., 14 January 1904.

34. Du Bois, *Souls of Black Folk*; Meier, *Negro Thought in America*, 176.

35. "Men and Events," *Star of Zion*, 5 March 1903 (emphasis added).

36. "Message to the Negro Race," *Daily Charlotte Observer*, 8 November 1903.

37. "Men and Events," *Star of Zion*, 26 February 1903.

38. Steelman, "Progressive Era," 253, 276–79; "The Election Returns," *Daily Charlotte Observer*, 6 November 1902. Local Republicans did not challenge the Democratic party in the municipal elections of 1901 and 1903. Although Republicans offered a slate of candidates for state judicial and congressional elections in 1902, Democrats won easily in Mecklenburg. See "Democrats Get Everything," *Daily Charlotte Observer*, 5 November 1902. For more on the North Carolina Republican party from 1900 to 1917, see Steelman, "Progressive Era," 399–417.

39. "More Backbone Is Needed," *Daily Charlotte Observer*, 4 February 1901; "Mayor McCall Replies," ibid., 5 February 1901; "The Saloon at the Bottom of It," ibid., 7 February 1901.

40. "Dr. Stagg's Point Well Taken," ibid., 10 February 1901; "Stop the Society Gambling," ibid., 8 February 1901.

41. "To the White Voters of Charlotte," ibid., 21 March 1901.

42. Heriot Clarkson, "Important Events of My Life," n.d., Heriot Clarkson Papers, SHC; "P. M. Brown Is Nominated," *Daily Charlotte Observer*, 10 April 1901; "Board of Aldermen Meet," ibid., 4 June 1901.

43. Whitener, *Prohibition in North Carolina*, 97. See also "The License Question," *Daily Charlotte Observer*, 7 December 1892.

44. "Will Resist the Dispensary," *Daily Charlotte Observer*, 2 February 1899; "Not a Preacher's Movement," ibid., 8 February 1899; "Dispensary Petition," ibid., 16 February 1899; "The Dispensary Hearing," ibid., 17 February 1899; "Mr. Osborne Blocks the Way," ibid., 19 February 1899; "At White Heat," ibid., 23 February 1899; *Raleigh News and Observer*, 24 February 1899, quoted in Whitener, *Prohibition in North Carolina*, 124.

45. *Daily Charlotte Observer*, 19 June 1894; "The Temperance Rally," ibid., 26 July 1894; "The Polyglot Petition," ibid., 17 January 1895; "A Temperance Chopping Party," ibid., 26 February 1897; "White Ribbon Tea," ibid., 20 April 1899; ibid., 17 May 1900; "WCTU Officers," ibid., 26 January 1901.

46. *Star of Zion*, 27 June 1895, 15 September 1898. Since Woodward claimed that

southern progressivism was for "whites only," it has been popular to emphasize the racial limitations of progressivism in the South. See Woodward, *Origins of the New South*, 373. See also Kousser, "Progressivism," 169–94. Lamon in *Black Tennesseans* challenges that interpretation by describing an entire array of progressive activities initiated by blacks in Tennessee between 1900 and 1930.

47. "Colored W.C.T.U. Meeting," *Daily Charlotte Observer*, 17 June 1901; "The Battle against Drink," ibid., 18 June 1901.

48. "Fight for Temperance," ibid., 21 January 1900.

49. "A Variety of Idle Comment," ibid., 24 March 1902. The arguments of Charlotte's businesspeople for prohibition in 1902 were similar to those of emerging middle-class shopkeepers in the antebellum North in their concern with creating a disciplined work force. In Charlotte, however, the arguments contained an additional layer of Social Darwinism. See Paul E. Johnson, *A Shopkeeper's Millennium*.

50. *Biblical Recorder*, 24 December 1902, quoted in Whitener, *Prohibition in North Carolina*, 113.

51. "Prohibition Is the Slogan," *Daily Charlotte Observer*, 15 December 1903; "Preacher for High License," ibid., 28 March 1904.

52. Records of the Anti-Saloon League, Heriot Clarkson Papers, NCDAH; "To Vote on Temperance," *Daily Charlotte Observer*, 5 January 1904.

53. "The Election," *Charlotte News*, 6 July 1904. For an example of Charlotte's subsequent role in the successful state prohibition election of 1908, see Executive Committee of the Anti-Saloon League of Charlotte, North Carolina, "It Helps Business and Is a Blessing," 1904, NCC.

54. S. F. Conrad, "The Effects of Prohibition in Charlotte: Remarkable Story of the Rapid Progress," Heriot Clarkson Papers, NCDAH.

55. "The Day Nursery," *Daily Charlotte Observer*, 8 August 1901; "A Woman's Club," ibid., 4 December 1901; "To Bless Working Women," ibid., 21 February 1902.

56. "Young Women's Home Ready," ibid., 23 March 1902; "To Bless Working Women, ibid., 21 February 1902.

57. "For Florence Rescue Home," ibid., 27 January 1903; "Rescue Home for Charlotte," ibid., 29 January 1903; "A Plea for Helpless Women," ibid., 1 February 1903; "Crittenton Meetings End," ibid., 3 February 1903; "24 Charlotte Girls Rescued," ibid., 25 October 1903.

58. "To Help Mill Operatives," ibid., 21 January 1902.

59. Doherty, "Alexander J. McKelway," 177–90; McKelway, "Child Labor Problem," 313, and "Child Labor in the Southern Cotton Mills," 269.

60. "Child Labor in the Mills," *Daily Charlotte Observer*, 14 December 1902.

61. "The Matter of Child Labor in the Cotton Mills," ibid., 11 August 1902; "Child Labor in the United States," ibid., 19 December 1902.

62. Powell, *North Carolina through Four Centuries*, 455.

63. Doherty, "Alexander J. McKelway," 179.

64. Powell, *North Carolina through Four Centuries*, 457–58.

65. See *Charlotte Evening Chronicle*, 23 August 1909; Minutes of the Mecklenburg Medical Society, Mecklenburg Medical Society Offices, Charlotte, N.C., September 1909; "The Hookworm Problem," *Charlotte Evening Chronicle*, 31 August 1909.

66. Grantham, *Southern Progressivism*, 125; "New Colored Pavilion," *Daily Charlotte Observer*, 2 May 1903.

67. "Jim Crow Street Cars," *Daily Charlotte Observer*, 27 September 1906.

68. "Reformatory Is Assured," ibid., 9 March 1907; "Jim Crow Street Cars," ibid.,

3 April 1907; "'Jim Crow' Street Car Law," ibid., 1 April 1907. The passage of the streetcar law sparked little interest in the press. The *Observer* did not comment editorially on the passage of the law, and articles summarizing the most important legislation of the 1907 winter term failed to mention it. See "Measured by the Results," ibid., 12 March 1907, and "Acts of the Legislature," ibid., 15 March 1907. Meier and Rudwick in "Boycott Movement" note that the following states implemented statewide Jim Crow streetcar statutes in the following years: Louisiana (1902); Mississippi (1904); Virginia (1906); and Texas, Oklahoma, and North Carolina (1907). Many southern cities, beginning at the turn of the century, passed municipal segregation ordinances. Both Atlanta and Montgomery passed such laws in 1900. See ibid., 756–75.

69. "Objected to Jim Crow Law," *Daily Charlotte Observer*, 16 April 1907; Meier and Rudwick, "Boycott Movement," 760; *Daily Charlotte Observer*, 3 April 1907; Floretta Douglas Gunn, interview with author, 17 February 1982. Meier and Rudwick note that "the boycott leaders, where they can be identified, were uniformly an elite group which consisted of prominent business and professional men, with at times a sprinkling of federal employees or a rare politician," and that ministers in some southern cities opposed boycott efforts. See Meier and Rudwick, "Boycott Movement," 767–69.

70. Floretta Douglas Gunn, interview with author, 17 February 1982; Meier and Rudwick, "Boycott Movement," 775. Meier and Rudwick discuss the conservative nature of the streetcar boycotts, arguing that the protests sought "to preserve the status quo" and "avoided a direct confrontation with the laws" (ibid., 770–71).

EPILOGUE

1. Meier, *Negro Thought in America*, 186; Harlan, *Booker T. Washington*, 431, 423; Haley, *Charles N. Hunter*, 172–88; U.S. Bureau of the Census, Census of the United States, 1900, 1910, and 1920.

2. *Colored Charlotte*, 2–3.

3. Ibid., 6.

4. *Charlotte City Directory*, 1897–98; Aurelia Tate Henderson, interview with author, 16 March 1982; Huffman, "Historical Sketch." In his study of Greensboro, Kipp notes a similar development, arguing that "the emergence of a system of formally sanctioned racial segregation and the hardening of informal social sanctions ironically opened up new opportunities for the black middle class." After white hotels, restaurants, and stores prohibited black patronage, enterprising blacks established businesses to cater to black needs. See Kipp, "Urban Growth and Social Change," 244–45.

5. Haley, *Charles N. Hunter*, 222.

6. Ibid., 226–27.

7. The Reverend Curtis Kearns, interview with author, 22 February 1982.

8. Aurelia Tate Henderson, interview with author, 16 March 1982.

9. Hanchett, "Rosenwald Schools," 387–444.

10. Aurelia Tate Henderson, interview with author, 16 March 1982.

11. Gaillard, *Dream Long Deferred*, 19–20.

12. Ibid., 3–8.

13. Ibid.

14. Ibid., 23–30, 113–14.

BIBLIOGRAPHY

. . . .

MANUSCRIPTS

Chapel Hill, North Carolina
North Carolina Collection, University of North Carolina
  "Address of Heriot Clarkson, Associate Justice, Supreme Court of North Carolina, Before the Woman's Christian Temperance Union," 1930.
  Executive Committee of the Anti-Saloon League of Charlotte, North Carolina, "It Helps Business and Is a Blessing: What Leading Business Men, Bankers, Farmers, Laborers, and Others Say about Prohibition," 1904.
  Southern Manufacturers Club—By Laws and House Rules. Charlotte, N.C.: Queen City Publishing Company, 1911.
Southern Historical Collection, University of North Carolina
  Edmund S. Burwell Papers.
  Marion Butler Papers.
  Heriot Clarkson Papers.
  Drury Lacy Papers.
  Daniel Augustus Tompkins Papers.
  Zebulon Vance Papers.

Charlotte, North Carolina
City Clerk's Office
  Charlotte Board of Aldermen Minutes, 1859–1900.
Mecklenburg County Courthouse
  Records of Corporation, Mecklenburg County, North Carolina, 1886–1900.
Mecklenburg Medical Society Offices
  Minutes of the Mecklenburg Medical Society, 1909.
Mint Museum of History
  Captain John C. Barnett, assistant superintendent of the Freedmen's Bureau, "Circular to the Freedmen of Western North Carolina," 1 October 1865.
Private collection of Rosa Smith
  Letter, J. T. Williams to W. C. Smith, 11 April 1905.
Public Library of Charlotte and Mecklenburg County, Robinson-Spangler Carolina Room, Vertical Files
  J. W. Smith, "Early History of Seventh Street Presbyterian Church, U.S.A, Now First United Presbyterian Church, U.S.A., Charlotte, North Carolina," 1976.

Raleigh, North Carolina
North Carolina Division of Archives and History
  Heriot Clarkson Papers.

Washington, D.C.
National Archives
  Records of the Bureau of Refugees, Freedmen, and Abandoned Lands, Record
    Group 105.

NEWSPAPERS, PERIODICALS, AND DIRECTORIES

AME Zion Quarterly Review, 1890–1900.
Branson's North Carolina Business Directory, 1872, 1877, 1878.
Catawba Journal, 1824.
Charlotte Chronicle, 1886–92.
Charlotte City Directory, 1875–76, 1879–80, 1897–98.
Charlotte Democrat, 1870–81.
Charlotte Evening Chronicle, 1909.
Charlotte Journal, 1847–51.
Charlotte Messenger, 1881–88.
Charlotte News, 1904, 1914.
Charlotte Observer, 1873–86.
Daily Charlotte Observer, 1892–1910.
The Land We Love (Charlotte), 1866–69.
Miner's and Farmer's Journal (Charlotte), 1833.
New Berne Daily Times, 1865.
New York Times, 1890, 1892.
North Carolina Prohibitionist, 1886–87.
North Carolina Weekly Standard (Raleigh), 1862–70.
North Carolina Whig (Charlotte), 1852–60.
The People's Paper (Charlotte), 1898–1900.
The Progressive Farmer (Raleigh), 1888–90.
Raleigh News and Observer, 1890, 1894, 1899.
Southern Home (Charlotte), 1870–76.
Star of Zion (Charlotte), 1880–1903.
Western Democrat (Charlotte), 1860–70.

CENSUS MATERIALS

U.S. Bureau of the Census. *Agriculture of the United States in 1860, Eighth Census.*
  Washington, D.C.: Government Printing Office, 1864.
———. *Census Reports.* Vol. 1, *Twelfth Census of the United States, 1900: Population, Part*
  1. Washington, D.C.: Government Printing Office, 1901.
———. *Census Reports.* Vol. 1, *Thirteenth Census of the United States, 1910: Population,*
  Part 1. Washington, D.C.: Government Printing Office, 1913.
———. *Census Reports.* Vol. 1, *Fourteenth Census of the United States, 1920: Population,*
  Part 1. Washington, D.C.: Government Printing Office, 1921.
———. *Compendium of the Eleventh Census, 1890: Population, Part 1.* Washington, D.C.:
  Government Printing Office, 1892.
———. Manuscript census schedules, Mecklenburg County, North Carolina, 1810,
  1830, 1850–80.
———. *Population of the United States in 1860, Eighth Census.* Washington, D.C.: Gov-
  ernment Printing Office, 1864.

————. *Report on the Products of Agriculture, General Statistics, Tenth Census*, vol. 3. Washington, D.C.: Government Printing Office, 1884.

————. *Seventh Census of the United States, 1850*. Washington, D.C.: Robert Armstrong, Public Printer, 1853.

————. *Statistics of the Population of the United States, 1870*. Washington, D.C.: Government Printing Office, 1872.

————. *Statistics of the Population of the United States, 1880*. Washington, D.C.: Government Printing Office, 1883.

INTERVIEWS

All interviews were conducted by the author in Charlotte, North Carolina.

Floretta Douglas Gunn, 17 February 1982.
Aurelia Tate Henderson, 16 March 1982.
The Reverend Curtis Kearns, 22 February 1982.
Rosa Smith, 15 March 1984.

BOOKS, ARTICLES, THESES, AND PAPERS

Abbott, Richard. *The Republican Party and the South, 1855–1877: The First Southern Strategy*. Chapel Hill: University of North Carolina Press, 1986.

Ahlstrom, Sidney. *A Religious History of the American People*. New Haven, Conn.: Yale University Press, 1972.

Alexander, J. B. *The History of Mecklenburg County, From 1740 to 1900*. Charlotte, N.C.: Observer Printing House, 1902.

Alexander, Roberta Sue. "Hostility and Hope: Black Education in North Carolina during Presidential Reconstruction, 1865–1867." *North Carolina Historical Review* 53 (April 1976): 113–32.

————. *North Carolina Faces the Freedman: Race Relations during Presidential Reconstruction*. Durham, N.C.: Duke University Press, 1985.

Anderson, Eric. *Race and Politics in North Carolina, 1872–1901*. Baton Rouge: Louisiana State University Press, 1981.

Ashe, Samuel A. *Biographical History of North Carolina*. Vol. 1. Greensboro, N.C.: Van Noppen, 1905.

Auman, William T. "Neighbor against Neighbor: The Inner Civil War in the Randolph County Area of Confederate North Carolina." *North Carolina Historical Review* 61 (January 1984): 59–92.

Baily, Hugh C. *Liberalism in the New South: Southern Social Reformers and the Progressive Movement*. Coral Gables, Fla.: University of Miami Press, 1969.

Baltzell, E. Digby. *Philadelphia Gentlemen: The Making of a National Upper Class*. Glencoe, Ill.: Free Press, 1958.

Barrett, John G. *The Civil War in North Carolina*. Chapel Hill: University of North Carolina Press, 1963.

Beatty, Bess. "Lowells of the South: Northern Influence in the Nineteenth-Century North Carolina Textile Industry." *Journal of Southern History* 53 (February 1987): 37–62.

————. *A Revolution Gone Backward: The Black Response to National Politics, 1876–1896*. Westport, Conn.: Greenwood Press, 1987.

Berlin, Ira. *Slaves without Masters: The Free Negro in the Antebellum South*. New York: Pantheon, 1974.

Berlin, Ira, et al., eds. *Freedom: A Documentary History of Emancipation, 1861–1867*. Series 2, *The Black Military Experience*. New York: Cambridge University Press, 1983.

Billings, Dwight. *Planters and the Making of a "New South": Class, Politics, and Development in North Carolina, 1865–1900*. Chapel Hill: University of North Carolina Press, 1979.

Black, Robert C. *The Railroads of the Confederacy*. Chapel Hill: University of North Carolina Press, 1952.

Blassingame, John. *Black New Orleans, 1860–1880*. Chicago: University of Chicago Press, 1973.

Blumin, Stuart. *The Emergence of the Middle Class: Social Experience in the American City, 1760–1920*. New York: Cambridge University Press, 1989.

Blythe, LeGette, and Charles R. Brockmann. *Hornet's Nest: The Story of Charlotte and Mecklenburg County*. Charlotte, N.C.: McNally, 1961.

Bordin, Ruth. *Woman and Temperance: The Quest for Power and Liberty, 1873–1900*. Philadelphia: Temple University Press, 1981.

Bromberg, Allen Bruce. " 'Pure Democracy and White Supremacy': The Redeemer Period in North Carolina, 1876–1894." Ph.D. diss., University of Virginia, 1977.

———. " 'The Worst Muddle Ever Seen in North Carolina Politics': The Farmers Alliance, the Subtreasury, and Zeb Vance." *North Carolina Historical Review* 56 (January 1979): 19–40.

Brown, Henry S., and Mary F. Hoffman. "Gold Mining on the Rudisill Lode and the Development of Charlotte, North Carolina." City of Charlotte, Community Development Department, n.d.

Buck, Solon Justus. *The Granger Movement: A Study of Agricultural Organization and Its Political, Economic, and Social Manifestations, 1870–1880*. Lincoln: University of Nebraska Press, 1913.

Burgess, Allen Edward. "Tar Heel Blacks and the New South Dream: The Coleman Manufacturing Company, 1896–1904." Ph.D. diss., Duke University, 1977.

Carlton, David L. *Mill and Town in South Carolina, 1880–1920*. Baton Rouge: Louisiana State University Press, 1982.

Cartwright, Joseph H. *The Triumph of Jim Crow: Race Relations in the 1880s*. Knoxville: University of Tennessee Press, 1979.

Cheney, John L., Jr., ed. *North Carolina Government, 1585–1979: A Narrative and Statistical History*. Raleigh: North Carolina Department of the Secretary of State, 1980.

Claiborne, Jack. *The Charlotte Observer: Its Time and Place, 1869–1986*. Chapel Hill: University of North Carolina Press, 1986.

———. *Unto the Least of These: The Story of the Alexander Children's Center, 1888–1988*. Charlotte, N.C.: Sherwood Printing Company, 1988.

Clay, Henry B. "Daniel Augustus Tompkins: An American Bourbon." Ph.D. diss., University of North Carolina, Chapel Hill, 1951.

Colored Charlotte. Charlotte, N.C.: AME Zion Job Print, 1915.

Connor, R. D. W. *North Carolina: Rebuilding an Ancient Commonwealth, 1584–1921*. New York: American Historical Society, 1929.

Crow, Jeffrey J., and Robert F. Durden. *Maverick Republican in the Old North State: A Political Biography of Daniel L. Russell*. Baton Rouge: Louisiana State University Press, 1977.

Cyclopedia of Eminent and Representative Men of the Carolinas of the Nineteenth Century. Vol. 3. Madison: Brant and Fuller, 1892.

DeCredico, Mary A. *Patriotism for Profit: Georgia's Urban Entrepreneurs and the Confederate War Effort.* Chapel Hill: University of North Carolina Press, 1990.

Doherty, Herbert J., Jr. "Alexander J. McKelway: Preacher to Progressive." *Journal of Southern History* 24 (May 1958): 177–90.

Donald, David H. "A Generation of Defeat." In *From the Old South to the New: Essays on the Transitional South*, edited by Walter J. Fraser, Jr., and Winfred B. Moore, Jr., 7–18. Westport, Conn.: Greenwood Press, 1981.

Dowd, Jerome. *Sketches of Prominent Living North Carolinians.* Raleigh: Edwards and Broughton, 1892.

Doyle, Don H. *Nashville in the New South, 1880–1930.* Knoxville: University of Tennessee Press, 1985.

———. *New Men, New Cities, New South: Atlanta, Nashville, Charleston, Mobile, 1860–1910.* Chapel Hill: University of North Carolina Press, 1990.

———. *The Social Order of a Frontier Community: Jacksonville, Illinois, 1825–1870.* Urbana: University of Illinois Press, 1978.

Du Bois, W. E. B. *The Souls of Black Folk: Essays and Sketches.* Chicago: A. C. McClurg, 1903.

Edmonds, Helen G. *The Negro and Fusion Politics, 1894–1901.* Chapel Hill: University of North Carolina Press, 1951.

Epstein, Barbara Leslie. *The Politics of Domesticity: Women, Evangelicalism, and Temperance in Nineteenth-Century America.* Middletown, Conn.: Wesleyan University Press, 1981.

Escott, Paul D. *After Secession: Jefferson Davis and the Failure of Confederate Nationalism.* Baton Rouge: Louisiana State University Press, 1978.

———. *Many Excellent People: Power and Privilege in North Carolina, 1850–1900.* Chapel Hill: University of North Carolina Press, 1985.

Foner, Eric. *Reconstruction: America's Unfinished Revolution, 1863–1877.* New York: Harper and Row, 1988.

Franklin, John Hope. *The Free Negro in North Carolina, 1790–1860.* Chapel Hill: University of North Carolina Press, 1943.

Friedman, Jean E. *The Enclosed Garden: Women and Community in the Evangelical South, 1830–1900.* Chapel Hill: University of North Carolina Press, 1985.

Gaither, Gerald. *Blacks and the Populist Revolt: Ballots and Bigotry in the "New South."* University: University of Alabama Press, 1977.

Gaillard, Frye. *The Dream Long Deferred.* Chapel Hill: University of North Carolina Press, 1988.

Gatewood, Willard B. *Aristocrats of Color: The Black Elite, 1880–1920.* Bloomington: University of Indiana Press, 1990.

Genovese, Eugene D. *The Political Economy of Slavery.* New York: Vintage, 1967.

Gilkeson, John S. *Middle-Class Providence, 1820–1940.* Princeton, N.J.: Princeton University Press, 1986.

Gilmore, Glenda Elizabeth. "Gender and Jim Crow: Sarah Dudley Pettey's Vision of the New South." *North Carolina Historical Review* 68 (July 1991): 261–85.

Goldfield, David R. "Pursuing the American Urban Dream: Cities in the Old South." In *The City in Southern History: The Growth of Urban Civilization in the South*, edited by Blaine E. Brownell and David R. Goldfield, 51–83. Port Washington, N.Y.: Kennikat Press, 1977.

Gould, Lewis L. *The Presidency of William McKinley*. Lawrence: Regents Press of Kansas, 1980.

Grantham, Dewey. *Southern Progressivism: The Reconciliation of Progress and Tradition*. Knoxville: University of Tennessee Press, 1983.

Greenwood, Janette Thomas. *On the Homefront: Charlotte during the Civil War*. Charlotte, N.C.: Mint Museum of History, 1982.

Griffin, Richard W. "Reconstruction of the North Carolina Textile Industry, 1865–1885." *North Carolina Historical Review* 41 (January 1964): 34–53.

Gusfield, Joseph R. *Symbolic Crusade: Status Politics and the American Temperance Movement*. Urbana: University of Illinois Press, 1968.

Hahn, Steven. *The Roots of Southern Populism: Yeoman Farmers and the Transformation of the Georgia Upcountry, 1850–1890*. New York: Oxford University Press, 1983.

Haley, John. *Charles N. Hunter and Race Relations in North Carolina*. Chapel Hill: University of North Carolina Press, 1987.

Hall, Jacquelyn Dowd, et al. *Like a Family: The Making of a Southern Cotton Mill World*. Chapel Hill: University of North Carolina Press, 1987.

Hanchett, Thomas W. "The Rosenwald Schools and Black Education in North Carolina." *North Carolina Historical Review* 65 (October 1988): 387–444.

———. "White-Collar, Blue-Collar, and Blacks: Spatial Development and Changing Concepts of Race and Class in New South Charlotte, 1880–1930." Paper presented at the annual meeting of the Organization of American Historians, St. Louis, April 1989.

Harlan, Louis. *Booker T. Washington: The Making of a Black Leader, 1856–1901*. New York: Oxford University Press, 1972.

———. *Booker T. Washington: The Wizard of Tuskegee, 1901–1915*. New York: Oxford University Press, 1987.

Harris, Carl V. *Political Power in Birmingham, 1871–1921*. Knoxville: University of Tennessee Press, 1977.

Harris, William C. *William Woods Holden: Firebrand of North Carolina Politics*. Baton Rouge: Louisiana State University Press, 1987.

Hart, Albert Bushnell. "A Cross-Section through North Carolina." *The Nation* 17 (March 1892).

Henderson, Archibald. *Washington's Southern Tour, 1791*. Boston: Houghton Mifflin, 1923.

Hewitt, Nancy A. *Women's Activism and Social Change: Rochester, New York, 1822–1872*. Ithaca, N.Y.: Cornell University Press, 1984.

Hicks, John D. "Farmers' Alliances in North Carolina." *North Carolina Historical Review* 2 (April 1925): 162–87.

Hoffman, Richard Lee. "The Republican Party in North Carolina, 1867–1871." Master's thesis, University of North Carolina, Chapel Hill, 1960.

Holt, Thomas. *Black over White: Negro Political Leadership in South Carolina during Reconstruction*. Urbana: University of Illinois Press, 1977.

Howe, Daniel Walker. *The Political Culture of the American Whigs*. Chicago: University of Chicago Press, 1979.

Huffman, William R. "A Historical Sketch of the Mecklenburg Investment Company Building." Charlotte-Mecklenburg Historic Properties Commission, n.d.

Isaac, Paul E. *Prohibition and Politics: Turbulent Decades in Tennessee, 1885–1920*. Knoxville: University of Tennessee Press, 1965.

Jeffrey, Julia Roy. "Women in the Southern Farmers' Alliance: A Reconsideration of the Role and Status of Women in the Late Nineteenth-Century South." In *Our American Sisters: Women in American Life and Thought*, edited by Jean E. Friedman and William Shade, 273–96. Lexington, Mass.: D. C. Heath, 1987.

Johnson, Michael, and James Roark. *Black Masters: A Free Family of Color in the Old South*. New York: Norton, 1984.

Johnson, Paul E. *A Shopkeeper's Millennium: Society and Revivals in Rochester, New York, 1815–1837*. New York: Hill and Wang, 1978.

Jones, Jacquelyn. *Soldiers of Light and Love: Northern Teachers and Georgia Blacks, 1865–1873*. Chapel Hill: University of North Carolina Press, 1980.

Kenzer, Robert C. *Kinship and Neighborhood in a Southern Community: Orange County, North Carolina, 1849–1881*. Knoxville: University of Tennessee Press, 1987.

Kipp, Samuel M., III. "Urban Growth and Social Change in the South, 1870–1920: Greensboro, North Carolina, as a Case Study." Ph.D. diss., Princeton University, 1974.

Kousser, J. Morgan. "Progressivism—For Middle-Class Whites Only: North Carolina Education, 1880–1910." *Journal of Southern History* 46 (May 1980): 169–94.

———. *The Shaping of Southern Politics: Suffrage Restrictions and the Establishment of the One-Party South, 1880–1910*. New Haven, Conn.: Yale University Press, 1974.

Lacy, Dan M. "The Beginning of Industrialism in North Carolina, 1865–1900." Master's thesis, University of North Carolina, Chapel Hill, 1935.

Lamon, Lester C. *Black Tennesseans, 1900–1930*. Knoxville: University of Tennessee Press, 1977.

Lebsock, Suzanne. *The Free Women of Petersburg: Status and Culture in a Southern Town, 1784–1860*. New York: Norton, 1984.

Lefler, Hugh T., and Albert R. Newsome. *North Carolina: The History of a Southern State*. 3d ed. Chapel Hill: University of North Carolina Press, 1973.

Lockman, Barbara B. *A Century's Child: The Story of Thompson Children's Home, 1886–1986*. Charlotte, N.C.: Thompson Children's Home, 1986.

McCarthy, Kathleen D. *Noblesse Oblige: Charity and Cultural Philanthropy in Chicago, 1849–1929*. Chicago: University of Chicago Press, 1982.

McKelway, Alexander J. "Child Labor in the Southern Cotton Mills." *Annals of the American Academy of Political and Social Science* 27 (January–June 1906): 312–26.

———. "The Child Labor Problem: A Study in Degeneracy." *Annals of the American Academy of Political and Social Science* 27 (January–June 1906): 259–69.

McMath, Robert C., Jr. *Populist Vanguard: A History of the Southern Farmers' Alliance*. Chapel Hill: University of North Carolina Press, 1975.

Meier, August. *Negro Thought in America, 1880–1915: Racial Ideologies in the Age of Booker T. Washington*. Ann Arbor: University of Michigan Press, 1963.

Meier, August, and Elliot Rudwick. "The Boycott Movement against Jim Crow Streetcars in the South, 1900–1906." *Journal of American History* 55 (March 1969): 756–75.

Moore, John Hammond. "The Negro and Prohibition in Atlanta, 1885–1887." *South Atlantic Quarterly* 69 (Winter 1970): 38–57.

Muller, Philip R. "New South Populism: North Carolina, 1881–1900." Ph.D. diss., University of North Carolina, Chapel Hill, 1971.

Noblin, Stuart. *Leonidas Lafayette Polk: Agrarian Crusader*. Chapel Hill: University of North Carolina Press, 1949.

Nordin, D. Sven. *Rich Harvest: A History of the Grange, 1867–1900*. Jackson: University Press of Mississippi, 1974.

O'Brien, Gail Williams. *The Legal Fraternity and the Making of a New South Community, 1842–1882*. Athens: University of Georgia Press, 1986.

———. "Power and Influence in Mecklenburg County, 1850–1880." *North Carolina Historical Review* 54 (April 1977): 120–44.

Overdyke, W. Darrel. *The Know-Nothing Party in the South*. Gloucester, Mass.: Peter Smith, 1968.

Paludan, Philip S. *Victims: A True Story of the Civil War*. Knoxville: University of Tennessee Press, 1981.

Parker, Inez Moore. *The Biddle–Johnson C. Smith University Story*. Charlotte, N.C.: Charlotte Publishing, 1975.

Penn, I. Garland. *The Afro-American Press and Its Editors*. Springfield, Mass.: Willey and Company, 1891.

Perry, Robert E. "Middle-Class Townsmen and Northern Capital: The Rise of the Alabama Cotton Textile Industry, 1865–1900." Ph.D. diss., Vanderbilt University, 1986.

Powell, William S., ed. *Dictionary of North Carolina Biography*. Vol. 1. Chapel Hill: University of North Carolina Press, 1988.

———. *North Carolina through Four Centuries*. Chapel Hill: University of North Carolina Press, 1989.

Prather, Leon. *We Have Taken a City: Wilmington Racial Massacre and Coup of 1898*. Cranbury, N.J.: Associated University Presses, 1984.

Price, Joseph C. "The Negro in the Last Decade of the Century." *Independent* 41 (January 1891).

Rabinowitz, Howard. *Race Relations in the Urban South, 1865–1890*. New York: Oxford University Press, 1978.

Rable, George C. *Civil Wars: Women and the Crisis of Southern Nationalism*. Urbana: University of Illinois Press, 1989.

Roberts, Bruce. *The Carolina Gold Rush*. Charlotte, N.C.: McNally and Roberts, 1971.

Robinson, Armstead. "Plans Dat Comed from God: Institution Building and the Emergence of Black Leadership in Reconstruction Memphis." In *Toward a New South?: Studies in Post–Civil War Southern Communities*, edited by Orville V. Burton and Robert McMath, 71–102. Westport, Conn.: Greenwood Press, 1982.

Rodgers, Daniel T. "In Search of Progressivism." In *The Promise of American History: Progress and Prospects*, edited by Stanley I. Kutler and Stanley N. Katz, 113–32. Baltimore: Johns Hopkins University Press, 1982.

Rorabaugh, W. J. "The Sons of Temperance in Antebellum Jasper County." *Georgia Historical Quarterly* 64 (Fall 1980): 263–79.

Russell, James M. *Atlanta, 1847–1890: City Building in the Old South and New*. Baton Rouge: Louisiana State University Press, 1988.

Ryan, Mary P. *Cradle of the Middle Class: The Family in Oneida County, New York, 1790–1865*. New York: Cambridge University Press, 1981.

Scarboro, David D. "North Carolina and the Confederacy: The Weakness of States' Rights during the Civil War." *North Carolina Historical Review* 56 (April 1979): 133–49.

Schweninger, Loren. *Black Property Owners in the South, 1790–1915*. Urbana: University of Illinois Press, 1990.

Shirley, James M. "From Congregational Town to Industrial City: Industrialization, Class, and Culture in Nineteenth-Century Winston-Salem, North Carolina." Ph.D. diss., Emory University, 1986.

Shore, Laurence. *Southern Capitalists: The Ideological Leadership of an Elite, 1832–1885*. Chapel Hill: University of North Carolina Press, 1986.

Sitterson, J. Carlyle. "Business Leaders in Post–Civil War North Carolina, 1865–1900." In *Studies in Southern History*, vol. 39, 110–38. Chapel Hill: University of North Carolina Press, 1957.

Standard, Diffee W., and Richard W. Griffin. "The Cotton Textile Industry in Antebellum North Carolina, Part 2: An Era of Boom and Consolidation, 1830–1860." *North Carolina Historical Review* 34 (April 1957).

Steelman, Joseph Flake. "The Progressive Era in North Carolina, 1884–1917." Ph.D. diss., University of North Carolina, Chapel Hill, 1955.

Stover, John F. *The Railroads of the South, 1865–1900*. Chapel Hill: University of North Carolina Press, 1955.

Tatum, Georgia Lee. *Disloyalty in the Confederacy*. Reprint. New York: AMS Press, 1970.

Thomas, Emory. *The Confederacy as a Revolutionary Experience*. Englewood Cliffs, N.J.: Prentice-Hall, 1971.

Thornburgh, Emma Lou. *T. Thomas Fortune: Militant Journalist*. Chicago: University of Chicago Press, 1972.

Thornton, J. Mills. *Politics and Power in a Slave Society: Alabama, 1800–1860*. Baton Rouge: Louisiana State University Press, 1978.

Tompkins, Daniel A. *Cotton Mills, Commercial Features: A Textbook for the Use of Textile Schools and Investors*. Charlotte, N.C., 1899.

———. *History of Mecklenburg County and the City of Charlotte*. Charlotte, N.C.: Observer Printing, 1903.

Trelease, Allen W. *The North Carolina Railroad, 1849–1871, and the Modernization of North Carolina*. Chapel Hill: University of North Carolina Press, 1991.

Tullos, Allen. *Habits of Industry: White Culture and the Transformation of the Carolina Piedmont*. Chapel Hill: University of North Carolina Press, 1989.

Tyrell, Ian. "Drink and Temperance in the Antebellum South: An Overview and Interpretation." *Journal of Southern History* 48 (November 1982): 485–510.

Wade, Richard. *Slavery in the Cities: The South, 1820–1860*. New York: Oxford University Press, 1964.

Walls, William J. *The African Methodist Episcopal Zion Church: Reality of the Black Church*. Charlotte, N.C.: AME Zion Publishing House, 1974.

Watson, Harry. *Jacksonian Politics and Community Conflict: The Emergence of the Second Party System in Cumberland County, North Carolina*. Baton Rouge: Louisiana State University Press, 1981.

Wedell, Marsha M. "Memphis Women and Social Reform, 1875–1915." Ph.D. diss., Memphis State University, 1988.

Whitener, Daniel J. "The North Carolina Prohibition Election of 1881 and Its Aftermath." *North Carolina Historical Review* 9 (April 1934): 71–93.

———. *Prohibition in North Carolina*. Chapel Hill: University of North Carolina Press, 1946.

Wiener, Jonathan. *Social Origins of the New South: Alabama, 1860–1885*. Baton Rouge: Louisiana State University Press, 1978.

Williams, Max R. "The Foundations of the Whig Party in North Carolina: A Synthesis and a Modest Proposal." *North Carolina Historical Review* 47 (April 1970): 115–29.

Williamson, Joel. *After Slavery: The Negro in South Carolina during Reconstruction*. Chapel Hill: University of North Carolina Press, 1965.

————. *The Crucible of Race: Black-White Relations in the American South since Emancipation.* New York: Oxford University Press, 1984.

Winston, George T. *A Builder of the New South: Being the Story of the Life Work of Daniel Augustus Tompkins.* Garden City, N.Y.: Doubleday, Page and Company, 1920.

Woodman, Harold. *King Cotton and His Retainers.* Lexington: University of Kentucky Press, 1968.

Woodward, C. Vann. *Origins of the New South, 1877–1913.* Baton Rouge: Louisiana State University Press, 1951.

————. *The Strange Career of Jim Crow.* 3d ed. New York: Oxford University Press, 1974.

Wright, Gavin. *Old South, New South: Revolutions in the Southern Economy since the Civil War.* New York: Basic Books, 1986.

INDEX

· · · · · · · · ·

Index

Bittersweet Legacy paints a surprisingly complex portrait of race and class relations in the New South and demonstrates the impact of personal relationships, generational shifts, and the interplay of local, state, and national events in shaping the responses of black and white southerners to each other and the world around them.

Janette Thomas Greenwood is assistant professor of history at Clark University.